MOB STAR

MOB STAR

THE STORY OF JOHN GOTTI

Gene Mustain

Jerry Capeci

ALPHA

A member of Penguin Group (USA) Inc.

International Standard Book Number: 0-02-864416-6
Library of Congress Catalog Card Number: 2002108503

06 05 04   8 7 6 5 4

Interpretation of the printing code: The rightmost number of the first series of numbers is the year of the book's printing; the rightmost number of the second series of numbers is the number of the book's printing. For example, a printing code of 02-1 shows that the first printing occurred in 2002.

Printed in the United States of America

For Jake Mustain, and for his beautiful mommy.

For Chuck Caruso—uncle, mentor, and friend who always stood by his buddies, and always rooted for the underdog.

CONTENTS

PROLOGUE

EARLY IN 2002, JOHN GOTTI finally shut up. But it wasn't because anyone made him. That he would definitely want you to know. He lost his ability to speak to throat cancer, and then only after he fought it, as he would say, "tooth and nail" for nearly four cruel years. In an operation meant to prolong his life a little while longer, the most voluble of men was silenced. Ten years after he went to prison for life, he was imprisoned further—locked in, as well as up.

He may be dead, or still clinging to life when you read this. Either way, the end of the John Gotti story has arrived. He must have died inside when he lost his ability to talk, for Gotti lived to talk. He loved to gather his men and hold court. He loved to gab, muse, banter, cajole, and abuse. He loved to reminisce, speculate, and editorialize. He was good at it, too. His way with words distinguished him from other gangsters. In his gruff, crude way, he was lyrical, clever, and vivid. He could use words like knives. Backed by guns, he rose to power on them. Unable to stop talking, he lost power because of them.

After he went to prison for good, his way with words was all he had left. "Right now, I'm cursed," he said early in 1998, after six years in solitary confinement at the toughest prison in America and eight months before the cancer came. "I'm stuck in this joint and that's the end of it. This is my realm, right here. That's the end of it."

On that day, during a visit with his daughter Victoria and brother Peter, he used his way with words to artfully spin his legal history and life story. "You know why I'm here? It took them $80 million in three lying cases and seven rats that killed a hundred people in the witness-protection program to finally frame me! You understand?" A little later, he added: "My life dictated that I take each course that I took. I didn't have any multiple choice. My time, all the doors were closed."

He spoke for four hours that day and four the next. He raged at the decimation of his crime Family since he went way, and he lamented a case that had fallen on his son Junior and another case about to fall on his son-in-law Carmine. He said he felt increasingly estranged from his relatives and complained of being forgotten—except by strangers who sent fan mail.

Despite the doom and gloom, he sounded as egomanical as ever—"listen to me carefully, you'll never see another guy like me if you live to be 5,000." Talking about his mail, which did come in bundles after his name was in the news for something, he was so over the top he sounded delusional. "I get mail from all over the world where people wish they could be my grandchildren or my children ... I got mail last night from Australia, South Africa, New Zealand—this was all last night! ... I got a million people who, if they could come here to see me now, they would cry just to be able to be here and see me."

He quoted some letters at length, including that of a 14-year-old Idaho girl writing a school paper on celebrities. She wanted him to write back and answer a few questions. "She says, 'You know, I don't know if you know it, there are millions of people out here (who) really love and adore you and respect you. I guess you and America was what was meant to be!' This is a 14-year-old kid! None of my relatives ever write that!"

Between quoting letters, he insisted he didn't care about them. It was obvious that he did, and it made you feel sorry for him. "I got a letter from England. (From) a couple, they just had a baby. They own a bunch of curio shops ... they're affluent people. The kid's got carrot-red hair ... you gotta see the letter! They named the baby 'Gianna,' like for Johnny in Italian. These are English people from London! 'We'd be honored'—they sent me pictures of the kids and all that—'we would be honored if you'd be the godparent' ... this is what the real world thinks!"

Gotti was well aware that his words, as so many more he spoke during what was supposed to be his secret life in crime, were being preserved. All visits between inmates and visitors at the United States Penitentiary in Marion, Illinois—a deliberately harsh hellhole for convicts deemed dangerous or incorrigible—are recorded on video and audiotape to discourage plotting of any kind. His words that day, January 29, 1998, and the next are among the most compelling in this book, which uses many Gotti words to tell his story.

His words help us finish the picture we sketched when the first edition of *Mob Star* came out in 1988 and ended on a note of triumph for Gotti. Though the real ending wasn't yet available, the first *Mob Star* remains a good story. It was the first book ever published about a mob boss who was, you might say, still in office. The main story is his rise to power. A key subplot tells the story of two men near him who lived dangerously—for years, they regularly informed on him to the FBI. Still-secret reports on these men's contacts with the FBI will take the reader inside Gotti's world during or after most major episodes of his pre-1985 life in crime in New York.

These many years later, we can't think of a better book title than we thought of then, even though the title had unintended consequences. "Mob Star" captures the idea that in his realm, he was a star, and that he came to have the things we associate with traditional realms of stardom—money to burn, the best tables, magazine covers, autograph hounds. In truth, it came to us as we considered the word, "mobster." Mob-ster. We were looking to make the second syllable into something. Mob Man ... Mob Boss ... *Mob Star!*

The title implied adulation we never felt. It fed Gotti fantasies, his and others. Just as it was for us, it was a thrill for him to see copies of *Mob Star* filling Fifth Avenue shop windows. The book's cover, if not the story inside, made him feel heroic. It became part of the mythical identity he created in America and a large part of the world during his time at the top. His time lasted five years. That is the story we tell in the eight new chapters that begin with Chapter 28, "The Fix."

Over those years, by winning trials in the world's media capital and swaggering in the ensuing spotlight, Gotti did become famous or infamous, take your pick. In the hype-around-the-clock culture just taking off when he came on the scene, fame and infamy are the same thing. It happened because of who he was and what people expected. He was a perfect picture of what everyone imagines Mafia bosses to be. He was gravel-voiced and smart-alecky, and handsome in a dangerous-looking way. He was good on his feet. He did for the Mafia what JFK did for politics 25 years before; he made it entertaining.

A master criminal he was not, but what he was and came to stand for are at least fascinating. "Best I ever did was a couple hijackings," Gotti once said. But people don't know or care about rap-sheet details. What mattered with him was perception. He was what we imagine gangsters to be. He looked like one. He sounded like one. He was straight out of a shared experience, the gangster movie. "He was a James Cagney, Edward G. Robinson-type of gangster," was how a former New York detective, Joseph Coffey, described him during a documentary a couple years ago.

Gotti brought the movies to life, which made it possible to invest real emotions in him: awe, envy, fear. Early on, when the press began pulling back the curtains on his life, the public learned that in 1980 a Gotti neighbor drove his car into one of Gotti's children and killed him. It was a horrible accident, but some months later the man was thrown into a van by several men and was never seen again. The case was never solved, but everyone believes Gotti ordered the man killed, and he no doubt did. He had the power and will to do what many of us would feel like doing if we lost a child that way, and he got away with it, which we could only dream of doing.

Where it got more fascinating with Gotti was that he saw himself a gangster actor, too. He relished the role and was good at it—in public, anyway. In private, as the Marion tapes show, he was often repulsive. (He railed on about "coons," "niggers" and Jews, and called his wife—in front of their daughter—a pig, a tramp, and a witch.) But in public, with his silvery showiness and sly smirks, he fed the public's fantasies, which fed his.

It is hard to overstate the imprint *The Godfather* tale left on the minds of people who dream about living by one's own rules, and on the minds of the Mafiosi who actually do. The movie version, with its even more romanticized treatment of Mafia life, came out in 1972. In the underworld then, the popular but mistaken notion was that it was based on the life of Carlo Gambino, leader of the Mafia Family known by his last name and which included then 31-year-old John Gotti, just out of the joint for hijacking.

When his crew leader was forced to lay low a while, Gotti took the man's place in meetings with the aging Gambino. It was no doubt heady stuff because a year later, after his arrest on a disorderly conduct charge, Gotti gave his name as John "DeCarlo" (son of Carlo). Gambino didn't much look like a gangster, but he talked like a godfather. He was prone to selectively quoting from *The Prince*, Niccolo Machiavelli's treatise on power. Soon, so was Gotti. "Fear is a stronger emotion than love" became one of his favorite lines.

By the time Gotti murdered his way to the top late in 1985, the godfather tradition was in steep decline. The federal government was putting all the big bosses away for life with new laws and sur- veillance capability that made it risky to even whisper about crime. Gotti went against the grain by beating a federal case and two state ones. That put him in the crosshairs of everyone with a badge. But he could not change who he was. Instead of retreating out of sight to try and operate on the sly, he paraded in public. Madison Square Garden one night, Rainbow Room the next. Worse, he required his men to attend weekly shapeups at his social club on a busy street in lower Manhattan. There and a block away on Prince Street, he took daylight "walk-talks," titillating passersby and taunting cops, agents, and "girl" prosecutors.

On the Marion tapes, many years of numbing incarceration and terrible sickness later, he had only this to say about whether he should have done things differently, and, for once, he had trouble getting the words out:

"I take credit for my, my, my bad doings. I made mistakes."

The Marion tapes were recorded about 18 months after Gotti, in prison, got what he may have never gotten before, at least not since he was a boy—a good beating. The scene was set during one of his cherished breaks from solitary confinement, when he and other inmates were allowed to exercise in an indoor recreation area just off his cell.

"Get out of my way, you piece of shit," Gotti barked at another con who didn't show enough respectful space quickly enough. "Don't you know who I am?"

The inmate, a black man about 20 years younger than the then 56-year-old Gotti, did indeed know who Gotti was, and he let Gotti by, with a scowl. The next time they were in the recreation area, however, the heavily muscled inmate sucker-punched Gotti, then beat him bloody before guards tore him away.

No one in the Gotti camp ever spoke publicly about it, least of all Gotti, and for sure not during tape-recorded visits with his relatives where he knew he ran the risk that tapes could be leaked, as these indeed were, to us, and the world would get the story of him getting his. Given what he wouldn't talk about, it's amazing what he did.

Aside from the vicious epithets for his wife Victoria, he criticized his son Peter for ignoring his advice and failing to write. He criticized daughters Victoria and Angela for failing to send timely photographs and letters and burdening him with problems he was helpless to do anything about. He said his son Junior and some codefendants in a case just filed "should all be sent to the insane asylum" for their criminal mistakes. He called son-in-law Carmine Agnello a "slob" who "conducts himself like a barbarian."

"You can't be more disappointed than I am in my family, utterly impossible," he said to his brother Peter, after daughter Victoria briefly stepped away from their Marion visitors' cubicle. "If I could go home, I say it right out, I wouldn't go near them with a ten-foot-long fucking pole."

The most powerful moment on the Marion tapes came when a Gotti grandchild—dressed in a suit, as though bound for a wedding or a funeral—entered the cubicle to say hello. The meeting began with gentle razzing. Then Gotti told the child that if he did well in school, some day he could be a lawyer. The child already had some-one to emulate—his mother Victoria, a successful writer. After her father went to prison, she wrote a top-selling mystery novel and a book about a heart ailment she suffers. His notoriety fueled curiosity buying of the novel, but at least her words were being put to honest use, and she would go on to write two more mystery novels.

With his mother now back in the cubicle, however, the child said he would rather be a professional athlete. His grandfather insisted on a lawyer: "To be a good basketball player or baseball player, first of all, you got to be a good liar. A good lowlife and an imbecile."

The child said nothing and squirmed in his chair.

"And you got to take steroids! You must take steroids, and anybody who takes steroids is a garbage pail."

Finally, softly, the boy replied: "Fine, then I will be a crook."

The words were a sharp slap to Gotti's face, sharper than the grandchild probably knew or meant. Briefly speechless, Gotti leaned back, stared, and then exploded.

"I don't care if you'll be nothin'! You think you're being … spiteful with me? You'll get an ass-kicking from me! I know how to raise children!"

The boy stayed silent.

"You ain't doing me no favor coming to see me talking sass to me! I will put my foot right up your ass, you hear me?"

The boy fidgeted and peered through the glass barrier separating him from Gotti, cradling one of the cubicle's telephones on his shoulder.

"You'll never forget the ass-kicking you'll get from me. You understand? Don't you look at me like that. I'm more serious than cancer. You can look as sad as you want. Now, give that phone to your uncle and get outta here!"

The boy fled, head down. His mother soon left too, after agreeing that her child did deserve a whipping for smarting off.

A couple moments later, Gotti said to his brother: "That's why these visits, I told you, I got to keep them to a minimum. When I go back upstairs (to my cell), it breaks my heart ... let's try and salvage some of this visit. You know anything good? Anything good anyone wants to talk about?"

A long silent ensued. "Not really, everything's normal," Peter finally said.

"That's perfect," Gotti answered, "that's terrifying. Normal. Normal in this family is terrifying, that's for sure. Normal in this family is terrifying."

Later, with daughter Victoria back in the cubicle, Gotti turned to another topic obviously stuck in his gloomy craw: His family failed to send him a photograph of his kids and their kids for the Christmas just past. He blamed Victoria the most, but she protested she had. He kept insisting she hadn't.

"I don't want to hurt you," he told her. "I want to die before you have a toothache. But I got nothing! I got no group picture!"

Victoria remained silent as Gotti raised his voice and sarcastically fumed that he received group photographs from many other admiring families, just not his own. "I didn't get none from mine! I got nothing! Nothing!"

Victoria then exited the cubicle again. Gotti turned to Peter: "What, am I wrong? I gotta beg them for a group picture of my grandchildren! When you come [the next time], come the fuck alone!"

His loss of power and freedom and the bleak terms of confinement—until he was hospitalized, he lived in a gray, closet-sized cell with only a 13-inch black-and-white television for company—were enough to put Gotti in a permanently agitated state, but his son Junior's legal troubles contributed to his hair-trigger mood the days of the visit. Junior and others were indicted a week earlier in a case based partially on evidence hidden behind a basement wall in a building owned by a friend of Junior's; the evidence included lists of "made men" in three Mafia Families and men who gave Junior cash when he got married—plus the cash itself, all $350,000 of it.

"These people here, if ever found guilty, they should never be sent to jail," Gotti yelled at Peter. "They should all be sent to the insane asylum. From keeping the wedding money down in the basement, right down the line. I want to know what part of this was intelligent!"

At least with Junior, Gotti paused to say how it was impossible for him to love Junior more than he did. Then he compared Junior to his uncle, Gotti's brother Gene, who went to prison for heroin dealing. "He's a tough kid, he's a smart kid, but he's another (Gene). They think they know everything and they don't. It's heartbreaking."

Gotti said he was sick of getting only bad news. He then took off after daughter Angela for failing to tell him about such good news as a new house. He complained he hadn't received a letter from son Peter in two years.

"I wish one day you would bring me good news," he told his brother. "I really wish one day you would bring me good news. You know more about Angela's house than I do."

Peter protested that he didn't even know where the house is.

"You know more than me ... I know absolutely nothing!"

His voice rising higher, Gotti growled that son Peter not only failed to write, he ignored his wishes. It hurt because men of "lesser ilk" had sons who do what their fathers say.

"If I tell him, 'Go this way,' he goes that way," Gotti said. "If I tell him, 'Go that way,' he goes this way.

"I don't know absolutely nothing about none of them. I don't know if they're home, who's living together no more, who ain't living together no more, who's talking.

"And I don't want to know. They choose that route, ahh, let them take that route."

With Victoria back in the cubicle, he started up again, complaining that he is forced to extract information about some relatives, such as her husband.

"So what's the story with Carmine?" he asked.

"Whaddya mean, what's the story with him?" she replied.

"Is he feeling good? Is he not feeling good? Is his medication increased? Decreased? Is it up? Down? Does he get in the back seat of the car and think someone has stolen the steering wheel?"

"It's the same," she said, answering only the question about medication.

Gotti predicted that hot-tempered Carmine, who operated a car-salvage business between minor dustups with cops, would be the next member of the clan to get in serious trouble. "He's gonna get in-dicted any day, this moron. He's built himself a gallows. He's bought the noose."

Near the end of a visit saying much of what there is to say about John Gotti doing hard time, Gotti recalled for Peter that one of their early Mafia mentors had warned that it was best for mobsters if they never married.

"He was right. In this life, you can't get married. You're better off if you don't have no fucking body, and this way, that's the end of it."

Author (and now New York newspaper columnist) Victoria Gotti wasn't the only person to benefit from Gotti's notoriety. We did. Besides the original *Mob Star* and this update, we wrote another book about him, and a third about some of his Gambino friends and enemies. We also did television documentaries, magazine pieces, and a thousand or so talk-show appearances. Our association with the story brought friendly newspaper and magazine interviews and profiles from New York to Hong Kong, and reasonable status at the *Daily News*, where we used to work. One of us, that's Jerry, owns and operates a very popular website, ganglandnews.com; it gets 200,000 hits a month.

Others also did well on the Gotti beat. John Miller, first for local television, now ABC; Michael Daly, who wrote the first major Gotti profile, in *New York*; the late Mike McAlary, who wrote several great columns for *Newsday*, the *Post* and the *Daily News*, and virtually all the reporters chosen to cover the 1992 trial—with its bomb threats, its tapes, showdowns, and staredowns, it dominated the news in New York for three months.

It wasn't just we reporters. Bruce Cutler, Gotti's lawyer, benefited. So did Gerald Shargel, another Gotti lawyer. They got profiles in *GQ* and *The New Yorker*, and all the other media they could possibly want. They were good; now they're big. John Gleeson, the lead prosecutor in the 1992 case, is now a federal judge in Brooklyn. Co-prosecutor Laura Ward became a judge, too, on the state bench in

Manhattan. Bruce Mouw, boss of the FBI's Gambino squad, won a big Justice Department award. Gotti case agent George Gabriel now has his own squad. Remo Franceschini, a Queens detective on many Gotti cases, got what most cops don't, a book about his career: *A Matter of Honor: One Cop's Lifelong Pursuit of John Gotti and the Mob.*

Going out wider, many other institutions and individuals also benefited. HBO got a ratings record out of *Gotti*, which was based on our second book. Other networks and cable channels, publishers, distributors, and bookstores, they all got a bounce out of Gotti. All the publicity also helped create an audience for HBO's *The Sopranos* series. Two members of the show's cast, Tony Sirico and Vincent Pastore, were first in *Gotti*, the movie. They and all the other make-believe gangsters from *Gotti* shaped up at Elaine's, a media hive on Manhattan's Upper East Side. It is a few blocks from where Gotti, when he was out and about, used to hoist glasses of Cristal Rose with the late Anthony Quinn, who—the circle keeps turning—portrayed Gotti's gangland mentor in *Gotti.*

The Sirico-Pastore crew called themselves GAG, for Gangster Actors Guild. "*Gotti* started everything for me," said Pastore; his character was killed off at the end of the second *Sopranos* season, but he has many other roles coming out or up. "Before that, I had bits and pieces. *Gotti* was the beginning of it all for me."

Gotti was the beginning of this reporting and writing partner-ship, too. It was hard keeping up with him, so four hands were bet-ter than two. Our view of him kept evolving because the bigger he became, the more material we kept getting. He did not, of course, give formal interviews, although one of us, that's Gene, spoke with him for 40 minutes once. Everything else, we got through records, tapes, sources on both sides of the law, and observing him in court.

The 40-minute talk was the serendipitous result of being a pool reporter on a pre-trial day in 1992 when the lawyers and judge stepped into chambers and left Gotti free to engage in banter with a writer who wasn't about to encourage him to shut up by asking a hostile question. At the outset, we gossiped about Bill Clinton, Gennifer Flowers, Mike Tyson, and other individuals and current events of the time. He was quick, funny, and cordial, much to the annoyance of the FBI agents and guards also in the room.

As we veered onto some issues in the case, he became theatrical. His voice rose, his shoulders shook, he wagged his fingers. He accused the FBI of crimes. He accused the judge of favoring prosecutors. He accused the lead prosecutor of a personal vendetta going back to the federal case Gotti won in 1987.

"This guy," Gotti shouted, referring to lead prosecutor John Gleeson, "learned how to talk by listening to my voice! This guy, you know what he says to his wife when he gets up in the morning? 'Hi ya, John!'"

It was a marvelous performance, and naturally the *News* and many more media front-paged it. By 1992, the Gotti story was far more about media than crime. He used the media to speak to his audience and the media used him to win one. Successful Mafia bosses would be men who die in their own beds and leave organizations that carry on under their names. Gotti gets neither. His organization is in ruin. No one wants to be boss. His social club is now a women's boutique. What he achieved was a stage.

The show continues. Our other Gotti book still sells. The movie remains popular in stores. Salvatore Gravano, the ex-underboss who took the stand against Gotti, also got a book-and-movie deal. In the summer of 2001, nine years after Gotti went away, even a comedy program, *Politically Incorrect with Bill Maher*, found material in Gotti. Its staff focused on him in three of the five half-hour shows they cooked up about the Mafia in a week-long ratings drive.

On one of the Gotti shows, the daughter of a man Gotti murdered was one of the guests. She wore a deep tan, black slacks, and a backless, satin top. In an only-in-modern-America few moments, Cindy DiBernardo recalled her father adoringly, then used the language of gangster movies to mythologize Gotti further.

She said Gotti was convicted because he was "given up" by a turncoat "who didn't want to do his time." Anyone who knows the facts of Gotti's trial knows it isn't true. Gotti convicted himself when he got caught on tape in his club. Salvatore Gravano, the "turncoat" DiBernardo was referring to, was just icing. But as far as she was concerned, Gravano was a bum and Gotti was … a man.

"Whatever John Gotti's agenda was, he is doing his time like a man," she said.

At least one of the show's other guests, Bruce Mouw, retired boss of the FBI's Gotti team, squirmed in his seat. Here was a woman whose father was murdered by Gotti, and only because—as Gotti said on tape played at his trial—of a rumor that he gossiped about

Gotti's leadership style behind Gotti's back. But DiBernardo went on: "Whatever (Gotti) is condemned for, whatever he has done wrong, he is doing his time like a man."

It was left to Mouw to try and provide the law enforcement view, that Gotti was just a thug who took power by murder, but DiBernardo and others on the show weren't buying. They, like most people, vaguely sensed he was something more. It was just hard to put fingers on. But he was. For a while, he was what he wanted to be, which is only what we all want.

We are sitting here at our desk. Piles of Gotti paper and records strewn about. We leaf through the notes detailing his declining health, the controversies over whether he was getting adequate treatment, and how he was fighting cancer tooth and nail. We look at the transcripts of various trials, the secret accounts of his secrets. But we keep going back to the Marion prison tapes. We keep being amazed by the self-absorption, then finally see it's how he survived six years alone in a hole and four more of merciless disease.

Here at the end, it's impossible not to feel empathy and a little admiration. He was delusional, but he tried living an impossible life. He tried to live up to expectations. His words and the words of others were the proof he tried hard.

Heroic anti-hero carrying the flag of a dying tradition people outside it don't want to let go. That's a hard role.

"What did I tell you the other day?" he asked Victoria, as they discussed how his son and her husband were following him into prison. "I'm tired, I'm tired. But I'll always be me. I'll always be me until the day I die."

THE CAST

Joseph Armone—former heroin dealer who became underboss of the Gambino Family in April 1986.

William Battista—former hijacker who became a bookmaker for John Gotti and others.

Thomas Bilotti—briefly the underboss of the Gambino Family; murdered in December 1985.

Dominick Borghese—burly bodyguard who belonged to crews headed by Junior Gotti and Jack D'Amico.

James Cardinali—confessed murderer and star witness against John Gotti.

John Carneglia—former hijacker, drug dealer, used-car parts dealer, and soldier in John Gotti's crew.

Paul Castellano—boss of the Gambino Family from 1976 until his murder in December 1985.

Michael Coiro—former attorney for John Gotti and other members of the Bergin Hunt & Fish Club.

Bruce Cutler—former assistant district attorney in Brooklyn; later an outspoken attorney for John Gotti.

Jack D'Amico—longtime Gambino soldier who became part of John Gotti's inner circle and a capo.

Raymond Dearie—former U.S. attorney in Brooklyn, now a federal judge.

Frank DeCicco—replaced Thomas Bilotti as underboss of Gambino Family; murdered in April 1986.

Aniello Dellacroce—mentor of John Gotti; underboss of Gambino Family from 1965 to his death in December 1985.

Victoria DiGiorgio Gotti—wife of John Gotti, mother of their five children.

John Favara—John Gotti neighbor involved in an accident that killed Gotti's son Frank; later disappeared forever.

George Gabriel—FBI agent assigned to get-John Gotti case after Gotti was acquitted on March 13, 1987.

Joe N. Gallo—Garment Center executive and longtime *consigliere* of the Gambino Family.

Carlo Gambino—boss of the Gambino Family from 1957 until his death in 1976.

Thomas Gambino—eldest son of Carlo and, at one time, a candidate to replace Paul Castellano as boss.

Diane Giacalone—assistant U.S. attorney in Brooklyn and lead prosecutor at 1986–87 racketeering trial of John Gotti.

I. Leo Glasser—federal judge in Brooklyn who presided over the 1992 racketeering trial of John Gotti.

John Gleeson—assistant U.S. attorney in Brooklyn; co-prosecutor in the 1986–87 and 1992 racketeering trials of John Gotti.

Gene Gotti—second-best known of the Gotti brothers, and a defendant in a major heroin case.

John Gotti—former hijacker who rose to top of large New York Mafia Family; became known as Teflon Don; made cover of *Time*.

John A. Gotti—son of John Gotti; inducted into the crime Family and groomed to follow in father's footsteps.

Peter Gotti—older brother of John Gotti; former sanitation worker who became a capo for his brother, and later his acting boss.

Victoria Gotti—daughter of the don who became a novelist, columnist, and champion of her father.

Salvatore Gravano—former member of the white-collar wing of the Gambino Family who became John Gotti's top aide and killer.

Willie Boy Johnson—longtime associate of John Gotti and the Bergin Hunt & Fish crew.

Lewis Kasman—Garment Center businessman and self-described "adopted son" and champion of John Gotti.

Frank LoCascio—Bronx-based capo who served Gotti as underboss and later as *consigliere*.

Dominick Lofaro—underworld informer whose information led to bugging of the Bergin crew.

Andrew Maloney—former U.S. attorney in Brooklyn and co-prosecutor in the 1992 racketeering trial of John Gotti.

Edward Maloney—former kidnapper and career criminal who became government witness against Gotti.

Joseph Massino—longtime friend of the Gotti brothers and boss of the Bonanno Family.

James McBratney—small-time hood shot dead in Staten Island bar in struggle with John Gotti and two others.

Robert Morgenthau—influential District Attorney in Manhattan investigating the murder of Paul Castellano.

Bruce Mouw—supervisor of FBI "Gambino squad" that began investigation of Gotti after 1986–87 racketeering trial.

Eugene Nickerson—federal judge in Brooklyn who presided over the 1986–87 racketeering trial of John Gotti.

Romual Piecyk—refrigerator mechanic who accused John Gotti of assault, then wanted to forget about it.

Salvatore Polisi—an underworld figure who became a government witness against Gotti.

Anthony Rampino—longtime associate of John Gotti who once described himself as "John's man."

Angelo Ruggiero—friend of John Gotti since childhood; codefendant of Gene Gotti in major heroin case.

Salvatore Ruggiero—brother of Angelo and a major New York heroin dealer while a fugitive from justice.

Gerald Shargel—attorney for many organized crime figures, including John Gotti and Salvatore Gravano.

Barry Slotnick—attorney for Aniello Dellacroce and other mobsters and former law partner of Bruce Cutler.

Matthew Traynor—bank robber and drug dealer who became star witness for defense at Gotti trial.

Carlo Vaccarezza—Upper East Side restaurateur who became a John Gotti pal and outspoken supporter.

Joseph Watts—loan shark and longtime crony of Gambino Family leaders; became part of John Gotti's inner circle.

Agencies

Eastern District of New York—prosecutes violations of federal laws in Queens, Brooklyn, Staten Island, and Long Island.

Eastern District Organized Crime Strike Force—federal agency that investigates and prosecutes organized-crime figures. Its work was taken over by Eastern District U.S. Attorney in 1989.

Manhattan District Attorney's Office—state agency that prosecutes violations of state laws in Manhattan.

New York State Organized Crime Task Force—state agency that investigates and prosecutes organized-crime figures in New York State.

Southern District of New York—prosecutes violations of federal laws in Manhattan, the Bronx, and some upstate New York counties.

CHRONOLOGY

1940—John Joseph Gotti, Jr., is born in the Bronx on October 27.

1951—U.S. Senate Kefauver Committee issues report stating there is a "sinister criminal organization known as the Mafia."

1956—John Gotti drops out of Brooklyn high school, joins street gang.

1957—*May:* John Gotti arrested for the first time after gang fight.

October: Albert Anastasia murdered, Carlo Gambino becomes head of Family.

November: Carlo Gambino and brother-in-law, Paul Castellano, attend national conference of Mafia men in upstate New York.

1960—Victoria DiGiorgio quits high school, falls in love with John Gotti.

1963—John Gotti goes to jail for first time, serves 20 days.

1966—Underworld figure known as Wahoo becomes FBI informer. John Gotti associates with gang reporting to Carlo Gambino.

1967—John Gotti arrested after JFK Airport hijacking.

1969—John Gotti incarcerated at United States Penitentiary at Lewisburg, Pennsylvania.

1971—Joseph Colombo shot at Columbus Circle after founding Italian-American Civil Rights League.

1972—John Gotti released from Lewisburg, returns to Gambino gang.

1973—John Gotti indicted for murder after James McBratney is shot.

1975—Roy M. Cohn, representing John Gotti, negotiates plea enabling Gotti to plead guilty to attempted manslaughter in McBratney case. Gotti incarcerated in state prison.

1976—*October:* Carlo Gambino dies after another heart attack.

November: Paul Castellano becomes boss; Aniello Dellacroce remains underboss.

1977—John Gotti released from prison, becomes "made" Gambino man and "acting captain" of Bergin crew; crew associate known as Source BQ begins talking to FBI.

1980—*March:* Frank Gotti, 12-year-old son of John, is killed in accident involving neighbor's car.

July: The neighbor, John Favara, disappears.

1981—*September:* Diane Giacalone begins investigating John Gotti.

November: Angelo Ruggiero's telephone is tapped.

1982—*April:* Angelo Ruggiero's home is bugged.

May: Salvatore Ruggiero dies in plane crash.

October: President Reagan orders crackdown on the mob.

1983—*March:* Castellano's White House is bugged.

August: James Cardinali arrested, becomes government witness as Angelo Ruggiero, Gene Gotti, and others arrested in heroin case.

1984—Romual Piecyk accuses John Gotti and another of assaulting him.

1985—*March:* Federal Strike Force chief predicts acquittal of John Gotti two weeks before Gotti is indicted in federal case; annex next to Gotti club is bugged by state task force.

June: Aniello Dellacroce's home is bugged, Angelo Ruggiero refuses to turn over transcripts of heroin tapes.

December: Dellacroce dies; Castellano names Thomas Bilotti underboss; Castellano and Bilotti murdered.

1986—*January:* John Gotti becomes boss of Gambino Family, names Frank DeCicco underboss.

March: Piecyk can't remember who assaults him, case dropped.

April: Gotti's federal racketeering trial begins; Frank DeCicco murdered; Gotti jailed after bail revoked. Trial postponed.

August: Federal trial begins again.

1987—*March 13:* Jury in federal trial of John Gotti reaches verdict. FBI "Gambino squad" begins "get-Gotti" investigation.

1988—*February:* FBI points video camera with a telephoto lens on the front door of the Ravenite Social Club to capture the comings and goings of John Gotti and his friends.

August: Willie Boy Johnson is shot to death in front of his house as he leaves for work.

1989—*January:* John Gotti is arrested in Manhattan for assault in the 1986 shooting of a carpenters union official.

May: After two mistrials, federal jury reaches a verdict in the third trial stemming from the electronic surveillance that began in 1981 at the home of Angelo Ruggiero.

November: A bug in an apartment two floors above the Ravenite Social Club picks up its first conversation.

1990—*February:* State court jury in Manhattan reaches a verdict in the assault case against John Gotti.

December: John Gotti and Salvatore Gravano are arrested and detained without bail on racketeering and murder charges; Gotti and Gravano hear taped conversations made in the apartment above Ravenite Social Club.

1991—*August:* Federal Judge disqualifies Bruce Cutler and Gerald Shargel, lawyers for Gotti and Gravano, from representing them at trial.

November: Gravano agrees to testify against John Gotti and other members and associates of the Gambino crime family.

1992—*January.* Jury selection begins in racketeering and murder trial of Gotti and *consigliere* Frank LoCascio.

March: Gravano takes the witness stand against Gotti and LoCascio.

April: Federal jury reaches a verdict.

June 23: Gotti and LoCascio are sentenced to life in prison; Gotti supporters rally and riot outside Brooklyn Federal Court; Gotti is flown to Marion Federal Penitentiary.

ACKNOWLEDGMENTS

Over the sixteen years—on and off—that it took us to write this book, we spoke to many people whose lives intersected with John Gotti's. We can't thank many of them publicly, but they know who they are, and we especially salute them for trusting us so that we might tell a good story.

Over the same time, we wrote hundreds of articles and columns about the mob star and his grimy world; we covered his trials and most other major events in his public life, and came to read or possess many secret documents describing his not-so-public life. Gotti left a very large paper trail.

We can publicly thank many people, including these current and former members of the United States Attorneys' offices in New York: James Comey, Patrick Cotter, Raymond Dearie, Fran Fragos, John Gleeson, Douglas Grover, Karyn Kenney, Walter Mack, Andrew Maloney, Kenneth McCabe, Edward McDonald, Leonard Michaels, James Orenstein, Charles Rose, and Laura Ward. At the Federal Bureau of Investigation, we thank William Doran, James Fox, George Gabriel, Greg Hagerty, George Hanna, Jim Margolin, Bruce Mouw, Arthur Ruffels, Philip Scala, Lewis Schiliro, and Joseph Valiquette.

At the New York state law enforcement level, we thank Ellen Corcella, Michael Cherkasky, Ercole Gaudioso, Barbara Jones, Eric Krause, Robert Morgenthau, Pasquale Perrotta, Jeff Schlanger, and Eric Seidel.

Though they often wouldn't say much, we also appreciate courtesies shown us by defense lawyers Benjamin Brafman, Anthony Cardinale, Charles Carnesi, Bruce Cutler, David DePetris, Jeffrey Hoffman, Susan Kellman, Albert Krieger, James LaRossa, John Mitchell, Richard Rehbock, George Santangelo, Michael Santangelo, Gerald Shargel, and Barry Slotnick. We also thank Lewis Kasman and Carlo Vaccarezza, two friends of John Gotti, for speaking to us on the record.

We also thank some journalism buddies who often made covering Gotti a lot of fun—Pete Bowles, Bill Boyle, Leonard Buder, Ying Chan, Irene Cornell, Ed Frost, Pablo Guzman, Hap Hairston, Beth

Holland, Patricia Hurtado, David Krajicek, Terri Lichtstein, Michael Lipack, Arnold Lubash, David Martin, Eric Meskauskas, Phil Messing, John Miller, Mary Murphy, Juliet Papa, Karen Phillips, Tom Robbins, Faigi Rosenthal, Philip Russo, Larry Sutton, and JoAnne Wasserman.

At Alpha Books, we thank Development Editor Jennifer Moore and Production Editor Billy Fields for the special care they afforded us, and we convey an extra special thank you to Gary Goldstein, the Acquisitions Editor who sought us out, encouraged and reinforced our efforts, and was the brainchild of this updated edition of *Mob Star*.

Lastly, we thank the people we love the most and who will always be tops in our book—Ms. Doreen Weisenhaus and Jake Mustain, and Barbara, Matthew, Kim, Haley, Jenna, and Craig Capeci.

Gene Mustain, Jerry Capeci
June 5, 2002

1

TABLE FOR SIX

THE POPE LIVED ON A HILL called Death.

His home on the hill was a stately mansion his followers called the White House. He owned or controlled many businesses in New York, New Jersey, Connecticut, Pennsylvania, and Florida. He was a national expert on unions and labor contracts. He was an elegant dresser, dined in expensive restaurants, and rode to meetings in a chauffeured car. He said he was a butcher.

Only some of his followers called him the Pope. Others called him Paul, Paulie, or Uncle Paul; outsiders called him Big Paul. His natal name was Paul Constantino Castellano. He was born in Brooklyn on June 26, 1915, the son of immigrants from the oppressed island of Sicily. His father *was* a butcher.

Presenting himself as merely a butcher who wound up a successful businessman and labor consultant was an unpapal pose, a shield for his family against the whispers of strangers. His three sons were successful businessmen; his daughter was happily married, although for a time she was not, and this had made the Pope very angry.

It was the way he presented himself to his followers that enabled him to acquire great wealth. As a young man he fell in with other men whose families came from Sicily, where thrived a culture outside the law. In the new land of opportunity, they felt isolated and discriminated against. And so they resorted to native customs, which included the use of violence and intimidation to get what they wanted. Crime became their profession.

The young pope was talented—and lucky—and in 1976, he became the most powerful criminal in America.

That was the year he customer-built his White House on Todt
Hill, or Death Hill to the Dutch settlers of *Staaten Eylandt*, which
became one of the five boroughs of the capital of crime, New York
City. He succeeded his brother-in-law, Carlo Gambino, as the
"boss" of a large "Family" of criminals—the largest of the Crime
Capital's five Families and the nineteen others around the country.
Gambino, a boss for twenty years, died of old age. His Family, out
of respect, carried on as the Gambino Family.

Most of the time, the Families found it advantageous to cooperate and to recognize each others' criminal spheres of influence. In
1931, Salvatore Maranzano, a boss who had great power—and was
an admirer of the military system developed by Julius Caesar—
imposed on each Family a highly organized structure. The boss
would be aided by an underboss and assisted by captains who would
command individual crews of soldiers. Each Family also would
retain a counselor, a kind of in-house lawyer. The spoils would flow
upward from the soldiers.

The system was designed to insulate the boss and protect him
from prosecution. For a long time, in the Gambino Family, it did.

The Pope alienated some followers right at the start. In succeeding his brother-in-law, who also was his cousin, he vaulted over
Aniello Dellacroce, the Gambino Family underboss since 1965.
Castellano's solution to this potentially fatal situation was to relin-
quish to Dellacroce near total authority over some Gambino Family
crews, including one led by a Dellacroce protégé, an ambitious former hijacker and degenerate gambler, John Gotti. Over the next
several years, an aberrant situation arose: a Family within a Family.

The styles and deeds of the Family branches overlapped, but distinct identities did emerge. The Castellano wing was more white
collar, because of its labor racketeering and bid-rigging in the construction, cartage, meat, and garment industries. The Dellacroce
wing was more blue collar, because of its preoccupation with gambling, loan-sharking, and hijacking.

Until Neil Dellacroce's death in December 1985, there was peace
if not harmony.

On December 16, two weeks after Dellacroce died of cancer and
other illnesses, the Pope rose early and padded around his house.
He was a large, bespectacled, seventy-year-old man with a big hawk

nose, weary jowls, and thinning hair combed straight back. The last
two years had been difficult. Caesar's system had finally failed the
Gambino Family. The Pope was a defendant in two federal racketeering cases. The trial in one case—in which he stood accused of
being the puppeteer of a murderous gang of international car
thieves—was underway.

Beset by his own worries, Castellano had not gone to Dellacroce's wake, a serious lapse of judgment for a man who already
had enough trouble with the Family within the Family.

Today, he was savoring a twenty-four-hour break in his trial. He
wouldn't have to fight rush-hour traffic to get to the United States
Court House in the borough of Manhattan by 9:30 A.M., his daily
duty for the last two months. For him, the worst part of the trial—
the testimony of the only witness directly linking him to the stolen-
car ring—was over. In three days, the trial would recess for two
weeks, and the judge had given him permission to take a holiday at
his condominium in Pompano Beach, Florida.

Today was to be leisurely. He had a meeting at noon near his
house with the boss of another Family and with one of his loyal captains, James Failla. Then he intended to drop by unannounced at his
lawyer's office, on Madison Avenue in Manhattan, and present
Christmas envelopes to the secretaries. He was going to be in
Manhattan later anyway. He was to meet Failla and another
Gambino captain—Frank DeCicco, who was a Failla protégé—and
two other men for dinner.

"Sparks, 5 P.M.," read the entry in his diary.

Sparks Steak House is located at 210 East Forty-sixth Street, just
east of Third Avenue in midtown Manhattan, one of the world's
most pedestrian-congested areas, especially at that going-home
hour. Grand Central Station, with its ribbons of steel to the suburbs,
is at East Forty-second Street, one block west of Third.

That week the restaurant had been named the city's best steak-
house by *New York* magazine. A woodsy, manly place, it was popular
with businessmen from the surrounding office towers and with
diplomats from the United Nations complex, two blocks east on
First Avenue. Castellano, the owner of the Meat Palace, a supplier of
fine cuts, was an occasional customer; he knew the Sparks beef was
top quality.

The Pope had helped Sparks's management win a sweetheart
union contract. He didn't expect to be treated like a butcher when

he went there, and he wasn't; but in a secretly recorded conversation
with two union leaders, he had complained that Sparks wasn't
respectful enough to pay for his meal. The Pope was a complex
man. Although generous with secretaries, he could be surprisingly
grubby about money in his business relationships.

"Ya know who's really busy making a real fortune?" he began.
"Fucking Sparks ... what those guys do is good for a hundred grand
a week. I don't get five cents when I go in there."

His colleagues expressed surprise that Sparks allowed the Pope to
pay for his dinners.

"Pay, hell, I don't get a thing. You know, they don't buy you a
drink. Forget about it." "Forget about it" is a common expression
among New Yorkers seeking to shrug off the everyday absurdities
and ironies of life.

The Pope would be chauffeured today by forty-seven-year-old
Thomas Bilotti. Bilotti was not an ordinary chauffeur. He was an
official of a concrete company on Staten Island and thus a member
of the Family's white-color wing. He had become Castellano's aide-
de-camp in the last few years, and Castellano had just named him to
succeed Neil Dellacroce as underboss.

The rise of Bilotti, rather than John Gotti, the protégé of Dellacroce, was another disappointment to the Family within the Family.
Dellacroce had been its buffer against misfortune.

Gotti, at age forty-five, was the swashbuckling "skipper" of a
large crew in Queens, the Crime Capital's largest-sized borough. He
was a dangerously handsome man who dressed to kill. He regarded
himself as Dellacroce's successor, although in recent years his position had been undermined by drug charges against some of his crew
members. Like Carlo Gambino, Paul Castellano had forbidden drug
dealing.

Gotti had a reputation for ruthlessness. He cultivated it by speaking to subordinates and enemies in a ferocious manner. His image
was not based on words alone, as some tragically knew, but he did
use words like knives. Hundreds of times, Gotti's voice had been
secretly preserved on government tape recordings; it was an occupa-
tional hazard for all Family men, especially during the 1970s and
1980s.

"I like to go and crack fucking heads," he had recently said about someone who offended him," and I'll put them in the dumpster. I'd take a few guys and have a little fun. I love batting practice. I go regular, ya know?"

Gotti, who began with nothing, had an ego as expansive as any in Yankee Stadium, Trump Tower, or City Hall. He sometimes became giddy when he realized how far he had come, as when he recalled what had happened at the recent wedding of the son of Frank DeCicco, a Castellano man whom Gotti had befriended:

"Hey, Bobby, whose wedding was that this weekend we went to?"

"Ahh, Frankie DeCicco's son."

"Whose wedding did it look like it was?"

"Yours."

"How many people come and bother me until what time in the morning? They put a chair next to me."

Three o'clock. Three-fifteen."

"Every good fellow [Family member] and every non-good fellow came and bothered me. My brother Pete said he clocked seventy-five guys. I say he undersold me. I'd say there was more than seventy-five guys came and talked to me."

Gotti was listed as an employee of a plumbing company, but detectives who followed him hundreds of times never saw him fixing faucets or laying pipe. Since 1982, they had spotted him meeting with Failla, DeCicco, and other captains in what was seen as an effort to foster relationships with the Family around the Family, which the men themselves sometimes called "the other mob."

Thomas Bilotti lived only two miles from the Pope. He arrived at the house on the hill just before noon. Castellano walked out through the big double doors, past a large Christmas wreath, and got into Bilotti's black Lincoln for the short drive to the day's first "sitdown," which is how Family meetings are described.

At a nearby diner, they met Failla and John Riggi, boss of the small but prosperous DeCavalcante Family in New Jersey. It was important for the two bosses to maintain contact because Gambino crews operate in New Jersey. In addition, Riggi was the business agent of a laborers' union and often sought the counsel of Uncle Paul, who manipulated many unions and their members.

About 2:00 P.M., Bilotti and Castellano left for Manhattan to drop off the envelopes, visit with Castellano's lawyer, and have dinner at Sparks. A table for six had been reserved. They drove toward the Verrazano-Narrows Bridge, a silvery span named after the Italian explorer who discovered Staten Island in 1524 and the Narrows, the mile-wide Atlantic Ocean gateway to the deep water of New York Harbor.

The Lincoln glided across the bridge to Brooklyn, the "Broken Land" of the early Dutch settlers. Then it veered onto the Gowanus Expressway and headed northeast, parallel to the waterfront docks of South Brooklyn, which the Gambino Family had corrupted long ago.

In Red Hook, the Lincoln left the highway and went underground, entering an opening in the East River bedrock known as the Brooklyn-Battery Tunnel. It emerged a few minutes later onto the southern tip of Manhattan, where tourists gather for excursion rides to the Statue of Liberty and Ellis Island, where many sons of Sicily landed in America. The Lincoln veered left through an underpass and then onto the Franklin D. Roosevelt Drive, locally known as the East River Drive, which was the road to midtown sitdowns.

Around 2:30 P.M., Castellano and Bilotti arrived at the office of attorney James LaRossa, on Madison Avenue near Twenty-fifth Street.

Recently, the news in Castellano's stolen-car case was good. Originally, the indictment charged the ring with some two dozen murders, including that of the Pope's former son-in-law, who was said to have cheated on his pregnant wife, which was said to have caused a miscarriage. In a setback for prosecutors, a judge had since broken the indictment down into several smaller, more defendable cases.

In the first of these, the only evidence directly linking Castellano to the stolen-car ring had been the testimony of the nephew of Gambino captain Anthony Gaggi. The nephew had testified he took stacks of money to Castellano and heard him discuss with Uncle Anthony one of the brutal murders attributed to Uncle Paul's henchmen.

Under cross-examination, however, the nephew admitted first linking Castellano to the ring on the eve of the trial even though he had previously undergone two hundred hours of interrogation. The implication was that the nephew had embroidered his story to help prosecutors out of a last-minute jam. Castellano felt the man came across as a liar when he denied it; he hoped the jury did, too. Many prosecutors consider New York juries the most skeptical around, but one never knows about juries, not until they free you or jail you.

"We talked very little about the car case, we thought we had it locked up," LaRossa would say later. "We were in a vacation mode, a holiday mood."

Bilotti and Castellano left LaRossa's office about 4:00 P.M., an hour before their sitdown with Failla, DeCicco, and two other people at Sparks.

"See you in court tomorrow," Castellano told LaRossa.

With an hour to kill before going to Sparks, Castellano decided to pick up a special Christmas gift, a bottle of perfume, for a LaRossa secretary who had been especially courteous to him. He directed Bilotti to a store on West Forty-third Street, where they parked the Lincoln in a no parking zone. They could have afforded a garage; Castellano had $3,300 on him, Bilotti $6,300.

Bilotti opened the glove compartment and removed a card issued by the New York City Patrolmen's Benevolent Association; it had originally been given to a newly promoted police sergeant. Bilotti placed it on the dashboard but it didn't do any good; the Lincoln was ticketed.

The middle part of Manhattan is a tiny grid: avenues run north and south; streets go east and west. Now, at 5:00 P.M., the grid was locked with people and cars—it's always a honking zone of despair during the Christmas season—and the boss and his new underboss were caught in a crosstown snarl.

They would be late for their executions.

In the vicinity of Sparks, in the fading light of day, about a dozen men empty of goodwill waited anxiously for the Pope's arrival. Several sat in parked cars on Second and Third Avenues. At least three waited on benches located in a small street-level plaza at Forty-sixth Street and Third Avenue or paced the side street, pausing in apartment doorways to light cigarettes.

Diplomatic bodyguards, a passerby decided.

One of the three men on the street was gangly, pockmarked, and had eyes as dark as tombs. Another was short and tense like a cobra. They wore trench coats and dark, cossacklike fur hats.

"Where the hell are they?" one grumbled to another, loud enough for someone to recall later. "They were supposed to be here by now."

At 5:25 P.M., Bilotti turned the Lincoln onto East Forty-sixth Street. It was dark now, and the car reflected a rainbow of seasonal colors. Both men were unarmed. The Pope had a rule about wearing weapons to Family sitdowns: Don't do it. But there was no need for weapons—they were meeting members of the Family, in the middle of midtown, at a crowded restaurant. All of which made it a perfect setup for the hit men in fur hats.

At 5:26, the Lincoln stopped in a no standing area in front of Sparks. Weapons drawn, two assassins moved directly in front of Castellano as he began to get out on the curbside; one confronted Bilotti as he emerged from behind the wheel.

There was a flash of recognition; the Pope knew at least one of the men who were about to kill him.

And now with a flash of blue-orange and a rapid crackling sound bouncing off the buildings, the bullets flew in from .32- and .38-caliber semiautomatic handguns and blood and bone flew out. The Pope and Bilotti were hit six times each, in the head and the upper body. A bystander recalled watching one of the gunmen leaning over and firing a be-sure shot into the Pope's head.

Castellano sank to the ground, his body wedged between the open car door and the passenger seat. His left hand clung to the bottom of the car door, a death grip; a half-smoked cigar glowed a few inches away, near his shattered glasses. Bilotti fell face up on the street, the car keys near his outstretched right arm.

Murder still gets a rise out of New Yorkers. Many screamed and darted into doorways or ducked down behind two large stone lions guarding Chez Vong Restaurant of Paris and New York, adjacent to Sparks. The killers tucked away their weapons—one was equipped with a silencer—and walked east on Forty-sixth Street to Second Avenue; the tense cobralike one whispered into a walkie-talkie, no doubt to a man in one of the cars.

At the corner, in front of the Dag Hammarskjöld Tower Condominium, another Lincoln pulled up and the assassins climbed in; the car slipped into the southbound traffic and disappeared. They and the men in the other cars, who were on standby in case anything went wrong, now relaxed and pounded the dashboards in exhilarated relief. Nothing had gone wrong.

A witness saw three men leave Sparks shortly after the gunfire ended. Two of them resembled police mug shots of James Failla and Frank DeCicco. Whoever the men were, they ignored the hysteria, and the little red rivers on Forty-sixth Street—and faded away as anonymously as the car full of happy hit men.

A Sparks bartender called 911 and the street soon filled with flashing lights. As word of the victims' identities was beeped around the city, a rowdy convention of homicide detectives, police brass, and reporters was convened. FBI agents arrived from New York University Law School; a University of Notre Dame professor, an architect of the controversial racketeering law used to indict Castellano in both his pending cases, had been holding a seminar there.

The excitement outside Sparks was palpable. The adrenaline rush the investigators and chroniclers of murder get when they come upon the smell of a big case and a big story always produces moments of thrilling confusion. A Family boss murdered in midtown the week before Christmas was big. Bosses had been slain in other boroughs, but one hadn't been executed in Manhattan since 1957, when Carlo Gambino's predecessor was assassinated in a hotel barbershop.

Reporters crowded cops for tidbits. Chief of Detectives Richard Nicastro, asked what effect the slaying might have on the other defendants in the car-case trial, said he wouldn't speculate. As for the Pope, however: "They don't have to prove guilt or innocence anymore. That's over."

Later, a detective—an expert on the Family—was astonished when told that the victims did not have bodyguards, considering the uncertain climate Neil Dellacroce's death was known to have caused. It was like the president and the vice president walking around without the Secret Service.

"They were always together. They made it easy."

The double hit provoked the usual expressions of outrage.

"The decent citizens of this country are demeaned in the eyes of the world if brazen cold-blooded murders can be perpetrated on a street in New York," said federal Court of Appeals Judge Irving J. Kaufman, chairman of the President's Commission on Organized Crime.

"The waste of a human life is shocking, no matter who it is," commented federal District Court Judge Kevin Thomas Duffy, who was presiding over Castellano's car case, as he adjourned the trial for three weeks to weigh motions from codefendants for a mistrial that was eventually denied.

The Pope's table at Sparks had been set for six. Failla, DeCicco, and an unidentified man were seen leaving as two other would-be diners lay in the street. Someone hadn't come to dinner.

The prime suspect in the drama, not the cameraman but the director, was at home that night in Queens. He was watching television with his longtime wife in their suburban Cape Cod-style home in the un-New York City-like neighborhood known as Howard Beach. The home had a rotating satellite dish on the roof; John Gotti had learned how to tune different worlds in or out.

"Gotti will emerge as the head of the other captains," predicted Lieutenant Remo Franceschini of the Queens District Attorney's detective squad the next day. "That's what this struggle is all about."

Over the next few days, the little that was known about Gotti was published and broadcast many times. He was said to have many double-breasted suits, his own barber's chair, and a fear of flying. New Yorkers with a sense of history raised their eyebrows at one unnamed cop's claim: "Gotti is the most vicious, meanest mobster I've ever encountered."

With justification, the cop might also have added "most reckless" or "boldest." A few months before, even though aware that his words were being taped by government agents, Gotti had threatened to kill a nightclub owner if the man didn't make a payment on a $100,000 loan.

"Your partner was here the other day asking me to shoot him in the head, and I would have if he didn't tell me in a taped joint," Gotti began. "You deserve to get hit, but the reason why you ain't ... is because I gave my word [that] if you come up here to straighten it out [you wouldn't be killed] but that is gonna be off, if you don't come up with it."

"Johnny, you're the best," the man replied.

The months before the murders had been especially tense. Dellacroce's health had faded as the long-simmering conflict over drug dealing had heated up. Members of both Family branches had become jittery.

"Everybody's running scared, John," one of Gotti's crew members had said to him.

"Well, fuck them, we ain't."

"I'm telling you what it is."

"I ain't running scared. I run scared ... when I bet three games and lose the three games. Then I run scared."

After the Sparks hits, a few reporters tried to talk to Gotti, but he demurred. He also declined, through his attorney, to submit voluntarily to an interview with FBI agents, because he knew "nothing about the murders."

Gotti also declined to attend the wake of Castellano, who had declined to attend the wake of Aniello Dellacroce two weeks earlier—a miscalculation compounded by appointing Bilotti underboss.

In fact, all except blood family boycotted Castellano's wake, which was held in the same funeral parlor as Carlo Gambino's, located in Brooklyn, in a peculiarly named section of the Pope's childhood borough: Gravesend.

2

THE NICE N EZ BUG

FOR A MURDER SUSPECT, John Gotti was a bold man in the days following the Pope's timely demise.

He was more irritated than worried that once again NYPD detectives and FBI agents shadowed him as he moved around the dense, tense city in a chauffeured car. The chauffeur was a necessary luxury; like the rest of him, Gotti's foot was aggressive. His motor vehicle rap sheet included several speeding beefs and a drunk-driving conviction, for which his license had been suspended.

He was not widely known in the lawful world, although he had been identified as the "new Godfather" of the "Gambino gang" in some premature newspaper handicapping in March, after Castellano's second racketeering indictment. He was widely known in the unlawful world, where Johnny, Johnny Boy, or John all described the same explosive force, John Gotti.

As Neil Dellacroce's health faded away, Gotti had assumed more responsibility for the Family's "other mob," which controlled a large gambling network. This was turning the proverbial distillery over to an alcoholic; Gotti was an astounding gambler—losses of $30,000, $40,000, $50,000 a weekend on horse racing and sports contests were common. He once won $225,000 on the Brooklyn number—an underworld lottery—and lost it in two nights of shooting craps.

Gotti's crew included three of his six brothers and men he'd known since his teenage street-gang days. "We're the fucking toughest guys in the fucking world," he proclaimed in a voice as coarse as a gravel pit, as he berated someone who owed him money.

Some members of his crew were afraid of him, only partly because of stories he told about himself. One of these—about a fight

with someone he later learned was a cop—revealed a man who took
delight in humiliating a beaten man.

After describing how he had broken the unidentified officer's legs,
ankles, and jaw, Gotti said "I told him, 'You want to play anymore?
You want to play, you cocksucker?' I open his mouth with my finger
and put the gun in. 'You want to play anymore?' He can't talk, he's
crying like a baby."

Like Castellano, Gotti also was under federal indictment. His trial
was only four months away; he faced 40 years of imprisonment if
convicted. He was out on bail, a time to lay low—unless you were
Johnny Boy.

The detectives and agents following Gotti were investigating a
double murder and keeping watch for rumors of war. The murder
of a Family boss was always cleared with the other New York bosses.
Had the tradition held? Would there be revenge? Who would seek it?

The day after Sparks, they knew where to look for answers.

Gotti and many other captains had offices in what they euphemis-
tically called social clubs. Legitimate social clubs, where friends meet
to play cards or pass time, are common in many New York neighborhoods, but the Families adapted them to other purposes.

In Manhattan, the surveillants saw Gotti and Frank DeCicco at the
Ravenite Social Club, an unimposing storefront that was Dellacroce's
longtime command center. They tailed DeCicco to Brooklyn, where
he met his mentor and Sparks companion, James Failla, at the
Veterans and Friends Social Club.

Later, they saw New Jersey Family delegates visiting Gotti at
his headquarters, the Bergin Hunt and Fish Club in Ozone Park,
Queens. As Gotti's notoriety grew, an early reporting error would be
institutionalized and the name of this equally unimposing storefront
would be spelled as "Bergen," even though photos of the club's sign
show Bergin is correct.

Outside the Bergin, the men watching Gotti also counted dozens
of Gambino men entering and leaving. Were they readying for war,
or making the peace?

On Sunday, December 22, 1985, Kenneth McCabe—then an
NYPD detective for the Brooklyn District Attorney's office—saw
Gotti at the Veterans and Friends. McCabe had never seen Gotti
there during hundreds of stakeouts. Gotti was accompanied by Joseph
Massino, a longtime friend who had recently become acting boss of

the Bonanno Family. McCabe also saw DeCicco, Failla, and several other captains, who in groups of two and three kept shuttling between the club and a nearby restaurant.

"There appeared to be a meeting at the location," McCabe later testified. "They would go in the club, come outside, go into the restaurant, back and forth into the club ... so they would not be overheard."

On Christmas Eve, Gotti and DeCicco were back at the Ravenite. So was Andrew Rosenzweig, chief investigator of the Manhattan District Attorney's Investigations Bureau. Gotti and DeCicco retreated to the narrow streets of Little Italy for several private talks, and at one point they walked within earshot of the unassuming, undercover Rosenzweig.

"They've got to come to me," Gotti said.

The same day, from a surveillance van 100 feet away, NYPD Detective John Gurnee took photographs of two hundred men coming to see John Gotti. Outside the Ravenite, as one shiny car after another pulled up, he saw the men bypass all the others and go directly to Gotti, who they embraced and kissed on both cheeks.

Gotti was always treated deferentially at the Ravenite Social Club, but never before like this. "It was very similar to the respect accorded Aniello Dellacroce," Detective Gurnee said.

It now seemed to McCabe, Rosenzweig, Gurnee, and all the other detectives and agents that there would be no war. Gotti was enjoying a peaceful Christmas Eve and many wiseguys—a New York term for gangsters—were rallying around his tree to wish him goodwill toward them.

Without inside information, which is not always shared by the Crime Capital's anticrime forces, the surveillants could only speculate who the new boss would be. They didn't know the inside details that were available; these indicated that Gotti took control of the Family on December 20. A symbolic vote would be held in a few weeks, but Gotti was boss a day after the Pope was buried.

One captain rallying around Gotti was Ralph Mosca, who also had a Queens crew. He was a Castellano man, but fond of Gotti and sailing with the prevailing wind. After meeting with him on December 20, Mosca briefed his crew, which included Dominick Lofaro, 55, a U.S. Army veteran, concrete worker, dice-game operator, numbers runner, illegal-loan collector, thief, and murderer who had spent two days in jail during his life.

"Johnny says everything's goin' be all right," Mosca told Lofaro. "We won't have to carry no guns around."

Mosca instructed Lofaro—whom Gotti was considering for a new gambling operation—that he now must communicate with Gotti through an intermediary, a sure sign that a power shift was afoot.

A lot was afoot that Mosca didn't know about. At the time, Lofaro was wearing two masks. He was working for Mosca and for the New York State Organized Crime Task Force; he was a perfect example of the rationale behind one of the few policies Castellano had laid down for both the Family and the other mob: no drug dealing.

The policy had nothing to do with the destruction of lives or neighborhoods and everything to do with self-interest. New York punished a drug dealer as severely as a murderer, and the Pope believed anyone arrested on a serious drug charge would be tempted to tattle on the Family if prosecutors dangled a deal with a dainty sentence. Serious was only four or more ounces of a controlled substance such as cocaine or heroin.

For men who make their living illegally, the profit in drugs was frequently too strong a lure. Many interpreted the rule this way: Don't get *caught* dealing drugs. They dealt on the side, secretly; they called it going "off the record." It was a gamble, and many who got caught were killed by Family antidrug police.

Dominick Lofaro had "rolled over" two years earlier after a 25-to-life heroin arrest in upstate New York. He was there to manage a gambling operation, but off the record he was making between $30,000 and $50,000 a kilo (2.2 pounds) for simply buying and reselling heroin to local dealers. He informed the arresting officers he was a "made" Gambino soldier in Ralph Mosca's crew.

A made soldier is a formally inducted member of the Family. In a secret ceremony, the soldier promises loyalty to the Family above all else. It's sometimes called "getting your button" or "getting straightened out." Made men are also known as "good fellows" or "nice fellows" or "friends of ours." Many men spend years as "associates," waiting for the day when they'll be deemed able money earners with the right character traits. They must be of Italian blood.

Made men are required to take a vow of noncooperation with the authorities. This is why Lofaro was so prized by the state's Organized Crime Task Force—only a few have ever broken the vow. There could have been only one explanation for his admission when he was arrested: He wanted to deal.

"We had him turned that night," recalled the director of the Task Force, Deputy New York Attorney General Ronald Goldstock. "He was facing big time, but we think he was more afraid he would be killed by Mosca or Castellano. Mosca was an old-timer; he would have enforced the no-drug rule."

A body transmitter was added to Lofaro's wardrobe. No court had to approve this action because legally, a person can secretly tape his own conversations in New York. Lofaro wore the device many months before he met John Gotti and taped him discussing an illegal gambling operation.

Lofaro's taping of Gotti gave the Task Force what it needed—evidence of a crime—to undertake an electronic mugging that would have been illegal without a court order. It asked a judge for permission to plant a listening device—a bug—in an annex to Gotti's Bergin Hunt and Fish Club; and in March of 1985 the bug crawled in and alighted somewhere, according to a court paper, "within two rooms located behind the red door immediately adjacent to the Nice N EZ Auto School," which was one door down from the Bergin club.

Over the next several months, the bug—and, later, a phone tap—raised a secret window on the life of John Gotti, although none of his "overheards" could be used in the federal racketeering case pending against him and others because they were recorded after Gotti was indicted.

The Task Force's eavesdropping order expired in October 1985. After the December murders, Ralph Mosca's conversations with informer Dominick Lofaro were cited in an affidavit requesting approval to reinstitute surveillance. Beginning on December 27, the two rooms behind the red door next to the Nice N EZ Auto School were rebugged and the phone was retapped.

"Gotti is [now] the central figure in the Gambino Family, and seems to have decided that the Family members need not carry weapons; therefore, Gotti must necessarily have knowledge of the facts behind the killings of Castellano and Bilotti," the affidavit said.

Only a few of the overheards on the preexecution and postexecution bugs and taps have ever been revealed. Almost all—and the affidavits supporting them—have remained secret, until now.

On December 27, 1985, the first day the reinstalled bug was in place, Gotti and a crew member referred to an article in that day's *New York Times* attributing to law enforcement sources a theory that Bilotti was the real target of the assassination.

The unidentified man was heard describing the article as "some kind of fuckin' off-the-wall story." The story was later broadcast on local television. "They said that he, that ah, the hit wasn't meant for Paul, it was meant for the other guy."

Gotti's response was partially inaudible, but the bug did hear him say it didn't matter whom Castellano was with that day. "No one was to—Paul, whoever it was, whoever went there, was gonna get shot."

In a separate conversation, agents monitoring the bug heard Gotti utter a tantalizing remark about whether the hits were sanctioned by the other Crime Capital bosses, who included Gotti's friend Joseph Massino, the acting Bonanno boss.

The conversation was with a childhood friend, his closet friend and henchman Angelo Ruggiero, a burly schemer who already had been recorded, bugged, and tapped more than any other Gambino, and probably more than any Family man ever. Ruggiero was under indictment, too, in a heroin-dealing case, and he was about to succeed Gotti as captain of the Bergin Hunt and Fish crew.

Gotti and Ruggiero talked about many matters, including other bosses, which prompted Gotti to say: "One half sanctioned us, the other half said, they're with them, we sanction ya."

Though hardly proof of who the actual murderers were, it was obvious the remark meant that two of the other four bosses backed a plot against Castellano and that two others went along.

Early in January 1986, as the boss-elect acquainted himself with the reins of power, a personal note in his life went unnoticed. In Manhattan, a judge slapped his youngest brother, a non-crew member, with a six-years-to-life term for selling cocaine to an undercover agent. No family members attended the sentencing and Vincent Gotti, age 33, went directly to jail.

Another brother, Gene, age 39, was an important crew member and a defendant with Angelo in the heroin case; he would be by his brother's side as the heir-certain contemplated his moves—unaware of the electronic plot taking place against him. One of John Gotti's early ideas, which he shared with Ralph Mosca, was hiring Dominick Lofaro to run his Queens gambling operation.

"This could mean a promotion for you," Mosca told Lofaro.

Mosca also said that once Gotti approved Lofaro to run the Queens operation, Lofaro would not need the okay of other captains to operate within their areas—whatever a boss wants, he gets.

Gotti stated this principle to a soldier who expressed concern about stepping on a captain's toes.

"No big deal," John said.

"But he's a captain."

"I'm your boss!"

Gotti was thinking a lot about how a boss should conduct himself as the day of his coronation approached. For instance, Angelo brought him a problem about a loan-sharking customer, but Gotti replied, "I don't deal with this anymore."

Gotti elaborated while discussing what he would say to a soldier who wanted to propose a business deal directly to him. "I'll tell him, 'Listen, your skipper will keep me up to date, you keep your skipper up to date.' I can't socialize with these guys. I can't bring myself down. I'm a boss, you know what I mean? I gotta isolate myself a little bit."

On January 10, Gotti held a similar discussion with Angelo in which he revealed—no surprise here—that he had chosen Frank DeCicco as his underboss.

"What we're gonna suggest to you is, everybody comes and sees us [captains]," Angelo said. "We'll see Frankie [DeCicco], we'll decide if we think it's important, then we'll bring it to you."

"Frankie's an underboss at least," Gotti replied.

"All right, so …"

"They have to go through a skipper, then go to [the] underboss."

The bug in the room next to the Nice N EZ Auto School captured many conversations that demonstrated Gotti was fully ready to exercise his power. He told Angelo that no new men would be made for six months to a year. He discussed which soldiers he would move to which crews—"We got to clip these guys' wings a little bit." He also boasted: "I could break every one of the captains now … a new boss does that as soon as [he's elected]; [then] he gets up and makes a speech."

He didn't intend to demote the captains, but felt he was entitled to their resignations. He was the new president and they were the old cabinet. Gotti told an associate he had threatened to strip the skippers in a meeting with the aging Joe N. Gallo, the counselor, or *consigliere*, of the Gambino Family since the Carlo Gambino era. Gotti considered Gallo a yes-man.

Gotti's description of this meeting, also attended by several captains, or *capos*, indicated how thoroughly he enjoyed Family politics.

He recalled Gallo giving a speech in which he agreed the new boss had the power to break up the cabinet. Gotti believed that Gallo was merely granting the point, to stop him from demoting Gallo as the Family counselor. The boss let Gallo know he couldn't be fooled.

As Gotti explained:

"I said, 'Joe, don't flatter yourself.' I said, 'You ain't no Paulie. You think you're dealing with a fool? I break twenty-three captains [and] I put ten in. They vote you down. I break them, put my original captains back and you ain't no *consigliere!*'"

Gotti, as many other recorded conversations had and would demonstrate, regularly regaled friends, soldiers, and associates with tales of his Family prowess. "[Gallo] told Angelo," he said, summing up the meeting, "'Where the fuck has he been? How did he figure this out?'"

On January 13, 1986, Gotti appeared publicly for the first time since the Castellano-Bilotti murders. He attended a pretrial hearing on his racketeering case at the U.S. District Court House in Brooklyn. The borough president of Queens had just attempted suicide, after a friend agreed to spill his political-corruption guts to a grand jury. A huge scandal involving organized crime of an aboveworld sort was on, but even so, the press showed up to take a look at the new underworld boss and fire a few hallway questions.

Gotti was jovial and coy when asked if he was boss of the Gambino Family: "I'm the boss of my family—my wife and kids at home."

It was unusual for a Family man, let alone a boss, to answer any questions, even the most innocuous, but Gotti—a *GQ* model of good grooming and style with his double-breasted gray suit and camel's hair overcoat—acted like a politician too dignified to respond to his opponents' gutter charges:

"We don't know nothing ourselves. We hear [the boss talk] the same place you [reporters] get it. We get it from the FBI."

Gotti and WCBS radio reporter Mary Gay Taylor arrived at the courtroom door at the same time.

"I was brought up to hold the door open for ladies," he smiled, a twinkle in his eye, as he grasped the door with his right hand and waved her in with his left arm.

After the brief session, he climbed into his lawyer's black Cadillac and rode off—having left a fairly positive impression, considering that the case against him and six codefendants involved three murders.

3

MEET THE NEW BOSS

AT AN UNGODLY HOUR at some unbugged location on January 16, 1986, John Joseph Gotti Jr., at the comparatively young age of 45, was officially selected as boss of the Gambino Family, the largest, most powerful organized crime group in America.

As expected, Frank DeCicco was confirmed as underboss and "for now" Joe N. Gallo remained counselor, according to Ralph Mosca, who attended the swearing-in ceremony and immediately informed Dominick Lofaro and other Mosca crew members.

DeCicco, who held a no-show International Brotherhood of Teamsters job, was given his own squad, the crew of the late Thomas Bilotti, and Angelo Ruggiero took over Gotti's Bergin Hunt and Fish crew, which, besides Gene Gotti, included Peter and Richard Gotti. Peter was a year older than John, Richard two years younger. They had minor criminal records, but Gene—in addition to the heroin case with Angelo—was a defendant with John in the Brooklyn racketeering case.

After a meeting, Angelo accompanied Gotti back to the club. Angelo had come down a long dirty road with Gotti, a road with many bodies alongside it. They had suffered similar personal tragedies. Angelo relished this triumphant moment and felt partly responsible—he had served Gotti dishonorably well.

"Meet your new boss," Angelo beamed to crew members as he and John walked into the Bergin.

"It's gonna be nice, you watch," Gotti told the men.

His election had as much suspense as a meeting of the electoral college an hour after the polls close. The fact that Gotti was under indictment made no difference. The fact that he could be sent away for the rest of his life made no difference. The only thing that made a difference was him, John Gotti—he had measured the odds, put all his chips on the table, and busted the house.

Almost everyone had already forgotten about another legal detail nagging the boss, whose victory was celebrated by the purchase of a $60,000 Mercedes-Benz SEL.

He also was under indictment in a state case, accused of assault and theft—the embarrassing result of a temperamental scuffle with a refrigerator mechanic over a double-parked car in Queens in 1984. Gotti was accused of slapping the man; an associate of Gotti's was accused of taking $325 from the man's shirt pocket—out of spite, not larceny, but it read like theft by both in the newspapers, which made it acutely embarrassing.

"The crime is beneath him," his attorney would point out.

Except for the unseemliness of the idea that he had mugged a mechanic, the case was a nuisance to Gotti, compared to the federal case. The state trial was set for March, but he believed it could be handled. Somehow.

The day after his inauguration, Gotti griped about the miserliness of the old boss. Theoretically, a boss gets a cut of the operations of each captain, who get a slice of each soldier's. But Gotti learned that Castellano had been taking $5,000 every Christmas from the life savings of the wife of an elderly captain who had only $2,000 coming in from an untypically moribund crew.

Castellano was a "fuck" for doing this. "Well, listen to me, that's ended," Gotti told an associate. "[It] don't mean [however] that you don't have to try to hustle and put something together for us."

Other aspects of the Family's far-flung money-making ventures crossed Gotti's desk his first day on the job. He revised the payments that an unspecified industry was making to Castellano and Bilotti so that a soldier in the scheme got a bigger share. He discussed a plan to stop a threatened labor action against concrete plants if they would "sweeten the pie."

Many conversations over the next several weeks showed the graduate of the blue-collar Family within a Family becoming a white-color boss, or trying to. On January 18, Gotti told Angelo about a deal headed his way with a representative of an unknown group: "He won a deal, supposed to get a job. Three and a half million in [contracts], a hundred and ninety-five thousand dollars in kickbacks or more than that. He says it all goes to Johnny Gotti."

On January 23, the new Gambino troika—Gotti, DeCicco, and Gallo—traveled to the Helmsley Palace Hotel in Manhattan to meet with recording industry executives seeking venture capital for an album by a new artist. The introductions were made by a longtime captain, Joseph Armone.

Someone tipped off the police as well as a network television crew working on an industry payola story; they arrived as Gotti and the others stepped off an elevator into the lobby. The ambushed mobsters declined interviews, but sinister footage of a handsome, well-dressed man described as an unknown gangster with record-industry contacts was telecast nationwide.

A few days later, back at the Bergin annex, after someone brought a copy of the singer's sample tape, Gotti was uncertain about the idea. It was risky to invest in a new singer—and the recording industry was too dishonest.

"They change two or three sounds and they make their own [record] and you get fucked."

The duties of a boss were many, and one was punishing miscreant subordinates. He grumbled about one offender this way: "This kid is as high as he's ever gonna get in life. This kid, I'm just trying to think of the way to punish him now. Enough to know how I didn't like that. Teach him what bitterness is. Give him something fuckin' [to] really feel sorry about. This ain't a ball game here. This ain't no ball game. This ain't no game."

Gotti was amazed after his ascension that at least one captain—Anthony Gaggi, uncle of the car-case witness against Castellano—had not adapted to the new game. He learned this during a telephone call from a soldier reporting about a dispute involving a Brooklyn restaurant. Family members had just bought into it and the landlord wanted to check them out.

The soldier said Gaggi had told him to "bring" Gotti to a sit-down with the landlord and the new partners.

"He's under me!" Gotti shouted. "You tell him, [to] get his ass up here to see me!"

In the meantime, concerning the inquisitive landlord, Gotti told the soldier to tell Gaggi and the others not to engage in any more "warning shit" until a sitdown. After all, people could be reasoned with.

"People ain't stupid, they know what we are," Gotti said. "So what are we gonna do? What, are we gonna worry about cops now?"

Three days after these comments, Angelo complained of having to visit someone about the same problem, which was "still up in the air." Forty-eight hours passed, and then a fire damaged the restaurant; authorities proclaimed it arson.

As this restaurant problem was being solved, another was beginning. Some men, believed to be members of a carpenters' local union, were vandalizing Manhattan construction sites using non-union labor. More than $30,000 damage was inflicted on the Bankers and Brokers Restaurant near Wall Street. It was owned by a Gambino soldier and previously owned by Castellano's four children.

The business agent of the carpenters' local, the largest in the country, was John F. O'Connor, 51. Gotti instructed two men to find out who O'Connor was "with"—not whether he was connected to a Family, but which one. In the Crime Capital, when it came to the construction industry, Gotti's assumption was historically justified.

At the time, O'Connor was the target of an investigation into whether he accepted bribes from the contractors to allow them to use non-union carpenters. When Gotti learned that O'Connor might have ordered the restaurant sacked, he said the union official was "becoming overconfident" and wondered whether he ought to "bust him up."

Over the next few weeks, inquiries went out to members of the Genovese Family, who reported that they had only partial control of the carpenters' union and were "embarrassed" because a Gambino Family place had been trashed by a renegade element.

Weeks later, O'Connor was shot several times in the lobby of his union's office building; the gunman, who fired four times, escaped. The victim crawled into an elevator, called for help, and survived. A few months later, O'Connor was indicted for taking thousands of dollars in bribes.

Sometimes the men in the Bergin annex were more paranoid about bugs than at other times. Years earlier, the pay phones in an empty storefront on the other side of the Bergin, which crew members used to place bets, had been tapped. So now and then they would whisper or turn up the volume on a television or radio, or run tap water while they talked.

This made it difficult to decipher some conversations, but usually at least a revealing sentence or two was picked up—such as when Gotti discussed a gambling operation using illegal slot machines: "He's with me, the stops are mine, the machines are mine."

Good "overheards" showed that while Gotti may have been a little uncertain about some aspects of his new position, he was not uncertain about himself. Late in February, he told Angelo: "You present the case, paint it up a little bit ... This has got to earn some [money] here. For us, not for other Families, but for us first ... I don't know about concrete, steel, and construction, but I got a lot of spies in the street and I know everything."

Again, early in March, underboss Frank DeCicco expressed concern about a "bad situation," most likely a jurisdictional conflict between the Gambino and Genovese Families, possibly over a construction project just north of the city that involved Family-connected unions.

"I'm thinking all night long how the fuck to resolve this motherfucker," the underboss said.

"You gotta understand we gotta be a little strong," the boss replied. "We gotta be strong against other people who are strong."

Gotti told DeCicco they didn't want to be lulled into a false sense of security, like Paul Castellano was.

"Frankie, you know what I'm saying ... that's what this guy allowed himself to be tricked into, Frankie."

Not all of the new boss's business was about such serious enterprises as concrete, steel, and construction. The boss was wherever a buck was, or might be.

A periodic topic on the Nice N EZ bug was an ice cream company in New Jersey. Gotti, Angelo, and two members of the DeCavalcante Family had somehow acquired part ownership three years before. Gotti, who said he owned seventeen percent, wasn't very happy with his lack of return or the company's prospects.

On January 10, NYPD detectives tailed Gotti to a meeting in which he reviewed the matter with the DeCavalcante fellows. Beforehand, he told Angelo the agenda: "Do I want my money out of it, or get rid of it?"

The next day, at the Bergin annex, he gave a report. "So I said, 'What's this company worth?' They said, 'Four million right now. If we sold it, we owe nothin'.'"

Gotti was displeased that his investment would yield nothing, but the men insisted that "in two weeks" the company's fortunes would turn around. The boss agreed to wait, but wasn't convinced.

"I told my partners, all nice fellows, I said, 'If conversation had calories in it, I'd be the fattest guy in the world, 'cause that's all I'm getting, conversation.'"

In March, the subject came up again when an associate of Gotti apparently came in with the latest nonprofit statement.

"You tell me the ice cream business is worth this? This?" the boss fumed.

Gotti compared his investment to what he could earn by investing the same money in loan-sharking—the illegal lending of cash at usurious interest rates. He cited a loan-shark rate of 1.5 percent of vigorish, or interest, a week, and launched into an amusing tirade:

"This guy told me in two weeks we're gonna see money! That's two and a half months ago. I'm not his fuckin' kid! We'll make Dee Bee [a Gambino captain] buy me out. Corky [a DeCavalcante man] buy me out. Any fuckin' body buy me out. I'll sell it for fifty dollars!"

"No you won't," the associate said.

"Fuck I won't. My end, I'll sell it."

Gotti was clearly weary of it all. "Afraid this ain't my fuckin' day," he added. "Ain't my fuckin' day."

He wondered if he should visit the company, investigate why ice cream wasn't profitable in New Jersey, but the associate advised against it: too many surveillants around.

"This is pathetic," Gotti complained again. "I don't even get ice cream out of it. If I want ice cream I have [to see another person]. I love those fuckin' frozen red somethin's. We got the company three years, never saw a dime. Never seen an ice cream bar out of it! If you took [the money] and you put it on the street for a point and a half, we'd be rich over three years! We'd be rich without all the ice cream meltin' or nothin'."

Gotti's impatience was easy to understand. He was in a much higher world of commerce now. On March 6, an unidentified man asked him to meet three others seeking to acquire control of gambling casinos in Puerto Rico. The men already owned a casino in the Bahamas. What the bug overheard was limited, but it appeared that the men wanted to give Gotti a piece of their action if he would solve a problem they were having with a disposal company they owned.

It was probably no problem at all. James Failla was an official of the Manhattan Trade Waste Association, the management group, and other Family men dominated the sanitation unions.

Another man, identified only as Joey, enticed Gotti with a story about gasoline. Two soldiers in another Family recently had been indicted by a grand jury because of a scheme to skim money from the sale of gasoline by not paying federal and state taxes. But Joey said that didn't mean similar opportunities were not available.

"A fuckin' twenty-eight cents [a gallon] you can steal," Joey said. "I'm talkin' about doing twenty, thirty million gallons a month."

Gotti did some quick figuring, noting that even at two cents a gallon on 30 million gallons, "It's six hundred thousand dollars."

"Wow," an unidentified person in the room said.

"I gotta do it right now," Gotti said. "Right now, I gotta do it. I gotta call this guy …"

Gotti picked up a telephone, dialed one of his bodyguards and asked him to contact someone he referred to as "Bobby the Jew" and "tell him to call me."

Gotti was free to receive such propositions because he had been granted bail after his indictment in the federal case. Ironically, a young and well-educated movie producer, who also was a capo in the Colombo Family, was being held without bail and preparing to plead guilty and pay $15 million in restitution for the largest gas-tax ripoff in history. The case was before the same judge who would preside at Gotti's trial.

Somewhere in a schedule clogged by men bearing gifts, deals, and problems, Gotti was able to find time for his lawyers. To properly manage his Family, take advantage of opportunities, and enjoy his status, he had to stay out of jail.

The nagging business with the Queens mechanic he was accused of assaulting and robbing was about to come to trial. The case had taken a few remarkable turns since the events in December—unusual is usual in Family cases—and by the time it was over, there would be many more.

Even after the case was officially closed, the turbulence around Gotti would keep it unofficially open.

4

I FORGOTTI!

THE CASE OF THE MECHANIC versus the mobster began September 11, 1984, the day an empty double-parked car blocked the impatient way of Romual Piecyk. He was a gruff, burly man who earned a living wage fixing cooling equipment, including the large walk-in refrigerators used to hang animal carcasses.

Piecyk was 35 years old, and no saint, at least not from 1972 to 1979, when on different occasions he was arrested for drunkenness, possession of a weapon, and assault. He was 6 foot 2 and considered himself a tough guy.

He ran into some other tough guys while in Maspeth, a tough working-class neighborhood in Queens. His car was blocked by the double-parked car outside two gambling dens under John Gotti's control, a social club and the Cozy Corner Bar. He got in his car and leaned on his horn. Again and again.

Out of the Cozy Corner Bar came an associate of Gotti's, Frank Colletta. He reached in through the open driver's window and smacked Piecyk in the face, according to the testimony of police officers who interviewed Piecyk moments later. Piecyk had just cashed his paycheck, and Colletta lifted $325 from his shirt pocket, apparently a fee he charged for aggravation.

Piecyk left his car and the pair began scuffling. Gotti then appeared and slapped Piecyk in the face; Gotti stepped back, glared, and made a motion with his hand, as if he were drawing something from the waistband of his trousers.

"You better get the fuck out of here," he said.

Piecyk did, and so did Gotti and Colletta.

Someone had called the police, and a car from the 106th Precinct arrived within minutes. Sgt. Thomas Donohue and Officer Raymond Doyle found the refrigerator man standing on the corner of Seventy-second Street and Grand Avenue. His face was puffy and he had cuts and blood on one hand and an arm.

"Two guys just beat me up and took my money," he said.

"All right, we'll make out a report," Doyle replied.

Piecyk pointed toward the Cozy Corner Bar, but it was now empty. Piecyk then looked through the window of a restaurant next door.

"There they are!"

Inside, Gotti and Colletta were sitting at a table with eight other men. Piecyk pointed them out and Sgt. Donohue told them they were under arrest and ordered them to stand.

In a showy display of solidarity, everyone at the table stood, and Sgt. Donohue, in a brief, tense scene, ordered all but Gotti and Colletta to sit down.

"Do you know who I am?" Gotti wanted to know.

"Step out," said Doyle, who didn't.

"Let me talk to this guy," Gotti said as Sgt. Donohue handcuffed him.

He wouldn't, and the heir to Carlo Gambino was led away like a miserable Times Square mugger.

Piecyk went to the precinct on his own and charges were filed based on his story. Gotti was booked and released on his own recognizance, pending action by a grand jury. A lawyer later involved in the case described it as "an example of one bully meeting another, except the first bully would be reformed."

———————————

At the time, FBI agents were regularly meeting with two daring men who knew a lot about the Gotti crew—they were part of it. They were not cooperating witnesses like the secretly wired Dominick Lofaro. They were informers. Years earlier, for revenge, for money, and to buy a little insurance against their own criminal acts, they had begun talking about Gotti and others as long as they never had to testify. Their tips enabled the FBI to make many arrests and recoveries of stolen goods. One, a personal friend of Gotti's, had been talking since 1966. The other had "gone bad," which is how the Family described such men, in 1976.

For legal reasons, the information they gave to the FBI was never made a part of Gotti's federal case in Brooklyn, but it is documented in secret FBI files. Every time an agent met or spoke with them—and there were hundreds of contacts—a memo went into the files.

To keep their identities secret, even within the FBI, the informers were known by code designations. The longtime personal friend of Gotti was Source BQ 5558–TE, "BQ" for Brooklyn-Queens and "TE" for Top Echelon, the highest informer rank in the RBI. The other was called Source BQ 11766–OC, "OC" meaning Organized Crime. The first source also was known as "Wahoo."

FBI agents always contacted their sources after a major event in Gotti's life such as the Piecyk incident. As in this case, the sources didn't always have startling information; sometimes they just had little brush strokes, little interesting details.

Source BQ 11766–OC, for instance, said Gotti told the officers who arrested him that he had $3,000 in his pocket and did not need to grab money off Piecyk. He said Gotti was shocked to learn that Piecyk didn't know him and had filed charges. Source Wahoo told how Neil Dellacroce reacted to his top captain's arrest. Neil told Gotti, he said, not to "interfere with the victim" because it will "bring heat on the Family."

A few days after the incident in Maspeth, Piecyk testified before a grand jury, which returned an indictment against Gotti and Colletta on felony assault and theft charges. The authorities said Piecyk was told Colletta and Gotti were wiseguys; he later said he was only told they were "punks." More than a year later, after the Sparks murders, a trial date was set, but now Piecyk began to read and hear more than he wanted to about Johnny Boy, who obviously wasn't just a punk, or even just a wiseguy.

Piecyk began looking over his shoulder. He bought a gun, which prompted his pregnant wife to temporarily move out. Exactly what happened during the next three months will most likely never be publicly known, but Piecyk did decide not to say any more nasty things about Gotti and Colletta. A lawyer familiar with the case said Piecyk couldn't get his mind off the idea of being found dead in one of the meat refrigerators he repaired.

Piecyk dictated a letter to his wife—which came to light later—in which he recounted the Cozy Corner encounter and said: "As time went on, my wife and I saw the name of one of the men who assaulted me, John Gotti, appearing in the [*New York*] *Daily News*. The media printed that he was next in line for godfather. Naturally, my idea of pursuing this matter dropped, and I cut off communication with [the Queens District Attorney's office]."

Piecyk said that after the cops arrived in Maspeth, "everyone connected with Gotti came out of the restaurant, looked my car over, and took the [license] plate number down." He sold the car, but "everyone knows who I am and probably how to find me."

Piecyk said he was told by cops that he would have to testify only to the grand jury—his name would not be revealed and the file would be sealed. For a man who had been arrested several times, this was a remarkable statement; it would seem that he was familiar enough with legal processes to know that a defendant has a constitutional right to face his accusers in court.

"I feel I have been lied to by the laws that are supposed to protect us," Piecyk wrote. "I have been a pawn in the power game between the government and the mob. I help to expose the bad factors of one organization, and then neither needs me anymore ... I can't and will not live the rest of my life in fear."

On February 24, 1986, Sgt. Anthony Falco of the Queens District Attorney's detective squad visited Piecyk to discuss the trial, now only a few days away.

"I ain't testifying," Piecyk said.

Sgt. Falco recalled later: "He stated he was in fear of his life, as well as the safety of his wife. He was afraid for his life because of Gotti's people."

Piecyk told Falco he had been receiving anonymous phone calls at odd hours from people who hung up. He said the brakes on his mechanic's van were cut, but that he did not want the police to investigate because "he was afraid our presence might further endanger his life."

On February 28, an assistant district attorney in Queens, Kirke Bartley, asked a judge to withhold the names of jurors in the case. He cited a "strong likelihood of juror tampering or harassment" and said Piecyk had received death threats.

On March 5, on the eve of court arguments on the juror question, Piecyk was interviewed by Stewart Ain, a *Daily News* reporter.

He denied receiving death threats or having his brakes cut. He said he would appear in court—on Gotti's side.

"I'm not going to go against Mister Gotti. I'm going in his behalf. I don't want to hurt Mister Gotti."

All the press coverage was upsetting another member of the Gotti family, Mrs. John J. Gotti Jr. She wrote a letter, too, to the *Daily News*, complaining of harassment and attacking all press "vultures," particularly another *Daily News* reporter, David J. Krajicek.

In another time, when she and Gotti were first married and they were struggling financially, she had aimed her anger at him and taken him to court. But that had been patched up and now Victoria Gotti passionately came to her husband's and family's defense.

She said John Gotti was too rich to steal: "In 1981, I inherited a little under a million dollars from a beautiful, hard-working lady whose family before her ... came to this country for a better life. That lady was my mother. The point is, my husband needs nothing. Not three cents, much less three hundred dollars."

Victoria Gotti also was perturbed by a column Krajicek wrote for the Queens section of the newspaper in which he described John A. Gotti, age 22, the couple's oldest son, as a "baby bully" and poked fun at the way he talked. Young Gotti's mother said he had been graduated from New York Military Academy, upstate on the Hudson River, and didn't have a grammar problem.

"After reading that bit of trash you passed off as journalism, I'm not surprised that people like Sinatra, Madonna, and Diana Ross kick, punch, and spit on you ... you are tantamount to vultures that will print anything, no matter how inaccurate, to sell a paper, or make brownie points with the boss."

At the time, John A. Gotti was facing assault charges, too. He was accused of striking an off-duty cop during a fight at a Howard Beach diner. His mother wrote, "My son 'Baby Bully' went to the aid of a friend who was getting hit by two cops, who did not identify themselves as such."

She added that she didn't wish the "pain and agony in my heart on anyone." She ended her letter with what she described as an "old Indian saying": "Don't criticize your neighbor until you have walked a mile in his moccasins." The letter was handwritten on embossed stationery and mailed via certified delivery. Its authenticity was never questioned, except by her husband's lawyer, who said the *Daily News* should not print the letter, "whoever it is from."

In his column, Krajicek said that when he and a photographer appeared outside the Gotti home in Howard Beach, young Gotti threatened to "start choppin' heads off" if they didn't leave.

The 22-year-old Gotti was president of Samson Trucking Company in Brooklyn. A few days earlier, Angelo Ruggiero had told him that a Gambino captain friendly with the president of a Teamsters local was told that the local could toss jobs young John's way. The electronic surveillance at the Bergin annex also demonstrated how and where the young trucking executive may have developed his proclivity for the use of menacing words.

In a conversation on March 2, the same day Krajicek's column was printed, John Gotti complained to his son about someone who had mentioned his name over the telephone, an unauthorized and intolerable breach of Family etiquette.

"I'm gonna give him a kick in the fuckin' ass," father Gotti said. "The fuckin' guy uses my name on the fuckin' phone."

"You serious? This guy's so full of shit it ain't funny."

"You tell [the person] next time, don't be mentioning no fuckin' names on the phone or I'll put him in the fuckin' hospital. And before you do anything or he does any fuckin' thing, you tell me first ... There's fuckin' reasons why I don't want people to go bothering people on the fuckin' phone."

"All right."

"Now make sure tomorrow you see me and I'll tell you what I want you to do there."

"All right."

On March 8, a Queens judge, Ann Dufficy, denied the request to withhold jurors' names in the Piecyk case—state law didn't allow it—but ruled their business and home addresses could be kept secret. Jury screening began that day.

Jury selection in Gotti's case in federal court in Brooklyn was not far off either. In fact, a lot would be happening in Gotti's two cases over the next few weeks, not all of it publicly reported.

On March 13, Gotti placed a mysterious, apparently pre-arranged, call to a public telephone booth in Manhattan and spoke to a man who identified himself only as "Frank." They talked about the Piecyk case. Frank thought he could be helpful.

"Hello, is this John?"

"Yeah."

"My name is Frank, John, I'd like to meet with you. I think I got something to help you out. I'm sure of it. In fact, I, it'd be worth, very worth your while."

"What's it like? What about it?"

"It's about your case in court."

"Yeah? Which one? I have two cases pending, uh, Frank."

"The one with the, the, the, the jerk-off there that took the three hundred and twenty five dollars off of, the one that ya got all the publicity about."

"Yeah."

"I know it's a nothing case but they, they could break your balls considering who you are."

"Yeah, well that's for sure. You, you can't tell me what it's about …"

"I don't want to talk over the phone, John."

"Huh?"

"[I'm] totally paranoid about talking over the phone. It'll only take five minutes of your time. I'm sure it will be helpful to you."

"You're sure this is gonna be helpful to the case now, Frank, this is not gonna …"

"… Guarantee you don't get convicted, how's that?"

"You guarantee I don't get convicted?"

"I can't guarantee you get acquitted, but I can guarantee you don't get convicted, you understand that?"

For a courtroom veteran like Gotti, it wasn't at all hard to understand. "Frank" was promising a mistrial, probably in the form of a hung jury, probably by buying a juror. Of course, such a guarantee had its price.

"I ain't workin' for nothin'," Frank said.

"Yeah."

The men made plans to meet at Teachers Too, a Manhattan bar, at ten o'clock that night.

"All right, I hope you're gonna be helpful," John said.

"It's more than helpful, John."

"Okay, buddy."

Gotti stood up Frank later that evening. Organized Crime Task Force agents who conducted surveillance also did not spot any Gotti men. A man who answered to Frank was in the bar, but was not identified. At least four scenarios were possible: Frank had a Piecyk

juror in his pocket, and Gotti decided to pass; he was a scam artist
working a bold one; or an undercover agent on a law enforcement
sting; or a nut case.

Opening arguments in the Piecyk case were held March 18. John
Gotti's trial lawyer was Bruce Cutler. Like Gotti, Cutler was a stout
dynamo out of Brooklyn, and good at what he did, which was to take
the prosecution's evidence, spin it, scuff it, twist it, and pound it to a
pulp, until it was nothing more than a lumpy pile of reasonable
doubt—just as he did with opponents when he was an undefeated
high-school wrestler and a college-football linebacker.

Up until 1981, Cutler was a prosecutor for the Brooklyn District
Attorney's office. For several years afterward, new lawyers were still
being told stories about his cunningly ferocious courtroom style; but
he was working the other side of the street now, a familiar career path
for lawyers whose skills are worth Manhattan apartments and homes
in the Hamptons.

Piecyk was drunk and picked the fight, Cutler told the jury as the
trial began. Gotti intervened because he knew the 46-year-old Colletta
had a heart problem. "And so he goes to pull this bully off the little
man," Cutler explained.

Piecyk was due to testify the next day, but failed to appear. He was
located two days later in a hospital where he had admitted himself
for elective surgery on his shoulder. He was taken into custody on a
material-witness warrant. In the Queens District Attorney's office that
night, he began to cry and asked to speak to Sgt. Falco alone.

"He apologized for his behavior," Sgt Falso said later, "and stated
he wasn't really mad at us. He did not want to testify. He was afraid
for himself, his wife, and he again stated that he was afraid of Gotti's
people."

On March 24, the reluctant witness, wearing dark glasses and
chewing on his fingernails, took the stand and took an oath to tell the
truth, which was that he was scared out of his mind.

The court was crowded with reporters and spectators. They fidgeted as the assistant district attorney, Kirke Bartley, led Piecyk
through a set-the-scene thicket of questions, anxious for the moment
when Bartley would ask him to identify the defendants. At the defense
table, John Gotti, employing a style he would employ again, was as
nonchalant as an easy chair, a man bored with the channel.

When the questions came close about the day in Maspeth, Piecyk
invoked the Fifth Amendment. This was because a lawyer had advised

him to seek immunity for anything he said—because the assistant district attorney could use Piecyk's grand jury testimony to prosecute him for perjury if his story changed at trial.

A recess was called, and Piecyk got his immunity.

Finally, Bartley asked Piecyk whether the men who "punched and smacked" him were in the courtroom.

"I ask you to look around the courtroom," Bartley said.

"I don't see them now," Piecyk said, without looking up.

"You don't see them now?"

Piecyk now looked around. He glanced toward the rear of the court. He looked to the left, he looked to the right. He cast his eyes here and there until finally, briefly, on the easy chair of John Gotti.

"I do not," he said.

Bartley tried to save the day, but it was a lost cause. He asked Piecyk several more questions about the dispute outside the Cozy Corner Bar, such as whether he recalled how the man who first slapped him was dressed.

"To be perfectly honest, it was so long ago I don't remember."

Piecyk didn't remember who slapped him either. "I don't remember who slapped me ... I have no recollection of what the two men looked like or how they were dressed."

The media played the story big. "I FORGOTTI!" said a large headline in the *New York Post*.

The next day, the judge ruled the prosecutor could not admit Piecyk's grand jury testimony into evidence because "The witness is not missing or dead." But "surely his memory is missing or dead," Bartley argued.

The judge then granted a defense motion to dismiss the charges and Gotti left court through a mob of reporters and bodyguards—one case down, one to go.

"The confusion has all been cleared up," he said.

Piecyk was cornered for a comment, too. He said he was not frightened into forgetfulness, but added: "Any human being would lie to save his life."

Piecyk went off to nurse his ego, which would suffer more self-inflicted wounds in the days and months ahead. Gotti went off to Ozone Park to celebrate and that night all the king's men came to Queens to cheer him. Almost all, and the king reminded one of his subjects of this the next day.

The absentee celebrant was Joseph LaForte, an elderly Gambino captain from Staten Island, who claimed the press of other important business and then apologized:

"You know I'm not selfish, John, you know I'm not selfish. You know it."

Gotti responded in a typically hyperbolic way. "Hey, Joe, you're trying to tell me then that everybody else, Angelo, Frankie, his Uncle Joey, Joe Gallo, ah, all of Eighty-sixth Street [in Brooklyn], all our people there, Jersey people, all these guys [are not] as important as you. They run cities, they run towns, countries!"

LaForte said he wasn't saying that.

"You pick up the fuckin' *Post* to find out how your fuckin' friend made out in court."

In the aftermath of victory, Gotti felt so lucky that he called a bookie.

"What are they bettin'?" he asked after calling a number subscribed to by a car wash in Ozone Park.

"They're goin' with Boston tonight," a man he called "Carmine" replied, referring to the Boston Celtics professional basketball team. "They're bettin' Boston, Washington, they're taking the points with Atlanta."

"Yeah."

"Uh, oh, they're bettin' that Wyoming [wins] in the college game."

"They're crazy. What's the spread there?"

"Five and a half, Ohio State."

"I love Ohio State."

"Ya like them that much?"

"I swear to God."

The boss who loved Ohio State steered the conversation to horses running that day at Roosevelt Raceway. He placed bets on the first two races and on the Daily Double. He bet the way he felt, on the favorites, to win.

On March 31, 1986, the plane-fearful boss traveled to Florida by limousine. His federal case was due to start April 7, and the sun would coat his face with a healthy polish in time for jury selection.

His family stayed behind, but his Family went along. He was accompanied by his driver, Bartholomew Borriello, and Joseph Corrao, a captain close to the late Paul Castellano. In Florida, he was spotted aboard a yacht with Ettore Zappi, a captain now based in Miami; James Failla, the captain from Eighty-sixth Street in Brooklyn who was Frank DeCicco's "rabbi," and Frank Dapolito, an official of a New York Teamsters local.

On the day Gotti departed, one of his codefendants in the federal case, Armond Dellacroce, disappeared. Armond was the son of Gotti's mentor. He was 30 years old and had dropped out of high school to emulate his father. He had pleaded guilty to racketeering after his father died late in 1985 and was on bail awaiting sentencing; he faced up to 20 years.

Maybe two decades in jail is why he failed to show for sentencing; maybe it wasn't. He had been regularly contacting the pretrial services division since the plea hearing, when his bail was set at $250,000. He was a good bail risk, his lawyer had said then, because bail would be secured by a deed to a Manhattan town house owned by his aunt and uncle. No Armond, no more town house.

"There is no question in my mind but that the moral commitment that Mr. Dellacroce has to these people is alone sufficient to ensure his presence," said defense lawyer Gerald Shargel.

Diane F. Giacalone, an assistant U.S. attorney, agreed that the bail arrangements were sufficient. Giacalone, age 36, was now steering the case toward trial after leading the three-year investigation that produced the indictment. The process had been bruising and controversial, but Giacalone was dogged and tireless. She had also attended a Catholic school in Ozone Park, Queens, and had given her life over to the pursuit of Gotti and the others.

Young Dellacroce's guilty plea was a victory for justice, she would certainly say, but also a victory for her, a scalp to silently wave at her detractors, which included other government attorneys in the courthouse and some FBI agents.

At the plea hearing, she pointed out that she had originally favored a higher bail. "Mr. Dellacroce, through his father's influence and power ... which reached throughout the United States, was capable of sustaining himself outside of this jurisdiction for a long period of time," she said. "It made possible his flight."

The death of the underboss changed her mind. Armond "no longer has the ability to call upon his father's influence and money ... his financial resources are changed and his position within the community ... has changed. [His] position ... was to some extent derivative of his father's position."

"We are surprised he did not appear," Giacalone said on March 31.

Five days later, John Gotti came back to New York on Interstate 95. The Florida sun had been soothing, and now a different kind of fireball lay just over his near horizon.

5

BLOWN TO BITS

FATE ROLLED JOHN GOTTI a 7-11 combination at the start of his federal trial in Brooklyn. It began on April 7 in Courtroom 11 of the United States Court House, a squat gray-white block of granite on Cadman Plaza East, near the Brooklyn Bridge.

The sudden disappearance of Armond Dellacroce had already cast a Piecyk-like shadow over the case. The truth, or Armond, might never surface, but his former codefendants were not happy that he had pleaded guilty. Armond was not scheduled to testify, but his plea would become part of the evidence against them.

Other shadows would roll in during the first week of the trial as the vexing task of finding a jury of unbiased, unafraid, and unlikely peers of John Gotti got underway.

On the trial's first day, Eugene H. Nickerson, age 67, a tall, droll, silver-haired man who looked the part of a federal judge, ordered that the names of witnesses be kept secret until they were about to testify. Diane Giacalone requested the unusual procedure and cited the 1976 murder of a witness in a state case involving the brother of a Gotti codefendant, John Carneglia, a soldier in the Bergin crew.

The victim was Albert Gelb, a court officer in Brooklyn who was shot four times a few days before Carneglia's brother, Charles, stood trial on a gun-possession charge. Gelb, who had arrest powers, had confronted Charles Carneglia in a diner after a woman companion noticed Carneglia was packing a gun.

In the current case, Gotti and the others were accused of violating a federal law making it a separate crime to commit crimes as part of an illegal enterprise—such as the Gambino Family. John Carneglia, for example, stood accused of killing Gelb to help his brother, a member of the enterprise. Charles Carneglia was indicted, too, but, like Armond Dellacroce, he was gone with the wind.

On the trial's second day, Giacalone seeded a storm by charging that twice in the past week, two men had approached a prospective witness about the Albert Gelb homicide: Dennis Quirk, president of the court officers association. In the first incident, two men, posing as detectives, went to Quirk's former home to ask where he now lived. In the second, which took place on the trial's first day, two men in a dark Mercedes pulled alongside Quirk's car in traffic, shouted they wanted to speak to him about the murder, and then sped off.

Ominously for the defendants, Giacalone said if anything similar happened, she would seek to revoke their bail—which meant going to jail. Bruce Cutler said that none of the defendants had contacted anyone but their lawyers. Even so, Giacalone's sensational charge led to another round of large headlines, further complicating the jury screening.

On the fourth day, the defense attorneys complained to Judge Nickerson about a "carnival atmosphere" created by the press and asked for a gag order, which they correctly expected would be denied. Cutler was particularly agitated by a *Daily News* editorial urging Giacalone to follow up her bail-revocation threat if any witnesses or jurors were harassed.

"They are making my client into a monster," Cutler said. The press had created an impression that "anyone who looks at Mr. Gotti disappears and is afraid." A "crescendo of hysteria" had spawned a notion "that my client is somehow a wild man."

When jury selection resumed, several potential jurors admitted they could not keep an open mind about the case. One man was excused after he admitted commenting to another, "Why did we have to get hoods?"

By week's end, the prospect of a twelve-member jury was far off and so was an early forecast the trial would last only two months. Over the weekend, the search for untainted jurors became a futile exercise and the optimistic forecast went up in smoke.

On Saturday, John Gotti spent part of the day reviewing his gambling debts with Angelo Ruggiero. He owed money to "the tall kid," who was 6 foot 5 Joseph Corrao, the Little Italy capo; a man named "Eddie"; and men he referred to only as "Jersey," who, like his ice cream company partners, probably belonged to the DeCavalcante Family. One debt was costing him $1,000 a week in "vig"—interest.

The two men were counting money as they talked, probably the cash receipts from a sports-betting operation that they shared with Anthony Corallo, boss of the Luchese Family, according to a state Organized Crime Task Force affidavit.

They talked about who got what. They talked in terms of thousands, not dollars.

"So I got to give you forty-five and you want to give, give what's-his-name ten," Angelo said. "Ah, what's his name? Bruce Cutler?"

"That's the man," Gotti said.

"Yeah. Bruce Cutler."

As Gotti's attorney in both the Piecyk and racketeering cases, Cutler undoubtedly earned much more than that, probably in cash, the standard—and perfectly legal—way mobsters pay their bills.

Angelo suggested to his old street-gang friend that one of Gotti's debts could be forgotten—because "we pulled this deal for everybody, you know?"

"My fuckin' friendship is better than nothin', eh?" Gotti laughed.

———————————

The next day, April 13, Frank DeCicco's friendship with Gotti came to an end near his mentor James Failla's social club on Eighty-sixth Street in Brooklyn. As DeCicco sat down in the front passenger seat of a parked car, a bomb exploded beneath him.

The blast, probably triggered by remote-control, sent a black mushroom cloud upward and a flaming DeCicco outward. Some burning debris struck Frank Bellino, a Luchese Family soldier and an official of the concrete and cement worker's union, who was standing beside the car waiting for DeCicco to hand him business cards from the glove compartment. About 100 feet away, NYPD Officer Carmen Romeo forgot about the summons he was issuing and came to the aid of both men. Bellino, age 69, lived, but the underboss died at Victory Memorial Hospital.

The mangled car, a 1985 Buick registered to an official of the hotel workers' union, was parked across the street from Tommaso's Italian Restaurant, the site of the post-Sparks shuttle diplomacy among Gotti, DeCicco, and others after the December hits. DeCicco and Bellino had just left a regular Sunday meeting of Failla's crew at the Veterans and Friends Social Club.

Within hours, the Bergin Hunt and Fish Club began to fill up with men, but their information was as scanty as the early radio bulletins. No one knew who killed DeCicco, or why.

"We don't know," Angelo told an early arrival. "We've just got to get to the bottom of it, that's all."

"What a shame," the man replied, but not just because his under-boss was dead. "That's the shame of it, Angelo, we don't know nothin' yet."

When Gotti arrived, someone asked, "How are ya, Bo?"

"I was doing good till a couple hours ago … the bomb was fuckin' something … the car was bombed like they put gasoline on it … put a bomb under the car … you gotta see the fuckin' car, you wouldn't believe the car."

Later that night, Kenneth McCabe and three detectives investigating the DeCicco bombing visited another Brooklyn social club where DeCicco hung out. The club on Bath Avenue had no name, but it did have ten men inside, apparently on a war-alert.

"Open the door!" shouted McCabe, who had left the NYPD for a coveted criminal investigator's job with the U.S. attorney's office in Manhattan.

Through a window, Detective William Tomasulo of the Brooklyn South Task Force saw a man hurriedly load a bullet into a handgun, which he then anxiously pointed at the door.

"Police!" McCabe shouted this time. "Open up!"

All of a sudden, guns started dropping to the floor and the door to the no-name club was opened.

Inside, the detectives arrested Robert Fapiano, age 43, on a charge of illegally possessing a handgun. They also recovered three other handguns, including a .38-caliber revolver stolen in 1973 from a shipment at John F. Kennedy Airport, which by then had supplanted the waterfront docks as the prime place of Family pilferage. Twenty-three guns were heisted that day; in 1976, one was recovered from Peter Gotti, now occasionally one of his brother's many bodyguards.

In the 1950s, Peter had preceded younger brothers John and Gene into a street gang in which all received their criminal baptismals. But both John and Gene had preceded Peter into the Gambino Family. Peter, a former city sanitation worker and the former target of an FBI investigation into cocaine trafficking, was made after John took over.

Amid much Monday-morning speculation in the newspapers, the Gotti trial resumed in Brooklyn federal court. Hypotheses abounded; the most popular was that DeCicco was blown up as a payback by the Pope's soldiers, who believed DeCicco had helped set up Castellano at Sparks. In time, this gave way to the idea DeCicco was targeted by revenge-minded civilian friends or relatives of short-lived underboss Thomas Bilotti, acting on their own.

Many police investigators, unable to recall a Family hit in the Crime Capital in which a remote-controlled bomb was used, came to accept this notion of DeCicco's death.

Arriving at court, unlike other times, Gotti strode through the stampede of reporters without tossing off any disingenuous replies. He seemed grim and tense and was heard to complain to his attorney:

"It's difficult being a gentleman around here."

Cutler asked Judge Nickerson to delay the trial, citing "a rash of publicity this morning regarding Mr. DeCicco, his body blown to bits yesterday." He said articles saying "some of Mr. Gotti's friends may have had complicity or involvement" had "broken and shattered" his client's presumption of innocence.

The judge denied Cutler's motion. At day's end, Gotti went home to Queens accompanied by several bodyguards. What he knew about DeCicco's murder was what most newspaper readers knew, which was only a dense package of details in search of a conclusion. Gotti went home weary of court and wary of war.

Enter the "Zips," a slang word for native-born Sicilians involved in crime. Ralph Mosca came back from a meeting with Gotti that night and instructed his men, including secret informer Dominick Lofaro, to contact all the friendly Zips they knew and put them on "standby." The Zips were considered willing gunmen and some cops even considered those loyal to Castellano as suspects in the DeCicco hit.

Lofaro told the state Organized Crime Task Force that Mosca was ordered by Gotti to meet the next day with two officials of an asphalt worker's union, which employed many muscular Zips. Lofaro also said that Gotti had issued instructions for all Gambino soldiers to attend DeCicco's wake, held over two days at a funeral home on Eighty-sixth Street, near the two-foot hole in the pavement and single black shoe left by the April 13 bomb.

In a driving rain on April 15, about 300 men made their way to the wake. *The New York Times* had published a story that morning by Selwyn Raab saying Gotti may have been targeted for assassination due to internal Family strife and unhappiness over his rule and personal demeanor. Unidentified sources said some Family men did not like his "Hollywood-style" clothes.

"One thing mob bosses don't like is scrutiny and notoriety," added an anonymous federal investigator. "Because of his legal problems, Gotti seems to be on television every night, strutting around the courthouse and relishing it."

Though Gotti may have been wondering about all that as well, he was not ducking public appearances, or dressing down. Clad in another of his many hand-tailored double-breasted suits, he arrived at DeCicco's wake in his new Mercedes, which had tinted windows and wipers for the headlights. Naturally, there was a peeping crowd of reporters and investigators, including Kenneth McCabe and Detective John Gurnee, both of whom had spied on Gotti during the post-Sparks shakeout, when he began to receive boss-like kisses and hugs.

Now, "there was a definite increase in the amount of respect shown John," McCabe said later, "as he entered the funeral home, [as he left] the funeral home, people holding umbrellas for him, people stepping out of the way, people kissing him."

"It appeared to me that he was accorded more respect than he was on Christmas Eve," Detective Gurnee added.

Outside the wake, Gurnee said Gotti "had very, very hushed conversations" with several captains. At one point, he took a ride with Castellano loyalist Thomas Gambino, the owner of many Manhattan garment district trucking firms and a son of the Family patriarch Carlo Gambino. Gotti and Gambino returned 40 minutes later.

At the wake, McCabe also saw Bruce Cutler and Barry Slotnick, then law partners and an odd couple. Slotnick's courtroom style was the opposite of Cutler's, though historically as successful. He was cunning, too, but in a softer way. He also was a physical opposite; he was tall and slim, and sported a salt-and-pepper beard.

Slotnick's public profile then was much higher than Cutler's. He had represented many organized crime leaders and several major politicians, and was then defending Bernhard Goetz, the seemingly mild-mannered man whose bullet-filled meeting with four black teenagers in a subway car in December 1984 was worldwide news.

Dodging raindrops, Cutler, Slotnick, and all the other mourners departed the wake of the abruptly absent Frank DeCicco, who was buried later in the week in a cemetery on Staten Island, the same burial ground where the Pope also lay.

———————————

Extensive coverage of the wake once again hampered jury selection in Brooklyn, which resumed the next morning. Not much was accomplished, although Judge Nickerson warned Cutler and Gotti to stop laughing at the comments of potential jurors.

The warnings came after Nickerson asked one candidate whether he had read anything about a Mr. Castellano."

"You know, I read the names," the man replied. "They don't stick with me. You know, it is not something I would retain in my head."

The sounds of incredulous laughter reached Nickerson, who ordered Cutler to a sidebar.

"I get the distinct impression that you and Mr. Gotti are trying to intimidate these jurors by the way you are laughing," the judge said.

Cutler denied it was so, but Nickerson persisted.

"You keep a poker face. You tell your client to do that."

Cutler denied it again.

"It certainly was intimidating, and I took it as such," said the judge.

The laughter was a tonic for the last few days. The murder of DeCicco preyed on Gotti's mind. At night, encamped with soldiers in the fortress next to the Nice N EZ Auto School, he tried to figure it out, and what he would do if he had a clue.

For instance, a few hours after he was rebuked by the judge, the boss and his driver, Bobby Borriello, were taped discussing an article in the *Staten Island Advance*. Before the bombing, the newspaper received, but did not publish, a letter predicting DeCicco's death. The anonymous letter writer said a revengeful relative was recruiting an inmate on Rikers Island, a city-run prison, to carry out a contract on the life of DeCicco.

Gotti speculated that the bombing might not have been the work of a relative, but "a crackpot"—after all, "it happens."

"It can't be a crackpot," Borriello said.

"Well … so we gotta put some investigation on it right away," Gotti said.

Borriello did not think this would be so easy. After all, Rikers Island had about 7,000 inmates confined to overcrowded cells in the middle of the East River.

"No, not that," Gotti said impatiently, before explaining what he meant:

"We don't take the guys who did this, we take the guys that sent them ... you gotta get the guys who're paying them. Know what I'm saying?"

Two days later, Gotti discussed the DeCicco hit with his brother Gene, five years younger. The brothers were similar, though Gene had a little less of all of John's traits, good and bad. It was a reason they quarreled a lot, but not now.

"Isn't it a shame that we lost him?" Gene said. "Isn't it a shame?"

John agreed that it was and the two brothers speculated about the possible culprits.

"Them kids ain't got the smarts for that," Gene said about one unidentified group. John said the same about another unspecified party, before wondering:

"You know who it might be? That Irish mob."

Gotti was referring to the Westies, a notorious gang of Irish-American thugs from the hardscrabble Hell's Kitchen area on the West Side of Manhattan. In the past, some Westies had been employed by Paul Castellano to kill people; in the near future, Kevin Kelly, a 31-year-old Westie, would be indicted in the shooting of the carpenters' union official Gotti had complained about. Presently, they were the target of many investigations and trials. Their number-two man had "rolled over" and become a federal witness.

In time, it became clear that only those responsible knew who blew up DeCicco; for the second time in five months, talk of war subsided. And so the Zips went back to the asphalt trucks and the Westies went into hiding or jail. The specter of jail soon surpassed DeCicco in the worry department of John Gotti's mind.

6

WE'RE READY FOR FREDDY

EUGENE H. NICKERSON was an extremely patient judge, and determined to move forward in the Gotti trial despite all of the *ex-parte* distractions.

For two weeks after the DeCicco murder, he kept trying to screen candidates—more than 200—for the juror pool. At one point, he had to take nine steps backward and eliminate those who admitted talking about the case among themselves. Finally, on April 28, citing all the contaminating publicity, he threw in the gavel and delayed the trial until August, when he said he would adopt a more elaborate screening process and consider seating jurors whose identities would be kept secret.

"I'll get banged around some more with this," Gotti said afterward.

It was an accurate prediction. That same day, assistant U.S. attorney Diane Giacalone said she would ask the judge to revoke the bail of John and Gene Gotti and two other defendants—a move she had been contemplating for several days.

Not just the defendants were shocked by her announcement. Upstate in White Plains, where the state Organized Crime Task Force had its main office, many agents were upset—if Gotti were in jail, he wouldn't be talking on the Nice N EZ bug, which they felt was certain to produce indictable crimes, eventually.

Giacalone was not officially aware of the bug or tap, but she and co-prosecutor John Gleeson suspected that the state agency had something cooking on Gotti because of the cautious way it had responded to her during her investigation. Still, Giacalone and her boss, Reena Raggi, then the interim U.S. attorney in Brooklyn and soon to be its first woman federal judge, believed they had to immobilize Gotti, for fear that witnesses would be located and intimidated while the trial was delayed.

Hearings on Giacalone's bail-revocation motion were held in early May. She had to show "probable cause" to believe that Gotti violated his bail by committing any local, state, or federal crime. She attacked on three grounds: Gotti had continued to participate in the criminal affairs of the Gambino Family; he attempted to intimidate a federal witness, Dennis Quirk, of the court officers association; and he did intimidate a state witness, Romual Piecyk.

Giacalone called twelve witnesses to the stand, including local and federal organized crime experts, the detectives and cops who surveilled Gotti during his takeover or were involved in the Piecyk incident, and Dennis Quirk. The state Task Force tapes remained secret and unavailable to her.

Surprise testimony about the Piecyk matter came from Edward Magnuson, a Drug Enforcement Administration agent. Curiously, because the case did not involve drugs, the DEA, not the FBI, had been the principal federal law-enforcement agency involved in the investigation leading to Gotti's indictment. Behind this drama lay an interesting tale of federal intrigue no one wanted to talk about, at the time.

Magnuson testified about the statement of a DEA informant who had been talking about the Gotti crew and organized crime for the past year. The informant said members of Gotti's crew told him Piecyk "had received a kick in the ass," a warning not to testify. Other than Piecyk's own initial statements, which he later denied, the informant's remark was the most damaging indication that the mechanic had been physically threatened.

Putting his spin on it, Bruce Cutler argued that Piecyk frightened himself into silence, after reading about Gotti's "violent and impulsive" reputation. As to Giacalone's other witnesses, he ridiculed their statements as "regurgitation of newspaper articles," "comic-book gossip," and multiple hearsay from unknown informants.

Nickerson issued a written opinion on May 13. He said that while the testimony showed Gotti did become boss of the Gambino Family while on bail—and "it is a bold, not to say reckless, man who will act in that way"—Giacalone's witnesses did not show that he engaged in Family crimes. As to the Quirk incidents, while they did lend "credence to the inference that [Gotti] was and is prepared to subvert the integrity" of his trial, there wasn't enough evidence to link them directly to Gotti or his men.

Gotti had been playing a game of chance for months and had just landed on two more lucky squares, but on Giacalone's third move—Romual Piecyk—he drew a Go-to-Jail card.

"The court concludes that there is substantial evidence that John Gotti, after he was admitted to bail, intimidated Piecyk," Nickerson wrote, "and that if continued on bail John Gotti would improperly influence or intimidate witnesses in this case ... the court revokes the release of John Gotti and orders that he be detained ..."

Earlier in his opinion, Nickerson explained why he rejected Cutler's argument about Piecyk's memory loss.

"Had Piecyk acquired a generalized fear of John Gotti solely because of his reputation, Piecyk would have simply claimed he made a mistake in his original identification. He would hardly have tempted Gotti's displeasure by accusing 'his people' of making telephone calls and tampering with brakes. Those specifics are not the kind of thing Piecyk would readily concoct. Indeed, they have the ring of truth ... Gotti had a clear motive to prevent Piecyk from testifying and the boldness to accomplish that end."

The government dropped its effort to revoke a second defendant's bail, and Nickerson denied its motions on Gene Gotti and John Carneglia, though he ordered them to stay out of social clubs and each other's company. Nickerson said Gotti would have to surrender on May 19.

As expected, Cutler mounted an appeal; unexpectedly, he invoked a new ally—the now-famous refrigerator mechanic, Romual Piecyk.

On the day stories about the decision were published, Piecyk had called Cutler. "He indicated to me that he was concerned that an injustice had been done," Cutler later said.

Piecyk went to Cutler's office and denied all of his previous statements to Sgt. Anthony Falco. Cutler then prepared an affidavit, which Piecyk signed.

"At no time was I ever warned, threatened, coerced or in any way persuaded not to testify against John Gotti, or anyone else," Piecyk's affidavit said.

The next day, Cutler filed the document with Nickerson and asked for a new hearing so Piecyk could testify that he was not

intimidated. He offered a surprising theory as to why he had not
called Piecyk as a witness earlier. He said he had relied on a ruling
by Nickerson that details of the Piecyk-Gotti encounter could be
admitted into evidence at the bail-revocation hearing—"but not for
the purpose of showing [Gotti] committed a crime while on bail."

Gotti was not on bail at the time of the incident, but the issue at
the hearing was whether the crime of intimidation occurred while he
was on bail. Cutler's briefs and examination of witnesses seemed to
indicate that he fully understood this. But now he was making a
fourth-down-and-big-yardage play, trying to force overtime, by loft-
ing an inference he had been faked out.

The judge's words, Cutler said, had led him to believe that "the
Piecyk incident would certainly not be the linchpin upon which
the court based its decision … and wouldn't even be considered by
the court during this hearing."

Cutler's hail-Gotti pass fall short, but not before Diane Giacalone
expressed her barbed astonishment.

"Your Honor, [these are] the remarkable and extraordinary
lengths to which counsel has gone and are highlighted by the affidavit of Mr. Piecyk … the government is convinced that if called to
testify, [he] would not deviate from the words in that affidavit. …
Mr. Piecyk is scared to death, [his] fear would fill this courtroom."

She said the court had provided Gotti ample time to attend to his
family affairs before entering federal prison, and that Cutler, in conversations with her, had rejected moves to expedite a hearing at the
court of appeals. "Mr. Gotti has no family business to wrap up except
the business of the Gambino Organized Crime Family," she said.

Cutler responded with a jab at Giacalone—the antagonism between the pair and between her and the other defendants' attorneys
would flare again when the trial resumed, and grow ugly as time wore
on, until it was genuine personal contempt and not just legal combat.

"Whenever I speak to Ms. Giacalone out of court, your honor,
there are misunderstandings and quotes from me that are not so. I
don't know what to do about this, other than to try and speak to her
as much as possible on the record."

"The motion is denied," Nickerson said.

An appeal to the court of appeals was still available, and Cutler
began preparing one, but no one was counting on a reversal of
Nickerson's decision.

Suddenly, Gotti confronted a harsh reality. When he surrendered in four days and entered jail, and the doors clanged shut, he might never leave. His trial wasn't scheduled to start until August 18, and for the same reasons he was going in, he would probably have to stay in while it was being conducted. If found guilty, he was vulnerable to a 40-year sentence, and it was unlikely he would be freed to await the outcome of an appeal.

Even so, the boss went about making plans for a short absence.

Many leaders had bossed their Families from prison. Vito Genovese, whose Family still carried his name, did it for ten years. His successor, Anthony Salerno, and Carmine Persico, the Colombo boss, were doing it now, from the same facility Gotti would be at—the Metropolitan Correctional Center in Manhattan.

Gotti intended to do the same. In the last few days, he had been mulling a replacement for Frank DeCicco. His brother Gene had urged him to consider "the tall kid, Joseph Corrao."

"I know you got candidates for that," Gene said, "But why don't you just ... entertain it?"

John had other ideas, and as the brothers talked, it was clear that Paul Castellano was still a factor in Family politics.

"Ah, just think about it, John. You know better than I do. Just put him in one arm and see what you come up with. He, he, he's good friends with, uh ..."

"The other side," John filled in. "Good with Paul."

In a few days, informants told the FBI that Gotti had chosen Joseph Armone, who wasn't so good with the other side, as the new underboss. Armone was the capo who set Gotti up with the record-industry producers at the Helmsley Palace Hotel. He had been convicted in the French Connection heroin scandal of the mid-1960s—a few years after the Gambino Family had first banned drug dealing, but during a "grace" period for getting out.

During Armone's trial, a Playboy bunny and nightclub dancer, Patricia De Alesandro, visited a juror, a shoe salesman, at the store where he worked. She bought a pair of white go-go boots and invited him to dinner, where she revealed herself to be a friend of Armone's, and could the salesman use a trip to Europe, his own shoe store, and $5,000?

"No thank you," the shoe man said. De Alesandro got 5 years for attempted bribery.

Armone was now 66. His advancing age might have been his biggest attribute. His glory was behind him. A younger man might be more tempted to make a play for the top spot while Gotti was away in jail.

On Gotti's last weekend of freedom, spent entirely in Queens, he was bird-dogged by FBI agents, detectives, and reporters, including Mike McAlary of *Newsday*, whose story included these details:

On Friday about noon, Gotti ignored several red lights as he sped from his home in Howard Beach to the Bergin. Over the next nine hours, several men came in and out of the club and several were seen hugging and kissing him on the sidewalk along 101st Avenue.

On Saturday, Gotti stopped to have his silvery mane trimmed at the V. G. Stylarama Hair Design shop a few doors from the Bergin. Later, he played stickball in a bank parking lot with his 12-year-old son, Peter, and other kids. At one point, he struck out.

He went home to freshen up for dinner that night with his brothers and crew members at Altadonna's, a restaurant in Queens that was always open for Johnny Gotti.

"I'm just going out to get something to eat," he smiled at detectives as he left his house. "I'll be right back. Why don't you wait for me here?"

On Sunday, he relaxed in the front yard of his home with his young grandchildren before holding court at the Bergin for two hours. Then, in a scene almost too perfect to believe, he went to a nearby church for a baptismal ceremony. He was to be the baby's godfather.

Afterward, the godfather stood on the church steps and fed the baby from a bottle. Several churchgoers came up and kissed him on the cheek.

"It's a beautiful day," Gotti said. "You have to admit that much."

"John is ready for whatever happens," added Richard Gotti. "He's a man."

Some non-Family citizens of Ozone Park and Howard Beach were in genuine mourning the following morning as the airwaves filled with stories about Gotti going off to jail. They chose to see him as a strong, dashing, self-made man who hosted big Fourth of July fireworks displays and barbecues. They saw him in the narrow light he allowed, a friendly, godfatherly glow. At worst, he might be a bookmaker or loan shark, but they, like him, felt that only the law called these crimes.

He left his house early that day and drove his Mercedes to the Bergin. He then switched to a Lincoln piloted by Bobby Borriello. He was due to surrender at noon in Brooklyn, but he rode into Manhattan first, to visit Joseph Corrao at his social club, the Andrea Doria, in Little Italy.

The Andrea Doria, which was listed in the phone book as the Hawaiian Moonlighters Society, was down the street from the late Neil Dellacroce's Ravenite Social Club, which was listed under the name Martin Lucan. It featured two display windows with ceramic sculptures, one of Christ and one of San Gennaro, the patron saint of Naples, the homeland of Gotti's forebears. Over the door to Corrao's club was a gag plaque:

ON THIS SITE IN 1897 ABSOLUTELY NOTHING HAPPENED

The club was virtually in the shadow of the Metropolitan Correctional Center, where Gotti would be confined following his surrender. Gotti had spent about five years of his life behind bars; compared to slammers he'd known, the MCC, as it was called, would be easy time.

It is a modern, 12-story, dormitory-style facility near the complex of civic buildings and monuments around Foley Square. It has six units of sixteen 9' by 12' rooms otherwise known as cells. Each unit has a communal area with color television, pool tables, exercise equipment, and games. The computerized security is almost invisible and heavy plastic panels, rather than iron gates, separate the units.

Dressed in a tan safari suit, Gotti left the Hawaiian Moonlighters and walked across the street to Caffe Biondo, a place where Little Italy tourists dine with live mobsters. It was owned by Corrao, who got it—and a Gambino crew—from his late father, James "The Blond" Corrao. "Biondo" is Italian for blond.

About 11:30 A.M., Gotti climbed back into the Lincoln, which headed across the Brooklyn Bridge to the courthouse on Cadman Plaza. "I feel good," he told reporters as he got out of the car, a few minutes before Bruce Cutler arrived with a small reprieve—a three-hour delay while a panel of the court of appeals considered an emergency appeal.

"Hey, John, we got time," Cutler said. "We got till three o'clock."

Appearing before the appellate judges that morning, Cutler had asked for a stay of Nickerson's order. He argued that the lower court had not heard from Piecyk himself. "There's not a scintilla of evidence to connect my client with threats," he said.

Cutler, who had become fond of his client and regarded him a friend, went off with Gotti back to the Caffe Biondo. While there, Cutler checked in by telephone and glumly learned the news.

"The stay is denied—that's it," Cutler told Gotti.

Gotti arrived back at the courthouse a few minutes after 3 P.M. and was soon in the middle of another mob of media and bystanders. The throng weaved through the large, concrete antiterrorist planters protecting the courthouse entrance. Gotti took off his tan loafers and slipped into a pair of Reebok sneakers.

"Let's go," he said. "We're ready for Freddy."

"Freddy" was the undertaker in a comic strip, *Li'l Abner*. The boss was keepin' 'em laughin' all the way to the joint.

Inside, he was searched, fingerprinted, and photographed—a familiar routine. He was placed in leg irons and handcuffs, and with five other prisoners was put in a van and driven out of the courthouse garage. He smiled agreeably at reporters as the van emerged, and then disappeared across the Brooklyn Bridge to the MCC.

Cutler would keep fighting, vainly, in the court of appeals, where a full hearing was held on May 29. "Hopefully, we will win on appeal, and if not, we'll win the trial," he predicted—boldly, the way his client would.

At the MCC, Gotti was processed. He had to give up his diamond pinky ring and gold watch. Inmates were not allowed to wear anything worth more than $25—which put Gotti's Reeboks in technical violation. He would be treated the same as the MCC's 799 other inmates, a prison official announced.

That night, dinner consisted of fried fish, macaroni and cheese, beets, salad, and Jell-O—a healthy meal but a pale mockery of the hearty feast of stuffed clams, veal marsala, and spaghetti carbonara he might have ordered at Altadonna's.

By 10:30 P.M., he was, as required, in his 9' by 12' room for the night, an eerie time in prison, a time when men settle into their enemy foxholes, when the quiet makes loud the odd sounds of torment emanating from distant cells.

Gotti was used to it, though he had successfully avoided it since 1977. He silently measured the dimensions of his new compartment and acquainted himself with the desk, the chair, the wash basin. Then he undressed, flicked off the light, pulled the prison-issue blanket back, slid into bed, and stared down the darkness.

So much had happened in his life, so fuckin' much.

7

THE ROCKAWAY BOY

From the day that Adam and Eve made the Garden of Eden their domicile, human society has struggled against lawlessness.
—*From a Report to the President and the Attorney General, April 1986*

THE DAY AFTER JOHN Gotti became a grandfather in 1984, he won $55,000 playing "the numbers"—the widely patronized though illegal Family lottery. He celebrated by buying his grandson a $10,000 bond, worth $20,000 at maturity.

"Second day of his life, the kid has twenty thousand dollars," John told Dominick Lofaro. "Me, I had two fuckin' cents."

John Joseph Gotti Jr., born October 27, 1940, in the Bronx, also had a dozen brothers and sisters. He was the fifth child of a construction worker and his wife, Fannie. Two brothers and twin sisters, all less than 5 years old, preceded him. And over the next 11 years they were joined by four more boys and two girls. Two other siblings died during childhood.

John Joseph Gotti Sr. was a hard-working but low-earning man of Neapolitan origin. With 13 kids in 16 years, he was barely able to provide. When the namesake son's freedom was at stake in Brooklyn more than four decades later, his lawyer painted a portrait of a proud man whose fastidious appearance lay in the fact that he overcame a childhood of severe deprivation.

"He doesn't apologize for growing up poor," Bruce Cutler would say.

The family lived in the South Bronx, now a wasteland, then a livable area of apartment complexes containing working-class families. Like others his age, John's earliest memories include his family gathered around a radio, listening to the latest war news.

Though many Italian-American longshoremen demonstrated their loyalty by securing the docks of New York against sabotage, many citizens descended from other nationalities regarded immigrant Italians suspiciously, good for economic exploitation, but not much else. Public slurs were common. A *Life* magazine profile of baseball hero Joe DiMaggio, for instance, mocked the Italians for being "bad at war" and said DiMaggio was a "testimonial to the value of general shiftlessness" who, amazingly, kept his hair slick with water "instead of olive oil."

Like black heavyweight champion Joe Louis, *Life* concluded, DiMaggio was "lazy, shy, and inarticulate."

For a boy with many brothers to tag along with, the South Bronx had many attractions. The Harlem River was a haven for urban Huck Finns and only a few blocks away. The Bronx Zoo was a short ride on the elevated train, but best of all, a boy could walk a few blocks up the Grand Concourse, turn left at 161st Street, and find himself at Yankee Stadium, where Giuseppe Paolo DiMaggio didn't hang up his cleats until 1951.

Just across the river, in northeast Manhattan, was the largest colony of Italian-Americans in the country. At that time Italian Harlem was a teeming town of 150,000 immigrants, mostly Sicilian and southern Italian, jammed into a one-square-mile area of five-story tenements.

The customs of the old country survived in these aromatic streets. In open-air markets along the main drag, Pleasant Avenue, housewives haggled for fresh fruits and vegetables and sifted through the racks of merchants for bargains in clothes and household goods. In private social clubs, men swapped stories and played cards. In cafés and restaurants, couples sipped espresso, and sampled fresh cannoli and sfogliatelli.

Most people worked hard and obeyed the law. They played the numbers, but, as now, few considered it illegal. If a rich man could play for millions on Wall Street, why couldn't a poor man bet a 30-cent combination on Pleasant Avenue? Everyone knew the lottery was run by men who belonged to secret Families. The same men also loaned money—the interest was high, but banks gave credit only to the rich.

The men were known to be violent when they fought over gambling territory or when someone fell behind on a loan. Some extorted tribute from shop owners, but better to pay them than the police. They were bad men to cross, but good men to know if you needed a favor or something hard to get—such as, during the war, gas for your car. One such man, Carlo Gambino, a Sicilian who came to America as a 19-year-old stowaway in 1921, was making a fortune dealing in stolen gas-ration stamps.

Walking the streets of Italian Harlem with his family, little John Gotti glimpsed a world soon to be fragmented by black and Hispanic migration and by immigrant assimilation. In time, when John joined the aging Family men of this world, they would favor him—partly because he had briefly seen the way it was.

The same forces that affected Italian Harlem caused John's family to move away from the Bronx during the middle of his fourth year at P.S. 113. They moved into a two-story wood-frame house on East Thirteenth Street in Sheepshead Bay, a tranquil community in the far southeastern corner of Brooklyn, near the Atlantic Ocean.

John enrolled in P.S. 209; classmates included kids whose parents had achieved more prosperity than the Gotti clan. John began to see that in some minds a kid's status was unfairly tied to his parents' status, which was measured by income. It wasn't his fault he was poor; a little river of resentment began to flow through John, and occasionally it bubbled up as a cocky strut and a sharp tongue.

The nation was at war again, in Korea, and hysterical about communism and fearful of the Doomsday Bomb. The toughest guy in fiction was Mike Hammer, a crudely violent hero created by Brooklyn writer Mickey Spillane.

Television was becoming a consumer phenomenon; in New York City, the most-watched program in 1951 was a U.S. Senate hearing in Manhattan on organized crime. After days of testimony by bookmakers, pimps, and thieves, the Kefauver committee concluded:

> "There is a sinister criminal organization known as the Mafia operating throughout the country with ties in other nations. ... The power of the Mafia is based on a ruthless enforcement of its edicts and its own law of vengeance to

which have been credibly attributed literally hundreds of murders throughout the country."

Young Brooklyn boys like John Gotti learned about the Mafia on the streets, not in classrooms, and so they knew little about its origin. "Mafia" is a derivative blend of Sicilian and Arabic expressions for many concepts: place of refuge, the righting of wrongs, and protection from the powerful. Regarding individuals, it came to mean strength of body, mind, and spirit. In Sicily, Mafia was a way of life; a Mafioso was a man.

Sicily was exploited by generations of conquerors. Unable to take part in the rule of their own land, subjugated by the whimsical laws of other cultures, the Sicilians developed a strong distrust of any governmental authority. They turned to their own families for protection and justice. Loyalty became owed only to the family. *Sangu di me sangu.* Blood of my blood.

The ideals of family loyalty and the Mafia way of life developed together. Over time, plundering and feuding over depleted resources caused groups of families to form large Families led by powerful *vomini di rispettu,* men of respect, who co-opted the past and became as lawless as their former oppressors. By the time Italy was unified in the nineteenth century, so-called "Mafia bosses" ruled Sicily. Many followers or their descendants came to the United States to seek opportunity or survive a purge by Benito Mussolini.

In this country, they had no power and little knowledge, except for the Mafia way of life. They altered their tradition further by accepting into their Families other immigrants the Old World Mafia bosses regarded as flashy, emotional, and recklessly violent: the Neapolitans.

In 1952, the future crime boss completed the sixth grade. This was the year 12-year-old Johnny Gotti, according to Bruce Cutler's trial portrait, went off "on his own"—and the year the Gotti clan was forced to move again after their house was sold.

John's parents had few housing options. They finally moved to the Brownsville-East New York area of Brooklyn, a neglected working-class community that was home to thousands of southern Italian immigrants and Eastern European Jews who had abandoned stacked Manhattan ghettos.

The best-known people in Brownsville-East New York were criminals, and among the area's numerous teenage street gangs they were regarded in the way other boys regarded sports heroes. One superstar of crime was Albert Anastasia, who had murdered his way to the top of the Family that included Carlo Gambino. A Brownsville alliance of Italians and Jews disposed of many men for Anastasia, who was called the Lord High Executioner by the newspapers. In ten years, they executed eighty people, many at the behest of Families now called the Mafia. They became infamous as Murder, Incorporated.

Young John enrolled in Junior High School 178 on Dean Street. Most students in this school were poor and they came from homes in constant stress. They tended to measure status by toughness. Only the weak earned their reputations in the classroom; smart-aleck boys with cocky walks chose the street.

In 1954, John showed how tough he was. Clowning around with friends, he had an encounter with a cement mixer, which ran over his feet. He spent the summer in Lutheran Hospital, East New York. It took him more than three months to heal, and by the time he was discharged and walked into high school, it was without benefit of the second toe on his left foot.

Teens at Franklin K. Lane High School had many competing street gangs to choose from. John joined the Fulton-Rockaway Boys. Brother Peter already was a member; brothers Richard and Gene signed up later. Another member was Angelo Ruggiero, a pudgy-faced, pigeon-toed kid who was called "Quack Quack" and became John's pal. As was the custom, the Fulton-Rockaway Boys, whose name came from a street intersection a few blocks from school, adopted special colors; theirs were black and purple, the color of bruises. In such gangs, poor teenagers found self-esteem and group identity. The year John joined the Fulton-Rockaway Boys, Marlon Brando starred as Johnny, the rebel hero of *The Wild One*, a popular film about a gang taking over a town.

In 1956, the year a new singer, Elvis Presley, sang "Jailhouse Rock" in New York and nearly caused a riot, John quit school and became a full-time Rockaway Boy. He was 16 years old.

School records indicate he had scored 110 on an IQ test, which was in the average-intelligence range. Much later, he told people he had taken another test in prison and scored 140—near genius. Maybe he exaggerated, but aside from two future probation officers who weren't impressed by him, he seemed to impress most people as having more than average intelligence.

By the year John dropped out, other sons and daughters of immigrants who came from the poor villages and farms of Sicily and southern Italy had begun moving into the mainstream of American society. Their parents or grandparents still worked with their hands, but they had been encouraged to obtain an education and enter the professional world of doctors, lawyers, and executives.

But Johnny Boy came from a particularly large family and had been on his own since he was 12. And when he turned 16, he obtained the legal right to quit school regardless of what his parents might have said. He hit the unsavory streets of Brownsville-East New York with too little education and too much time on his hands.

Another boy who later got in trouble with heroin, went to prison, and testified before a presidential commission said the neighborhood's tough teenagers knew who the racketeers were. And that once they began running with a street gang like the Rockaway Boys, the next logical thing was to work their way up to the big time—the Families.

A secret New York City probation report compiled years later stated that John, after dropping out of high school, "became involved in antisocial behavior." This was an officially understated way of saying that he became a punk.

As a Rockaway Boy, he cultivated a defiant image. At age 16, he was 5 foot 7 and 150 pounds; he was solid and strong and he went around with a straight back, squared shoulders, and a glare that said *I dare you.*

John's gang formed an alliance with the Fulton-Pitkin gang and together they faced off against black gangs such as the Brownsville Stompers, the Mau Mau Chaplins, and the Ozone Park Sinners. On May 15, 1957, a gang fight led to John's first arrest. The charge was disorderly conduct. Two months later, he beat the charge. It was a good way to start a rap sheet. He didn't even have to put up a defense; the judge dismissed the case.

The gang rumbles over turf were a fierce New York tradition, romantically evoked at the time in a Broadway play, *West Side Story.*

The Rockaway Boys also feuded with the Ridgewood Saints, a particularly violent gang, according to Matthew Traynor, an ex-Saints gang leader who went on to bank robbery and other crimes. In one fight, a Rockaway bled to death after he was stabbed and tossed through a window. Another incident involving a Rockaway landed Traynor in jail.

"I stabbed a guy from John's gang," Traynor recalled. "I was fifteen, the guy was nineteen or twenty, a real jerk. He was in our neighborhood without permission. We found out he was over at some girl's house. We rang the bell. And when he came down I stabbed the shit out of him. I was pretty violent in those days."

In a world in which violent death was possible, gang members were measured by their ability to control fear. In John's mind, he became the Rockaway Boy against whom all should be measured. He feared no one. Thirty years later, he told a friend how this had benefited him:

"I never have to lie to any man because I don't fear anyone. The only time you lie is when you are afraid."

Men who manage fear become candidates for leadership. And Traynor said John exhibited command presence in another way.

"Most of the people in the gang were crazy, nuts, but not John. He was tough, but also a politician. He could talk to people and they listened. It was the difference between him and the others. He didn't have to be wild to impress people."

Eventually, the neighborhood's older gang members, who called their gang a Family, heard about this boy who talked like a politician and wasn't afraid. Pivotally, two of these adult-gang members were Carmine and Daniel Fatico, who, the boy-gang members knew, were connected to a large Family led by Albert Anastasia, who was so important his name was only whispered.

The Fatico brothers operated out of a storefront they called The Club and were active in hijacking, extortion, gambling, and loan-sharking. They killed only when necessary, the boys thought. Carmine was older and cagey; he had been pinched more than a dozen times but had hardly spent any time in jail.

Besides the Fatico brothers, plenty more of the wrong role models lived close by. Two of them, Wilfred "Willie Boy" Johnson and William Battista, would become important members of John's crew in Ozone Park. Willie Boy was a sausage stuffer by day, a bookmaker by night, a part-time boxer, and part American Indian. He had a violent and justifiably tough reputation, having fatally stabbed his brother-in-law and survived a bullet to the head fired by the dead man's friend.

Battista was a gambler, too, but his early fame was based on a truck hijacking he had staged using inside information from a secretary who lived on Bergen Street, around the corner from John. Battista waited until the truck driver took his coffee break at the time and place the girl indicated, and then just hot-wired the rig and drove off with $75,000 worth of new clothes.

The Fatico brothers were always looking for a few good men. In time, Willie Boy and Battista would be recruited. So would Angelo Ruggiero and his younger brother Salvatore. And John and Gene Gotti. And another pair of brothers who hung out in the neighborhood, John and Charles Carneglia.

Two days before John's seventeenth birthday, the neighborhood crooks led by the Fatico brothers got a new boss. As sometimes happened, the transfer of power was bloody and resulted in a new name for one of the five Families. The director of death, Albert Anastasia, was executed in the barbershop of the then-Park Sheraton Hotel in Manhattan.

It was the type of murder—public, flamboyant—that Families reserved for bosses. Soldiers and associates were stuffed into car trunks, concrete or scrap-metal recyclers; bosses were dismissed in offices or restaurants. The distinction was a final sign of respect that had practical benefits: the body would be found, and people would know someone else was in charge.

Other Family leaders didn't trust Albert the Executioner, whom they called "The Mad Hatter." They believed he was power-hungry and might actually be mad. In the 1930s, he proposed killing Thomas Dewey, a special prosecutor who later ran for president. The Families never killed prosecutors or cops; it caused too much heat. Besides, cops were simply doing their jobs.

Anastasia had taken control in 1951, when Family boss Philip Mangano was killed and his brother Vincent vanished. By 1957, he had left Brooklyn and wasn't an easy target; he lived in Fort Lee, New Jersey, in a fortified mansion overlooking the Hudson River. The plotters were led by the Genovese boss, who had taken over his own Family in a similar way. He persuaded the number-two man in Anastasia's Family, Carlo Gambino, to join them. Gambino arranged for Anastasia's bodyguards to exit the barbershop while the boss was given a final shave.

Betrayal and inter-Family intrigue thus accompanied the dawn of what became known as the Gambino Family, which included a crew led by Carmine Fatico, who was about to recruit some promising boys from the neighborhood.

One Anastasia soldier who vowed to avenge the boss's death was a violent hood named Aniello "Neil" Dellacroce. But Dellacroce also was a realist and after another would-be avenger disappeared, he accepted Gambino's invitation to sit down and talk about his future. To his surprise, Gambino made an offer too good to refuse: Neil became the new underboss.

A few weeks after the hit, more than 60 Family men from around the country were arrested in an upstate New York community after a raid on a farmhouse sitdown called by Vito Genovese to review inter-Family rights and wrongs. Carlo Gambino was driven to the farm by his brother-in-law and cousin, Paul Castellano, who would later prove his mettle by doing a year in jail rather than answer a grand jury's questions about the so-named Apalachin Conference.

He did talk about it much later, in May of 1983, while he was being secretly taped. In a conversation with his son, Paul Jr., and his nephew, Thomas Gambino, he recalled how the conference of bosses adopted two rules: no drug dealing, no cop killing.

The reasons were simple—both brought too much pressure. Defendants facing drug charges also had a habit of betraying Family secrets.

What was feared in 1957 was more feared in 1983, as a conversation a month later between Castellano and *consigliere* Joe N. Gallo demonstrated. They were taped while discussing whether because of extenuating circumstances an unidentified drug-dealing violator should be given a pass; the usual punishment was murder.

"The problem is," said Gallo, "give a guy a pass, Paul, twenty years later, somebody comes in and makes a federal [conspiracy] case [against us]."

At the time, the Apalachin Conference was considered to be evidence of a nationwide criminal conspiracy, and the extensive newspaper coverage was a handy primer to all the restless dropouts of Brooklyn, who would someday seek a pass from Paul.

The more time he spent with the Rockaway Boys, the more John gave himself over to the notion he was not going to succeed in life on the square.

Unlike other gangs, the Rockaways were not just a forum with which to establish tough teenager credentials. The Rockaways began to deal in "swag," stolen merchandise fenced by neighborhood thieves and hijackers. It began to resemble a sort of farm team—for the Family league.

En route to the majors, John made rookie mistakes. At 17, he was arrested for burglary after he and a few confederates were caught in the act of stealing copper from a construction firm. He pleaded guilty and was placed on probation.

The terms of his probation required him to shun unsavory places and characters—a nearly impossible burden for anyone in Brownsville-East New York. Now a committed juvenile delinquent, John continued to hang out in poolrooms, bars, bookie joints, and racetracks.

In 1959, he was arrested for the first time as an adult. The charge was unlawful assembly; he had been caught in a raid on a gambling location. Theoretically, he had violated his probation and could have been jailed immediately. Instead, he was allowed to remain free. Nearly a year later, after he had been arrested again and fined $200 for disorderly conduct, the unlawful assembly charge came up on the court calendar.

John was given a 60-day sentence, but it was suspended. He sauntered out of the courtroom a free man. Two months later, his probation expired and he was "discharged as improved." John naturally had a hard time taking seriously a system so easy to beat.

As in Italian Harlem, gambling was rampant in John's neighborhood. It seemed like everyone played the Brooklyn numbers. The Faticos also made sure that anyone could also bet on a horse, the Giants, Dodgers, and Yankees, or anything else that moved. John grew to love the action.

Gambling required money. Still a novice at crime, John needed a job and went to work operating a garment-pressing machine in a Brooklyn coat factory. He thought too highly of himself to do such mundane work, but it was pocket money and gas for his car—and it pleased his parents. In the back seat of the car, in case of emergencies, he kept a billy club; and when he was curbed by the cops in May 1961, it would be found and he would be arrested again.

John Gotti was clinging to familiar terrain at the same time John F. Kennedy was promising a New Frontier. But John didn't know too much about the world beyond his home turf, though he had heard about a handsome Italian kid from Belmont Avenue in the Bronx, Dion DiMucci, who as lead singer of Dion and the Belmonts had all the Italian girls drooling over such songs as "Lonely Teenager" and "A Teenager in Love."

One of these girls was Victoria L. DiGiorgio, a pretty, raven-haired girl with brown eyes, a petite figure, an outspoken nature, and a new boyfriend named Johnny Gotti. She was two years younger than he and had dropped out of Brooklyn's Erasmus Hall High School in her senior year. She was the daughter of a sanitation worker and his wife.

Her parents hoped she'd find a boy who had finished school and begun a career more promising than that of a coat presser. Victoria was strongly attracted to John. She saw a rakish young man, now barely over 5 foot 8 and 170 pounds, who had a strong, memorable face and dark hair which he dashingly combed back into a duck's tail that brushed the collar of his black leather jacket. He was a rebel and talked smart, like he knew all the angles. But around Victoria, he was surprisingly gentle and well-mannered—Marlon Brando's Johnny and Victoria's Dion in one tightly wound package.

Victoria didn't see bad Johnny; all she saw was good Johnny. Soon she was pregnant.

In 1986, as her husband was going on trial in Brooklyn, Victoria told a *New York Post* reporter she had been married 26 years, which would mean she got married in 1960, the year she dropped out of high school. A secret report written in 1969 by a probation officer who interviewed John, Victoria, and other family members states the couple was married on March 6, 1962.

Whatever the case, the couple's first child, Angela, was born in April 1961. After her father became a Gambino capo, he told an acquaintance he was so poor when the baby was born he sneaked into the hospital at night and took mother and child home without paying the bill.

———————————

After the baby's birth, John left the coat factory and took a job as a truck driver's helper for the Barnes Express Company. By design or happenstance, it was an astute career move. He learned how to value goods and how shippers and warehouses operated. Concepts and words previously vague—wholesalers, bills of lading, shipping manifests—became understood. Unlike the abstract lessons he had rebelled against in school, this was worthwhile knowledge.

He wasn't making much money, however. Between the family and the car and the hanging out, he was always broke. And he and Victoria kept having kids: three in three years. Angela was followed by another girl, Victoria, and a son, who was named John. Money woes and his nocturnal touring of pool halls, gambling dens, and honky-tonks caused the young parents to fight; they separated several times.

Some separations were forced. In 1963, John went behind bars for the first time—20 days in a city jail after he and Salvatore Ruggiero, Angelo's brother, were arrested in a car reported stolen from the Avis rent-a-car company. Salvatore was a bright boy who would go far in crime, too, but not as a Family man. Sal would become a very rich drug dealer.

John's scrapes with the law troubled Victoria, but he was not the type to take his wife's advice; in 1965, he demonstrated this repeatedly. In January, he was arrested for unlawful entry and possession of bookmaking records in Queens. In March, he was caught breaking into a tavern on Long Island. In October, he was accused of attempted petty larceny in Brooklyn.

He was acquitted of the January charges, but pleaded guilty to the attempted theft and was jailed for several months in 1966. This cost him his job with the Barnes Express Company and a lot of goodwill with his wife. Struggling to support three small children whose father was a jailbird caused her to seek public relief from the New York City Department of Welfare and to file support petitions against him in Domestic Relations Court in Brooklyn.

Any reluctance to completely embrace crime as a way of life melted away in the wake of these humiliations. In the next year, John would not find another job; he would become a professional hijacker.

John was only 26, not too old to seek the education or training which might have opened a legitimate door of opportunity. But he was too impatient and too scornful. He had a wife, three kids, and expensive appetites. He had them *now*. What could he be? A store manager? An insurance salesman? *Forget about it.*

When John thought of successful men, he thought of Carmine and Daniel Fatico. They wore fine clothes and drove big cars. At the track, they could lose with cheer as opposed to despair. They were respected, maybe not by the wider world, but by the young men of John's world.

He also knew the story of the new boss of the Faticos, Carlo Gambino, who came to America as a stowaway and through guile and cunning rose to the top of an exciting and dangerous empire— an empire known by many names: Mafia, mob, syndicate, the outfit. It was there, he didn't create it. Some men pray, others prey. This was the way the world was. In the story of Gambino, John saw a message: Not all the doors to opportunity were closed.

Something else pushed John toward crime. Blacks were moving into the old neighborhood. John needed money so he could follow the Italian-Americans who had fled north and east, into Queens, and even out of the city onto Long Island, where the building lots were bigger, the houses better, and the people whiter.

Carmine Fatico, for instance, had moved to Long Island and bought a house in West Islip; he now commuted to the social club he had in Brooklyn, at the corner of Rockaway Avenue and Herkimer Street, near John's former home on Dean Street. The club was called the Bergin Hunt and Fish Club. The "Bergin" may have been a misspelled salute to Bergen Street, two blocks away.

Even before he lost his job as a truck driver's helper, John, through his friendship with the well-connected Angelo Ruggiero, was occasionally at the Bergin. Now that he was to be a hijacker, the club became his office.

The Rockaway Boy became a Bergin Man.

8

VELVET TOUCH

AS JOHN GOTTI BECAME an associate of a Gambino crew, a prisoner in the Queens House of Detention became an informer on the Gambino Family.

The prisoner decided on this dangerous occupation shortly after he was brought to Queens for sentencing on a burglary charge. He described himself as a Gambino "muscle man."

"He expressed disgust for the syndicate," an FBI agent wrote in the first of many secret memos, "and feels he has been used by them and that his wife and children have not received the financial help that the syndicate should have extended to them." Because he never "wants to be separated from his wife and children as a result of confinement," the prisoner "wants to cooperate right away."

So he did, and so he would, for nearly two decades, beginning that day with the identification of photographs and information about a counterfeiting case. During nearly all of Gotti's years in crime, this new informer—Source BQ 5558–TE, who sometimes used the code name "Wahoo"—would be there chronicling the story—first out of revenge, and then later, when he believed he was immunizing his own illegal conduct, out of self-interest, but always for cash.

Such was the world John Gotti was entering, but it looked good to him. The man holding the door was Carmine Fatico, who exuded style and authority, though he stood only 5 foot 4. At the racetrack, Carmine entered the gate reserved for members, horsemen, and owners, though he was none of those. At the Bergin, he lectured the men on their personal behavior.

In 1966, under the 56-year-old Fatico's direction, the 26-year-old Gotti began to learn firsthand about the Gambino Family. He learned, for example, that for all the world knew, Aniello Dellacroce was a $200-a-week salesman for a soda distributor, but in reality he was Carlo Gambino's second-in-command, and Fatico, as a *caporegime*, or crew leader, reported to him regularly in Manhattan.

Gotti learned that just a few miles away from the Bergin was a vein of riches mined by all the New York Families—John F. Kennedy International Airport, a vast facility spread over 5,000 acres, the equivalent of Manhattan from the southern tip to Times Square.

The former truck driver's helper would get a chance to put his knowledge to use when Fatico moved the Bergin even closer to JFK and set up shop in a bland, three-story brick building on 101st Avenue, on the other side of the Brooklyn border, in Ozone Park, Queens. Gotti and others under Fatico's control began to treat JFK like a giant candy jar, using as many devious means as they could contrive to take away goodies. Sometimes it was easy, but not always productive.

———————————

At 6 A.M. on November 27, 1967, probably after an all-night card game, Gotti telephoned George Beatty, a cargo agent for United Airlines at JFK. He identified himself as a representative of a well-known freight forwarding company.

"What have you got waitin' there for us?" Gotti asked.

"Just a minute," said Beatty, who rummaged through papers and read off a list of airway bills of lading.

"Okay, fine, I'll be right over. So long."

About 15 minutes later, Gotti arrived at the United cargo area in a rented Hertz truck. He was accompanied by a younger, slimmer man later said to have looked like Gene Gotti.

"Where's our stuff?" John asked Beatty.

"Right over there, we'll help you load it."

The two hijackers, aided by two cargo agents, loaded forty-seven cartons containing $30,000 worth of women's clothing, electrical gear, and aircraft and machine parts into the truck.

Beatty handed John the airway bills. "Got everything?"

"Sure, no problem."

"I'll need your signature."

"No problem."

John signed the name of the man he had impersonated. He and the slim man then got into the truck and drove away, leaving behind the most valuable carton of all—a box of furs.

Three days later, in Glen Oaks, Long Island, the truck, which had been rented by a man using phony identification, was found abandoned with most of the load still on board. Only ten cartons of women's clothing were missing.

The mostly intact load was evidence of a poorly conceived crime, a random stab at grabbing anything, which resulted in the most valuable item—the furs—being left behind. It showed that John Gotti had room to grow.

Most of the load was hard to fence; among the sidewalk salesmen and flea markets of New York, no great demand exists for aircraft and machine parts. Not so with women's clothes. What didn't wind up adorning the frames of wives and girlfriends found their way onto the racks of neighborhood merchants eager to beat wholesale prices.

After better scores, the hijackers gambled and partied. It was a time of great turbulence in America, the Vietnam era of protest and cultural change, but it had nothing to do with them. Gotti patronized a gambling club located above a car wash on Eastern Parkway run by a former Fulton-Pitkin ally. At night, he retired to such shot-and-beer establishments as the 101 Bar, Bullock's Lounge, Tutti's Bar, and the Colony Bar, according to Matthew Traynor, one of Gotti's former gang rivals. Traynor began hanging around the Bergin in the late 1960s and told the FBI he helped in more than twenty hijackings.

The Colony was in Brooklyn, and Traynor said that after Gotti acquired a taste for loan-sharking he acquired part ownership of the bar when the owner went arrears on a loan. That same year, Gotti threw a party and strutted around the bar charging round after round to the house.

Gotti's personal family now included a fourth child, a boy named Frank. He was living with Victoria and the kids in a new Brooklyn apartment. It wasn't the home of their dreams, but it was a step forward. Gotti was recovering from near financial and personal ruin.

Gotti's new profession, however, was risky. On December 1, 1967, only four days after the United Airlines score, he rolled snake-eyes.

Security at JFK was provided by the Port Authority of New York and New Jersey police, supplemented by the FBI, which investigated interstate thefts. Lately, the airplanes and shippers had been more upset than usual because of the rampant pillaging of cargo. A periodic crackdown was then in effect.

From nearby surveillance posts, FBI agents saw a rented U-Haul truck pull up to a pallet of cartons in the cargo area of Northwest Airlines. They saw two people—one walked kind of funny, the other had dark hair combed back—load twenty-three cartons into the truck and drive off.

Agents tailed the U-Haul as it drove away from the cargo area, until it stopped and a Cadillac driven by a younger, slimmer man pulled alongside. They arrested Gene Gotti, driver of the Caddy; Angelo Ruggiero, driver of the truck; and John Gotti, found hiding in the truck behind the cartons.

Gene had acted unsuccessfully as the lookout. But after he was arrested he acted the way an accomplice was expected to. Say nothing. He even refused to say John was his brother. The car was registered to Angelo's wife. The rental truck contained $7,691 of—once again—women's clothes.

All three got out on bail after an appearance at the United States Court House in Brooklyn. They knew the federal charge likely meant time in prison, which is more serious than time in a city jail. Jail is inconvenience; prison is incarceration. They didn't know a state case was then being made against John for his impersonation act on George Beatty and United Airlines.

The cargo agents who had helped load the truck identified John as the driver and the man who signed someone else's name. They thought Gene was the other man, but weren't sure. John was arrested in early February 1968—in two months he was a two-time loser. Angelo posted his bail.

A condition of Gotti's bail, of course, was that he obey the law. *Forget about it.* A man who scorned legitimate work had to make money somehow, even if it meant he had to step up to a high level of crime: kidnapping. It happened during the third hijack, on April 10, two months after his second arrest.

The case was known as the Velvet Touch caper. The Velvet Touch was a bar in Ozone Park, another Bergin crew hangout and the focus of a police investigation into a stolen-car racket that led to a wiretap on the bar's phone.

On April 10, cops monitoring the wiretap heard several conversations between men at the bar and men who had grabbed two parked tractor-trailers filled with cartons of cigarettes—about a half-million dollars worth—near a restaurant on the New Jersey Turnpike. The drivers had been forced into a car and driven by Gotti to a street on the Brooklyn side of the Verrazano-Narrows Bridge. Though no ransom was demanded, and the men were released unharmed, Gotti would be charged with kidnapping.

The Velvet Touch wiretaps showed that the hijacking did not go smoothly. A future bookmaker for John—the veteran neighborhood hijacker William Battista—had driven one of the tractor-trailers to a drop in Queens, but Gotti's ten confederates, including Angelo and John Carneglia, couldn't get the second truck in gear. They called Battista, who had gone to the Velvet Touch, and others seeking tips but were never able to drive the second truck away, so they left it.

"I remember the guys in New Jersey also were worried about what their girlfriends were doing at the Velvet Touch with their friends," an investigator on the case recalled.

One year later, Gotti was indicted in Newark, charged with conspiracy and interstate theft in addition to kidnapping. By that time, he had already been sent away to a federal penitentiary on the Northwest Airlines airport theft.

Michael Coiro, a 39-year-old Queens lawyer who defended many hoodlums, had represented John, Angelo, and Gene in federal court in the Northwest Airlines case. It was the first of many assignments that he undertook for the Gotti brothers and Angelo over the years; his services would later earn him unwanted national recognition as a "mob lawyer," as well as a serious legal jam of his own. Coiro had been recommended by Carmine Fatico, then in trouble, too: He was named in a plot to murder a businessman.

Coiro advised his clients to plead guilty and bank on the judge's goodwill. Gotti faced eight years, but was sentenced to four, which usually translates to about 30 months actual time. Gotti would have to come back to New York from prison to deal with the state's hijack case and the Newark federal case.

Before sentencing, a probation officer interviewed Gotti and prepared a confidential report for the judge. He wrote that Gotti "appeared lackadaisical and unconcerned about his present situation" and was "very vague and evasive when questioned about his personal life." Gotti had filed no income tax returns the last three years and had "no verifiable employment" in the last four, although his father-in-law had told the officer that Gotti had a "standing offer" of employment at Century Construction, but "failed to avail himself of it."

The officer described Victoria Gotti as a "rather intelligent" woman "who closed her eyes to [her husband's] criminal tendencies." The report carried this final notation: "Leader of crew for this crime, [has] organized crime ties."

A few months after he was sentenced, as he had agreed to do, Gotti surrendered to federal marshals. Unbowed and unashamed—just unlucky, he probably thought—he was transported to the United States Penitentiary at Lewisburg, Pennsylvania.

It would be difficult to find a worse place to send a mobster-in-the-making.

9

CLUB LEWISBURG

THE HIJACKER WITH ORGANIZED-CRIME connections arrived cuffed and shackled at Lewisburg federal prison on May 14, 1969, after a six-hour ride from New York in a mobile cage. From inside the prison bus, John Gotti saw a medieval-looking stone fortress with gun towers rising against low, dark hills.

Once inside, he and others were ordered from the bus and led past guards with machine guns to a reception area enclosed by wire mesh and steel bars. He was given a sheet, a pillow, a blanket, a towel, a toothbrush, and a job emptying garbage cans and mopping floors.

Gotti knew Lewisburg wasn't going to be like a city jail. It was a long-term home for hard-core criminals. It had two sets of laws: institutional and inmate. The trick was not to offend either and do your time as peaceably as possible. At least he would have some company—his *gumbah*, his good friend Angelo Ruggiero, had been sent to the same prison and so had a heroin dealer named Anthony Rampino, who would become, later on, Gotti's chauffeur, or "John's man," as "Tony Roach" Rampino described himself.

At the time, 2,000 men were incarcerated at Lewisburg, including many big-time Family men from the Crime Capital. The biggest mobster was 5 foot 3 Carmine Galante, the fiery fifty-seven-year-old boss of the Bonanno Family, who was doing heroin time after deciding that the Apalachin drug ban didn't apply to him.

The prison had 1,200 black inmates, but the 400 Italians were more unified and thus dominated prison life. "Mafia Row" extended its umbrella of protection and influence to all prisoners of Italian descent, especially those with Family ties. It introduced them to the prison's underground economy, its bookmaking operation, its network of friendly "hacks" who could be counted on for favors. They might even get invited to "Club Lewisburg," a room where Galante and others played cards, ate purloined steaks, and drank liquor hidden in after-shave bottles. Another Lewisburg inmate, former International Brotherhood of Teamsters president Jimmy Hoffa, had designated Club Lewisburg as Teamsters 865. Outside prison, Galante was ill-tempered and ruthless, but inside he did not allow fighting; everyone was expected to keep their cells clean and the noise level down.

Gotti spent the summer on the sanitation crew, but in September he was transferred to the yard detail, a sign he was moving up fast in prison prestige. He began putting on extra muscles by pumping Lewisburg iron.

In October, Gotti was driven back to New York to stand trial in the state's hijacking case pending against him in Queens. If convicted, he might have to go directly to state prison once his expected 30-month Lewisburg tour was over. The federal Velvet Touch caper was still hanging over him, too.

Gotti was kept in the Queens House of Detention as jury selection began. Once again, Michael Coiro was his attorney and after the jury was seated, Coiro once again came up with a deal Gotti couldn't pass up. Gotti would plead guilty and would get no additional jail time.

For several more years, Michael Coiro would often demonstrate an amazing touch with the officials in Queens.

Feeling fine, considering, Gotti rode back to Lewisburg and Mafia Row and settled once more into the abnormal routine of prison life. He had more than two years to go, two more years with some of the most incorrigible criminals in America. In Washington, D.C., people were trying to figure out what to do about such men.

Six years earlier, another descendant of immigrants from Naples, Joseph M. Valachi, had started a national debate on how to fight organized crime by revealing the secret ways of the Families. Valachi, a Genovese Family soldier, told his story to a U.S. Senate committee after killing a man—at the U.S. Penitentiary in Atlanta—who he mistakenly believed intended to kill him. Valachi thought that his boss,

Vito Genovese, had ordered him killed because Genovese believed he had cheated him out of money.

Facing the death penalty in Georgia, Valachi contacted the U.S. attorney in Manhattan, Robert Morgenthau, and agreed to cooperate with the federal government. Soon he was a star witness before a Senate rackets committee and on the front page of newspapers across the country.

Valachi gave a new name to the Families—*La Cosa Nostra,* our thing. He named bosses and described their schemes and methods; he discussed his own 30 violent years in crime. His testimony pushed the Republicans to a law-and-order campaign in 1964 and prompted the victorious Democrat, Lyndon Johnson, to announce "a war on crime" that would include a Presidential Commission on Law Enforcement and Administration of Justice, which would appoint a special task force on organized crime.

The task force issued its report in 1967. It urged Congress to adopt many anti-organized-crime weapons; over the next three years, many were. Special federal Organized Crime Strike Forces of specially recruited prosecutors were created in cities with a Cosa Nostra Family. Under certain conditions, wiretapping and other electronic-surveillance methods were legalized. The power to empanel grand juries was taken away from judges and given to prosecutors, who also received greater power to immunize witnesses and a program to protect and relocate those who jeopardized their lives by testifying. Finally, a sweeping new law, the Racketeering-Influenced and Corrupt Organizations Act, was passed. "RICO" made it a separate crime, punishable by long imprisonment, to belong to a criminal organization.

Many Italian-American groups were upset by the publicity given Valachi's disclosures. They protested that the feverish coverage of a 4,700-member secret network of criminals was a libel on 15 million law-abiding citizens of Italian heritage.

Protest was then at its peak in America. For every cause there was a movement, and in 1970 a most surprising protest leader came forward—Joseph Colombo, boss of the Colombo Family in New York. In April, his son was arrested for defacing U.S. currency; Colombo picketed the offices of the FBI in Manhattan, claiming harassment. Over the next few months, the size of his demonstrations swelled and he founded the Italian-American Civil Rights League. It had an amazing but brief history, and so would Colombo.

In its first year, the league sponsored a Unity Day, which drew 50,000 people and most major city and state politicians to Columbus Circle. It was a protest against discrimination and offensive stereotyping of Italians in television commercials and the media. The league became a forum for airing legitimate grievances, but Colombo was a cynical leader with a hidden agenda. He wanted the government to cease its Family investigations so that he could operate as freely as he wanted.

Colombo's gambit backfired. The government retaliated with stepped-up investigations of all the Families. Gambino Family underboss Aniello Dellacroce, for instance, was hauled before grand juries in Manhattan and Brooklyn. He refused to talk to either— even after offers of immunity—and was later jailed for a year. The Internal Revenue Service also opened a separate tax case that would result in another jail term.

After only one year, Carlo Gambino had seen enough. His wife had just died and the government was trying to deport him. Colombo's high-profile activities had jeopardized Gambino's goal of living out his final years quietly. He and other bosses spread the word among unions and along the docks—where Gambino's support was the greatest—that attendance at the second annual Unity Day would not be appreciated.

On June 28, 1971, only 10,000 people showed up, one-fifth of the previous year's crowd. Even so, Colombo was besieged by reporters and photographers in Columbus Circle. One lensman was only acting. He was really a hit man and he shot Colombo in the head and neck. A few seconds later, the hit man was hit, by a man who fired three fatal bullets and melted into the crowd.

Colombo survived, but was paralyzed and incapacitated; he died in 1978. By his side that day was a young Brooklyn lawyer admitted to the bar at age 21. Barry Ivan Slotnick, who would wind up representing Aniello Dellacroce, had helped Colombo start the Italian-American Civil Rights League.

A few days after Joseph Colombo was hit, three Italian-Americans in Lewisburg got a gift from the law gods. Prosecutors in the Velvet Touch hijacking case pending against Gotti, Angelo Ruggiero, and John Carneglia moved to dismiss the indictment. A new state wiretap law had been declared unconstitutional and recordings from the bar phone were useless as evidence.

Gotti had gotten a sentence break on his first case; Coiro had made the second go away; and now the government had taken away the third. He got the news in the middle of July 1971. He now had only six more months to serve. For the three hijackings he was caught in, he would do less than three years.

10

HOODLUM'S HOODLUM

JOHN GOTTI GOT OUT OF Lewisburg in January 1972. The thirty-one-year-old ex-con joined Victoria and the four kids—the oldest was almost 10 now—in an apartment at 1498 East Ninety-first Street in Canarsie, a safe and solid neighborhood south of Brownsville-East New York.

Gotti outlined his plans to his parole officer. He said he had a job waiting for him, working with his father-in-law—Francisco DiGiorgio, a retired sanitation worker—now involved with his own son in the Century Construction Company in a northern suburb. On February 15, 1972, the parole officer put a note in the file indicating Gotti had begun to work at the Dee Dan Company, a Century subsidiary, as a $300-a-week job superintendent.

The job looked good on paper, and that's about all it was. Gotti really had no interest in the construction business, except for the money to be made fixing contracts or causing labor problems. Thirty months in the joint merely confirmed what he had become—a hoodlum; merely pointed the way to what he would become—a "hoodlum's hoodlum," to use the words of a future admirer caught praising Gotti on a hidden tape recorder.

No doubt further seasoned in crime by the career crooks of Lewisburg, Gotti was poised for opportunity. With Bergin Hunt and Fish Club boss Carmine Fatico growing older, he was eager to pursue his future and his fortune.

The Bergin was a few miles away from Canarsie in Queens, in Ozone Park on 101st Avenue, a street of small merchants and small dreams, except for those of the new guy on the block—John Gotti.

Most of the original residents of Ozone Park were of Italian or Polish descent and they remain a dominant force. Over time, many left their jobs in Manhattan, which they call "the city" or "New York," as if they aren't part of it. In many ways, they aren't. Manhattan is an hour away by train; shopping and entertainment are more accessible in Nassau County on Long Island. Many work close to home, at nearby Aqueduct Racetrack or JFK International Airport. Their Ozone Park is a small, manageable world on the edge of the frantic universe of New York City. They mind their own business and let the men at the Bergin Hunt and Fish Club mind theirs.

In 1972, the Bergin was still a center of gambling, loan-sharking, robbery, and hijacking. One crew member had opened a chop shop for dismantling stolen cars for resale as parts and, while John was away, brother Peter also got into something new—cocaine, according to what Matthew Traynor, the ex-Ridgewood Saints gang leader, later told the FBI.

Traynor had moved to Florida and met a cocaine dealer. On a trip back to New York, he saw Peter in the 101 Bar and told him about his connection. Traynor flew the first of many cocaine sorties to Florida on behalf of Peter, then still a city sanitation worker. Peter had been previously arrested in 1968, on a felony assault charge that was later dismissed.

In time, Traynor said Peter began to direct him to a different source, a man later identified as a major southern Florida dealer with Family connections. Traynor said he usually delivered the cocaine to Peter at the Bergin or the 101 Bar. Usually he was paid over $500 for smuggling the coke, but once Peter rewarded him with $200 and a stash of barbiturates, 500 Tuinol tablets. Traynor didn't complain about the smaller fee; he had also brought back 50 .25-caliber handguns and was having no trouble selling them in Queens bars.

Although he placed Gene as being present at this transaction, as well as another, Traynor never put John Gotti in a room where drugs or cash were passed, though he did say he believed John knew what was happening. This was the first of many conflicting stories about John Gotti and drugs. He would never be charged with a drug crime, though in three different investigations, he would be named in connection with drug dealing. He would preach against it to younger associates, but close around him, older associates would get into trouble over drugs time and time again. Source Wahoo would say

Gotti was not involved in drugs; the other FBI informer, Source BQ, would say he was—in a big way. As an ambitious man, Gotti knew he had to appear faithful to the no-drugs policies of Gambino and later Castellano. If his faith was genuine, he can at least be said to have looked the other way, many times.

It was not in John Gotti's nature to look the other way. One night, four months after his release from Lewisburg, John, Peter, and their father were in the Crystal Room, the bar that Traynor said Gotti partly owned. A likely bar topic was the sensational murder of Joseph "Crazy Joe" Gallo a few days before at Umberto's Clam House in Little Italy. The victim was the reputed operations director of the hit on Joseph Colombo, the surprising Italian-American civil rights leader, and doubtless it was Colombo's friends who took their revenge with machine guns.

On this night in the Crystal Room, a patron began arguing with the barmaid and Gotti intervened. Cops were called and he was arrested and charged with menacing and public intoxication.

As he was booked in the 75th Precinct station house in Brooklyn, he used an alias for the first and only time. Perhaps as a joke, perhaps as a tribute, the young Carlo Gambino-affliliated hood gave the name "John DeCarlo." Gotti was able to pay a $50 fine and forget about it.

Besides the Crystal Room, another place Gotti now favored was the Sinatra Club, a storefront on Atlantic Avenue near Eighty-seventh Street in Queens. It featured the singer's albums and all-night card games, and it's where he met a future nemesis, Salvatore Polisi.

Polisi was a degenerate lowlife who entered the world of crime at about the same time as Gotti, after faking his way out of the Marine Corps on a psychological discharge. Over the years, he would also fake his way out of several criminal charges by reading medical journals and learning to act convincingly crazy; he would fool more than two dozen psychiatrists.

Polisi was once diagnosed as "a chronic, undifferentiated schizophrenic with a passive dependent personality disorder, with sociopathic tendencies." It was all the result of a scam, except for the sociopathic tendencies.

"I could put myself up as looking odd and strange sometimes," he later testified.

Polisi went into the Marine Corps to beat a robbery case, and wanted out after a couple of days so that he could rob again. He received a sizable, completely fraudulent disability pension for many years. He stole tape players from cars, robbed gas stations, and carried around a "blue box" to cheat on his telephone calls.

When Gotti met him, Polisi had become associated with the Colombo Family through a bookmaking operation he and his uncle operated. Polisi bragged about conning the Marine Corps, and so he became known on the street as Sally *Ubatz*, the last name a slang rendering of *pazzo*, crazy.

Though associated with the Colombos, Sally Crazy began hanging out a little at the Bergin Hunt and Fish Club in 1972, he would later testify. He was friendly with a Bergin associate named Ronald Jerogae, who was known as "Foxy." That same year, Sally Crazy and Foxy also went into the cocaine business.

Sally Crazy said John and Gene Gotti were at the Bergin nearly every day. Other club men included the brothers Fatico, the brothers Ruggiero, and the brothers Carneglia. Willie Boy Johnson and William Battista, the hijackers and bookmakers from John's old neighborhood, also were part of the scene, as was Tony Roach Rampino, now out of Lewisburg, too.

"Some days we hung around and did some gambling," Polisi said. "There was other days we conspired to commit crimes."

Polisi said it was clear who at the club had power and respect. As crew leader, Carmine Fatico, now 62, had the most, followed by his brother Daniel. Because the Faticos treated him with respect, John Gotti was next in line, followed by Angelo and Gene.

The elite five, at various times, were called upon to approve high-interest loans to bettors. Loan-sharking is a natural complement to a gambling operation. They are like peanuts and beer; the more the customer eats, the more he drinks. More losses, more loans. If the bettor can't pay his debt, he had better come up with something valuable—a piece of his business, a tip about a horse or an unguarded truck, the key or layout of a warehouse; in Ozone Park and its environs, the bars, hangouts, and union halls were full of bettors.

During scores, the two pals, Crazy and Foxy, played Smart and Stupid—Polisi, of course, was Stupid, although he believed he was Smart. That spring they heard about a hijackable truck. As they were with different Families, permission from spokesmen for each was needed. When Foxy got his from John Gotti, it was clear in Crazy's mind that Gotti was going places. Gotti himself had quit going out on jobs and contented himself with management duties— another sign of his emerging status.

A dispute over the proceeds of a hijacking also showed Gotti rising fast in the Bergin world. Gotti had teamed up Crazy and Foxy with a man who had inside knowledge of a fur shipment, and when the furs were fenced by Angelo and Danny Fatico for a price Polisi thought unfair, Gotti told him, "Tough. You got to take it,"

A few months later, the FBI heard of this hijack from Source Wahoo. It was apparent then why Polisi had complained. The FBI valued the load of 5,577 mink and muskrat pelts at $100,000, but Polisi and Foxy got only $4,500 each.

In May 1972, Gotti benefited from Carmine Fatico's misfortune. Fatico was indicted in Suffolk County, Long Island, on loan-sharking charges; the authorities said he was collecting more than 200 percent in annual interest on several loans.

Carmine was already on probation due to a conspiracy conviction for his role in the 1968 murder plot against a Long Island businessman. Needing to lay low and prepare for his trial, Fatico began to avoid the Bergin. With the consent of Neil Dellacroce, Gotti filled the vacuum. At 31, he became acting captain of the Fatico crew, even though he was not a made man. It was impressive, but another ex-Brooklyn Neapolitano, Al Capone, had done better: He ruled all of Chicago at age 32.

No one at the club was surprised. Johnny Boy Gotti was aggressive and political and a more able leader than Danny Fatico. Men around him now rose in stature. For instance, Polisi said that Willie Boy Johnson began to be "treated with a great deal of respect because he was a close friend of John's."

Willie Boy's father wasn't Italian and thus he could not be inducted into the Family, but over the years Willie Boy became like Family to Gotti. He was a versatile and likable criminal and, among many other things, wound up managing his own gambling operation.

In addition to the Crazy-Foxy tip, Source Wahoo had also told the FBI about a hijack drop used by William Battista and John Carneglia. Now Wahoo filed his first report on John Gotti, post-Lewisburg, and his control agent put a note in the file.

Gotti was "a big hijacker" and Angelo and Salvatore Ruggiero worked for him. Every Saturday, he reported to Neil Dellacroce at the Ravenite Social Club in Little Italy. He would be made a member of the Family soon. As an aside, Wahoo said the Bergin crew was "starting to wonder" about Billy Battista, who was asking too many questions about a man wanted on an FBI warrant.

The visits with Dellacroce shot Gotti into the big time. A year earlier, another United States Senate committee had issued a report calling Dellacroce "the most powerful boss in New York today. His influence is enormous. His power is incredible."

The Senate committee was overstating a bit, but Gambino was slowing down and Dellacroce, born and bred in Little Italy, seemed an obvious choice as the new *don*, or lord of the Family. Few outsiders knew much about the man who was emerging as another possible successor, the low-key cousin and brother-in-law, Paul Castellano.

Dellacroce's high profile was a possible disadvantage. At the time Carmine Fatico was indicted on the loan-sharking case, Dellacroce was indicted on an income-tax charge. He was accused of reporting an income of only $10,400 in 1968 when he actually made $134,150; it was a net-worth case, meaning that the government had to prove his guilt by proving how much he had spent. The prosecutor said Dellacroce "had lived the life of a professional hoodlum all his life." Dellacroce, however, was confident he could beat the charge. He had beaten so many.

John introduced Angelo and Gene to Dellacroce, who now supplanted Fatico as John's mentor. The young Bergin hoods fawned over the chief Ravenite hood. Angelo called him "uncle." When they went to sit down with him, they wore suits and ties; going into "New York" they felt sharp and looked sharp—in their own way. For John, who came from a house of hand-me-downs, it was the start of an obsession with fine clothes.

Late in 1972, after all appeals had been exhausted, Dellacroce had to go to jail for snubbing a grand jury despite having gotten immunity. More bad news broke in January. His sanguine attitude about his tax case evaporated in a conviction. The evidence included testimony that Dellacroce, as "George Rizzo" in three days of gambling in a casino in Puerto Rico, had lost as much as he reported in income for the entire year. He faced five more years after his grand-jury contempt sentence expired in June.

———————

John Gotti went about his business as best he could. As acting captain, he matched talent with tips. Early in 1973, he hooked Crazy and Foxy up with Sal Ruggiero and another hijacker so they could swipe 57,000 watches from a storage area at JFK Airport. Soon everybody at the Bergin had new watches to go with off-the-truck suits from an earlier hijacking.

Source Wahoo told the FBI about the stolen watches and said Gotti had started hanging out at another social club, the Nevermore, which was in Maspeth—still Queens, but far from the Bergin. At the club and a nearby bar, the Sportsman's, Gotti was loan-sharking with the son of a top official of a dirty Teamsters local.

With Dellacroce behind bars and Carmine Fatico laying low, Gotti began seeing Carlo Gambino himself. FBI agents saw him—on several occasions—entering and leaving Gambino's apartment on Ocean Parkway in the Sheepshead Bay neighborhood.

John took great pleasure in passing along Carlo's orders. For instance, early in 1973, John told the troops that the old man wanted them to lay off trucks connected to companies associated with various Families; he wanted them to avoid committing certain crimes: counterfeiting, stock and bond fraud, drug dealing, and the kidnapping of other criminals.

All these crimes are violations of federal laws; Gambino was well aware that federal agencies had been granted sweeping new powers to attack the Families; he knew the federal law bureaucracy was less corruptible than the state's. He had banned kidnapping other criminals for an additional, personal reason. His 29-year-old nephew Emanuel Gambino, who operated his own version of the Bergin's beer-and-peanuts business, had been grabbed off a Manhattan street the previous May.

Given all the criminal opportunities in New York, it's a wonder crooks should choose to kidnap other crooks, especially a nephew of a powerful crime boss. But at the time, at least two gangs of kidnappers specializing in bookmakers and loan sharks were prowling around card games and after-hours bars.

Emanuel Gambino's kidnappers contacted his wife and demanded $350,000. She collected about $100,000 from relatives, turned it over to an unknown person, and waited for her husband to come home. He never did. On January 26, 1973, he was excavated from the grounds of a federal ammunition depot in New Jersey, a bullet in his head.

James McBratney, age 32, was not a part of the Gambino kidnap scheme, though some people may have believed it. He was a large, ruddy man who belonged to another gang; unlike the first gang, whose members were all Irish, McBratney's gang cut across ethnic lines. It had recently kidnapped a Staten Island loan shark and gotten $21,000. But some neighborhood kids saw the snatch and passed along a license-plate number to neighborhood Family members.

McBratney and his partners soon learned they were wanted, but not by the police. One partner was Edward Maloney, who ran away from an orphanage to begin a New York crime career at 15. He would have a bad night in Gotti country a decade later, but now he fled the city. McBratney put a machine gun in his car and stayed put on Staten Island. A bad mistake.

11

MAKING HIS BONES AT SNOOPE'S BAR

ABOUT 11 P.M. ON MAY 22, 1973, John Gotti, Angelo Ruggiero, and another Gambino aspirer, Ralph Galione, entered a homespun tavern on Staten Island called Snoope's Bar & Grill.

The barmaid, Miriam Arnold, age 26, a part-time student, later said Snoope's was so well-lit that it was possible to read a book and so she recognized the trio instantly. She remembered that they were in the bar a month earlier, and that they looked around, acted suspiciously, and left without having a drink, although the one she later learned was John used the men's room.

This night, they were preceded by a few minutes by a large, fair-skinned man who sat at the bar next to a regular customer, Lawrence Davis, age 29, a mechanic. The barmaid didn't know Jimmy McBratney, who had left his machine gun outside, but when he ordered his drink she said it sounded like he had a bad cold.

McBratney sat quietly sipping his 65-cent crème de menthe on the rocks as John, Angelo, and Galione came in and strode to the rear of the bar, past a half-dozen or so tipplers. Miriam Arnold, who was serving three friends celebrating a birthday, remembers sensing danger when the trio of men turned and walked back toward the big Irishman.

Quickly they surrounded him: Angelo on his left, Galione on his right, and John behind; Galione had a gun; Angelo had a pair of handcuffs. All began pulling McBratney up and away from the bar.

"You're under arrest," Galione said to McBratney, who was trying to pull away. "You've been this route before; don't give us any trouble."

"Hey, who are you?" a patron named Red McManus yelled.

"We're police," Galione said.

"Let's see a badge."

Galione fired a shot into the ceiling, ending further requests for identification. Two customers fled the bar; two darted into a cellar. Galion ordered the others to stand against a wall, but Miriam Arnold, keeping her cool, had already slipped to the end of the bar—and onto a pay telephone.

McBratney was off the bar stool now, struggling to free himself from Angelo and John. But the Bergin buddies had Lewisburg muscles and McBratney, though he, too, was strong and actually managed to drag all of them several feet toward the end of the bar, couldn't get free.

John and Angelo, with McBratney wedged between them, ended up in front of Miriam Arnold, on the phone with a 911 operator. "I realized I was in a rather bad position, if something was going to happen," she recalled. "So I moved away."

"Where do you think you're going?" demanded Galione, who now had the rest of the bar under his control.

"The hell out of your way. I don't want anybody to get hurt."

Too late for that. Galione walked toward McBratney, a standing duck between John and Angelo, and fired three times at close range, producing in the smoky air streams of a fine pink mist. McBratney would kidnap no more.

A few Family men have said an associate will not be made until he participates in a murder. This frustrates infiltration by undercover agents. The rite of passage was once described as "making your bones." Gotti, then 32 years old, was making the best of his bones. The victim was a Family menace.

Even so, it was a sloppy murder. Why not wait for McBratney to leave the bar? Why not attempt to conceal faces? Who would buy the cop charade without a badge to display?

In July, two of McBratney's killers, Angelo and Galione, were picked out of a police photo spread by Miriam Arnold and Lawrence Davis. They were quickly arrested, but the police had no idea who the third man was. They probably never would have if Gotti hadn't succumbed to the common habit among criminals of boasting about their crimes.

A month after Angelo and Galione were arrested, Source Wahoo heard Gotti bragging about the McBratney hit and Carmine Fatico vainly advising him to lay low. The FBI tipped the NYPD, which showed a photo of Gotti to the witnesses, and on October 17, a few days before his thirty-third birthday, a state grand jury indicted him on a murder charge. This time he listened to Carmine Fatico and went into hiding. He left Victoria and the kids, but not the Crime Capital.

The police called on an FBI hijack squad to help search for the fugitive. The FBI called on Source Wahoo, who "was given a specific assignment to locate John Gotti and set him up for apprehension." Nearly a year after the murder, Wahoo reported in. He said Gotti avoided the Bergin, but "on a daily basis" was at the Sportsman's Bar or the nearby Nevermore Social Club in Maspeth "with the exception of weekends when he goes off with his wife." He was driving a Mark IV Lincoln registered to an Ozone Park restaurant. He got messages from a pay phone across the street and regular visits from his brother Gene and Foxy the hijacker and cocaine dealer. He was often in the company of Tony Roach Rampino, the heroin dealer, Bergin hijacker, and "John's man."

"Source stated Gotti, to his knowledge, is not carrying a gun and will not resist apprehension," an FBI memo said.

On June 3, 1974, as Gotti and Rampino chatted in the Nevermore, FBI agents arrived, arrested the murder suspect and turned him over to the NYPD. Wahoo "was the sole basis for the apprehension of Gotti, who is a bonafide organized crime figure under Carmine Fatico and Dellacroce," an FBI agent wrote in support of a $600 payment to the source.

Gotti was held on $150,000 bail until his parents and his inlaws— who had helpfully provided a job cover after his release from Lewisburg—put up their houses to secure a bond.

His in-laws were already doing a lot for Gotti, their daughter Victoria, and their grandchildren. They had recently purchased a house for them in Howard Beach, directly south of Ozone Park on Jamaica Bay. Finally, Gotti had made it out of Brooklyn apartments and into a Cape Cod house in a suburb by the sea. He hoped he wouldn't have to go off to prison too long.

The Gotti house was white with black trim. It had five rooms on the first floor and three bedrooms upstairs. This was plenty of room even though Victoria was pregnant and soon expected to give birth to another boy, who they would call Peter. The house was on Eighty-fifth Street in the Rockwood Park section of Howard Beach, an area containing about 3,000 single-family homes built in the early 1950s on filled-in marshland.

Howard Beach lies directly beneath the airplane approach to Runway 31-L at JFK Airport, but most residents don't even notice the big jets anymore. Generally, they are more prosperous and professional than their neighbors in Ozone Park; but they share the same community attachment, the sense of having escaped the madness of the metropolis, of live-and-let-live, and of minding your own business.

In midday traffic, the Bergin Hunt and Fish Club was now a six-minute drive from Gotti's home.

Free on bail, Gotti was hopeful his lawyers could work something out. He had more than the usual reasons for wanting to avoid prison. Carlo Gambino was growing old, Dellacroce was in jail, *consigliere* Joe N. Gallo was laid up with a heart attack, and Carmine Fatico had just been indicted on another loan-shark charge. The new case was instructive: Fatico was accused of collecting usurious interest from ten businessmen on loans of five hundred to several thousand dollars. When debtors fall behind on such loans is when underground bankers acquire part of seemingly legitimate enterprises as well as a way to wash illegitimate money.

Gotti had a few enterprises to tend to. Back at the Bergin after a few years in Florida, Matthew Traynor was told Gotti had acquired a piece of a motel and a Chinese restaurant. Source Wahoo said Gotti was the hidden owner of a Queens disco and that he ran a crap game with Carmine Fatico's money in a second-floor loft on Church Avenue in Brooklyn.

Gotti now kept a private office at the Bergin, "which could not be entered without an appropriate reason," an FBI agent wrote after interviewing Traynor, who said it was clear that "John was the boss." Angelo was John's top aide and in their absence Gene was in charge.

At day's end, Traynor hung around with crew members in the 101 Bar, another establishment he was told Gotti had gotten a hook into. Source Wahoo was getting expense money from the FBI to hang out in such joints, and he kept delivering. His tip led to the recovery of a load of Canon calculators and cameras from a Gambino Family drop in New Jersey.

———————————

At the time, Wahoo's control agent was Special Agent Martin J. Boland, then stationed at an FBI office in New Jersey. Boland debriefed Wahoo on the phone or met him at quiet places in Brooklyn and Queens; he occasionally summed up for his superiors how valuable Wahoo was:

"Source converted to top-echelon criminal informant [in] February, 1971. Since then [source has been] responsible for solving numerous FBI cases which resulted in arrests of Cosa Nostra figures and recovery of over $300,000 in stolen property, national publicity in [a Luchese Family fraud] case and the arrest of Sal Polisi in a bank robbery."

Informants whose value depends on maintaining criminal credibility can be troublesome. They test the patience and resourcefulness of agents, as Special Agent Boland noted:

"Case agent has handled this informant single-handedly; has had to contend with the informant being arrested [for] counterfeiting, ... receiving stolen property ... and armed robbery ... the above arrests and informant's activity within the underworld has presented problems which Agent Boland has handled efficiently without recourse to higher bureau authority. It is noted Agent Boland received a letter of commendation in [a fraud case] for handling liaison with the Brooklyn District Attorney."

———————————

Matthew Traynor acted as a wheelman in several hijackings pulled by the Bergin crew after his return from Florida. One of his drinking companions was Tony Roach Rampino, a gangly man with sinister eyes, hollow cheeks, and pockmarked skin who favored sharkskin suits and gaudy ties.

Rampino was a worker bee in the Bergin gambling games; he also collected loan-shark debts. He boasted that his menacing appearance accounted for his successful collection rate. He told Traynor that Gotti helped kill "the Irish guy" for "the little big man, Carlo," and that everyone in the crew benefited.

"We're going to take over everything some day," John's man added.

Rampino advised Traynor to tell businessmen who needed money to see John Gotti, as the acting Bergin boss wished to go "legitimate." This was after Rampino returned from Canada with money he collected for Gotti from the "Greco brothers." Rampino wanted to get close to the brothers.

"They're big dope guys," John's man said.

Many years later, Angelo would get close to one of the Greco brothers; it was on a big heroin deal that caused grave problems for the Family within the Family.

Traynor was told by another Bergin associate that Gene Gotti might be dead had it not been for John. Gene had gotten into a dispute in a Manhattan bar and slapped around a relative of a Gambino captain, who threatened mayhem. John stepped in and restored everyone's dignity with negotiated regrets about the misunderstanding.

The older hoods liked the younger hood—he was capable and respectful, even if sometimes a little too outspoken and aggressive. "Dellacroce will sponsor Gotti to Cosa Nostra membership when Gambino opens the books. Gotti is a well-respected hoodlum and has gained much stature since the killing of McBratney," Boland wrote after another Wahoo chat.

Gotti no doubt was disappointed that Gambino had closed the membership "book" and was making men only when members passed away. Carlo was worried about adding men affiliated with Dellacroce, who would surely want to take over once Carlo was gone. He also wanted to keep the Family a manageable size and was wary of initiating an informer or anyone connected to drugs. At the time, the Family was said to include 500 made men and 1,000 more associates, making it far and away the nation's largest.

Although Carlo was keeping Gotti waiting, FBI informers were saying that around the Bergin the acting captain would refer coyly and mysteriously to special favors that the old man had called upon him to provide.

"He didn't get specific about the favors," an FBI agent said. "He let them use their imaginations."

A story going around in Queens bars that the FBI later heard had Gotti killing a man and chopping off the victim's head and storing it in a hatbox in a refrigerator. Gotti "got credit, in the minds of some crew members, for hits he did not do. But a story like that, even if it isn't true, embellishes a guy's reputation," the agent said. "It helps build a mystique."

The police and the FBI were not always able to sort out all the details, but at the end of some tales about Gotti and his crew they found dead bodies. Such was the case with Sally Crazy Polisi's hijack buddy, Foxy, who passed away on December 18, 1974, the victim of three .38-caliber slugs, two to the head.

Four years after the fact, Traynor talked to the FBI and to Queens detective John Daly about Foxy's murder. He said the Gotti brothers were angry at Foxy for skimming hijacking proceeds and he was asked to drive two Bergin associates to Foxy's apartment in nearby Howard Beach and wait in the car while they went inside. They returned in a few minutes.

"I guess we'll have to go to Foxy's funeral," one said.

Traynor had heard no shots, and the man didn't elaborate, but three days later Traynor was in his Cadillac with Richard Gotti, driving to Foxy's funeral. During the funeral, Traynor heard Gene Gotti ask Foxy's sister to turn over to him a boat her brother had. She later did.

Traynor said crew members decided to concoct a story and pin the murder on one Tommy DiSimone, yet another hijacker who preyed on the JFK Airport as a member of a gang associated with a Luchese Family capo, Paul Vario.

Traynor would give this version of Foxy's death to federal agents again—essentially the same way—in 1986. In between the two stories, Sources Wahoo and BQ insisted to the FBI that Tommy DiSimone, aided by his brother-in-law, did in fact kill Foxy over a girl, not money. The girl would not talk to the police about it, but she did tell Gotti, and he swore revenge.

Sally Crazy heard of Foxy's demise as he began an eight-year stretch in Lewisburg federal prison. Angelo was then on a return visit to Lewisburg for another hijacking—a fellow inmate was convicted hijacker John Carneglia—and he told Polisi that Foxy was killed by Tommy DiSimone.

"Well, then, I will kill Tommy," Polisi responded.

"You can't kill Tommy. John and I are going to take care of Tommy," Angelo retorted.

In January 1979, not long after he got out of prison, not long after he was suspected of taking part in a stunning armed robbery—the theft of nearly $6 million in untraceable dollars from a Lufthansa German Airlines vault at the airport—Tommy DiSimone, who had gotten over the girl who fell for Foxy and married the daughter of a Gotti crew member, disappeared and was not seen again. His brother-in-law, Joseph Spione, had disappeared earlier.

Source BQ gave a chilling description of how Spione was dispatched. He said Spione was beaten with bats and dismembered by four crew members in the back room of the Bergin. The pieces were placed in several plastic bags and dumped in the ocean.

With regard to DiSimone, BQ gave a chilling account of Gotti's use of his power. He said Gotti ordered DiSimone's father-in-law, crew member Sal DeVita, to set up his son-in-law by bringing him to a street corner where two other crew members were waiting in ambush. The two gunmen were John's man, Tony Roach Rampino, and Michael Roccoforte, an eventual cocaine dealer.

Source BQ said Rampino and Roccoforte waited for five hours before deciding that Sal and Tommy weren't coming. Later at the Bergin, BQ saw DeVita crying and asking Gotti not to be angry with him, but he just couldn't set up his daughter's husband.

"Tommy will be killed," John Gotti said, according to BQ.

Four days later, Gene Gotti told BQ that Sal DeVita would not have to worry about setting up Tommy anymore; Tommy was gone. Source Wahoo said Tommy was taken on a sea voyage, weighted down, and thrown overboard, thus joining his brother-in-law in the Jamaica Bay cemetery off Howard Beach.

12

DYING IN A STATE
OF GRACE

IN 1975, THE ACTING CAPTAIN of the Bergin crew wasn't acting like a man out on bail for murder. John Gotti went about his and the Family's business as though nothing had changed.

He was moving up fast and there was no time to waste—he might have to go to prison for the killing of James McBratney. Looking for the best possible deal, Source Wahoo said, "Carlo and the capos chipped in" and hired Roy M. Cohn to help Johnny Boy out.

Cohn was one of the best-known and most powerful lawyers in New York. His client list was eclectic: leading businessmen, politicians and entertainers, the Roman Catholic Church, and several Family leaders, including Aniello Dellacroce.

The McBratney case had seen a few major developments since Gotti, Angelo Ruggiero, and Ralph Galione were arrested. For one thing, Galione, age 36, had been ambushed and murdered in the hallway of his Brooklyn apartment building early one morning.

Angelo had gone to trial without Galione, had gotten a hung jury, and was now facing a retrial with Gotti, who had been apprehended later. In the first trial, witnesses for Angelo had said he was in New Jersey the night McBratney died. Cohn knew the hung jury meant the prosecution might want to deal down the charges against both Angelo and Gotti. He sent feelers to the authorities on Staten Island and once again Gotti wound up with a great deal.

He and Angelo, whose earlier defense was that he wasn't even in the state at the time, pleaded guilty only to attempted manslaughter. It meant time, but not heavy time. At a hearing on June 2, 1975,

Cohn made it all sound so noble: "After a long and difficult reflection and discussion ... realizing the jury did in fact sharply disagree at the last trial ... we nevertheless did determine that the interest of justice would be served in the acceptance of a plea."

Now the District Attorney's Office on Staten Island did Gotti another favor. As a pre-sentence investigation was being prepared by the Probation Department, the D.A. declined to attempt to classify him as a persistent felony offender, though he was—and it might have meant a longer prison term.

A probation officer who interviewed Gotti noted the D.A.'s action on another confidential report prepared for the judge who was to sentence him. In this report, the officer gave Gotti's account of the McBratney incident and his account of Gotti, which was not flattering.

Gotti told the officer he didn't know Galione was armed and that he merely came to the aid of his friends when they began tussling with McBratney. Gotti would say something similar in 1984, when he and a friend were accused of assaulting a refrigerator mechanic in Queens: He was only helping his friend.

"The defendant showed no remorse for his involvement and appears to take his [presumed] incarceration as one of those things," the officer wrote.

Gotti said he was not connected to any organized crime group. He had worked day-to-day jobs as a construction worker since his release from Lewisburg, but had no documentation. He said he was a gambler who won most of the time and that his in-laws would help out his family while he was in prison again.

The probation officer didn't buy any of it. He wrote, "Prior investigations indicate the defendant is irresponsible and has exhibited a criminal pattern of behavior since 1958. [He] has found theft and other antisocial and illegal behavior more profitable and desirable than gainful legitimate employment."

Understandably, the officer was gloomy about Gotti's future. "This defendant is an individual of average intelligence who has not met his family's needs and it appears that he has embarked upon an amoral type of existence to the exclusion of all other responsibilities. The defendant's prognosis is extremely poor and there is no indication that he has made any attempt to reform."

Gotti did not care what the probation officer said. What was important was what the judge said.

"Four years," Judge John A. Garbarino said on August 8. Gotti knew that this was likely to mean two, and it would. He would do less time for a body on the floor at Snoope's Bar than he had done for hijacking $7,691 worth of women's clothes at JFK Airport.

Gotti now entered the crisis-prone New York State corrections system, which guards more inmates than the entire U.S. Bureau of Prisons. He would do most of his time in the Green Haven Correctional Facility, 80 miles north of Howard Beach. Green Haven was one of three prisons for the state's most recalcitrant and recidivist criminals. One who went in at about the same time was Johnny Boy's friend, Willie Boy Johnson, who had been sent away for armed robbery in Brooklyn.

Gotti and Johnson and 1,700 other hard-core convicts were jammed into lockups built for 1,200 prisoners. The yard, the mess hall, and the cells were segregated along ethnic lines. Guards were inexperienced and poorly paid. Tensions ran high. In 1976, two inmates were murdered and prison officials announced a shakedown; literally dozens of homemade weapons, assorted drugs, and bottles of liquor were confiscated.

Gotti swept floors once in a while, lifted weights, attended classes in Italian culture, played cards, and survived. Even if he was able to wind down at night with a dry martini, it was a hellish way to throw away two years of his life. The thought of going away to such a prison was too much for some men. Salvatore Ruggiero, Angelo's brother, was such a man.

Salvatore was not as rugged as his brother, and not as interested in the Family, although he was a hijacker and was interested in money. Source Wahoo met him in the early 1970s. In 1974, he reported that Salvatore also was in the real estate business with Anthony Moscatiello, who leased the Cadillac that Gotti was then driving and who later became a kind of accountant for the Bergin crew. Wahoo said Salvatore had amassed $500,000 worth of Long Island properties.

Two months later, Wahoo said Salvatore had decided to make his money grow by going into another business, the *babania* business. *Babania* was a Family word for heroin. Soon Salvatore was making a lot of trips to Florida and spending money like an oil baron; several years later, the crew still talked about a party he held aboard a yacht and the $70,000 he spent providing food, booze, entertainment, and girls for his guests. By May 1975, Salvatore was a millionaire and had been indicted as a large supplier of heroin for the drug addicts of Harlem.

Angelo admired his younger-by-five-years brother and his deal-maker charms. "He coulda been anything he wanted in life," he once said. "A doctor or lawyer. This kid, he could sit down with anybody."

Salvatore did not want to sit in prison, so he went into hiding just before he was indicted; at the time, he also was under investigation in a tax-evasion case. He learned that he might be indicted in the heroin case while watching a television news report at his summer home in the Hamptons. Angelo was later overheard on tape talking about his brother's decision to become a fugitive:

"[Sal] said, 'Listen, I'm gettin' indicted on income tax. I'm goin' on the lam.'"

"'For what? Income tax,' I said."

"He said, 'Angelo, listen. I got a feelin' somethin' else is comin' down.'"

"I said, 'Don't go home. Don't go no place. Get in the fuckin' wind.' And that's what he did."

Salvatore kept a stash of cash—$500,000—for such a purpose. He told Angelo, "I don't care if I'm broke, 'cause I'm not goin' to be broke. In case anything happens, I take the five hundred thousand dollars, the two kids, my wife, and I go."

Angelo's brother got into the wind before the heroin indictment was returned; as he predicted, he also was indicted on an income-tax charge, as was his wife, Stephanie. In between, he also was indicted in a hijacking case. By 1977, when John would leave Green Haven, Salvatore was wanted on three federal warrants. Only a few people knew where he was, and sometimes he wasn't far away, not from the Bergin and not from *babania*.

In 1976, Source BQ 11766–OC, Source BQ for short, began appearing in FBI files, and proved helpful right away. He told his control agent, Patrick F. Colgan, the Bergin crew had recently grabbed $150,000 worth of frozen lobsters from the wrong fishermen; the company that owned the lobsters was owned by another Family.

The crew wisely decided to return the seafood, but Source BQ alerted Colgan, who alerted the hijack squad, who arrested two men as they left a warehouse to throw back the lobsters. With Gotti away, the semiretired Carmine Fatico had to be called in to smooth things over in a sitdown with the other Family.

Two months later, Source BQ tipped off the FBI to another hijack—of 2,555 mens' suits, but these were peddled before the FBI could do anything. After he was arrested and decided to talk to the FBI, Matthew Traynor also talked about hijacks the crew pulled while its unofficial leader was away.

Besides hijackings, Gene Gotti, the new unofficial leader, looked after his brother's interests in another way, Traynor said—a way that required a dose of John's now-famous verbal ferocity.

Both Sources Wahoo and BQ had said many times that John had become a secret owner of a discotheque on Northern Boulevard in Queens; it was the nightclub that "Son of Sam" killer David Berkowitz followed one of his victims home from one night. According to Traynor, the main owner of the disco fell behind on a debt to John, which prompted a visit from Gene, the fearsome-looking Rampino, Traynor, and others—most of whom were armed. Traynor said Gene told the owner he would get "whacked" unless he made good. Traynor said that the Bergin men never paid a cover charge or for their drinks when they visited the nightclub.

Traynor said that he also made a few more cocaine runs to Florida on Peter Gotti's behalf. He said Gene was present when Peter gave the Florida merchandise to three men in Cono the Fisherman, the Maspeth restaurant where John would be arrested for the Romual Piecyk assault. Peter gave Traynor $1,500 and a quarter-ounce, seven grams.

"Here're some scrapings for you," he said, according to Traynor.

Traynor said he also shared the proceeds of a burglary with Richard Gotti, who gave him a tip about Fortunoff's, a store on Fifth Avenue known for its expensive merchandise. He said a friend of Richard's was an "alarm man" and if Traynor smashed the display window, he would have a "safe three minutes" to grab the merchandise and run. He would and he did, with gold chains he later sold for $1,500. He said he paid Richard $200 for the alarm tip.

On October 15, 1976, Carlo Gambino, who looked more like a lovable uncle than a crime boss, lay in his bed in Massapequa on Long Island. In a half-century of crime, he had spent 22 months in jail, for operating a half-million-gallon whiskey still in Philadelphia. Now he was 74 years old and frail from three heart attacks that had successfully thwarted the government's attempts to deport him. He asked to see a priest, was given the last rites of the Catholic Church, and then died "in a state of grace," according to the Reverend Dominic A. Sclafani.

In the obituary columns, Gambino also was identified as a former consultant in SGS Associates, a labor consulting firm, whose clients included the owners of the Chrysler Building, a New York landmark. He was preceded in death by his wife, the former Kathryn Castellano, and survived by three sons and a daughter. He had sent one son, Thomas, to a private school to be educated with the future shah of Iran and the future dictator of Nicaragua.

Thomas Gambino and his brothers owned many trucking and manufacturing firms operating in the midtown Manhattan garment district, where most of the wardrobe of America's women was designed and produced. The Gambino and Luchese Families had dominated the district since the 1930s. Joe N. Gallo, the Gambino *consigliere*, was the major force in the Greater Blouse, Skirt and Undergarment Association, a trade group that negotiated contracts with the district's 700 employers. By controlling the association and the trucking companies, the Families controlled the price of clothing and the lives of thousands of frequently exploited workers.

Over the next few days, the newspapers ran many stories on Carlo Gambino's possible successors. Aniello Dallacroce was the most popular choice; Paul Castellano was hardly mentioned. In fact, however, Dellacroce was in jail and Castellano was already in charge; like the nation, the Families move fast to replace a fallen leader.

Carlo had passed the word that he wanted Cousin Paul to replace him. *Consigliere* Gallo and crew leaders such as James Failla and Ettore Zappi immediately gave Castellano their allegiance. But like John Gotti a decade later, Castellano did not officially become boss until a few weeks later, after Dellacroce got out of jail on Thanksgiving Day.

The transfer of power presaged another. Paul, too, was under federal indictment, accused of running a loan-sharking ring that charged 150 percent vig. His nephew, who had worn a wire in Paul's presence, was the chief witness. A cousin of Paul's had already pleaded guilty. The case went to trial November 8, three weeks after Carlo had passed away.

When the nephew took the witness stand, he demonstrated a familiar condition—amnesia. He couldn't remember conversations he secretly recorded. No witness, no crime. "What happened here is that somebody got to this defendant," the assistant U.S. attorney complained to the judge.

The nephew was sentenced to two years in prison for criminal contempt. Paul Castellano had gotten off as boss just the way John Gotti would when Romual Piecyk forgot who assaulted him. He'd beaten the charge.

Paul's coronation took place a few weeks later in a house on Cropsey Avenue in Brooklyn. The house was owned by Anthony Gaggi, a soldier soon to be a capo. Gaggi's nephew, Dominick Montiglio, lived upstairs. Montiglio was a thief and a loan shark and eventually became a drug addict. He later betrayed Castellano and Gaggi by testifying against them at the stolen-car trial.

Gaggi taped a gun underneath the kitchen table prior to the arrival of Castellano, Dellacroce, Gallo, Failla, and other Family leaders. He told Montiglio to take another automatic weapon and go to his upstairs apartment, which looked out on the driveway.

"If you hear any shots from the kitchen, shoot whoever runs out the door," Uncle Anthony said.

Guns weren't necessary. Paul didn't like them. He offered Dellacroce virtual control of the Gotti-Fatico money tree and other crews, as long as they avoided drug dealing. Castellano, who had driven Carlo Gambino to the Apalachin Conference, was reaffirming the drug ban as a plank in his platform. Dellacroce, a free man after four years in jail because of his tax conviction, accepted Paul's terms, just as he had accepted Carlo's terms twenty years earlier when Carlo took over for Dellacroce's mentor, Albert Anastasia.

"Paul's the new boss," Gaggi told Montiglio after the visitors left. The sitdown had lasted only 20 minutes, but long enough to plant the seed for a Family within a Family.

Back at the Bergin, the men anticipated Gotti's release from Green Haven. Gene had been acting captain to the acting captain, but there was no doubt that John would take over as soon as he turned in his prison broom. Source BQ told the FBI on July 21 that Gotti was getting out in a week and the crew had bought him a new Lincoln. And, like a lot of crew members, Source BQ thought that Dellacroce was running the Family, and he told Special Agent Colgan this boded well for John Gotti.

Gotti got out on July 28, 1977, a little less than two years after he went into prison for the McBratney murder. After visiting Victoria and his quintet of happy children, he tried out his new blue and brown Mark V Lincoln, with New Jersey license plates, and found it satisfactory. At the Bergin, he hung a plaque that his former fellow inmates had given him during a party the night before his release.

The plaque read: To John Gotti—a Great Guy.

13

JOHNNY BOY GETS HIS BUTTON

FRESH OFF THE DISABLED LIST, John Gotti reclaimed his position in the Bergin lineup, acting captain of what was still technically Fatico's crew.

Carmine Fatico was now 67 years old. Recently, he had been cheered up by a doubleheader sweep—he won both his loan-sharking cases. The first fell apart at trial after, on successive days, two alleged victims refused to tell what they had told a grand jury. One had worn a hidden microphone to a loan conference with Fatico, enabling agents to overhear him, but the meeting was not recorded and thus there was no way to rebut the man—and therefore no case.

"Justice prevailed, that's all," said Carmine as he left a Long Island courtroom with his dismissal.

Four months later, the second case ended similarly: The main witness said he had lied to the grand jury.

Carmine still wanted to lay low, however. He had been convicted in a hijacking case with his brother Daniel and the brothers Carneglia, and was awaiting sentencing. Carmine and Daniel had copped pleas, betting they would get probation rather than prison.

The Great Guy of Green Haven, antsy to climb the Gambino ladder after two years in the can, was hoping they would lose the bet, according to source BQ; Gotti believed he could step up faster if his one-time mentor was out of the way.

"Source spoke to John ... and he is actually hoping that both Faticos get jail time," Special Agent Patrick F. Colgan wrote after talking to BQ, who said Gene Gotti felt the same way. Jail time for the Fatico brothers would enable "the Gotti brothers to obtain more power and influence."

Gotti was especially restless because Angelo and Gene had been made while he was away. But now that he and his new mentor, the powerful Neil Dellacroce, were out of jail and Paul Castellano had opened the membership book that Carlo Gambino had shut, crooked Johnny Boy would finally get straightened out.

No Gambino man has ever testified about the ceremony in which associates are baptized as soldiers. Members of other Families have. Although some differences are likely, so are similarities.

"Jimmy the Weasel" Fratianno, a West Coast mobster, recounted his initiation while testifying at a 1980 trial. He described a room full of Family men and a table on which a gun and a sword formed a cross. Then: "They all stood up. We held hands. The boss said something in Italian. It lasted two or three minutes. Then they prick your finger … until blood draws. Then you go around and meet each member of the family. You kiss them on the cheek and you are a member."

Fratianno said the membership rules were then listed. "The first thing they tell you [is], you can't fool around with narcotics. Secondly, you can't fool with anybody's wife or their daughters or girlfriends. Third, they never kill an FBI agent or any officers because it creates too much heat."

By testifying, Fratianno was violating *omerta*, the code of noncooperation with the law originating in feudal Sicily. "You can't never divulge anything about the organization," he said. "You can't talk to any officials of any kind. You can't go to any grand juries and tell the truth. You can't take depositions … They also tell you, 'You come in alive and go out dead.' There is no way out of the organization."

Q.: What happens if you violate any of these rules?
A.: As a rule, they kill you.

Eight other men were inducted into the Gambino Family the same night as John, according to Peter Mosca, the son of Ralph Mosca, the Queens capo. Many years later, Peter was caught reminiscing about the night while in the company of Carmine Fiore, a Mosca crew member, and Dominick Lofaro, the secret state Task Force informer whose body wire helped agents record the conversation:

MOSCA: The night I got straightened out, I met Johnny. He was with me. I was right behind him.

FIORE: They held it up for him. They were waiting for him to come home [from prison].

LOFARO: They used to make a lot of guys in those days.

MOSCA: Oh, it was good … coming home that night. Oh, it was marvelous … That night was nine.

Gotti's parole terms required that he have a job. Fortunately, the Bergin was located near the Arc Plumbing and Heating Corporation, which was owned by two brothers, old friends of his. In theory, Gotti now became a salesman for Arc, which would provide similarly helpful services for Angelo Ruggiero and his drug-fugitive brother, Salvatore.

Over the next several years, Arc Plumbing prospered. It won pieces of many substantial city contracts, including construction of the new police station for the 106th Precinct, which served Ozone Park and Howard Beach. Arc Plumbing secured other public jobs at city parks, housing projects, Shea Stadium, and the National Tennis Center in Flushing Meadow.

At one point, the company was barred from doing business with the city for three years. Arc president Anthony Gurino failed to mention, when the company submitted its bid on the construction of a new city jail, that he and his brother Caesar were under indictment for helping Salvatore Ruggerio elude the law. This led to a hearing at which Anthony Gurino was asked what type of sales work Gotti did.

"What John does is point out locations," he said.

A month after John Gotti's release, Matthew Traynor made another cocaine trip to Florida for Peter Gotti. He was to meet a supplier in a Fort Lauderdale parking lot, but the police had been tipped off. The supplier got away, but Traynor was arrested. He was released in a few days and returned to New York empty-handed.

Traynor decided to go into banking. At gunpoint, on September 1, he withdrew $25,000 from a bank on Long Island. A few days later in the 101 Bar, Gene demanded a cut because he considered Traynor part of the crew, which was entitled to a tribute—"or you will be hurt or arrested."

Traynor handed over $10,000 and flew off to Las Vegas to spend $7,000 more.

A month later, Traynor was shot during another bank job and arrested. Recovering from his wounds, Traynor, an unmade man trying to help his case, decided to talk. The FBI opened a drug investigation on Peter, Gene, and John Gotti.

"Traynor advised that he is an 'errand boy' and 'courier' for John and Peter Gotti who operate in Queens County," an agent wrote. "Source advised John Gotti ... remains in the background insofar as the narcotics ... operation is concerned."

The FBI closed this investigation 18 months later when Traynor flunked a lie-detector test in connection with another story he had told about a fellow inmate's plot to murder a police officer. Traynor's wife had provided corroborating evidence of his trips to Florida, but his polygraph performance discredited him as a witness.

Sources BQ and Wahoo said John Gotti—leery of violating his parole—was careful not to discredit himself in the months following his release from Green Haven. Though he still lived an underworld life and made illegal money, he made no waves.

BQ said that Gotti and Willie Boy Johnson ran a gambling operation, which, along with loan-sharking, was providing Gotti with "a small but steady income." Wahoo said Gotti avoided riskier crimes like hijacking and fencing.

Gotti instructed his men "not to bring heat on the club," BQ added. He told them to stop loitering in front of the Bergin and to park their cars elsewhere.

In February 1978, Gotti's 81-year-old father-in-law died and his mother-in-law moved to Florida. In November, the mortgage on the Howard Beach house they had bought for him and Victoria was transferred to her, and she legally assumed the monthly payments. Angelo, who had gotten out of Lewisburg a second time, now lived in Howard Beach, too, in a home owned by his wife's parents. He, too, was supposedly working for Arc Plumbing and he was then the father of four children; the oldest was a boy named John. An occasional babysitter, who also had moved to Howard Beach, was John Joseph Gotti Sr., now retired.

In between these domestic matters, Carmine Fatico was finally sentenced to five years probation after several delays engineered by Roy Cohn, his lawyer.

After so much time away from the Bergin, it didn't matter that Fatico got probation instead of prison, which is what his brother Daniel would get a year later. Gotti had undisputed control, although now and then he would seek the old man's advice. They would meet secretly in a tailor shop near the Bergin.

About the same time the Faticos faded away, Source Wahoo's control agent, Martin J. Boland, was transferred to Tampa and replaced by James M. Abbott. Source Wahoo was wary, but agreed to continue informing "on the condition he never be compromised or told to testify." A memo explained: "He will not testify under any circumstances and would deny he ever cooperated in the event he was ever surfaced. Source is very sensitive as to his confidential relationship and was given assurances by agents Boland and Abbott."

In a final memo, which successfully requested that Wahoo be reimbursed for gambling losses at the Bergin, Agent Boland said: "Source has been very well accepted by individuals at the club."

Gotti continued to content himself with gambling and loan-sharking. "Until such time he is sure [that] the parole officers are not going to be bothering him, he will continue to earn money in this slower fashion," Agent Colgan noted after another BQ contact.

Source BQ, however, added an interesting footnote. He said drug-fugitive Salvatore Ruggiero, though he never risked being caught by coming to the Bergin, was in "occasional contact" with Gotti and with Angelo.

BQ would develop a different perspective than Wahoo on John Gotti and drugs. He would come to believe that Gotti was a major drug investor, whereas Wahoo, who was closer to him, would say he was not. BQ's suspicions first surfaced early in 1979, after Gotti told crew members not to deal drugs—an order that would be frequently and robustly violated. BQ told the FBI that the ban did "not mean that Gotti himself is not involved in a large-scale way ... investing money, in cocaine and other high-value drugs."

Most Crime Capital cops still regarded Neil Dellacroce as the Gambino boss and, in June 1978, the Manhattan D.A.'s detective squad opened an investigation of him. The investigation centered on his Ravenite Social Club, located on Mulberry Street in Little Italy—an island of narrow streets and tenements virtually surrounded by another ethnic neighborhood, Chinatown. Mulberry was Main

Street; a few blocks south of the club, tourists clogged cafés named after Amalfi Coast villages like Positano and Sorrento.

Dellacroce was no tourist. He was born and raised in Little Italy. Though he now had a home on Staten Island, he also maintained an apartment near the Ravenite; on 124 consecutive days of surveillance in 1979, the D.A.'s detective saw him at the club on all but 5 days.

The detectives had been rediscovering a familiar problem conducting surveillance in Little Italy. It was noted in an affidavit seeking approval to bug the Ravenite, inside and out:

"The denizens of that area are very alert to the presence of strangers and strange vehicles," Detective Joseph Borelli said. "The fact [that] even law-abiding inhabitants of that area will report the presence of strangers to the organized crime figures who frequent it is legend in the NYPD."

Detectives tried to eavesdrop while hiding in trunks of cars parked outside the club, but dropped the tactic after someone opened a fire hydrant and flooded the street. When they got permission to break into the club and install bugs, they met a large German shepherd named Duke.

On two occasions, Detective John Gurnee tried to neutralize Duke by feeding him meatballs spiked with tranquilizers. The first time, Duke still kept charging the door and Gurnee retreated. The next time, more powerful meatballs made Duke a puppy and Gurnee made it inside. Then a half-dozen men with baseball bats appeared outside the club and Gurnee fled through a rear exit—as several police cars filled the street.

One of the batsmen was Mickey Cirelli, the 76-year-old caretaker of the Ravenite who lived on an upper floor. A few days later, John Gotti, according to Detective Victor Ruggiero, was overheard telling Cirelli that the next time he discovered cops breaking in, he should shoot them and say they were burglars. Detectives saw Gotti at the Ravenite 35 times during the same 124-day period.

The detectives successfully planted bugs outside the Ravenite, hoping to overhear conversations on Mulberry Street, where it was obvious that club members and their visitors discussed business. The outdoor bugs, however, were soon discovered and destroyed.

The detectives next installed a parabolic microphone and video camera in an apartment overlooking the Ravenite, but not too long afterward Neil's son Buddy and another man placed a ladder against the building, climbed up, and confirmed their suspicions. Other men threatened to set the building afire.

Despite the obstacles, the district attorney's detectives did hear and see enough to warrant a grand jury investigation into loan-sharking and gambling. Neil, John, Angelo, and others were subpoenaed to testify, but the investigation went nowhere—not then, at least.

The recipients of subpoenas discussed among themselves who would plead the Fifth Amendment and refuse to testify, and who would answer questions and shadowbox with the grand jury. Dellacroce and Gotti sparred, and one day outside the grand jury room a police detective complimented Gotti on his elegant suit, now practically a trademark.

"I got it from a hijacked load," Gotti teased. "Solve that case."

Dellacroce had more than a Manhattan grand jury to worry about. In Florida, he had been indicted by a federal grand jury for ordering the murder of a loan shark. The contract allegedly was carried out by Anthony Plate, another loan shark accused—in the same case—of loan-sharking for Dellacroce in the Miami area. The indictment stated that Plate, on behalf of Dellacroce, had jumped onto the desk of a Florida auto dealer and spit in his face, which he threatened to "bite chunks" out of unless the businessman made good on a loan.

One day at the Bergin, Daniel Fatico, about to finally go to prison for three years for hijacking, gave this view of the Florida case to Willie Boy Johnson:

"If Neil would go to trial without this guy [Plate], he could beat the case, but he's going to sit next to him and the jury is going to find them both guilty."

In June or July 1979, a Bergin crony—who later became a government witness—was at the Ravenite with Neil, John, Angelo, Willie Boy, and Tony Roach. He said they had just returned from a trip, he didn't know where, but all were newly tanned. He said Angelo suggested that they should call Plate in for a strategy session on Neil's case and everyone laughed at the idea.

In August, the FBI reported that Anthony Plate had left the Tropicana Hotel in Miami Beach and disappeared. He was not seen again. The following spring, the government witness was at the Bergin when someone from the Ravenite called with a message.

"Neil got a hung jury. It's like a win."

During the summer Plate vanished, the Crime Capital underwent another fatal quake whose epicenter was the Ravenite Social Club.

Carmine Galante, the wild man of the Bonanno Family, was tamed by two shotgun blasts as he lunched on the patio of Joe and Mary's Italian-American Restaurant in Brooklyn. A Galante bodyguard also was killed, but the assassins botched the job and also shot two bystanders; one, the restaurant owner, was fatally wounded. His son, however, survived a bullet in the back as he dialed for help.

Galante had been out of prison for only a few months, but had unnerved the other Family leaders with his ambitious talk.

"With five heavies at the top, something like this was bound to happen," a detective said as Galante, a Medicaid card tucked into a trouser pocket, was carried out in a green bag.

Unfortunately for Dellacroce and his son Buddy, the cops watching the Ravenite had picked up fragments of conversation about an upcoming hit. The camera across the street had recorded four suspected plotters arriving at the club after the murders, which now became part of the Ravenite grand jury investigation.

Source BQ gave a report on the hit to Special Agent Patrick Colgan. The Bergin men knew in advance, but were not involved, and Gotti had left for Florida by car early the same day.

"Source stated John Gotti was driving and not flying because Gotti has a dreadful fear of flying," Colgan wrote. "Source also stated Gotti has a fear of boats, and once nearly killed an associate for going too fast."

After Gotti returned, and the grand jury stepped up its investigation, BQ said the Gotti brothers and Angelo discussed what to do if they came to suspect crew members who had "gone bad." They decided they would kill them, BQ said.

In time, six Gambinos, including Buddy Dellacroce, and two Galante capos were indicted for refusing to testify before a grand jury. Buddy would do a year in jail. Neil would battle the grand jury to a draw, but in 1985, in a federal conspiracy case, he was accused of ordering the hit to install Galante subordinates at the top of the Bonanno Family.

Intense press coverage made the public aware that the Gambino Family was the Crime Capital's most powerful mob. Neil Dellacroce was called its boss. The public still knew little about the real boss, Paul Constantino Castellano, and nothing about a new happily made man, John Gotti.

14

THE MAYOR OF 101ST AVENUE

*Q.: Do you know whether people who frequented the Bergin Hunt and
Fish Club had certain obligations to John Gotti?*

A.: Of course.

Q.: What were they?

A.: A hundred percent.

THE BERGIN HUNT AND FISH CLUB was now a part of
the Ozone Park fabric and John Gotti was the mayor of 101st
Avenue.

The Bergin men were good customers in the small cafés and
stores operating on slim margins. Around his neighbors, Gotti acted
like a gentleman; around him, they acted as though he were a successful salesman. He began saluting the community with Fourth of
July fireworks displays and barbecues; some residents began saluting
him by alerting the club when men resembling undercover detectives were around.

After falling and striking his head against a garbage truck, Peter
Gotti retired on a city disability pension and began managing the
Bergin for John. In time, brother Richard would manage a compan-
ion club across the street and around the corner, the Our Friends
Social Club, that John occasionally used for sitdowns. As was the
custom in the Family, the crew usually gathered once a week for

meetings. The Berginites met over dinner, which they cooked at the Bergin, usually on Wednesday nights.

Sally Crazy Polisi, out of Lewisburg prison on a psychiatric counseling scam, no longer came to the club because under his probation he wasn't supposed to consort with criminals. But the Bergin—the FBI had linked about 100 men to it—was not lacking in members or visitors with colorful nicknames.

There was Willie Boy and Tony Roach of course, but also: Frankie the Beard, Frankie the Caterer, Frankie Dep, Frankie the Hat, and Frankie Pickles; Mike the Milkman, Brooklyn Mike, Mickey Gal, and Mikey Boy; Tommie Tea Balls and Tommy Sneakers; Johnny Cabbage and Joe Pineapples; Little Pete, Skinny Dom, and Fat Andy; Joe the Cat and Buddy the Cat; Jimmy Irish, Joe Butch, and Tony Pep; Joey Piney, Joe Dogs, Donny Shacks, Eddie Dolls, Philly Broadway, Nicky Nose, Anthony Tits, and Jackie the Actor; Old Man Zoo, Redbird, Steve the Cleaner, and Captain Nemo.

Nicknames were a Family tradition with a sometimes useful purpose: If you don't use real names, cops and agents won't know who you're talking about, even if you're overheard on a tap or bug.

Gene Gotti was simply Genie; in addition to Johnny and Johnny Boy, John was Junior and *Cump*—a form of *gumbah*, which was a slang derivative of *compare*, which meant anything from good friend to adviser to godfather. Neil Dellacroce was the Tall Guy or the Pollack; he used "Timothy O'Neil" as an alias. At the Bergin, Castellano, who was Big Paul and Uncle Paul elsewhere, was known as the Pope, somewhat disrespectfully.

Into this ensemble early in 1979 came another man, James Cardinali, a handsome 30-year-old ex-heroin addict, armed robber, and future coked-out murderer. He had met Gotti at the Clinton Correctional Facility in upstate New York before both were transferred to different prisons, Cardinali to Attica, Gotti to Green Haven.

At Attica, Jamesy, as he was called, had met Angelo Ruggiero, doing his McBratney time. Angelo said he and Gotti were partners and invited Jamesy to drop by the Bergin when he got out.

Jamesy was going to Ozone Park anyway; his mother lived there and he had no other immediate prospects. He dropped by on his first day of freedom and stayed 18 months. In great detail, and more explosively than Polisi, Jamesy would testify about what he saw, heard, and did hanging out at the Bergin.

"Whaddaya gonna do, Jamesy?" Gotti asked at the outset.

Jamesy said another prison acquaintance had written him a letter of introduction to a local union.

"If you're going to be around me you can't work over there. I'll send you to another place."

Gotti instructed Willie Boy Johnson to deliver Cardinali to a trucking company in Maspeth, a firm once included in Carlo Gambino's no-hijacking-here edict.

"Johnny wants you to put this kid on the books," Willie Boy told a company executive.

Jamesy didn't quite get it. He actually went to work. During his first day on the loading dock, he beat up a fellow employee. He also saw time cards for Gotti and Willie Boy, though he never knew them to go to work there. After a few days, Willie Boy stopped by.

"What are you doing?"

"I'm working."

"Just punch the card and go. Don't worry about it."

Willie Boy left instructions for Jamesy's ghost employer: "If his parole officer comes around, just tell 'im he's out on a run."

Willie Boy also told Jamesy that Genie wanted to see him about beating up the co-worker.

"You can't raise your hands to nobody over there. You got to control yourself," Genie admonished.

Cardinali soon considered himself to be "with Johnny," which meant "You did anything he wanted." Johnny wanted Jamesy to hang around the club and be available for errands.

"Take a walk around the corner and pick up my salary from Arc [Plumbing]," Gotti would tell Jamesy.

In addition, Jamesy was also told to pick up a $22,000 check from Arc and go with Tony Roach to Staten Island to pick up another new Lincoln to replace Gotti's almost-new one.

"Neil picked it out for me," Gotti said.

Another time, Jamesy was in a nearby motel helping Angelo, Gene, and Willie Boy count $20,000 in small bills, when someone from the club called and told Jamesy to go fetch a new white shirt for Gotti, who had an important meeting.

Jamesy, who had some stature because he had done time, escaped some of the more tedious clubhouse chores. These fell to younger attendants, who picked up laundry or washed cars. At the club they answered the phones and dialed Gotti's personal calls, like secretaries whose boss had power and wanted people to understand it.

About the telephone Gotti told Jamesy, "Don't ever say anything you don't want played back to you someday."

Jamesy wanted to do more than run errands, but Gotti urged him to be patient.

"Everything is going to be all right," Gotti said. "Maybe I'll have you collect my small loans."

At the time, Source Wahoo said Gotti had $100,000 "on the street." Some was in the form of "knockdown loans," which Gotti explained to Jamesy required repayment in equal installments, with the interest—the "vig"—built in.

Gotti was particular about how money was delivered to him. Once a debtor dropped off an envelope with two names on it. One was Gotti's, the other an associate with whom the debtor had a separate relationship. The envelope was passed along to Gotti, in his car outside the club.

"If I ever see my name on another envelope, I am going to kill you," He shouted, tossing the envelope out the window as he sped away.

Jamesy was not patient, or candid. He had started using cocaine and was developing a monster habit that required more than the $100 or $200 a week Gotti paid him. Jamesy and his new friend, Neil's son Buddy, spent much more than that in a single night of snorting their way through discos in Manhattan and Queens.

As a heroin addict, Jamesy had beaten a priest during a robbery; on coke, he killed. In October 1979, he and another man shot two South American coke dealers and stole three kilos—six and a half pounds of disco nights.

Jamesy entered the coke trade even though Gotti had warned him about the consequences.

"If I ever catch anybody in my crew [selling drugs], I'll kill them. I'm not going to let no one embarrass me and I am going to make an example out of the first one I catch."

Gotti seemed confident that no one could deal drugs without his knowledge. Referring to another Bergin associate, Johnny told Jamesy: "He thinks I don't know he's [pushing drugs]; he is going to wind up dead."

At the time Gotti was warning Jamesy, Source BQ was telling the FBI he knew from "overheard conversations" that Gotti and Angelo were buying rolls of quarters and calling drug-fugitive Salvatore Ruggiero from pay phones. BQ also said Gotti was losing big at the track and on sports contests.

"Source states he does not know where Gotti obtains all his money in order to incur such losses and not be severely cramped in his lifestyle," Special Agent Patrick Colgan wrote.

Like Source Wahoo, Source BQ helped in many ways. Late in 1979, agents asked him to identify surveillance pictures taken outside the Bergin. BQ identified men previously unknown to the surveil-lants: William Battista, Peter Gotti, Willie Boy, and Tony Roach. As for Tony Roach, BQ said Gotti had decided not to propose him for formal Family membership.

BQ said Rampino had defaulted on certain "street deals" and was heavily in debt because his son was being treated for cancer. "Gotti, however, does trust Roach and will use him in any capacity," he added.

Though Gotti wasn't privy to all of Jamesy's sides, what he saw he apparently liked. In 1979, he invited him to his home on Christmas Eve, an honor accorded such men as Angelo, Willie Boy, Tony Roach, and John Carneglia. Jamesy was so touched he offered Gotti money from a non-cocaine robbery.

"Put that in your pocket," Gotti said. "All I want is your love and respect."

One day Jamesy felt that he was being tested by Gotti, who gave him what he said was $5,000 in small bills to exchange at the bank for larger denominations. The teller told Jamesy the wad totaled $5,500, which Jamesy later explained to Gotti, who shrugged and pocketed the money.

Jamesy was occasionally able to witness how Gotti handled himself in problem-solving situations: sitdowns. These ensued after men were "brought up on charges." In these tribunals, Gotti drove to the point in a bulldozer style laced with a smart dark humor that was uniquely his.

Jamesy accompanied Gotti to a Bronx sitdown. The charges involved a visit by members of another Family to the home of the wife of a mobster jailed on a drug charge.

"I wish it was me," Gotti told the Bronx men. "You would never be safe if you stopped and spoke to my wife while I was locked up."

"John, you are here defending a drug pusher."

"If every drug pusher in this room dropped dead, I would be the only one alive."

Typically, Gotti left a warning on the table: "You tell your skipper I said, 'You ever go to a guy's house while he is in jail, I'll kill you.'"

On another occasion, a problem arose when Michael Franzese—the son of a Colombo Family skipper—and another man sought to open a flea market near one run by a man who told them he was affiliated with Gotti.

"Fuck John Gotti," replied Franzese.

Franzese was a modern mobster. Cool, educated, almost a yuppie. He would graduate from promoting flea markets to producing movies—credits include such teenage gang movies as *Knights of the City* and *Savage Streets*—and to stealing millions in a sophisticated gas-tax ripoff that would later stir Gotti's interest. In hardball, however, he didn't play in the same league as Gotti.

"Watch this, I am goin' to take you to school," Gotti told Jamesy shortly before Franzese and his associate arrived at the Our Friends Social Club for a sitdown.

Gotti informed Franzese that flea-market rights in the area were taken and he must abandon any claim. "I don't care if you tell your father. I don't care who you go to. You can take it to Yankee Stadium, you can't win this."

As Franzese rose to leave, Gotti told him: "There is a guy running around the city saying 'Fuck John Gotti.' What do we do with a piece of shit like that? Should we beat him up? Kill him? He's a dog, right?"

"Yes, anybody who said that wouldn't be a friend, they would be a dog," Franzese replied.

Tails between their legs, Franzese and his associate left, two more recipients of Gotti's confident terrorism.

In Jamesy's version, Gotti never tired of displaying a bully swagger when he perceived a slight. Even Mike Coiro, the lawyer who had done such nice work for Gotti, was not exempt from a dressing-down.

Gotti arrived at the club one day ranting that Coiro had shown disrespect for him in a Queens restaurant. Coiro was dining with Jimmy Burke, then under scrutiny as the Svengali of the $6 million Lufthansa airline heist at JFK Airport, and failed to stop by Gotti's table and say hello. In Queens, at the time, Burke's reputation was as *bad* as Gotti's. He was aligned with the Luchese Family capo Paul Vario.

Gotti sent for Coiro, who was in too deep with the Bergin to overlook the invitation. As he had done before, Gotti urged Jamesy to pay attention.

"Watch what I am goin' to do," he said. "I might stuff him in the fireplace."

Coiro felt indigestion in the wake of Gotti's screams.

"I found you when you were a fifty dollar ambulance chaser. You are a piece of shit. You're supposed to run when you see me. You sit there with Jimmy Burke, don't get up to say hello to me. I'll kill you."

Coiro, a former cop for the city's Waterfront Commission, apologized. In time, Jimmy Burke was convicted for conspiring to fix Boston College basketball games and went to prison. None of the Lufthansa cash was ever found. Much is believed to have gone to the Luchese Family, some to the bosses of other Families. Many suspected hijackers and their accomplices or friends—13 in all—were found. Dead.

From prison, Burke began complaining about "unauthorized" murders of the suspected hijackers. His Luchese captain, Vario, told Gotti about Burke's complaints, according to Source BQ, who added: "John Gotti is the most powerful captain of any Family and does not want to hear any comments from Burke."

Gotti's court was not without irony. One day, two steaming-mad men arrived at the club threatening to kill a young man named Carmine Agnello, for a reason described only as "some beef."

Agnello was an industrious youth just starting out in the auto-salvage business. The young men who wanted to kill him brought the idea to John Carneglia, who they regarded as a mentor.

"Wait, you can't," Carneglia said. "Wait until Johnny gets here."

After Johnny got there and went across the street to Lolita's Café for breakfast, Carneglia sought him out. After a few minutes, Carneglia reemerged from Lolita's and told the angry pair, "Go ahead, do it, but don't kill him."

The next time Jamesy saw him, Carmine was as dented and scratched as the cars he salvaged. But alive.

A few years later, Carmine Agnello reentered John Gotti's life. He married Vicki, John's second daughter, a contestant in the Miss New York-USA beauty pageant. She was sponsored by Jamaica Auto Salvage, Carmine's company.

People didn't always come to Gotti to resolve disputes. Some merely sought advice, or ambience.

Such was the case with the actor Jon Voight, who had just won an Academy Award for *Coming Home*. Voight had grown up in nearby Yonkers and was then interested in a film about the life of Joe Sullivan, a hit man with Bergin connections.

Sullivan was the son of a cop and the only man ever to escape from Attica prison. He invited Voight and a producer to Ozone Park to visit with Gotti and as word of a movie star's presence spread, people got excited. Angelo Ruggiero's daughter called the club to ask if she could drop by.

Actors practice their profession when they seek out the real-life equivalents of characters they may portray. James Caan, "Santino" in *The Godfather*, befriended Colombo Family men while researching his role as the hot-tempered oldest son of "Don Corleone."

John, Gene, Willie Boy, and Jamesy were in the club when Voight and the others came calling. Eventually they retired to the Our Friends.

"We drank all fucking night," Jamesy later recalled in a phone call from prison. "Voight could drink. I think he started with Scotch, then he went with Remy Martins."

Jon Voight said he may have met John Gotti, but he has no recollection of it. He said Joe Sullivan introduced him to many people, "but I was only interested in Joe Sullivan." He said if he had known

Sullivan was associating with people involved in crime, he would have advised him not to.

Voight's foray into Queens would eventually be reviewed by FBI agents who questioned him as part of an investigation into whether Sullivan's lawyer, former Attorney General Ramsey Clark, had harbored a fugitive. No charges were ever filed.

John Gotti was at ease with Voight. He was a celebrity, too; he had cash, a big car, great clothes, many retainers, and a style that caused heads to swivel when he strode into a room. His fame was earned in another world, an underworld, but it was his world, and it was real.

———————

In some families, when a star eclipses another, trouble lies just over the horizon.

It was true of John and Gene Gotti; Gene had followed John into the Fatico-Dellacroce orbit and proven himself capable in crime. He was similar in many ways; he could be funny, menacing, and forceful, more than his brothers Peter and Richard, but not as much as John. He was both dependent and independent. With a childhood friend, Joey Scopo, a member of the Colombo Family, he had established a separate loan-sharking business, but its base was the Bergin.

Gene resided in the large shadow cast by John. He was the man left in charge; he was Genie. The blood bond was strong, but under pressure it was a spring wound too tight.

"I ain't nothin' over here," Gene once complained to Angelo. "I'm just a fucking workhorse."

On another boozy night at the Bergin, a dispute between Jamesy and another man over what to play on the jukebox led to an insult, which led to a fight outside. Everyone spilled out onto the sidewalk and tried to break it up. Jamesy described what took place next.

"Genie was like defending me. And Johnny wasn't actually defending anybody. [He was] trying to be a mediator. Genie was drunk. They had words. Johnny knocked Genie out."

Jamesy said he pulled John away from Gene. "I was holding Johnny. I tried to hold him in a headlock. He said, 'Get your hands off of me and that's an order.' I let go."

Jamesy felt responsible for the fisticuffs between John and Gene and apologized.

"It ain't you," Gotti said. "This has been coming a long time, me and my brother."

Later, after everyone had sobered up, John regretted the incident and rebuked Jamesy for starting it. "You can't raise your hands to anybody we hang out with."

"John, there are some things I can't overlook."

"I don't care how serious it is. You are going to get your hands chopped off."

The club had many such rules. Gene explained one to a fortunate soul one day. He and other crew members were at a wake when a clubhouse attendant called the funeral home to report that a school bus from a company headquartered on 101st Avenue had been stolen. Jamesy had been told by Angelo that he, John, and Neil were secret partners in the firm, which transported handicapped students under a city contract.

Peter Gotti, along with Jamesy and two other men, left the wake and returned to the club. The clubhouse attendant told them that whoever took the bus had loaded it with adding machines and typewriters and departed the premises by crashing through a gate. The men, figuring that it would be hard to hide a school bus, decided to look around the neighborhood.

The bus was quickly located lurching along on Rockaway Boulevard; the driver was having trouble operating the stick shift. As soon as the driver veered down a side street, the car full of Bergin men swerved in front and cut him off. Jamesy dragged the driver out and threw him in the car. Peter got in the bus. Both vehicles then returned to the club.

Gene called from the funeral home and Jamesy reported the news. "I got the bus and the guy."

"Hold him. I'll be right there."

The quivering thief was taken to a back room to await his fate. He was approaching meltdown when Gene burst in. But Gene was surprisingly mellow. Perhaps it was the effect of the wake.

"I don't mind [that] you are a thief. I am a thief. I don't mind you stealing, but you can't rob from us. Now go."

John Gotti was always explaining the rules to Jamesy. About guns, Gotti said "It's nice to have them close by, but don't carry them." Except for the few hidden at the Bergin, the crew stashed most of its guns in members' homes.

A don't-hang-out-with-kidnappers rule was adopted after Gotti learned that Jamesy had socialized at a disco with three men Gotti believed were kidnappers.

"I already killed a kidnapper," Gotti said, "and I don't want you around them."

Johnny told Jamesy that the only reason he pleaded guilty in the McBratney case was that Angelo was not going to get a plea offer unless he accepted the same deal. Angelo, who was identified by two witnesses, told Jamesy that he and his *gumbah* should have gone into Snoope's Bar with bags over their faces.

Jamesy saw Paul Castellano once. He remembered Gotti had said this about the Pope: "Paul's the boss, but we're with Neil. Paul has nothing to do with us."

The encounter took place at a Manhattan restaurant when Jamesy spotted Castellano dining with Neil Dellacroce and a few other Family men. Jamesy had been pulling a few robberies lately. Neil waved him over.

"How are you doing?" Neil asked.

"All right."

"What are you doing?"

"Robbing."

At that, Castellano looked up. "Good boy," he said.

Jamesy was never admitted to the Bergin's inner circle. He did learn, however, that once you belonged to the circle, you belonged to Gotti.

Jamesy was present when a crew member asked Gotti about the possibility of a "release" so that he might associate with another crew.

Gotti flashed a disbelieving smile and joked that Jamesy was the chairman of his "release department," which was never open. Gotti then faced the crew member; his smile had left as fast as it came.

"You don't get released from my crew. You have lived with John Gotti and you will die with John Gotti."

15

BOY ON A MINIBIKE

HOWARD BEACH WAS A safe place to raise children. It had none of the problems—poverty, drugs, crime, poor schools— that lay to waste so many other New York City children.

The Gotti home near the corner of Eighty-fifth Street and 160th Avenue was on a quiet block, as close to the Atlantic Ocean as the man of the house had been years before as a twelve-year-old boy in Brooklyn. His solidly middle-class neighbors lived in well-kept homes along wide, tree-lined streets patrolled by a civic association to which Victoria Gotti contributed money.

The Gotti family included five children now, two girls and three boys. The girls and one boy had entered their teenage years. The middle son, twelve-year-old Frank, was about to. He was a promising student who enjoyed sports. He and a son of Crazy Sally Polisi were on a junior-football team called the Redskins.

On March 18, 1980, Frank borrowed a friend's motorized minibike and went for a spin. He explored a trail next to the Belt Parkway, an expressway on the northern border of Howard Beach that isolated it between Ozone Park and the ocean. Near where Eighty-seventh Street dead-ended at a fence along the parkway, Frank turned south toward 157th Avenue; he was about six blocks from home.

It was late in the day. John Favara, the driver of a car westbound on 157th Avenue, was confronted by a low white sun. Favara, age 51, a service manager for a furniture manufacturer, lived with his wife and two adopted children on Eighty-sixth Street, directly behind the Gotti family on Eighty-fifth Street. His son Scott was good friends with the oldest Gotti son, John.

Favara was coming home from work. On 157th Avenue, near Eighty-seventh, a house was under renovation. A dumpster had been placed in the street to collect the debris. It was on Favara's right. Favara did not notice the boy on the minibike dash into the street from the other side of the dumpster, and his car stuck and killed Frank Gotti.

The sudden horror and violence of the boy's death left a gaping hole in the Gotti family heart. They fell into a deep, black depression, which no doubt was similar to the one that would soon visit the Favara household.

The grief felt by Victoria, whose life was mainly her children, was especially acute and tinged by a bitter rage for the presumed recklessness of Favara. For a long time, she dressed only in black. In her living room, a photograph of Frank was draped in black and hung over a setting of candles and flowers. A Queens detective who saw it called it a shrine.

In a few months, when Frank would have turned 13, Victoria, in what became an annual rite, placed two in memoriams in the *New York Daily News*. The first was from Frank's sisters and brothers:

Frankie Boy. Happy Birthday in Heaven, we miss you so.

Love, Angel, Vicki, Johnny Boy and Peter Boy.

The second came from his parents:

Frankie Boy. We love you always & long to be with you.

Love & Kisses, Mom & Dad.

Hundreds of people came to the wake to say good-bye to Frank Gotti. John Favara did not because he was advised by a priest and friends that his presence might be upsetting. Frankie Boy was buried in St. John's Cemetery in Central Queens.

FBI agents, who had begun shadowing Gotti—whose parole had not expired—and the Bergin crew a few months before, did not surveil the wake or the funeral. Out of respect.

"Losing a son is the worst thing that can happen to a man," said one agent, who recalled that a fellow agent in Queens had lost a son three years earlier. "Gotti probably doesn't believe it, but out of respect we didn't [conduct surveillance]. I don't think anyone did."

The NYPD traffic investigators ruled the tragedy an accident, but not everyone saw it the same way.

Two days after the boy's death, an unidentified woman called the 106th Precinct and said: "The driver of the car that killed Frank Gotti will be eliminated."

Favara found a death threat in his mailbox the same day, but he wasn't alarmed. "That kind of stuff only happens in movies," he told a detective who came to warn him about the call.

The day after the warning, an unidentified woman called the Favara home and made another threat. Two weeks later, Favara's car was stolen; it was found in another two weeks a mile away in Howard Beach.

Favara still wasn't concerned. But then a funeral card and a photograph of Frank Gotti were placed in his mailbox and the word "murderer" was spray-painted on his car.

John Favara was what he seemed, a mild-mannered family man, but he was friendly with Anthony Zappi, a Gambino soldier. Anthony's father, Ettore, had been one of Carlo Gambino's top capos. Anthony Zappi was treasurer of a Teamsters union local that had a contract with Castro Convertible Corporation, Favara's employer on Long Island. He and Favara grew up in Brooklyn together; though he went one way and Favara another, he was godfather to Favara's son Scott.

Favara adored his son, who had slept overnight in the Gotti house. He had transferred from the sales department of Castro Convertible so he could be with him on Saturdays.

"His sun rose and set on his son," Sgt. Gary Schriffen, a Nassau County homicide investigator, would say later.

Favara asked Zappi what he should do. He told his old connected friend that the threats had to be the pranks of children; he didn't believe adults would regard Frank Gotti's death as anything but an accident. Zappi told Favara to move away and get rid of the death car, a vehicle that enraged Victoria Gotti every time she saw it pull up to the house behind hers.

On May 28, Victoria attacked Favara with a baseball bat. He went to a hospital for treatment, but did not press charges against her. He and his wife Janet then put their house up for sale.

On July 25, John and Victoria went to Florida. Willie Boy Johnson told Source BQ that Gotti would be gone a week.

"My wife is still mourning my son and I took her down there to get her mind off things," Gotti later said. "She's still on medication."

On July 28, John Favara left the Castro Convertible plant at the end of his shift and walked toward his car, which was parked near the adjacent Capitol Diner. He had his eye on a new home in Nassau County and a buyer for his Howard Beach home had come forward. The deal's closing details would be taken care of in two days.

As he came near his car, Favara was surprised by a heavyset man who clubbed him with a large piece of wood. The assailant then lifted Favara by the belt of the trousers and threw him into a blue van. A watchman at the Castro plant and several people in the diner saw the abduction. The diner's owner, Leon Papon, came out of the back door and demanded to know what was going on.

"Our friend is sick," the heavyset man replied. "We are taking him home."

Another man got out of the van and into a green car that followed the van away from the diner. Both vehicles disappeared down the nearby Jericho Turnpike. Later, a third man drove Favara's station wagon away.

Neither John Favara nor his car were ever seen again.

The next day, Janet Favara reported that her husband was missing. Detectives from 106th Precinct, joined by Nassau County detectives, interviewed the witnesses and scoured the scene for clues. The witnesses identified Favara as the man who had been shoved into the van; a .22-caliber slug and bullet hole were found in a nearby house, at an angle suggesting gunplay during the abduction. Some detectives believe Favara may have started carrying a gun and gotten off a shot before he was overpowered.

A day later, three burly men visited the diner, sat at the counter and stared at the owner for 15 minutes. Leon Papon stopped talking to cops, sold the diner, and moved away.

John and Victoria Gotti returned from Florida on August 4. The FBI told Source BQ about the Favara incident the same day, and asked him to find out what he could.

On August 5, BQ reported back. This memo was placed in his file:

"Word at the [Bergin] is that the individual responsible for [Frank Gotti's death] was killed recently at Gotti's direction and Gotti wanted a solid alibi of not even being in New York at the time this killing took place ... Gotti did not initially want revenge ... but learned from witnesses [that] the man was speeding and had jumped a stop sign before striking the boy."

No one ever told the police that John Favara was speeding or ran a stop sign. "He just didn't see the kid, he just rolled over him, it was that simple," Sgt. Schriffen said. What the Bergin men may have been told is another story.

The memo also said: "Gotti's wife has been completely distraught since the death of her son and Gotti had promised her revenge ..." A subsequent BQ memo added that Favara's body would never be found.

Queens and Nassau county detectives—including Sgt. Schriffen—went to the Gotti home a few days later and were invited in by Victoria, dressed in black. She was asked if she knew what had happened to her backyard neighbor.

"I don't know what happened to him. I am not sorry if something did. He never sent me a [condolence] card. He never apologized. He never even got his car fixed."

Her husband wasn't home. Sgt. Schriffen asked where he was and what he did for a living.

"I don't know where he is. I don't know what he does. I am an old-fashioned woman. All I know is, he provides."

At the Bergin, Gene Gotti told the cops his brother was at his dentist's office. He said he would call them at the 106th Precinct when John returned.

Two hours later, Gene called. "My brother will meet with you now," he said.

Gotti was dressed in black that day, too. He apologized for having no coffee. He joked that everyone should watch what they said because the Bergin was bugged. He said he had lately been laid off from his job at Arc Plumbing.

"He was very self-assured," Schriffen remembered.

When the discussion turned to Favara, Gotti sounded very much like his wife.

"I don't know what happened. I am not sorry if something did happen. He killed my kid."

———————————————

As time wore on, Janet Favara knew her husband wasn't coming home. But she worried about the safety of her children.

The detectives tried to give her some peace of mind. They appealed unofficially to Anthony Zappi. Was there some way they might get a tip about where Favara's body was, so his family could arrange a proper funeral?

"What happened was Family business," Zappi said. "It's over. There will be no more trouble."

Detectives believe Favara and his car were compacted into a small block of bones and steel, but no evidence was ever found. In 1986, a court declared him dead.

At one point, the detectives got a tip that a notorious gang of killers and car thieves known as the "DeMeo crew" was responsible for Favara's death. The crew was led by Roy DeMeo, who reported to Anthony Gaggi, who was one of Paul Castellano's top captains.

The DeMeo crew would be accused of 22 murders, many in connection with a stolen-car racket, for which Castellano was on trial when he was murdered. One victim of the DeMeo crew was hacked to death, after which the killers went out for pizza, one later testified. Another victim was Castellano's former son-in-law, Frank Amato, who had strayed from Constance Castellano during their marriage and was held responsible for her miscarriage. Amato disappeared a few months after Favara.

Two years after Favara vanished, a newspaper updated the story and quoted Sgt. Schriffen, who then got a call from an agitated Victoria Gotti, who asked him to stop talking to the press.

"If my husband knew I was calling you, he'd kill me," she added. "Let my son die in peace."

16

FORGET ABOUT THIS PHONE

IN THE FALL OF 1980, the father of the boy on the minibike was gambling heavily and losing big—about $30,000 a weekend, according to Source BQ.

Gotti beat bookmakers out of many of his losses, but BQ said, "He does not have the money he used to." Meanwhile, crew members were beginning to grumble about their own financial woes, BQ added.

Crew associates Tony Roach Rampino, Michael Roccoforte, and the man told by Gotti to set up his son-in-law Tommy DiSimone for murder, Sal DeVita, were identified as "just a few" who were "considering taking action" on their own if Gotti didn't start arranging scores for them.

"Source states there is a lot of hard feeling and animosity among members of the club toward Gotti," Special Agent Colgan wrote.

Source BQ flatly predicted Gotti and the men closest to him would start dealing drugs in a big way—at the risk of getting killed by Paul Castellano if they got caught by the authorities.

Gotti would attempt to insulate himself by only putting up investment money, BQ said; Angelo, Gene, and Willie Boy would be more actively involved. BQ cited two bits of circumstantial evidence: Salvatore Ruggiero, with whom Gotti was once arrested in a stolen car, was recently in town and seen by Gotti and Angelo; in addition, a young dealer named Mark Reiter had begun hanging around the Bergin.

"The informant knows Reiter is heavily involved in the sale and distribution of cocaine," Agent Colgan wrote. In fact, Reiter would soon be indicted in Manhattan for selling heroin.

Though Gotti himself would be seduced by the easy money in drugs, he had recently condemned drug dealing, BQ said.

"Source states Gotti himself has laid the law down to his crew that he will not back them if they are in any way involved [in drug deals], but apparently Gotti was just following orders given him and is not abiding by these same rules."

At the time BQ was making his predictions, the Queens District Attorney's office detective squad was just beginning to investigate John and Angelo. They got underway after learning from Manhattan detectives that the pair hung out on Mulberry Street with Neil Dellacroce.

Detectives noticed that the men who hung out on 101st Avenue kept walking back and forth between the Bergin and a seemingly empty storefront only 10 feet away. The detectives then noticed that there were two pay telephone booths inside the store.

A check with the telephone company disclosed that the Bergin itself did not have a phone. New York Telephone records indicated that the name of the subscriber to the storefront phones was Vito Maccia's Candy Store; but neither Vito nor candy was inside, just a few chairs and the pay telephones along one wall.

The detectives installed court-approved pen registers, devices that track dialed numbers and count incoming calls. They gave a new name to the phantom candy store: "The telephone room."

The registers produced frequently called numbers. One was traced to an apartment in Ridgewood, Queens. Detective Jack Holder, a veteran of many gambling investigations, hid in the hallway outside the apartment. He kept hearing "Hello" without hearing a phone ring. Many bookmakers use phones that announce calls with a light instead of a ring so as not to annoy neighbors.

"Hello, yeah, who's this?" Holder heard the voice say. "Okay, go ahead ... one hundred twenty-eight for ten. Two hundred fourteen fox six ..." Holder now knew: The apartment was a "wire room."

Further surveillance showed the apartment was occupied from noon to 2 P.M. and from 6 to 8 P.M., the standard times bettors get down with bookies for the afternoon and evening action at tracks and stadiums.

Holder obtained a search warrant and found evidence of $5,000 in daily receipts. Tacked to a wall, he found a list of telephone numbers. Two belonged to the candy-store phones. One rang at Our Friends Social Club and another at Lolita's across from the Bergin. The other numbers were for phones in other social clubs or businesses in Queens and Brooklyn.

The occupant of the apartment, Peter Schiavone, was arrested on misdemeanor charges, pleaded guilty, and was fined $250. The detectives were certain that Schiavone was only a clerk, not the boss of the operation. However, they continued to watch.

Within weeks, Schiavone was spotted going in and out of a new apartment. The candy-store pen registers now showed calls to that address. Outside the Bergin, Detective Michael Falciano overheard Billy Battista and a man they knew as Frank Guidici talking about a bet that had been recorded inaccurately.

"That fucking ticket was for a thousand dollars. What does he mean, he put it in for five hundred?" Guidici said angrily. "As far as I am concerned, he owes five hundred yet."

"What the fuck you getting excited about? Call him on the fucking phone," Battista said.

Guidici entered the Bergin telephone room and called the new wire room occupied by Schiavone. The call and Guidici's words led detectives to believe that Guidici was Schiavone's boss. His actions were not those of a mere bettor. If the $500 "ticket" had been his bet, he hardly would have complained if he had lost; if he had won, he would be owed more than $500.

Back in September, Guidici had been listed along with Gotti and Angelo as targets of the Queens investigation. Here was evidence that Guidici was running a gambling operation with ties to the Bergin, which was the field headquarters of Gotti and Angelo—two disciples of the man thought to be the king of the Gambino Family, Neil Dellacroce.

The detectives intensified their investigation, taking time off only for Christmas.

On Eighty-fifth Street in Howard Beach, the Gotti home was dark; it was the first time it was unlit for Christmas holidays since the family moved there in 1973.

The still-acting boss of the Bergin, who usually went to the Yonkers or Roosevelt Raceway on Friday nights, continued to gamble and lose heavily in 1981.

The second weekend in January was a big football weekend. Gotti lost $21,000. The next weekend, he lost $16,000. Meanwhile, Source BQ said, crew members like Tony Roach, Sal DeVita, and Billy Battista could hardly afford to play the daily number.

When it came to gambling, there was more to Gotti than horses and games. On February 4, BQ told the FBI two days later, Gotti brought Atlantic City to Queens when he opened a gambling hall for Family men on the second floor of the Bergin. The main event was dice and the minimum bet was $500. It would be open six nights a week until 4 A.M.

On the first night, men from other Gambino crews and other Families dropped by. Frank DeCicco came and went away without $15,000. The hosts lost, too. Willie Boy dropped $13,000, Angelo $8,000, and Gotti $3,000. Later in the week, Mark Reiter, the future heroin defendant, won $20,000.

A month later, BQ said the game was going so well that Gotti would move it to Manhattan, to make it more accessible and to attract bigger gamblers, including "legitimate people" with Family connections. He might even admit women gamblers—an absolute taboo at the Bergin.

Early in March 1981, the game did move to Manhattan, to a building on Mott Street in Little Italy, around the corner from the Ravenite Social Club. The game, as it had in Ozone Park, rested on Saturday, but remained a boys-only event. "Street talk indicates at this time that this particular dice game of Gotti's is the best in the New York area," a FBI memo noted.

Because the dice men were up late, they slept late, and Gotti razzed those who didn't seem to show the energy he did. A call—secretly taped—that he placed one day about 6 P.M. to a groggy Willie Boy illustrated this. Gotti wondered why Willie Boy hadn't shown up at the Bergin yet.

"It's a new game now? Whoever goes to the fucking crap game can sleep all fucking day?"

"I'm there every night, John."

"And where the fuck do you think I am? ... There's things to be done here. I can't do them all by myself."

Source BQ said the house of dice began each night with a bank of about $40,000 put up by twelve partners, including DeCicco and the old JFK hijack squad, John, Gene, and Angelo. "According to the informant, the house has never lost," Special Agent Colgan wrote.

Gotti, however, continued to lose. Being an owner of the game, he could borrow against the house money. At one point, he became concerned about how much others had borrowed and ordered an accounting, which showed he was the largest debtor, for $55,000.

Gotti's losses endangered the game's profits. On May 13, he lost $30,000, causing Angelo to wonder whether the only way to detoxify his *gumbah* was to close the game. The next day, he called Gene Gotti to complain. They used "dollar" and "balloon" as synonyms for $1,000; they also used unflattering terms to describe a man they loved, most of the time.

"You gotta do yourself a favor and everybody else a favor, too," Angelo began. "We gotta see how we gonna close this fucking joint in New York."

"Yeah, what happened now?"

"That fucking hard-on, you know that hard-on, the guy that your mother shit out."

"Go ahead."

"He lost thirty dollars last night."

"We were on top sixty balloons! I left there one-thirty, we were on top sixty balloons! We didn't need him in the fucking game!"

"I'm by the club now."

"We were on top sixty balloons—what, is he kidding somebody or what, this guy? Who the fuck needed him there? So what is he looking to do now? Just take advantage of people or what?"

"Let's see how we got to do it, Genie."

"Oh fuck him, I don't give a fuck. What is he looking to do this, this guy? Is he abusing his position, or what?"

Angelo responded with a comment that indicated the night hadn't been a total loss.

"I won ninety dollars."

In June, Willie Boy Johnson was rewarded for lost sleep and won big, too. BQ said Willie Boy was not a good gambler, "but one of the luckiest individuals I've ever known."

Source Wahoo ran into bad luck on January 27. He left the Our Friends Social Club and was followed to his home in Brooklyn by the detectives working on the Bergin gambling case.

After Wahoo parked his car and opened the trunk, the detectives walked toward him. He saw them and began throwing money from his pockets into the trunk. The detectives then announced who they were.

"Oh good. I am glad it's you guys," Wahoo said. "I thought it was someone else. Go ahead. Take it. I don't see anything."

"What are you talking about?" replied Detective Holder, who looked in the trunk and saw bundles of cash.

"Take what is yours."

"What do you want me to take that for?"

"If my parole officer saw this, I would be in a lot of trouble."

Holder said he would take the bribe, but would have to clear it with his boss. Wahoo nodded and Holder arrested him on the spot for attempting to bribe him with the $50,000 in the trunk.

Wahoo was indicted by a state grand jury in Queens. The indictment was kept secret because he had decided to begin a second dangerous relationship. He did not inform the Queens district attorney that he was a Top Echelon informer for the FBI and he did not tell the FBI that he was now a confidential informant for the NYPD—a violation of the agreement he had made the previous March with his new control agent, James Abbott.

The D.A.'s detective commander, Lt. Remo Franceschini, tried to talk Wahoo into becoming more than an informant. He told Wahoo that he had a close working relationship with the FBI and the special federal Organized Crime Strike Force in Brooklyn and Wahoo would probably qualify for the federal witness-protection program; he would be able to get a new identity and be relocated in another state if he would actually testify at trials.

"I will never testify. I would rather go to jail," Wahoo said.

Over the next few months, for the Queens detective squad, Source Wahoo was a kind of talk-show expert, a studio commentator, on happenings in all the Families. He paid them well for his guest shots—his $50,000 was deposited in the police pension fund.

On a few occasions, Wahoo got specific. On May 18, 1981, he told Queens cops where to find the body of Alphonse "Sonny Red" Indelicato, a Bonanno capo who was caught on the losing side of yet another internal power dispute in that Family.

Go look in "The Hole," Wahoo said.

"The Hole" was a vacant lot near an auto-salvage yard on the Brooklyn-Queens border, near the Lindenwood Diner, where John Carneglia, who owned the Fountain Auto Shop, hung out with other Family soldiers and friends. Six days later, Sonny Red's body was found.

Indelicato was one of the plotters who had waited at the Ravenite Social Club with Neil Dellacroce two years earlier for the killers of Bonanno boss Carmine Galante to return from their assignment. Now Indelicato and two other capos who had plotted against Galante's successor had gone the way of Galante, which is how it goes in the Crime Capital.

The triple hit caused a few tense moments for the Gambino Family in the summer of 1981. Indelicato's son, Anthony, swore to take revenge and felt that his father's murder resulted from Dellacroce's mediating again in Bonanno Family problems. It was a logical suspicion; Anthony had helped murder Galante at the behest of Dellacroce.

Anthony, or "Bruno" as he was known, was considered violent even by Family standards. He was a big cocaine user, always armed, and he dipped his bullets in cyanide.

Vincent Gotti, the youngest Gotti brother, was another big coke user, according to Wahoo. Early in June, Wahoo told detectives that Vincent had gone into hiding after he was indicted in a cocaine-selling case.

Vincent, age 28, had begun a rap sheet in 1969 when he was arrested for rape. The charge was dismissed, but in succeeding years he pleaded guilty to misdemeanor theft and felony theft; in the latter case, while employed as a construction laborer, Vincent employed a fake gun to rob a gas station of $84. Agents say his degenerate gambler brother had banished him from the Bergin because of his degenerate cocaine use.

Dominick Polifrone, an undercover agent for the Alcohol, Tobacco and Firearms division of the Treasury Department, met Vincent in a Brooklyn bar. Polifrone had been asked to adopt an underworld guise by the NYPD, which was investigating illegal arms dealing.

Vincent told Polifrone he had "connections" to both guns and drugs. "He reminded me of John," Polifrone later recalled. "He was a typical wiseguy. He mentioned that his brother was an important wiseguy, but he was earning on the side. He didn't want his brother to know anything."

When the gun-running investigation stalled, a Manhattan grand jury led by a special narcotics prosecutor indicted Vincent for selling 2.5 ounces of cocaine to Polifrone for $5,400; but when the cops later went to arrest him he could not be found.

Vincent turned up in 1986, just as his brother was taking over the Gambino Family. After a routine traffic stop, upstate cops had discovered that his driver's license was phony; a computer search turned up the outstanding drug warrant from Manhattan. Vincent pleaded guilty in an empty courtroom and was sent away on a six-year-to-life prison term.

While on the lam, one alias he used was Frank Gotti. Source Wahoo also told the Queens detective squad about John Gotti's dice game in Little Italy.

Members of the squad, armed with 40 pairs of handcuffs and three paddy wagons, rode into Manhattan on June 24 and busted the game. Even at 1:30 A.M., the sight of 30 neighborhood celebrities being detained and questioned drew a large and mostly sympathetic crowd that razzed the raiders.

The Bergin was informed almost immediately.

"They just pinched the game," a caller told Peter Gotti at 1:50 A.M.

The cops confiscated $100,000, two loaded revolvers, a professional dice table, nine pairs of dice, and 775 poker chips. "This was not your average after-hours joint," one detective told reporters. "This was strictly for card-carrying gangsters who are high rollers."

Seven men were arrested, including Frank DeCicco, Tony Rampino, and Billy Battista, on charges of promoting gambling. Tony and Billy also were charged with being "dressed up," or possessing weapons. A 61-year-old Gambino man, Peter Tambone, also was arrested on the gambling charge, but he would face far more serious problems involving drugs in just a few months, and would feign craziness to save himself.

The arrestees were taken to nearby Manhattan Criminal Court for arraignment. The court, which operates around the clock, is so busy the ordeal of booking, fingerprinting, and checking suspects' records for outstanding warrants can take more than 36 hours, if all goes well. An arrestee can't be released until he is formally charged, admitted to bail, or pleads guilty. The dice men would sleep a night in the slammer.

Eighteen hours after the arrests, Tony Roach called the Bergin from jail to find out if Bergin lawyer Michael Coiro and his partner were on the case and if bail plans were being made. He spoke to Gene Gotti.

"They're there, they're on it, the bondsmen, they're on it," Gene said. "[The police] are fucking you around with your prints."

Tony Roach complained he was hungry and Gene teased him by saying, "We're eating now, mother fuck."

The next morning, with Michael Coiro by their side, all the men pleaded guilty to the misdemeanor gambling charge and were fined $500 each. The gun charges were put over for grand jury action because they were felonies. All were released.

Detective Victor Ruggiero, a veteran of the Ravenite Social Club investigation now assigned to Queens, conducted surveillance at the court. He saw Coiro with two men he did not know; Coiro gave one of them a copy of the arraignment papers, which indicated that the cops were tipped off by an unnamed informant. The man went to a pay phone in the lobby and Ruggiero slipped in beside him.

"Hello? Johnny Boy?" Ruggiero heard the man say. "You got a rat, a fuckin' rat … I'll personally take care of it … I'll kill the motherfucker."

Learning about an informant in the crew's midst was an important piece of information, but nothing over which to stop gambling. On the very next day, the game moved across Mott Street to a larger room, where the gaming tables were replaced, and the dice rolled again that night.

According to Source BQ, however, the game never really recaptured its former popularity. He said the tension caused by the Bonanno Family murders put a damper on attendance. Indeed, Indelicato's vengeful son waved a weapon at Angelo and Gene as they were driving on an expressway one day, but they were able to veer away before meeting up with any cyanide bullets.

Few people have the nerve or acting ability to play the games Sources BQ and Wahoo were playing, especially Wahoo, who was committing crimes while revealing only selected others to agencies unaware of his double-agency. He was dancing on a high wire without a net and, so far, getting away with it.

The day before the Mott Street raid, Wahoo checked in with the FBI. He said Willie Boy Johnson had become partners with Gotti in an auto-body repair shop. He said, however, that Angelo remained Gotti's "main man, emissary, and trusted messenger."

Wahoo also provided extensive details about the interior of the Our Friends Social Club—which was managed by Richard Gotti—across the street and around the corner from the Bergin. Such details would be useful if the FBI sought to install a bug or telephone taps. Wahoo had already supplied the layout of the Bergin itself, and now he told Agent Abbott about the telephone room adjacent to the Bergin. The sugarless-candy store was more than a telephone room. It was a fireworks depository; in a rear room, $20,000 worth of holiday explosives were stored.

On June 30, 1981, Manhattan cops, along with the FBI, rode into Queens and raided the telephone room. The cops, members of the Manhattan South vice squad, wanted the fireworks; the FBI wanted to scout the room to size up its bug potential. The FBI, by this time, had heard enough about the Bergin Hunt and Fish Club to open a formal investigation.

Special Agent Donald W. McCormick had been working the case since March. Inside the room, as the fireworks were being carted off, he went to one of the two pay phones to tell his boss the raid went well.

"Be careful what you say on the phone," Bergin associate Jackie Cavallo smiled. "Santucci's got a tap on it."

Santucci was John Santucci, the elected district attorney of Queens. McCormack smiled back and dialed Bruce Mouw, his FBI supervisor, and also called a sergeant on the vice squad in Manhattan.

Moments after Mouw was called, his boss, Ed Sharp, the special agent in charge of the FBI's New York office, got a call from someone in the Queens District Attorney's office congratulating the FBI on the fireworks raid. The NYPD vice sergeant also received a similar call. Cavallo wasn't kidding; the pay phone *was* tapped.

Later, Special Agent Mouw met with District Attorney Santucci and others to "discuss the conflict of interest between the FBI and the Queens D.A.'s office regarding electronic surveillance" of John Gotti and the Bergin, Mouw said later.

The Queens D.A. told Mouw that his men had tapped both pay phones and installed a bug in the rear of the Bergin. The bug never came to life; the taps produced many gambling tapes, enough to indict 15 to 20 people, but not much else. Santucci said taps at social clubs were not as good as bugs in the Family homes.

The meeting had a "competitive air," Mouw said, but the D.A. did agree to ease up on the Bergin surveillance and forget about trying anything similar at the Our Friends Social Club. But Santucci also indicated he would continue his investigation, hopeful of getting something more important than gambling charges.

In September, another meeting was held. The Queens officials said someone with access to secret documents was leaking information about their not-so-secret Bergin surveillance. "They were greatly disturbed [that] they had a leak or some sort of compromise in their office," Mouw said.

The Queens contingent also admitted the presence of another embarrassing situation. The D.A. had issued subpoenas for the telephone records of Angelo and crew associate Michael Roccoforte, but failed to insert a "do-not-notify" clause in the subpoenas; both men were told by the telephone company their records had been subpoenaed.

Mouw agreed to schedule a meeting between case-agent Donald McCormick and the Queens case-detective, Jack Holder, but this meeting was never held. Neither side really wanted to work with the other, a not-unusual example of a failure-to-communicate situation between rival law-enforcement agencies.

"We didn't feel that information would be secure by sharing it with the Queens D.A.'s office," Mouw said. "I never contacted [them] and they never contacted me."

Of course, Source Wahoo contacted the FBI. He said that Bergin lawyer Michael Coiro was "friendly" with an unnamed assistant district attorney in Queens. He also said that Gotti had recently told the crew, "We're all going to jail."

The candy-store taps went in on May 7, after the Queens D.A. used the surveillance by Holder and others, the pen-register information, and the arrest of Peter Schiavone to obtain the required court approval. The D.A.'s affidavit said the taps were necessary because:

"A misguided sense of loyalty, combined with the criminal wall of silence and the fear of personal reprisal, make it extremely unlikely that even after receiving immunity any member of the conspiracy or criminal associate of the targets would testify truthfully against any other members of the community."

The taps lasted only until August. The targets, who knew the candy-store numbers were found in the Schiavone wire room, were cautious on the phones. For instance, near midnight on June 2, Angelo called Gotti and began to speak about someone identified only as an "asshole," but Gotti cut him off.

"Forget about this phone."

Angelo then started talking about other subjects, but later returned to the first one.

"Please," Gotti said. "You know, you got a car. Why don't you drive here when you want to talk with people?" [Or] call me. I'll drive ... Just tell me you wanna talk to me. I'll get in the fucking car, you know?"

Gotti demonstrated similar restraint many times on the Bergin tapes, but when it was time to place a bet, he didn't care who was listening in.

17

I AIN'T GOING CRAZY NO MORE

IT IS ILLEGAL TO BE a bookmaker, but not to bet with one.

During the three months the candy-store taps were on, they sizzled with action. A constant melody of tips, hunches, lines, odds, and bets entertained monitoring cops. John Gotti sizzled—and fizzled—most of all.

Near the end of the first week, Gotti was heard calling the telephone room to learn how two horses he'd gotten tips on made out. One had "ran out," bolted the track.

"Fucking fuck bastards with their fucking tips," Gotti screamed when he heard the news. "I bet every bookmaker [I] could find."

"Ah, I believe that," the man answering the phone said.

With his multiple contacts and interests, Gotti was always getting tips. They came from other bettors, racetrack fiends, friends of track employees, stable owners—everywhere.

"The Pope gave me two tips," he told a man a week later. "Two seconds [second-place finishes], on my mother's life!"

When Gotti bet on a horse race, he bet to win, and almost always bet $1,000, a "dime" as he called it. A man who bet thousands like dimes demanded quality service.

"Give me a dime on him and a dime on Prospect," he told a bookie one day.

"Prospect is in the fifth race?"

"What the fuck's the difference what race? You know the horse, so you look for the race!"

When Gotti couldn't get through to a bookmaker when he needed him, he turned the job over to one of his Bergin minions.

"Call around and see if you can get me in the fourth race, Sun Ray Classic," he ordered a minion one night.

"In the fourth?"

"Yeah. It's a nine-oh-eight post time, so you got about twenty minutes. See what you can fucking do."

"Sun Ray, what did you want on it?"

"A dime!" Gotti was incredulous. "What do I want on it?"

In a similar conversation a few days later, Gotti gave a possible clue about his attraction to gambling.

"Call me in a bet on the last race, too, all right?" he told a different Bergin man.

"How much? Dime?"

"Yeah, what the fuck. I'll get myself really in fucking jeopardy."

One of the few times Gotti was overheard betting less than $1,000 was on May 20, when he hunch-bet $500, a "nickel," on a horse whose name he liked: John Q. Arab.

"That's all?" the surprised bookie replied.

"That's all, I ain't going crazy no more."

Gotti broke the vow that very night, and was furious because he almost was not able to get a dime down in time for a late race; it was all because a bookie had left his wire room a little early that evening. Later that night, he tracked the man down and complained.

"I don't even remember what happened to the horse," he added.

What happens to the horses determines the winning numbers in the illegal Family lotteries. The Brooklyn number, for instance, is determined by the last three digits of the total pari-mutuel handle at whatever New York track is open that day

The day after he almost failed to get his bet down, Gotti was on the phone with Billy Battista, who handled some of his sports betting. He asked Battista his running "figure" for the week—a gambler's week begins Monday and ends Sunday; he settles with the bookie, usually, on Tuesday or Wednesday. He also asked for the baseball line. He wanted to bet on a day game, but bookies don't like to open wire rooms in the afternoon when only one game is scheduled.

Gotti told Battista to "make a beef" about this with such a bookie. "What have you gotta do for accommodations?" he asked.

"He don't come in when there's only one afternoon game," Battista replied.

"What kind of bullshit is that? He's got a beef with this cock-sucker."

"I told him that. He says he don't stay open."

"Ah, he's full of shit."

Battista gave Gotti the line on several night baseball games, and Gotti bet a dime on each. In sports betting, a dime can be more than $1,000 because bookies establish the odds on a basic unit of $5. For example, if the Bergin team were a 6-7 favorite to beat the Ravenite team, a fan who bet a dime on the Bergin is "laying" 7, the higher number, 200 times. So the bet is $1,400 to win $1,000. If the under-dog Ravenite wins the game, a fan who bet a dime on it wins $1,200—200 units of 6. The bookie gets $200—his vig—of the $1,400 lost by the Bergin fan.

Gotti would have so much riding on the outcome of some games that sometimes when he was at the Bergin, crew members would turn off the television set so that he wouldn't become upset.

His temper was something to behold, as a few nongambling con-versations on the Bergin tapes profanely illustrated.

One outburst came after Anthony Moscatiello—the former real estate partner of Salvatore Ruggiero who had leased Gotti a car—failed to promptly return Gotti's phone calls.

"Hi, Buddy," Moscatiello began cheerfully when he was able to get back to Gotti.

"Buddy, my fucking balls. What, I got to reach out for you three days in a-fucking advance?"

"Paul, my wife just called me."

"You know, let me tell you something. I, I got, I need an example. Don't you be the fucking example. Do you understand me?"

"Listen, John ..."

"Listen, I called your fucking house five times yesterday, now ... if you're going to disregard my mother-fucking phone calls, I'll blow you and that fucking house up."

"I never disregard anything you ..."

"This is not a fucking game ... my time is valuable ... if I ever hear anybody else calls you and you respond within five days, I'll fucking kill you ..."

Jamesy Cardinali was not allowed to attend the Little Italy dice game, the one that the Bergin bigshots were operating in 1981.

"The next thing you know, you'll be gambling...that's not for you," Johnny told Jamesy.

People might have lived if Jamesy had become addicted to gambling and not to cocaine; in March 1981, in a house in Brooklyn, he participated in another white-powder murder.

Jamesy didn't pull the trigger, but it was still murder. He sucked the cocaine dealer into seemingly idle conversation while an accomplice shot him in the face. The two killers wrapped the body in a painter's tarp, took it to Howard Beach, got on a boat, and deposited another corpse in Jamaica Bay.

> Q.: *Did you have to do anything to the body to make sure that it didn't float?*
> A.: *He was cut open.*

Jamesy doesn't remember exactly, but he got $9,000 to $12,000 for this murder "in dribs and drabs." Gotti heard he was selling drugs again and talked to him about it on June 1.

"Someone came here and said you were selling drugs."

"It's not true."

"If I find out it is true, I will kill you."

"Who told you?"

"Michael Castigliola."

The next day, Jamesy murdered Michael Castigliola as the victim sat in a car. Tommie LaRuffa, a 70-year-old comrade of Jamesy's, saw his wicked young friend pull the trigger.

Jamesy didn't go to the Bergin for a few weeks, but one Sunday night he was tapped out and dropped in to ask Gotti for a loan.

"Did you kill that guy?"

"Yes."

"Never do anything like that again. You come and ask me ..."

"John, if I asked you, you wouldn't let me kill the guy."

"You got to post everything with me. I knew it an hour after you did it."

"How did you know?"

"Somebody saw you."

Jamesy knew it was true. Incredibly, a Bergin man was turning onto the street at the time Jamesy shot Castigliola and saw it all.

Gotti told the now four-time killer that Castigliola was with another mobster. "But don't worry. I can handle [him], just keep your mouth shut."

About this time, Special Agent Paul Hayes began calling on Jamesy, who had turned up in surveillance photographs taken outside the Bergin. Jamesy wasn't supposed to hang out with criminals; the photos suggested that he had violated his parole. Sources BQ and Wahoo had identified the photos, for which some Bergin men had posed. One day they grew tired of seeing an FBI car outside the club and agreed to have their pictures taken if the agents would then leave.

The FBI wanted to talk to Jamesy about John Gotti and not, except as a possible lever, a parole violation. But Jamesy wasn't interested in talking, not then, and every time Agent Hayes came calling, Jamesy told John or Gene.

One time, after Hayes invited Jamesy to the FBI office in Queens, Gene gave him money in case "they keep you." John told him it was okay to go once. "But don't take no [lie] tests. Go and talk once, that's enough."

Naturally, Jamesy wasn't telling Agent Hayes about any murders either, and in August 1981 he put number 5 in the grave.

On cocaine, Jamesy was a greyhound chasing an elusive mechanical rabbit. He had to stay high to escape the low.

> *Q.: So you have to keep doing it?*
> *A.: Yes.*
> *Q.: You have to keep doing it and you have to keep doing it. You do it until it's all gone, right?*
> *A.: Then you go get some more.*

Jamesy went to the Riviera Motel near the airport to get some more, after friends told him about a coke dealer holding four kilos.

At the motel, Jamesy flashed a badge and handcuffed the flush dealer. He policed him into his car, drove behind the motel, and fired a fatal bullet into his neck. Jamesy and three partners each got a kilo, a thousand grams; a thousand disco nights for Jamesy if he weren't so greedy, which of course he was. He sold some, but most of the score went up his nose.

En route to his more timid friends, Jamesy, for once, felt "bad" because the victim "looked like a college kid."

Two months later, the parents of a young man wearing a University of Pennsylvania ring on his finger were informed his body had been found behind the Riviera Motel, near John F. Kennedy International Airport, Queens, New York City.

In the meantime, Jamesy was asked to appear in a police lineup for the Castigliola murder. He was not identified, but as he left the precinct, three state parole officers were waiting. At a hearing, he was found guilty of violating his parole. The charges were using drugs, failing to report for visits with his parole officer, and "consorting" with criminals. The evidence of the latter was a photograph of Jamesy with Willie Boy Johnson outside the Bergin. FBI Agent Paul Hayes angered Jamesy by giving pivotal testimony.

Jamesy went off to do nine months in a state prison. He was one thorn out of Gotti's crown, but others were on the vine.

On September 1, 1981, the criminal aspirations of a young Queens armed robber, Peter Zuccaro, were put on hold when he was sentenced to 12 years in prison by Brooklyn federal judge Eugene H. Nickerson, who would make John Gotti's acquaintance later.

Zuccaro had been convicted of taking part in two armored-car robberies, which netted about $1.1 million. He was the nexus that bound Gotti and a former Ozone Park schoolgirl, Diane F. Giacalone, in a fierce court battle to be fought five years later.

The Zuccaro case was prosecuted by Giacalone, who became an assistant U.S. attorney for the Eastern District of New York—Brooklyn, Queens, Staten Island, and Long Island—in 1979.

Giacalone, the daughter of a civil engineer, used to walk along 101st Avenue, past the Bergin, on her way to the Our Lady of Wisdom Academy. She used to wonder whether the men who hung out there worked only at night.

As John Gotti climbed in the Family, Giacalone climbed in the legal profession. After being graduated from New York University Law School, she went to Washington to work in the Justice Department's tax division. She then returned to New York, to live in Manhattan and work in Brooklyn.

The Zuccaro case began July 29, 1980—a time when Gotti was in Florida and a day after his neighbor John Favara was kidnapped and disappeared forever.

Zuccaro and three confederates waited in the parking lot of a Queens grocery store until an employee of IBI Security Services, an armored-car company, came out of the store with the day's receipts.

Two, maybe three, robbers followed the employee into the truck, waved their handguns, announced a robbery, and handcuffed him and the driver, Francis Higgins, an ex-cop. They drove the truck a short distance, gobbled up $310,000, and took off.

On December 26, 1980, the robbers struck again. Same truck, same driver, same routine, but in Brooklyn outside a bakery and for more than twice as much money—$750,000. They left the truck outside a *New York Daily News* printing plant. Ex-cop Higgins had had enough; he left IBI Security to work in a grocery store.

Zuccaro was indicted in March 1981; his accomplices remained free until one, Andrew Curro, became a suspect in the murder of his 19-year-old girlfriend, April Ernst. Investigating her death, police learned that April had threatened to reveal his role in the IBI Security Services thefts during an argument they had over another woman.

Cops began to pressure Andrew Curro. Early in August, he was arrested on charges of possessing a weapon, a violation of his probation. Bail bondsman Irving Newman got a call from a man who wanted to help Curro make bail—Angelo Ruggiero.

"He said that he knows the people well and not to worry about it," Newman recalled later. "He would see that I got the collateral and everything else."

A few days later, Newman was asked by others to guarantee more bail for Curro, after he was arrested again and charged with his girlfriend's murder. April Ernst had been strangled with a rope, taken to a motel, and dismembered with a machete.

The cops were told something else during their probe of Curro: He and Zuccaro also were car thieves who had sold cars and parts to the Fountain Auto Shop, owned by John Carneglia. Some of the IBI Security loot, an informant said, was passed on to the Bergin, and thus possibly to Neil Dellacroce.

All this was easier said than proved. But a few days after Zuccaro was sentenced, Diane Giacalone began "doing Neil and Johnny," as one participant of an initial strategy session recalled. The victorious prosecutor began laying plans for making a racketeering and conspiracy case against them, a "RICO" case.

RICO is an acronym for the Racketeer-Influenced and Corrupt Organizations Act, a legal sledgehammer conceived with the Families in mind. It had been federal law since 1970, but had only recently come into vogue at the Justice Department.

The government had conspiracy statutes prior to 1970, but RICO was a wider net. Its focus was entities, not individuals— Families rather than soldiers. Until RICO, federal law, for the most part, saw individuals committing criminal acts; it did not see organizations whose individuals committed crimes to benefit the organization. RICO introduced two new ideas: "criminal enterprise" and "pattern of racketeering."

A "criminal enterprise" was any organization or group of individuals "associated in fact," if not by law, which employed racketeering for group purposes. A "pattern of racketeering" was two or more violations of state and federal laws, against crimes such as murder, mail fraud, extortion, bribery, or 28 others.

Under RICO, it became a separate crime to belong to an enterprise that engaged in a pattern of racketeering. Even if the racketeering acts were committed by others, a member was guilty if he was shown to be a knowing and active member of the enterprise. RICO meant that some serious state crimes, such as murder, could be tried in federal courts.

The penalties upon a RICO conviction—up to 20 years and $25,000 in fines for each count—are much more severe than most of those provided by the 32 individual state and federal laws that can be cited in the pattern of racketeering. RICO also permits government confiscation of businesses or property obtained through the enterprise.

Defense attorneys say some RICO provisions are unfair, especially one permitting prosecutors, as part of the pattern of racketeering, to charge crimes for which a defendant has already been convicted and punished. This makes it possible, for instance, to convert two relatively minor violations into one serious RICO felony. Under RICO, a defendant may even be charged with a crime for which he has been previously acquitted, under a theory that committing the crime for the enterprise is considered a new crime.

A principal RICO author, G. Robert Blakey, now a law professor at the University of Notre Dame, defends RICO this way: "If you don't want any more trouble, stay away from crime."

RICO was part of a package known as the Organized Crime Control Act of 1970. It was proposed by Blakey and other young lawyers employed by a presidential commission under Presidents Kennedy and Johnson or by a Senate committee that held hearings on organized crime in the mid-1960s.

The testimony of Joseph Valachi—the Genovese mobster who first revealed the existence of *La Cosa Nostra*—had already helped RICO supporters guide other anti-mob measures through Congress, laws that gave prosecutors control of grand juries and greater immunity and surveillance powers.

"RICO was designed to zap the mob, not mobsters, but the mob," said Blakey, "But few prosecutors understood it."

Many within the Department of Justice, especially the FBI, had recently discovered this concealed weapon at professional forums and law-school seminars and were pursuing investigations which they hoped would yield RICO indictments.

As early as 1979, information from Sources BQ and Wahoo was going into a "Bergin Hunt and Fish Club (RICO)" file at the FBI office in Queens. Former federal judge William H. Webster had led the FBI into a wider assault on the Families than had his predecessor, FBI founder J. Edgar Hoover, who had four agents working Family cases in New York during the McCarthy era.

Aniello Dellacroce was now considered New York's second most powerful mobster; FBI agents had learned that Castellano was in fact the Gambino boss.

Still, by starting an investigation of Dellacroce and his top skipper, John Gotti, Diane Giacalone was entering territory normally patrolled by the Eastern District's special Organized Crime Strike Force. The Strike Force was located next to the U.S. Court House, where Giacalone worked, in the so-called IRS building. The two offices were distinct enterprises with their own methods and personalities.

Giacalone, who bears a physical resemblance to comedienne Lily Tomlin, already had an uneasy relationship with some FBI agents. In April 1981, because Strike Force prosecutors were occupied with several political corruption cases—the result of a spectacular FBI sting operation known as Abscam—a case the FBI had against Peter

Castellanna, a cousin of both Carlo Gambino and Paul Castellano, had landed on Ciacalone's desk.

Castellanna and two others had been arrested on extortion charges based on secret tapes made by the alleged victim as he was threatened with death. By September, Giacalone had not yet secured indictments. FBI agents thought she was dragging her feet; she thought the case needed more investigation.

Whatever the merits, the friction was undeniable. But Giacalone did not seem to care what they thought about her. The power and prestige of her office imbues some of its occupants with a sense of national mission and noble purpose that does not abide any distraction. She was outspoken, strong-willed, and occasionally tempestuous. In the mainly male world of cops and robbers, and agents and mobsters, she was a prickly outsider.

Many of the men whose cooperation she needed didn't think the 31-year-old former tax attorney was ideally suited for the task of taking down Dellacroce and Gotti in a complicated RICO case. She felt absolutely confident that she was suited, and that she would not have had the job if her bosses didn't think so, too.

Besides, it really wasn't that complicated. Obviously, the Gambino Family—an associated-in-fact illegal enterprise if there ever was one—existed. Neil and Johnny Boy were certainly members; there was evidence—court records, guilty pleas—that they had committed at least two violations of state and federal laws during their careers. The case was a tedious but doable matter of pulling all the pieces from all the files and persuading a few people to testify about them. This was more the work of lawyers than cops, and Giacalone was a thorough, tireless lawyer.

Giacalone's first strategy session was attended by Lt. Jack Fergerson of the NYPD's Organized Crime Control Bureau, and three detectives: Kenneth McCabe, then of the Brooklyn D.A.'s office; Joseph Coffey, then commander of the NYPD's Organized Crime homicide task force; and Billy Burns, who had worked on the IB case. Three federal agents also participated: Edward Magnuson of the DEA, and Richard Robley and Stephen Morrill of the FBI.

At the time, New York State did not have a law similar to RICO; it was common for the NYPD to assign detectives to cases better brought in federal court. Among other reasons, the DEA was interested because John, Peter, Gene, and Vincent Gotti, at various times, had been named in drug-dealing investigations. Significantly, although the FBI had special organized-crime squads for each Family, the two agents it sent to Giacalone's meeting were members of a property-crimes unit. The FBI was used to taking Family cases to the Strike Force, not getting them from assistant U.S. attorneys.

All the agencies had their own informants. To varying degrees, they felt loyal to them, a result of the ironic bond that develops between good guys and bad guys during years of secret meetings under dangerous circumstances. They tended to regard their informants in a proprietary manner; informants, of course, give information, a source of power.

One informant that the DEA brought to Giacalone at the outset was Kenneth O'Donnell, an armed robber who had been an informer for the NYPD. Detective Joseph Coffey would later testify that O'Donnell was the best informer he ever had, but he had to be closely monitored.

Though difficult to handle—after some undercover work one night, he committed a robbery—O'Donnell was effective. He had introduced ATF undercover agent Dominick Polifrone to Vincent Gotti; he had set up Frank DiCicco for a loan-shark charge, eventually dismissed. He had also set up one of John Gotti's barbers, Vito Scaglione, who had a shop on 101st Avenue and delivered a silencer-equipped pistol to an undercover agent for whom O'Donnell had vouched. Vito pleaded guilty.

Lately, O'Donnell had been helping the DEA make cases against drug dealers in New Jersey. He now told Giacalone he saw John Gotti give Peter Zuccaro, the man she had just prosecuted in the armored-car case, a "bag full of money" in front of the Bergin "for drugs." The charge was never publicly made, but it fired the interest of Giacalone and the others.

In the beginning of the Eastern District–NYPD–DEA–FBI RICO investigation, there was goodwill.

18

THE MERCHANTS OF OZONE PARK

SUCCESSFUL INVESTIGATIONS DEPEND ON SECRECY, and a big secret was kept from Diane Giacalone as she began her pursuit of Neil Dellacroce and John Gotti.

John, Gene, and Angelo were about to be named in a wiretap request as targets of a RICO investigation that Gambino Family specialists of the FBI and the Eastern District Organized Crime Strike Force already had underway.

Giacalone was not told; she worked for another agency. And neither the FBI nor the Strike Force believed that her RICO investigation, which had sprouted coincidentally out of the armored-car case, was any reason to shelve theirs, about which they naturally felt more loyalty.

An FBI squad in Queens—the "Gambino squad" involved in the Bergin fireworks raid—had been investigating the crew for nearly two years, collecting data from, among others, Sources BQ and Wahoo, who were described in an FBI affidavit as "never unreliable." FBI policy precluded Giacalone from knowing the identities of BQ and Wahoo, but in time she would ignite a revealing behind-the-scenes battle over how to use them.

Citing the informants, the Strike Force had received permission from the Department of Justice in Washington to seek a wiretap order on Angelo's home phone, which was granted November 9, 1981.

One of the other informants was 6 foot 9 inch, 400-pound George Yudzevich, the "heavyset man" in *Gloria*, a 1980 film directed by John Cassavetes. Yudzevich was with another crew, but had spent time on 101st Avenue in an unsuccessful effort to hook up with the Gotti squad as a loan-shark collector.

Loan-sharking and gambling were the initial focus of the FBI–Strike Force investigation, but not long after agents began monitoring Angelo's phone, the work *babania* was heard. Several amazing turns ensued; one featured the FBI investigating itself because, somehow, Angelo Ruggiero found out that agents had been listening to him and he went into hiding.

At the time, the FBI did not know how Angelo penetrated its official secrecy; in 1985, it would learn that he had obtained a draft copy of a bureau affidavit, which told him and others they were in deep trouble. The affidavit caused panic and deception within the Family within a Family, whose titular boss equated drug dealing with death. When it was all sorted out four years later, and John Gotti was the new boss of a unified Family, a few people would look back at November 9, 1981, the day the Angelo eavesdropping began, and say this was the day Paul Castellano really died.

The tapped telephone in Angelo's home was listed in his daughter's name. It was singled out because he had told informants it was "safe." They said that Angelo, only a few months after the Bergin wiretapping by Queens officials, was openly discussing—on the phone—the loan-sharking and gambling rackets that he, John, and Gene operated.

In its initial request to wiretap the telephone, the FBI listed Peter and Richard Gotti as loan-shark collectors and stated that Angelo was a "known murderer who would, without question, seek physical retribution and possibly murder a shylock victim who is unable to pay his debts."

"Shylock," another word for loan shark, has a literary etymology. In Shakespeare's *Merchant of Venice*, Shylock demanded "a pound of flesh" from delinquent borrowers. The unliterary underworld slurred the character's name into "shark."

"The shylock victim is generally a gambler who is deeply in debt," the FBI document continued. "For the victim, a shylock serves as a convenient, if menacing, answer to an immediate debt.

Accordingly, a victim is loyal to the shylock and seeks to protect him."

The second day of the wiretap, Angelo and John Gotti, the merchants of Ozone Park, were overheard discussing a meeting about a loan to two men who ran a firm in the garment district, Mercury Pattern Service.

Later, "Marty" of Mercury called Angelo to see if it was okay if "Tommy" dropped off some "shirts" the next day.

"It's all right to say 'money,'" Angelo told Mercury's Marty.

The tap also quickly showed that Angelo had not been able to cool Gotti's ardor for gambling, now devoted to professional football, whose season was in full swing.

On Sunday, November 11, Angelo called to see how Gotti was doing so far that day. Gotti, already a big loser, was beside himself.

"I bet the Buffalo Bills for six dimes, they're getting killed, ten-nothing. I bet New England for six dimes, I'm getting killed with New England … I bet six dimes on Chicago, they're losing. I bet three dimes on K.C. They're winning, [but] maybe they'll lose, these motherfuckers."

All told, Gotti was down for more than the $25,000 he allegedly made in a year allegedly working for Arc Plumbing. Angelo wondered which teams Gotti had bet on in the late-afternoon games.

"The Washington Redskins. I bet them for six dimes. Maybe they'll lose, too, against the Giants."

Angelo tried to steer the conversation into another area, but Gotti was distracted.

"We're getting killed, that's more important. I'm stuck almost thirty dimes here and nowhere to fucking go."

Angelo tried again. He told a story that ended with a reference to a man being loyal to his brother "all his life."

"Ah, Christ on the fucking cross. Right now I'd give my fucking life just to have fucking Buffalo win one."

On the following Sunday it was worse. As the late-afternoon games were ending, Angelo tracked Gotti down at the Cozy Corner Bar, which FBI agents suspected was the base of the gambling operation that Gotti's men ran for bettors besides themselves; the Berginites would bet with other bookies so as not to win their own money, if they ever won.

"Did you hang yourself?" Angelo asked as Gotti came on the bar phone. This time they used "dollar" as a synonym for $1,000.

"Forget about it. If I tell you what I lost you won't believe it."

"I could believe it."

"Forget about it. I got killed. Forget about it. I lost ... fifty-three dollars. You know the last time I lost fifty-three dollars?"

"I know all about it."

"On my son's grave, I ain't got fifty-three fucking cents."

Gotti then complained to Angelo he had just discovered that one of the men who managed the Cozy Corner operation had left a numbers bet in for him the last four weeks.

"He tells me another three dimes I owe ... fucking mother-fucker."

The same conversation showed Gotti used loan sharks, too, and one shark wanted to be fed.

"There's a problem," Angelo told his gambling *gumbah,* "with the guy who lent you fifty dollars. I was told not to say nothing to you."

Gotti sighed and complained that in the meantime "I got three days to go borrow" the additional $53,000 he had lost.

On November 21, the word *babania* popped up obliquely in a conversation between Angelo and Gene Gotti. Source BQ had recently told the FBI that the pair was contacting *babania* salesman Salvatore Ruggiero "just about every night from various public phone booths."

Salvatore was wanted on three federal warrants for heroin dealing, hijacking, and tax evasion. For the latter, his wife Stephanie also was sought. They had been on the lam for six years.

Salvatore could afford life on the run. He secretly owned hideouts in Fort Lauderdale and the Poconos and traded stocks and bonds under other names. He also owned a diner, a greeting card store, and other investment property purchased through a company called Ozone Holding. He had four cars, including a Mercedes, and ten watches worth $12,000 each. He was living in a leased home in New Jersey while another was being built for him through a company run by Anthony and Caesar Gurino, owners of Arc Plumbing and paper bosses of John Gotti and Angelo Ruggiero.

At the time of Source BQ's tip, Angelo—a big gambler, too, but not like Gotti—was broke. Six months later, he would cite a remarkable turnaround.

"I'm way out of debt now," he told an acquaintance. "I'm no fuckin' millionaire, [but] I'm sitting on four hundred thousand dollars."

The furtive-phone-calls tip was evidence of a conspiracy to conceal a fugitive. The FBI intensified its surveillance of Angelo, John, Gene, and other Bergin men.

On November 24, Anthony Moscatiello, who had been forwarding mail to his old real estate partner, Salvatore, was stopped and searched by FBI agents. Tony quickly called Sal's brother.

"Two guys just took me out of the car."

"You're kidding," Angelo said.

"Guns drawn"

"For what?"

"[They] told me [it] was the company I keep."

Angelo called another Howard Beach neighbor, Joseph Massino, soon to be acting boss of the Bonanno Family.

"I don't know what the fuck is going on over here," he told his and John's longtime friend. "Every time somebody leaves my fucking house ... agents grab them on the corner."

"What the fuck they want you to do?" Massino said. "Hang out with doctors and lawyers?"

Later that day, Angelo called John.

"There's a little green car circling your block and my block."

"Yeah, all right."

"Broken taillight."

"Yeah ... fuckers."

On December 1, the Angelo wiretap was removed because he moved from Howard Beach to nearby Cedarhurst, Long Island, to a house that he was having renovated. Angelo told informants it was a good move for him—the FBI wouldn't know where he lived. In fact, pen registers at the Our Friends Social Club had disclosed several calls to Cedarhurst and FBI agents were watching on the day Angelo moved in.

The agents had increased physical surveillance of Angelo and John, suspecting they might be doing what they had not yet talked about on the phone: dealing drugs. Source BQ had just reported that they booted heroin dealer Mark Reiter, age 33, out of the crew—"to have everyone at the club think that they are on the outs with him. In reality, Reiter is arranging deals."

On December 30, two telephones in Angelo's safe house were tapped.

If John Gotti resolved to stop gambling in the New Year, he broke his resolution on New Year's Day—and lost $90,000 on bowl games he bet on with three bookies.

"The man is fuckin' nuts," Angelo told Massino a few days later. "The man is mad."

Angelo frequently trashed John behind his back, the wiretaps showed. John was a "sick motherfucker" whose "fuckin' mouth goes a mile a minute." He was always "abusing" and "talking about people" and was "wrong on a lot of things." Even so, Quack Quack loved Johnny Boy "like a brother"—their bond was now three decades in the making.

By law, when they're "up" on someone's phone, FBI agents must suspend monitoring if the conversations "are not criminal in nature." This is known as "minimization." As a practical matter, however, personal or unrelated comments are frequently made during "relevant" conversations. Sometimes, on Angelo's phones, the results were amusing.

For instance, Gene was taped talking about a horror movie he was watching when Angelo called one day.

"I just watched them shrink a head!"

"Shrink whose head?"

The Amazons, creatures of the Amazons."

"Yeah?"

"They didn't show you capturing the guy, they just show you his head. Forget about it."

"Yeah? I got to go watch it."

On occasion, touching comments about family members became part of impersonal Department of Justice transcripts.

Angelo, now the father of six children, was taped telling John about telling his young daughter a bedtime story. "So I told her about 'The Three Little Pigs.' And I forgot to tell her about the third little pig with the brick house. [Would] you believe, this morning when I woke up, she said, 'What happened to the other pig, Dad?'"

Eighteen months after Frank Gotti's death, John was taped telling Angelo where he'd been that morning.

"I went to see some hard-on and I went to see the fuckin' cemetery."

"Oh."

"My route, my daily route."

On January 10, Angelo's "mad man" went to see the Pope on Death Hill on Staten Island. Out of respect for Carmine Fatico, Gotti wasn't "officially" captain of the Bergin crew yet, according to what Angelo told a friend, but he "reports directly to the boss."

Gotti was accompanied by John Carneglia and observed by FBI agents lurking outside the Castellano White House. The two Johns spotted the agents, who decided to come out in plain view and take down a license-plate number, to let the spotters know they knew they were being watched.

Three days later, Angelo told Gotti that the agents were trying "to put something"—a bug—in Castellano's home. Angelo had the right idea, but the wrong house—at that time, anyway.

Late on January 14, Queens detectives began arresting the first of many crew members on bookmaking charges. As usual, the legal arrangements were handled by Angelo.

About 3:30 A.M., Angelo woke up Gotti, sick with the flu and in a grouchy mood. After Angelo filed his report. Gotti wondered whether they might get busted, too.

"What are they going to get us for?" Gotti seethed. "Sucking a fucking cunt?"

Having lost nearly $200,000 during the last few months of the football season, Gotti was annoyed that he might be arrested. "Maybe they want to help me borrow to pay," he said about the Queens cops. " ... maybe they want to pay the [loan-shark] rate."

Angelo said ten, maybe twelve, men had been arrested so far.

"One bigger fuckin' bum than the other they locked up, uh?" Gotti grumbled.

"They're looking for your brother Richie."

"Like I said, one bigger bum than the fuckin' other ... no matter how many cocksuckers they get, they wanna bother the mother-fucker assholes in the world. I can't believe this."

Gotti's harsh reference to his brother Richard would not have surprised Source BQ. Only two months earlier, BQ had told the FBI it was "common knowledge" that John, Gene, and Richard "do not talk regularly" and frequently communicated through Angelo, who had known them all since childhood. BQ considered Gene the most intelligent of the Gotti brothers.

His tirade over, John said he had something important to tell Angelo, but not over the phone, and, in case anyone was listening in, he left this message:

"Meantime, these fuckin' bums, the money they're wastin' to tap these phones for release cases like us, they coulda went and spent it on good tapes. You know what I mean? Or lend it to us, these fuckin' bums."

The men listening in didn't think they were wasting tax dollars, but the more agents and their supervisors heard Gotti betting nickels and dimes on horses and games, the less optimistic they were about persuading a jury that a man who bet so heavily also was a big bookmaker.

As the sun rose, Angelo was back on the phone with Michael Coiro, the Bergin bail-out specialist.

"Being that this is only a gambling case, you know, you shouldn't run into any problem on the bail," Coiro advised.

Angelo next called Tony Moscatiello and assigned him to come by and pick up money, take it to Queens Criminal Court, and bail the Berginites out.

Finally, Angelo called Gene, who asked, "What's the story?"

"It's misdemeanors and stuff and fines. We're going to take the fucking thing and forget about it."

As it turned out, Angelo and Gotti were able to forget about being arrested themselves; and for a brief while, Gotti forgot about gambling. He stopped after Frank Guidici, who was suspected of running the Bergin bookmaking operation for John, Gene, and Angelo, complained he wasn't making any money because he had to cover John's personal losses with other bookmakers.

"He thinks he's got to go on welfare," John griped to Angelo.

Angelo said he would pacify Guidici by putting him on the payroll of Mercury Pattern Service, run by Marty and Tommy, who were still sending "shirts" to Angelo. The firm now also employed Angelo—or so its books might say—and soon Marty would even solicit more shylock customers/victims for him.

"I'll send him some place where [Guidici] can make a few hundred a week," Angelo added. "I make five hundred dollars a week myself."

Gotti laid off the action, at least through the 1981 Super Bowl on January 24. This surprised Johnny Boy-watchers like Neil Dellacroce, who was so informed when Angelo telephoned him to talk about their bets.

"Johnny's the only one that didn't bet," Angelo said. "He gave up betting. He's just going to watch."

"Who?" Neil asked. "Johnny?"

"Yeah."

"No kiddin'."

A few months after Angelo's phones were tapped, Diane Giacalone learned, unofficially, about the FBI–Strike Force wiretaps. In the world of agents and cops chasing the same suspects, especially among the fraternity of organized-crime experts, secrets are difficult to keep, despite official policy.

Although the wiretaps weren't hers, Giacalone decided to try to use them in her effort to link Dellacroce and Gotti to the IBI armored-car robberies. She would "tickle the wire"—prompt more conversation on the tapped phones—by issuing a grand jury subpoena for John Carneglia, the man Angelo sponsored into the Family. Two IBI robbers, Andrew Curro and Peter Zuccaro, were thought to have stolen cars for Fountain Auto Sales, a used-car lot and scrap-metal business run by Carneglia, whose rap sheet included several arrests for car theft and related crimes.

If the tickling turned up indiscreet talking about the cash disbursements of the armored-car jobs, the FBI agents monitoring the wiretaps would have to inform the property-crimes specialists working for Giacalone.

A subpoena commanding him to testify before an Eastern District grand jury under Giacalone's control was served on John Carneglia early on February 8.

"Two hard-ons just left here, gave me a subpoena," Carneglia told Angelo in a call a few minutes later.

"For what?"

"I don't know, something to do with ... that kid Andrew [Curro], or some shit."

Crazy Sally Polisi would later say that Carneglia offered to hook him up with Curro and Zuccaro so they could steal cars for him, which he could then sell to Carneglia. Now, however, Carneglia told Angelo that he told the agents he had nothing to do with Curro and Zuccaro.

"These kids are junkie motherfuckin' kids half my age," he quoted himself.

Carneglia said the agents replied they knew he didn't and the subpoena was "bullshit," but a "lady prosecutor" had insisted.

"What's her name?" Angelo asked.

Carneglia didn't remember offhand, but he had seen it on the subpoena, which was signed by a "real, real Italian lady."

Charles Carneglia also got a subpoena. Crazy Sally Polisi would testify later that Charles told him "we whacked out" a court officer—a reference to Albert Gelb, who was to testify against Charles in a gun-possession case. James Cardinali would testify that John Carneglia told him—as they talked about what they would do if a cop ever happened on a crime-in-progress—that he had "whacked" a court officer.

According to court papers, on the night Gelb arrested Charles Carneglia for carrying a weapon, Carneglia threatened to kill him. Over the next thirteen months, Gelb, who had won three medals for heroic off-duty actions, received many threats. He became "very fearful of testifying" but decided to go ahead.

Gelb, age 25, was shot dead in Queens early one morning a few days before the trial began. A man in a white car followed Gelb home from his job in Brooklyn Night Court, cut off Gelb's car, jumped out, and fired four times through the windshield.

If Giacalone hoped remembrances of Gelb would turn up on Angelo's tickled wire, she was disappointed.

Angelo and John Carneglia did talk several more times about the subpoena, but not incriminatingly. Angelo advised Carneglia that all he had to do was take the Fifth Amendment—refuse to answer any questions—if the real Italian lady didn't give him immunity.

A grant of immunity, Angelo correctly told Carneglia, would have to come from Washington.

"Takes seven to eight weeks to get it," Angelo said.

"Yeah?"

"They can get it in three weeks if they want."

"Oh ...?"

"Listen, the fastest they can get it is two weeks."

"No."

"They could have it waitin' for you, don't get me wrong."

Without immunity, Carneglia appeared before the grand jury on February 17.

"How'd you make out?" Angelo asked.

"Yeah, good, Fifth Amendment, that was it, no nothing, no immunity ... two seconds I was in and out."

James Cardinali got out of prison a few days after Carneglia got out of the grand jury. Police in Brooklyn considered him a suspect in the murder of Michael Castigliola, the man who told John Gotti that Jamesy was selling drugs. A witness to the murder, Jamesy's 70-year-old friend, Tommie LaRuffa, now went up in flames with his house. Jamesy said he believes he knows who torched Tommie and he wasn't him.

Under his new parole terms, Jamesy wasn't supposed to be seen with John Gotti, so he avoided the Bergin and hung out at a small storefront in Brooklyn that Willie Boy Johnson used as the base of a small bookmaking operation.

After a few months, Willie Boy told him that Gotti was wondering why Jamesy wasn't around. "You never go over there. Just go over there and show your face."

Jamesy went, but had only a hello–good-bye conversation with Gotti, who had people waiting in the Our Friends Social Club. A few weeks later, he saw him again, long enough for Gotti to say one of his former drivers, Richard Gomes, had the same parole terms as Cardinali, but occasionally came by anyway.

In fact, two months earlier Gomes had been arrested by FBI agents who found seven-and-a-half kilos of hashish hidden in the closet of a house in Providence, Rhode Island, where he was apprehended.

Indirectly, Jamesy said, he ran at least one more errand for Gotti. He and others brutally beat the owner of a Staten Island bodega— a Hispanic grocery—who was suspected of running a numbers operation in territory that Gambino captain Joseph LaForte considered his.

Jamesy said he got the assignment in a Toys-Я-Us parking lot from Willie Boy, who said LaForte had taken the problem to

Dellacroce, who passed it along to Gotti, who gave it to Angelo, who handed it over to him, Willie Boy.

"Give him a good beating, [but] make sure you don't kill him," said Willie Boy. After all, he added, the bodega owner "was warned to stop."

As Willie Boy watched from a car, the attackers hid in a van until the bodega owner, who had a limp right arm from childhood polio, emerged.

"We went to work on him with sticks and hammers," Jamesy said. "I thought he was dead."

Antonio Collado was unconscious for 28 days. As he blacked out, he dropped a bag containing about $8,000 cash, the day's receipts. Jamesy said the muggers didn't take it, but somebody did—for good.

Years later, Collado said a man who worked for the bodega's former owner had taken a few bets in the store and outside in the parking lot, but was not employed by him. He recalled that prior to the beating two men appeared in his store and demanded that he turn his numbers operation over to them.

"But I said I was no knowing about that thing. That was the other people."

Willie Boy later discussed the beating with Jamesy. "You did great. Everybody knows about it. Neil and Johnny said if you get arrested, everything will be taken care of. This was a personal favor. But you did get a little carried away."

Within days, Neil Dellacroce's son Armond introduced Cardinali to Buddy LaForte, son of the capo for whom he had beat up a polio victim. They met at the San Gennaro feast in Little Italy, where Jamesy had a $100-a-night job as a security man. The feast honors a bishop of Naples martyred by Romans.

"Here is James," Armond said to LaForte. "He did that thing in Staten Island."

"Thank you very much. I appreciate it."

Jamesy did not appreciate Special Agent Paul Hayes, whose testimony had sent him back to prison for 9 months. And when Hayes arranged a visit, Jamesy, who had forsaken cocaine for heroin, decided he would kill him.

"I was going to shoot him for lying at my parole hearing and causing my mother, who was on chemotherapy and dying, to make a trip to Sing Sing in bad weather," Jamesy said.

But on September 30, 1982, Agent Hayes, for the first time, arrived with another agent from Bruce Mouw's Gambino squad and Jamesy could not lure them out of their car to a building where he planned to shoot them. He tried to entice them with a heroin dealer he could "give" them.

In a recorded conversation, Jamesy told the agents he had spent $40,000 on heroin—"I need money, I need drugs"—and had "a nigger and a house with one kilo of pure" to offer.

The agents, trolling for bigger fish, were unmoved.

"I could fill up this back seat with heroin," Jamesy said.

"What if it leads me to Johnny Gotti?" Agent Hayes said.

Jamesy wasn't suspicious like Source BQ. He told Hayes that drugs would never lead to John Gotti. Never.

"If you're not talking about Johnny," Agent Hayes said, I'm not talking to you."

Because Jamesy wasn't hanging with Gotti out of parole paranoia, it fell to Willie Boy to offer a little godfatherly advice now and then.

"Everybody knows your business. You are killing drug dealers," Willie Boy said one day as they drove along an Ozone Park street in Willie's car.

Jamesy said he couldn't deny it.

"Leaving guys in the street. I am not saying that you are wrong."

Jamesy replied that he had to make money somehow.

"I am not going to tell you how to make your money, but you've got to be more secretive."

As to secrecy, Willie Boy cited the example of Anthony Plate. This was the Florida loan shark who was indicted with Dellacroce and who then vanished forever about the time John, Willie Boy, and several newly tanned crew members returned to the club after being away several days. Plate's disappearance had helped Dellacroce get a hung jury.

"You did that?" Jamesy asked.

"Yes."

During the time Angelo was advising John Carneglia to take the Fifth Amendment, he also was advising others on legal matters.

One recipient of Angelo's wisdom was his son John, who was charged with attempted murder after a fight with an unidentified person. Another was Michael Paradiso, a Gambino capo from Brooklyn, who was trying to withdraw a guilty plea.

Paradiso had pleaded guilty in another undercover weapons-buy set up by Diane Giacalone's new informer, Kenneth O'Donnell. He had drafted his own motion to retract the plea, and called Angelo seeking a lawyer to "read it" in court.

"Any lawyer," Paradiso said. "I could use a fucking twenty-two cent lawyer" because "he don't have to do the work 'cause it's all done."

"Yeah, but you don't want to get a fuckin' imbecile to do it either."

"No, but in other words, a guy that we trust, that's all, like ... Marty Light."

Marty Light, a former assistant D.A. in Brooklyn, was a childhood friend of many of the Family men he later represented in private practice. In 1984, after 15 years of trying to keep mobsters out of jail, Light was sentenced to 15 years in prison on a heroin-trafficking conviction. He later testified before the President's Commission on Organized Crime about "doing the right thing" as a "mob lawyer."

The right things included bribing cops and judges, suborning perjury, obtaining secret documents, intimidating witnesses, and, especially, conducting cases according to the wishes of Family leaders rather than the client's.

"It's always the Family comes first," Light said. "What's for the best of the Family is what counts."

Well, not always, Light added. The anti-drug-dealing policy adopted by the Families was routinely violated by "very important members" and "certain crews" searching for scores to replace the ones—such as hijacking, counterfeiting, and other kinds of fraud—that society had gotten better at preventing.

Q.: Why was it violated?
A.: Why? Because it was too profitable ... and the easiest thing for them to do was to deal with drugs.

19

BABANIA MADNESS

I think this drug business will destroy us in the years to come.
—Don Corleone, 1948, in The Godfather

IN LATE FEBRUARY 1982, the FBI–Strike Force team began to strongly suspect that John and Gene Gotti, Angelo Ruggiero, and John Carneglia were dealing drugs on a major-league level.

Their suspicions were based more on physical surveillance and informant reports than wiretapped conversations. Over a few days, FBI agents spotted a known drug dealer leaving Angelo's house and placing a package in the trunk of his car; saw Angelo and Carneglia visiting three known drug dealers in New Jersey; and spied Angelo as he entered a known drugcutting den in Queens.

Agents didn't see a transaction between Carneglia and Crazy Sally Polisi that Polisi later said went down about the same time. Though Polisi had become a big drug dealer, this deal involved real estate. He sold two buildings to Carneglia for $150,000. The buyer assumed a mortgage and gave cash for the equity value—about $90,000, all in twenty-dollar bills, all in a shopping bag.

Though unaware of the deal, agents believed they already had enough information to justify invading Angelo's privacy further by planting listening devices. In April, in an affidavit seeking approval to add bugs to wiretaps, the FBI, for the first time, told a judge that drug dealing was part of its investigation.

The document quoted an unidentified informant, probably Source BQ, as saying that John and Gene, Angelo, and Carneglia were partners in a major drug deal—"a fact which is kept from Gambino boss Paul Castellano due to his directive prohibiting Gambino members from [dealing drugs]." It said heroin dealer Mark Reiter had been evicted from the crew only to "appease" Castellano, but that he was dealing for the partnership. It quoted another informant saying that the partners were harboring Salvatore Ruggiero and also obtaining drugs through him.

A judge approved the bug request on April 5; within 72 hours, agents installed a bug in Angelo's basement den. Later, two others were secreted in the kitchen and dining room. The methods used to accomplish such FBI missions are top secret. Sometimes they involve a ruse—a plumber who isn't; other times, "surreptitious entry."

The affidavit did not cite other details that BQ had recently provided. Though supposedly an outcast, Reiter was staying at Angelo's mother's house. He was driving a Mercedes, had just spent $70,000 in cash for two boats, and was buying a $200,000 house, also with cash.

Source BQ also had told the bureau that he believed Willie Boy Johnson was one of the drug partners, none of whom would actually "touch heroin, because if they are arrested or charged, they would be killed." *Babania* transfers would be handled by non-Family men. BQ's suspicion was rooted partly in the past; in a 1976 trial, while John Gotti was in state prison, Willie Boy was acquitted of heroin-trafficking charges; so was one of his codefendants, Angelo Ruggiero, then an unmade man.

Only days after the first bug was planted, Angelo began to get jittery—an encounter with FBI agents near his house made him wonder if his phone was tapped. He reached out for a private electronics expert, Jack Conroy, a former NYPD detective recommended by Michael Coiro.

Conroy's arrival on the scene was a major plot twist. When he met Angelo, he lied and said he had been an agent for the Eastern District Strike Force. He let on that he was a big inside trader in the mob-intelligence market. He listened as Angelo described how he had been recently pulled over in his car by three men who "looked like fuckin' junkies."

"One guy reaches in, grabs me by the shirt. He's pulling me, I'm pulling him. Another guy uses his head, says, 'Hold it, hold it, we're

FBI agents.' [I say:] You're FBI agents, you'd better identify yourself 'cause you're gonna have a bad problem."

Angelo said one agent apologized that they had mistaken him for someone else, a fugitive, but to satisfy the others, would he mind showing his identification?

"They were looking for something," Conroy wisely said.

"When the car cut me off, I had a telephone number in my hand. In a half-hour I was gonna go call this other guy."

"Okay."

"The telephone number, I swallowed it."

"Oh, good."

Conroy agreed to come back to Angelo's house in a few days with the proper equipment to sweep it for taps and bugs.

Angelo again showed his alarm on April 13, in a call to his mother, who complained about noise on the line and asked:

"What is this, a party line?"

"FBI agents are listening in," her son said.

Despite Angelo's unease and despite obvious efforts to discuss matters in code, drug-dealing clues continued to pile up—mostly via the phone.

The same day that Mrs. Ruggiero talked to her son Angelo, her son Salvatore and another man met in Florida to arrange a heroin deal, an informant later told the FBI. Soon a drug courier was on his way to New Jersey with 13 kilos.

Late the next day, Angelo called his house and spoke to his 17-year-old daughter, Ann Marie, who said "Mark" had come by and left something for him.

"So long, Ann, don't say nothing," Angelo replied.

On April 15, a man named Arnold Squitieri called to say that someone had not yet shown up with their "bankroll." Squitieri was one of the three New Jersey drug dealers with whom Angelo and Carneglia had been meeting.

Two days later, Squitieri called to ask Angelo, "Did you get that furniture yet?" Another man, "Charles," also checked in: "The kid can't make a mortgage payment yet."

Squitieri made plans to come to Angelo's house for dinner with the other two New Jersey dealers, Alphonse Sisca and Oreste Abbamonte. Drug Enforcement Administration (DEA) records show that they and Squitieri all have convictions for multi-kilo deals and are related by marriage. Angelo met Sisca and Abbamonte while incarcerated at Lewisburg.

The night of the dinner, Angelo told his New Jersey pals that he had contacted Bonanno boss-to-be Joseph Massino, who had been indicted recently and gone into hiding, and that "everything was all right." Because so many of its soldiers were flouting the drug-dealing ban, the Bonanno family had just lost its seat on the Commission, the coalition of Family bosses, who, somewhat like a board of directors, set policy for all divisions.

On April 17, Jack Conroy lugged his phony credentials and electronic gadgets into Angelo's house. After conducting tests, he correctly told Angelo that two phones were tapped; but, as to bugs, Conroy pronounced the house clean. Because it knew Conroy was coming, the FBI had shut down the bugs.

Conroy now said he had a source at the telephone company, which is notified when phones are to be legally tapped, and he could find out who authorized the taps. A week later, he told Angelo this would cost $1,000—$800 for his telephone-company source, $200 for him and his partner. No problem, Angelo said.

In a few days, Conroy delivered a bill of goods. He said the taps were legal because of a March 18 federal court order in the Southern District of New York, which is Manhattan and the Bronx. This invention caused Angelo to speculate that he was only peripherally involved in an investigation aimed at someone else. Just in case, however, he told Conroy, who had just suckered Angelo out of $1000, that he would get some other phone numbers for him to check. No problem, Conroy said.

"I want to get your phone checked," Angelo told Gene, who dropped by after Conroy left. "I want to get the kid, Johnny Carneglia's, checked."

Angelo also decided to include John Gotti's phone and later told Conroy to contact his source.

"Why don't you tell him, make a package deal? I'll give you three, four guys and we'll have a package deal instead of charging us [$1,000 each]."

Gimme a price," Conroy said. "Give me a price for the four."

"Five hundred apiece."

"He'll do it ... Yeah, absolutely ... Fuck him."

After the scam was sealed, Gene professed confidence he had not been indiscreet on the phone.

"If they got my phone earlier, then there's nothing, you see, I mean, they might, but, you know who I speak to? There's only one person I speak to on the phone."

"Me," Angelo said.

"That's it. Nobody else calls my house."

Gene wanted to be careful now. "Watch this phone, Angelo."

"Ah, there's nothing I can do now, Genie. What should I do now? I'll make my kids answer the phone, my wife ... Find out who it is, tell them I'll call them back [from a pay phone]."

Angelo was impressed by Conroy's telephone tipster.

"The guy he's got, he's the guy who installed [the tap]. Gene, we got some fuckin', we got some score here. This is a helluva score."

Gene wanted to make sure that brothers were warned. "Tell your brother," he said to Angelo. "Tell my brother."

That day, after Conroy left, the basement bug overheard a Bonanno Family soldier arriving at Angelo's house to discuss "a shit load" of heroin.

"Try not to let too many people know who we are," Angelo said. "I got to speak to my brother at one-thirty today."

"I got thirty things of heroin," the Bonanno man said. "That's why I'm here."

The next day, Angelo told John Carneglia his phone would be checked for a wiretap. He said Conroy had been highly recommended by Michael Coiro.

"That's good," said Carneglia, who now saw Conroy as a long-term source of inside information. "You want to know the truth? This guy will become a hook."

"Oh yeah. I'm fattenin' him up already."

"This guy'll become a hook."

"I asked Mike Coiro today. He said 'Listen ... go to sleep with him.'"

After playing charades with his gadgets, Conroy delivered a report on the other phones: only John Gotti's was tapped. It was another fictional story, but very believable.

Angelo was ecstatic about going to sleep with Conroy. Source BQ told Agent Colgan that Angelo was "bragging" that Conroy had "direct access to court records and telephone company information." He said Angelo, Gene, and Carneglia told him they had "an ex-FBI agent in their pocket."

BQ was worried the ex-agent might know about BQ's secret role, but Colgan told him to forget about it.

Source Wahoo also tipped his control agent, James Abbott, who wrote: "There is a leak somewhere in the federal system and this leak is through [Michael] Coiro. This source does not know where the leak is, but Gotti and his associates get advance information on federal probes."

At the time, the FBI was not certain all of Conroy's claims were false. And though in fact there was no leak—not yet anyway—the bureau decided to pull its two property-crimes agents out of Diane Giacalone's Dellacroce-Gotti investigation.

From the FBI perspective, her investigation had been a bother from the start; it would undoubtedly tread on areas the Angelo team was working, posing possible prosecution problems down the road. Lately, there also had been a cantankerous dispute over whether the FBI or the DEA would take responsibility for managing Kenneth O'Donnell, the informer who told Giacalone that John Gotti gave an armored-car robber money for drugs.

It was suggested that the two agencies share the job, as well as the expenses of O'Donnell. The FBI said an informer as difficult as O'Donnell could not have two masters, and if it paid the bills, it would have to manage him alone. The DEA said no way, because O'Donnell was setting up drug targets in New Jersey. Some members of Giacalone's team felt the FBI just wanted to dominate the case.

The stalemate broke after the bug went in and the FBI investigation turned toward heavy-duty trafficking. The agents assigned to Giacalone were in an untenable spot: They were part of her team, but were not permitted to share the intelligence the surveillance was producing.

Why? In the wake of events at Angelo's house, the FBI was paranoid about "a leak somewhere in the federal system." An FBI participant in the drama recalled: "There was no certainty the information wouldn't be compromised."

Giacalone was insulted and perturbed, and got permission from her boss, Raymond J. Dearie, U.S. attorney for the Eastern District, to carry on against Dellacroce and Gotti without the FBI. Giaca- ' lone, age 32, a former tax attorney, was now boss of the first major organized-crime investigation in the country not involving the FBI.

Eventually, the Brooklyn District Attorney's office gave money to help support Kenneth O'Donnell. But when the money dried up, he became useless; on May 7, 1983, he held up a bank and later was sent to prison.

————————————————

Afraid of telephone taps, but not bugs, Angelo carried on, too. Late in April 1982, he invited into his house one Edward Lino, a Bonanno Family associate and former client of Marty Light.

Lino said Angelo would get "first shot" at an unspecified shipment that was due soon. Angelo said he would take a shot "if it's a very good price [because] I'd just like to [deal in kilos]."

The two men discussed the perils of modern-day heroin dealing. Angelo said the raw product couldn't be imported on planes any longer because the government was using an AWACs plane to identify low-flying aircraft. Even dropping bags of drugs into fields for later pickup had become hazardous.

"Forget about it! They got a helicopter that goes over the fields that picks up human bodies. They're very fucking ... they're up to date on us."

Throughout April, the bugs in Angelo's house produced a record that told the story of a murder plot that perfectly illustrated the death-defying game Ruggiero was playing with heroin.

The story began when two members of another crew "ratted out" Gambino soldier Peter Tambone. They told Neil Dellacroce that "Little Pete"—one of those arrested the year before in the Little Italy dice-game raid—was dealing heroin supplied, off the record, by Salvatore Ruggiero. It's not clear who told Castellano.

A hearing on the charge was not possible—if a "friend of ours" accuses another "good fellow," there is a presumption of guilt. The news upset the Pope, still agitated by the recent presence of agents outside the White House and more concerned than ever he might become the victim of some turncoat caught in a drug vise. He decided it was time to put bite in his bark and proposed to the other three bosses sitting on the Families' ruling council, the Commission, that they murder Little Pete, a 62-year-old grandfather.

Castellano summoned John Gotti to discuss his proposal, according to what Angelo told Edward Lino during one of their heroin sales conferences.

"Johnny, we got a bad problem with Little Pete," Angelo quoted the Pope. "You know that anybody that's straightened out that moves *babania* [gets killed]."

Angelo summoned Little Pete and told him the Commission was meeting to decide whether to kill him.

"How's the weather so far?" Little Pete asked.

"Half and half, Pete."

Angelo was telling Tambone that the commission was deadlocked on Castellano's proposal: two bosses for, two against.

The boss on Castellano's side was Vincent Gigante of the Genovese Family. Like the Castellano branch of the Gambino tree, Gigante's Family was making big money from labor rackets and wasn't as vulnerable to the drug virus.

Two years after the Little Pete episode was played out, John and Gene would tell Source BQ that during the 1970s "Chin" Gigante—a former boxer who used a punch-drunk act to beat a few cases—was used by the Commission to eliminate members who were caught hustling heroin. Those who dealt drugs—but got away with it—were not harmed. In the only attempt at humor found in the FBI memos, Agent Colgan summed up BQ's talk with the Gotti brothers this way: "However, those apprehended and/or convicted ... normally met with individuals associated with Gigante, and these meetings normally were their last."

Vincent Gigante himself had been convicted of dealing heroin in 1959, which was within the grace period for getting out that was established during the Commission meeting at the Apalachin Conference two years earlier. John and Gene told BQ that one of Gigante's first victims was a man named "Consalvo" who was pushed off the roof of a twenty-four-story apartment building in New Jersey. Indeed, police in Fort Lee say this is what happened to one Carmine Consalvo in 1975, while he faced trial on heroin charges. One Edward Lino was the victim's wife's uncle. Three months later, Carmine's brother Francis was found dead in Little Italy; the police said he had been pushed off a five-story building.

At Angelo's house, Little Pete was given some advice.

"Pete, listen to me like a brother," Angelo said. "I'm telling ya, worse comes to worse, get your wife and take off."

Angelo wanted Tambone to get in the wind because he suspected a murder contract would be handed to the Gotti crew—and possibly to him because he was a longtime acquaintance whom Little Pete might trust.

Considering his own activities and Tambone's connection to Salvatore, it was easy to see why Angelo was sympathetic and why he also told Tambone that he was worried about defending him too openly because people might think he was in with him. Even with Edward Lino, who was well aware of the grim incongruity of it all, he cited other reasons for opposing a Little Pete hit.

As it happened, these seemed noble enough. Tambone had claimed that one of the men who ratted him out was dealing drugs, too, and both had actually introduced him to the business. Although there is no evidence it ever happened, Angelo told Lino what would be done to punish this duplicity:

"Me and Johnny are going to whack 'em," Angelo said. "We have to wait a year. We can't do it right now."

The state of Family harmony and justice was enough to make Lino disinterested in being a made man—"What do I even need it for? I'm gonna get myself killed." He added, however, he would feel differently if "Johnny becomes the boss."

Angelo discussed the Little Pete situation somewhat more frankly with Gene. They debated asking Neil to ask Paul to back off, as a "favor" to the crew.

Angelo said John had suggested telling Neil that merely "chasing" Little Pete—kicking him out of the Family—was as good as killing him. But, as Angelo told Gene, this approach had a downside:

"The only thing that your brother made sense [on] was, we ask [Paul] for [that] favor, suppose something happens to us ...?"

"We ..."

"... we're using a favor up."

Gene didn't like any of it. "Whatever happens, whatever the outcome is with Little Pete, it's not good for us." He knew if the favor weren't granted, a contemporary example for drug dealers would be set; if it were, the favor box would be empty. In any case, Gene said Mark Reiter and Arnold Squitieri should be warned immediately. If they get fingered, they better hide, fast. Meantime, "all of us" should get out of the "business" within six months.

Gene also bemoaned having to ask an aging Dellacroce to intercede with Paul; he was used to a more aggressive underboss.

"It's a different story now," Angelo explained. "It's Paul ... him and Chin [Gigante] made a pact. Any friend of ours gets pinched for junk ... they kill 'em ... they're not warning nobody, not telling nobody because they feel the guy's gonna rat. And your brother says he meant that for Neil."

A few days prior to a final Commission meeting, Angelo and Gene discussed the dilemma again—in bitter, defiant terms that suggested a fatal collision someday. Both were fearful and contemptuous of Castellano and made clear their anxiety about killing someone for what the bugs indicated they were doing.

Gene said he could "take a guy out, a worm" because "I understand the rules," but Little Pete should not be killed because "there's a hundred guys that got passes" in similar situations. Gene did not want to be a *babania* "cop."

"So what do I got to do ... become a cop? ... [I]f I nail this guy, I gotta go become a cop because ... they'll nail anybody that steps out of line [and] I'm on order to kill them."

In light of the "conflicting stories" about the extent of Tambone's involvement, Gene wondered how the Gotti crew would appear to others if it "killed a fuckin' dear friend of theirs."

Gene was wondering a lot. He said Castellano, who inherited control of profitable labor-union rackets from Gambino, was against drugs only because "he never had to struggle for a quarter in his life."

Angelo noted that his heroin contact, Edward Lino, had recently "declared" himself off the record on drugs to Neil.

Gene's response to this news was remarkable for its irony—a soldier whose Family regarded labor unions only as places to plunder now recommended a union. For Family soldiers. "More guys like us should all come forward. All of them ... they should all do that. I wish they would start a fucking union."

Once organized, the soldiers should boycott all other operations: bookmaking, loan-sharking, whatever. Then, Gene added in his own ironic way, union racketeering is all the Caesars would have left—"because that's all they got, and [even those] will go [eventually]."

Angelo said he meant to tell Neil this: "I don't know what John Gotti wants to do, but I'm gonna tell you what me and Gene Gotti want to do, and this kid, Johnny Carneglia ... Anybody that we have with us, we're looking to take off record with us. As of now. Forget about Little Pete."

"Between you and me," Gene replied, "if this guy gets hurt, you listen to me, Paul becomes more hard-nosed about it. We could start wars ... we can't turn the tide on everything."

Gene's last remark brought out the Brutus in the forum of Angelo, who said: "Maybe it's time to turn the tide."

No tapes of John Gotti saying what he wanted to do were made; his exact role is unknown, except to a silent few. There were hints from others' lips, however, that he wanted the Pope to back off, too, though he wasn't as outspoken as his best friend and most influential brother.

The Tambone tension arose during a period of brotherly tension, as Gene illustrated in a remark to Angelo later that same day: "I'm not basin' my life around him. I'm not basin' my life around his fuckin' gambling."

The day before Angelo and Gene's second heart-to-heart talk, Angelo told Edward Lino that Chin Gigante might reverse himself and oppose Paul on the Commission; the former boxer had a soft spot for Tambone. This was a seemingly harmless forecast, but in speaking of Commission business to an unmade man, Angelo was violating a Family rule against even mentioning the Commission to anyone but soldiers. It was a major infraction, committed on FBI tape, and it would have devastating consequences throughout the Crime Capital.

On April 30, FBI Special Agent Arthur Ruffels called on Tambone to warn him he might be killed. Little Pete tuned in the Angelo channel for another weather bulletin.

All clear now, Angelo said.

Angelo had just come from a mercy mission to Neil's. Neil had told him to do with Little Pete whatever he wanted, it was now okay with Paul. Despite the speculation about Gigante, the Commission had deadlocked again. In a test case, the High Court of the Families couldn't issue a drug-dealing opinion—because the Family with the tiebreaking vote had been expelled for it.

Even so, Neil had left no doubt where he stood, Angelo said. If anyone around him—Angelo, the Gotti brothers, even his son Armond—got involved in narcotics, Neil would kill them, unless there were extenuating circumstances, such as a police frameup.

Angelo informed Little Pete what his punishment would be. He would have to lie to Frank DeCicco, who was then in the Pope's corner, and say he never touched heroin, only money. He would have to endure "a riot act" from John, but this would be only "a formality." After that, Little Pete would have to stay away for at least six months, although he would be able to have coffee with Angelo. Occasionally.

As he put out the Tambone fire, Angelo stoked his own. Edward Lino, the unauthorized recipient of Commission updates, was suspected of supplying only part of the fuel.

"Did you get an answer on these, uh, Quaaludes?" Angelo asked Lino on April 26.

"Yeah."

"Could you do anything if I got 'H'?"

"Yeah, I got a few good guys handling poppy."

"Call my brother, call him collect."

20

FOUR SOULS ON BOARD

ON MAY 6, 1982, across the George Washington Bridge in New Jersey, fugitives Salvatore and Stephanie Ruggiero awoke in the suburban home they had secretly leased and prepared to drive to a local airport to catch a 10 A.M. flight to Orlando.

In addition to Florida, Pennsylvania, and New Jersey, the couple had hidden out in Columbus, Ohio, for two of their seven years on the run. Lately, they believed the Garden State was as safe as any other. Salvatore, who had used the name Stephen Terri, had made several flights to Florida recently. He always flew in a Learjet he leased with a drug partner, Alfred Dellentash.

Dellentash had wanted the plane this day for a flight to the Bahamas, but deferred to his partner. Salvatore, age 36, wanted to size up a fast-food franchise near Disneyworld that he was thinking of adding to his *babania* empire, or so Dellentash later said.

"Okay, time en route—two hours," the Lear pilot told the Teterboro Airport tower prior to takeoff. "Four souls on board."

Pilot George Morton, age 38, had flown Salvatore south many times, usually on short notice, like today. Sheri Day, age 24, a last-minute substitute, was the copilot. He had 7,000 hours of flight time, she 1,550. The Lear "was flown only in conjunction with Mr. Dellentash's business," a federal document says.

It was a beautiful day to fly. The forecast was for clear skies all the way, and once the Lear climbed to 41,000 feet the Ruggieros had 700 square miles of unobstructed viewing along the curvature of the Atlantic seaboard. The couple had contemplated surrendering, but Michael Coiro was unable to negotiate agreeable terms, so they stayed in the wind. With three homes and piles of cash—for Christmas, Sal had given family members $50,000 in Kruggerands—life wasn't so bad, although the couple's two kids were being raised a little differently than other children.

Near noon, it was time to begin the descent toward Orlando International Airport. The Lear was over the Atlantic 35 miles southeast of Savannah, Georgia. Morton radioed the federal air-traffic control facility in Jacksonville, which gave him permission to descend to 39,000 feet. He disconnected the Learjet N100TA's automatic altitude hold and begin flying manually.

"One hundred tango alpha descending now," copilot Day told the Jacksonville tower. A tape of this transmission later revealed a high-pitched sound in the background.

In the cockpit, Morton and Day were startled by the sound and two red lights indicating problems with cabin pressure and Mach overspeed. The second warned that the Lear was going too fast for the descent pattern.

Radar instruments later showed that shortly after the alarm was sounded, the Lear pulled out of its descent and climbed sharply to 41,000 feet, where it began to descend again. At 37,000, it shot back up, and then down again, like a paper airplane tossed across a room. Morton had lost control.

For the next minute, at an increasingly steep angle, the plane with four terrified souls on board plunged in the wind toward the sea until it struck water nose first at shattering speed. Parts of the plane and its victims were recovered two hours later in placid waters. An investigation suggested that the cockpit alarms came from a malfunctioning instrument, causing Morton to make unnecessary adjustments that brought on the fatal dive.

The tragedy had many consequences, which soon surfaced on the bugs in a house now stricken with grief and greed.

Only three weeks earlier, another plane Dellentash leased had been seized in Mississippi with 1,000 pounds of pot aboard. Now, in New York, Dellentash was contacted and told he'd lost a plane and a partner. He in turn called Angelo and within hours, Angelo, Gene, and John Carneglia arrived at Sal's hideout and, says the FBI, removed all valuables and evidence linking the dead man to them or to drugs.

The next day, Michael Coiro, mulling semiretirement in Florida, flew up from the Sunshine State to console Angelo and help him clear up Salvatore's affairs. He chatted briefly with Frank DeCicco at Angelo's house.

"Gene found the ... heroin," Coiro said.

Meanwhile, Source BQ told the FBI the news. Agents got a warrant to search the already sanitized home for drugs and evidence of Salvatore's assets, which the government hoped to seize as the proceeds of an illegal enterprise. Agents began serving grand-jury subpoenas on the Gurino brothers, Sal's in-laws, and others.

The bugs overheard Angelo saying how difficult it was accepting his brother's death because the body was in "fuckin' pieces." He added: "If he would have been shot in the head and [they] found him in the streets—that's part of our life, I could accept it."

A memorial service was held in Howard Beach at Angelo's mother's house. Afterward, Angelo said his late younger brother "had a pretty good, nice sendoff. I mean, my whole fucking family [and] ... all the wiseguys in my Family were there."

Source Wahoo checked in May 10. He said Angelo—who had scheduled a secret rendezvous with Salvatore for that day—was making arrangements for the welfare of his brother's children.

Angelo was making many arrangements. On May 11, he and another man discussed Sal Ruggiero's "last load": six kilos of pure heroin that had previously arrived from Florida. " ... [H]e gave me three" and "I've already sold half-another," Angelo said.

On May 12, as he agreed to sell part of the last load for $240,000, Angelo told the buyer that he was not new to the business and was continuing his brother's "thing."

"I have to, I, you know, I got to keep doing it."

In the afternoon, Angelo got together with Gene and Michael Coiro to discuss the grand jury's interest in Salvatore's assets.

"They're going to think [Salvatore's] empire was turned over to me ... now [that] I'm taking over," Angelo said.

"They gotta prove it," the lawyer said.

"We keep our mouths shut, they're gonna say nothing," said Gene. "But see if this gets around that we're just talking like this, they're definitely going to put it [together]."

This same day, Coiro said John Gotti was angry at him for not visiting him since coming up from Florida. As Coiro told the story, Gene became incredulous.

"So I said, 'John, I was over there [at Angelo's] where I thought I had to be, doing what I had to do. I didn't know you were unaware of what was going on.'"

"You believe he's unaware of all this, huh?"

"I figure he knew about it, Genie."

Coiro said he explained to John that he knew it was "my duty and obligation" to visit John first—then Angelo and Gene—when he came to town. But he figured John would realize "at a time like this" Coiro would have to stay by Angelo.

Coiro said he tried to explain "you don't stand on the ceremony that we had before, that you expect me to come and see you first."

"So what did he say about that?"

"He said ... that we're leaving him out. We're doing everything without him."

"Why didn't he come where we were? Where were we? We were somewhere we weren't supposed to be?"

"I said, 'We didn't hide anything. We weren't doing anything without you.' I said, 'Right now Angelo is very, very much upset.'"

Coiro said John replied he understood Angelo was upset, but that Angelo and Gene were "leaving me to do all the work." Coiro said John recalled that the day his Frank was buried, he had to attend a sitdown.

At this, Gene's voice rose. "What the fuck does he want? So he shouldn't have went!"

"He was trying to say that Angelo should lay aside his grief."

"All I can say, Mike, is the man's got some fucking pair of balls. And I'll tell ya, the best guy to justify things. And it don't make no sense. It makes ya dopey and stupid about anybody that leaves their own family [on the day of a burial]."

During his career, Michael Coiro had blurred the line separating a lawyer from his clients many times, but now he would take a giant step across it.

"If I get some money, will you hold it?" Angelo asked.

"Yeah," Coiro said.

"Nobody is to know but us ...," Gene said. "You're not our lawyer, you're one of us as far as we're concerned."

"I know it, Gene, and I feel that way ... "

Over the next few days, the plot to sell Sal's last load and conceal his assets thickened. Angelo and Coiro discussed inventing a story to hide cash that Sal had paid for real estate. Angelo met another man to discuss selling the property to someone for "two hundred and fifty thousand dollars, no conditions." Angelo and Coiro urged three women—Stephanie Ruggiero's mother and two other relatives—to take the Fifth Amendment before the grand jury.

Stephanie's mother, who had visited her daughter's hideouts, was frantic. She feared the probe would jeopardize her husband's police pension. The two men tried to assuage her anxiety, and Angelo's.

"Don't worry," Angelo said. "If your lawyer knows the law, he's gonna tell you, 'Don't answer no questions.' Unless they give you immunity."

As Stephanie's mother pondered what to do, Angelo rambled on like the jailhouse lawyer he was:

"[If] they give you immunity, you tell them, 'I see my daughter every year' ... if they don't give you immunity, take the Fifth Amendment ... walk out and go home."

Later, when Gene was told what the two men had discussed with the in-laws, he asked Angelo:

"You sure these people weren't wired up?"

"[If] they were wired up, they gonna get their heads cut off."

Angelo was in a nasty mood because he had just been told—by one of his brother's heroin partners—that Salvatore had made another half-million in the last year, and that some people who owed money to Sal were now saying Sal owed them.

"My brother don't owe a fucking person," he growled.

Angelo said Sal had made much more than that amount in the past year, and he would "wind up breaking a lot of guys," if Sal's debtors didn't tell the truth.

"I don't want nobody lying to me," Angelo told one of Sal's couriers. "If I find out anybody's lying ... if they're holding back from my brother ... I promise you this. You are gonna die the same way my brother died—in pieces."

Summing up, Angelo demanded what he would soon try to hide from his "Uncle" Neil and their Uncle Paulie: "All I'm asking for is the truth."

Two weeks after Jack Conroy said John Gotti's phone was tapped, Gotti went to Florida. Consequently, the FBI omitted his name from the list of people it was citing each month as targets of "oral inter-ceptions." Although he had not been taped talking about drugs, he was still named as a suspected member of a conspiracy to distribute heroin, cocaine, and "digs"—slang for the synthetic downer Quaa-lude. Maybe it was because Source BQ kept insisting to the FBI: "Ruggiero is Gotti's main worker and a conduit for all information and money for him."

During this same period, BQ said: "Gotti is so powerful he has to do very little to maintain his position." Source Wahoo, the man more friendly with Gotti, rarely gave reports implying any criticism. For instance, at the time of BQ's report, Wahoo merely said that Gotti was being "groomed" to replace Dellacroce or even Cas-tellano.

Near the middle of May, Angelo doubted the completeness of Conroy's intelligence. If he was only peripherally involved in a Southern District of New York investigation of someone else, Angelo wondered, why did it seem like he was being followed all the time? Angelo asked Michael Coiro to make inquiries about any investigations in the Eastern District, and on May 21, Coiro said forget about it.

"Your guy says nothing is going on there?" Angelo replied. "This is fucking amazing."

Coiro said the Eastern District's investigation was nothing more than IRS agents snooping around for Salvatore's assets—no big deal.

"Mike, listen, you've always come through before, so I really believe ya."

Hedging their bets, Angelo, Coiro, and Gene decided to seek more intelligence and hatched a plan to buy a secret Gambino Family report from an unidentified police official on Long Island. They debated who should be told, if anything damaging turned up.

Gene said Angelo must decide who to tell the news to—if it was bad news. "It's his decision, he's an assistant ... captain."

"Big Ange," Coiro said.

"Big Ange Ruggiero," Gene chimed, "associate of captain, pow-erhouse captain John Gotti."

The next day, several of Salvatore's former business partners and nominees visited Angelo to discuss how to thwart the grand jury. Before that, they reviewed the gold-chain market.

"You bought busted chains, right? Chances are they get ripped off," one man said to Angelo.

"Yeah. The store up in Harlem does best."

"Yeah, I bet."

"Got all them fuckin' junkies and everything."

The men talked as if the grand-jury battle were no big deal, and over the next few days Angelo dove deeper into the heroin cesspool.

On May 30, he told John Carneglia that two other suppliers wanted to supply them, but if they turned out to be all talk and no dope, at least he and Carneglia had $450,000 in cash to shop around for other sources. That night they discussed hiking the price they would charge a distributor—William Cestaro, brother of Philip Cestaro, who ran the Cozy Corner Bar, allegedly for John Gotti. Sources Wahoo and BQ had also said William helped manage the Queens disco they had said Gotti partially owned.

"Angelo is taking over Sal's business," Source Wahoo told Agent Abbott the next day.

The heroin arbitrageur also was a venture capitalist, and he was soon heard making plans to cop six more kilos. On June 11, Gene dropped Angelo and Carneglia off at LaGuardia Airport. Using aliases, the pair flew to Palm Beach to meet one of Sal's friends. Back home the next day, Angelo told Gene they were assured delivery of another load. It hardly needed saying, but Angelo was intoxicated by the color green.

"There's a lot of profit in heroin," he said.

On June 18, the shipment arrived. Angelo told Gene he had just "picked up eight things," six kilos from agents of "them guys" in Florida and two from another supplier. A day later, he learned his efforts to badger his in-laws into silence were starting to unwind; one relative had come clean in the grand jury about her contacts with the fugitives over the years. It was bad news for Angelo—it meant the government might get a better line on Sal's assets—but Angelo was a runaway freight train and on the very next day he agreed to sell two kilos.

The exchange of money for 97 percent pure heroin took place on June 23 as government agents watched. William Cestaro and a man named Salvatore Greco were arrested; years earlier, Tony Roach Rampino had wanted to "get close" to the "Greco brothers," who were "big dope guys" from Canada—and now Angelo had. A week later, however, the FBI dropped the charges against them to avoid disclosing how extensive its eavesdropping had been. Cestaro, age 49, and Greco, age 51, were "mules"—small fry—and the heroin was off the street.

Agents also might have hoped that letting the mules out of the corral would tickle the boys. But Angelo hid out in his mother's house, certain of a security breach and now as worried as his in-laws about the grand jury. It's not known what happened to Cestaro and Greco, but they have not been seen since.

Predictably by now, the FBI's principal Bergin informants reacted a little differently to the arrests. Source Wahoo said Gotti returned from Florida and "jumped all over" Gene for his "close allegiance" to Angelo and "John's suspicion they are involved in narcotics activities." John was "outraged" that those arrested were hanging "around the club and unknown to him had been dealing drugs." BQ, on the other hand, said John and Angelo "definitely back large-scale narcotics transactions ... they use Willie Boy Johnson, Carneglia, and others." BQ said Willie Boy had side deals with Mark Reiter, and Wahoo added that Johnson had recently assaulted a loan-shark customer.

Wahoo and BQ did agree the arrests were a surprise and triggered inquiries by Angelo into possible buggings.

Somehow, sometime in late June, the Bergin crew finally demonstrated it could get accurate information. Angelo obtained a pasted-together version of the last of the FBI's six Angelo electronic-surveillance affidavits. The notes told him that Jack Conroy was not all he cracked himself up to be and that Coiro was not as wired into the Eastern District as he imagined. Critically, the FBI working papers confirmed the depth of the probe, and that it was supported by a three-bug invasion of his home.

I am a dead man, was among Angelo's many thoughts, said Source Wahoo. This memo went into the FBI file:

"Source advised Angelo Ruggiero is scared to death ... because he has been lying systematically to Big Paul and Neil insofar as he has constantly told them that he is not dealing in drugs by himself, but is merely cleaning up the loose ends of his brother's narcotics operation ... [if] they learn he was [lying] it is quite likely that Angelo might be hit."

Though Angelo thought Conroy had been merely incompetent, not insincere, Conroy suffered an attack of thanatophobia, too, and moved away. Much later, Conroy did surface briefly—as a cooperating trial witness against Angelo, which was when Quack-Quack finally knew he had been had.

At the time, Wahoo said that shortly after the FBI affidavit was obtained, "Angelo advised the Bergin ... that three bugs had been found in his house." In fact, Angelo had not found the bugs, but they were shut down because Angelo was not home to be overheard.

Even so, the leak astounded the FBI, which began investigating itself and everyone in the Eastern District with access to the affidavits. Three years later, agents would find the notes in the home of Anthony Moscatiello, pal of the brothers Ruggiero. The mystery of how the papers got to his house in Howard Beach has never been solved; neither has the mystery of why Moscatiello would bother keeping them around.

Although the government would not arrest Angelo and the others for more than a year, the greedy game was up, or so it seemed. "Angelo thinks he is a fugitive and is acting it," said a Wahoo bulletin. "Angelo is in hiding," added BQ.

John believed trouble was imminent, too, and avoided the Bergin. Wahoo, possibly unaware of the Commission's inability to reach a decision on the Tambone case, said, "Because it is policy to issue contracts on anyone charged with narcotics violations, Gotti feels he will most likely get instructions from both Neil Dellacroce and Castellano ... to carry out a contract murder on his good friend Angelo."

Despite all the danger, Angelo ventured outside at least once—to make another score, the FBI says.

In August, agents learned a major heroin deal was afoot; they followed the trail to a Long Island motel, where Angelo was registered in Moscatiello's name. They saw Quack-Quack, Carneglia, and others meet in a lounge and exchange envelopes. Still building a case, the agents did not intervene; afterward, Angelo and Carneglia decided to lay low in Florida.

Gotti hung out in Little Italy, waiting for the other shoe. He told Wahoo he feared he might be arrested on some cooked-up conspiracy charge. Wahoo understood because he had just reported that "John's man," Anthony Rampino, was peddling and using heroin.

"Source advised that at the present time he feels [the entire crew] with the exception of John Gotti have dealt or are presently dealing in drugs." Wahoo didn't say if this meant he had or was; he and BQ, who didn't know about one another, had been told that their FBI romances did not entitle them to commit crimes, except maybe for a little bookmaking.

Wahoo's opinion on the impact of the Angelo affair on Gotti contained a caveat: "Gotti's position has not been diminished or enhanced ... however, [if] Dellacroce died or is imprisoned, Gotti will not have the support he now enjoys ... Neil is a 'street guy' with power while Big Paul Castellano is not as streetwise."

Angelo, of course, was Gotti's biggest booster, despite the behind-the-back barbs. In June, two weeks before the heroin dam broke, he was sure John had emerged untarnished by Little Pete's tie to Salvatore Ruggiero. This was evident when Angelo told Gambino capo Robert DiBernardo about "a little rumor" he had heard:

"The rumor came right from [*consigliere*] Joe Gallo, that uh, they spoke. Paul, Neil, and Joe Gallo. They said that every Family has groomed or has put somebody on the side in case something happens to them, and we're the only Family that hasn't been doing this. And Johnny's name came up three times, Joe Gallo told me. He says, 'Tell Johnny to be cool.'"

DiBernardo, a loan shark and pornographer, was favorably impressed.

"And Joe Gallo is not a bullshit artist," Angelo said.

"Will Johnny give Angelo [Gallo's] position?"

"That I don't know. I believe in my heart that position is going to [Carlo Gambino's son] Tommy."

Angelo spread the little rumor a few days before he and Gotti, sporting a Florida tan, were spotted by U.S. Secret Service agents and NYPD detectives eating at the Sheraton Centre Hotel in Manhattan. President Reagan was coming to the hotel that day to address a state Republican party meeting, and the president's protectors told the pair they would feel more comfortable if they left beforehand.

"Gotti and Ruggiero are extremely proud of the fact that they intimidated the Secret Service and the NYPD as being potentially harmful to the President," BQ's Agent Colgan wrote.

Soon, the men from Howard Beach, especially Angelo, would feel differently about posing a potential threat to the man from Washington, D.C.—and all because Angelo was taped talking about Commission politics to an unmade man, Edward Lino.

When he spoke of the Commission while updating the Little Pete murder plot for Lino, Angelo caused hearts to stop—first among the Gambino-squad agents and then all the way up the line to FBI headquarters and the Justice Department in Washington. No one had captured the word on tape before; until this point, the Commission existed only on the word of informants cutting deals. The breakthroughs invited a RICO conspiracy attack on the Crime Capital bosses. Angelo's indiscretion would be used to help establish probable cause to go "up" on many, notably Paul Castellano, and, later, a dying Neil Dellacroce.

Over the summer, a battle plan was drawn up. One of its architects was Associate Attorney General Rudolph W. Giuliani, who came from humble beginnings in Brooklyn. He would be going home soon, as U.S. attorney for the Southern District. But before he did, he took part in a cabinet meeting that primed Reagan for a major announcement on October 14, timed to benefit GOP candidates in the midterm elections of 1982.

Then, at the summit of his popularity, Reagan strode into the Justice Department auditorium and, in remarks later given to the press, told department employees:

"It comes down, in the end, to a simple question we must ask ourselves: What kind of people are we if we continue to tolerate in our midst an invisible, lawless empire? Can we honestly say America is the land with justice for all if we do not now exert every effort to eliminate this confederation of professional criminals, this dark, evil enemy within?"

In the next few months, Congress approved plans to add 1,000 agents and 200 prosecutors. Ominously for the Families, the Justice Department removed a cap on electronic-surveillance applications, once limited to 100 a year. The value of electronic warfare had just been demonstrated; the Angelo bugs had thrown a light on the dark, evil enemy within.

Days before Reagan spoke, someone fired shots inside the Cozy Corner Bar, alleged center of the Bergin gambling empire. A man was shot nine times, but lived. It was the second attempt on Edward

Maloney's life within four months—and, amazingly, both times he was hit twice in the head.

"Enough is enough," Maloney said on his way to the FBI.

Maloney began in crime at age 15 after running away from home, and was one of two survivors of a gang that snatched loan sharks and bookmarkers. He outlived James McBratney—the man John and Angelo killed in 1973—and three others. Maloney says he did not take part in the murder of Carlo Gambino's nephew, although "my name popped up" because McBratney was a friend.

The FBI suggested to Maloney that John Gotti, settling the last debit on an old account, had issued a murder contract, and his book-maker Philip Cestaro had aided the second attempt by tipping off the gunman when Maloney came into the Cozy Corner.

Maloney agreed to wear a body wire. In meetings with Cestaro, who was known as "Philly Broadway," Maloney did not determine if Gotti was behind the plot—in fact, the hit had upset Gotti, Cestaro said; gunplay was not good for business in "Johnny's bar."

"You know how Gotti got his wings?" Maloney asked.

"I didn't know him [then]."

"This guy got his wings for whacking out a friend of mine, Jimmy McBratney, an Irish kid, fucking Irish kid from Staten Island. Gotti was the last fucking guy he saw in his life."

"I know he ain't involved," Cestaro said.

Maloney tried several more times to get Cestaro to bite; each time the answer as to a Gotti-backed plot was no. However, after the men warmed to each other and Maloney asked Philly Broadway to help him buy drugs, the answer was yes.

John Gotti: What me worry?
(Courtesy New York Daily News*)*

Gotti smiles.
(Courtesy New York Daily News*)*

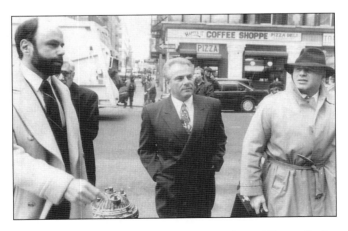

Gotti is sandwiched by Gerald Shargel (left) and Bruce Cutler,
the lawyers who gave him his last year of freedom by beating
the Manhattan assault charges.
(Courtesy New York Daily News*)*

Andrew Maloney, former West Point boxer and U.S. Attorney who sent Gotti away to prison for life.
(Courtesy New York Daily News*)*

Lisa Gastineau, the Rainbow Room woman whose Sinatra-concert plans were derailed by Gotti's arrest.
(Courtesy New York Daily News*)*

Brother Peter Gotti laughs and "adopted son" Lewis Kasman snarls outside Brooklyn Federal Court in 1992.
(Courtesy New York Daily News*)*

John Gotti, in a different fashion, circa 1975.
(Government photo)

Gene Gotti, left, and family friend Joseph Massino,
boss of the Bonanno crime family, are in step outside
Brooklyn Federal Court.
(Courtesy New York Daily News*)*

Willie Boy Johnson: Boxer, bookmaker, and much more.
(Government photo)

Diane Giacalone: Assistant U.S.
attorney.
(Courtesy New York Daily News*)*

Bruce Mouw, supervisor of the FBI
"Gambino squad" that got Gotti.
(Courtesy GangLandNews.com)

December 16, 1985: The body of the boss, Paul Castellano, on the sidewalk. The body of the underboss, Tommy Bilotti, in the street.
(Courtesy New York Daily News)

"Uncle Neil" Dellacroce gets an earful from Angelo Ruggiero.
(Government photo)

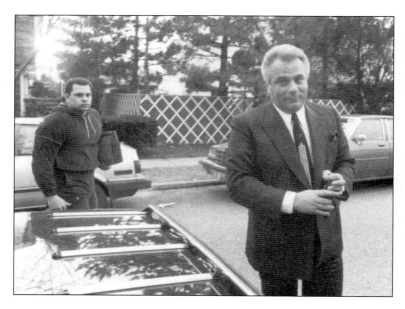

Junior follows in dad's footsteps on March 13, 1987, a few hours after dad beat the case in Brooklyn Federal Court.
(*Courtesy* Newsday)

(sketch) Gotti looks away as Gravano stares him down in this drawing of their courtroom confrontation by sketch artist Ruth Pollack.

Gotti, capo Jackie D'Amico (left), and Frank LoCascio's son Salvatore take in the fights at Madison Square Garden.
(*Courtesy* New York Daily News)

The victorious prosecution team. In the rear are prosecutor James Orenstein (left) and FBI agent George Gabriel. In front, from left to right, are prosecutors Patrick Cotter and Laura Ward, paralegal Karen Kenny, and lead prosecutor John Gleeson.
(*Courtesy* GangLandNews.com)

Salvatore Gravano, when he was John Gotti's right hand man, and as he autographs a copy of his book about his life before going back to federal prison for drug dealing.

(Government photos)

21

ON THE CARPET WITH BIG PAUL

The government is looking to make us be one tremendous conspiracy.
— *Paul Castellano, May 31, 1983*

IN THE SPRING OF 1983, Death Hill was occupied by the FBI. Agents had a bunker near the White House; after a four-month campaign, they had broken in surreptitiously. The Pope was bugged now, too, thanks to Angelo and the Reagan White House.

John Gotti had visited Castellano many times during the previous year, but he never turned up—in person, anyway—on the White House bug, probably because he suspected that Death Hill was a place to avoid. During one of his 1982 visits, he and John Carneglia had spotted agents and, afterward, Gotti and Angelo speculated that the agents were up to more than routine surveillance.

Though suspicion was everywhere and thunder was coming from all directions, the Angelo-bugs tension had slipped away as the months had passed by without an indictment. Angelo and Carneglia had come home, ready to try and ride out the storm if the truth was ever washed ashore. Neil was sick with heart trouble, and Gotti—as he had with Carmine Fatico a decade earlier—was picking up the slack, and underboss experience.

Castellano had no special fondness for Gotti—now, at last, the Bergin crew's official boss. He did respect Gotti's forcefulness and had used him, as Thomas Bilotti was heard describing it, "to lay down the law" to a union official who needed a lesson in the Family code. The Pope regarded himself as a businessman who regrettably associated with unsavory people out of loyalty to the past. He was happier sitting down with a man like Frank Perdue, whose company supplied chickens to the East Coast, and discussing how to improve Perdue's business.

Sources Wahoo and BQ formed opinions in a Bergin context. Except for BQ—once in 1985—neither ever indicated that anyone besides Gotti was in line for the top spot. Neither was privy to the Castellano context, however, and thus they did not know two men were at the White House frequently: Thomas Gambino and Thomas Bilotti, who also regarded themselves as businessmen.

One day, Gambino—Carlo's oldest son—brought Castellano a problem involving Gotti, Angelo, and Marty and Tommy of Mercury Pattern Service. The firm was still paying large-size "shirts" to Angelo, who, after a raise, was now on the payroll for $700 a week. As Uncle Paul told Nephew Tommy what to do, it sounded like a boss tutoring his intended successor.

Beforehand, they chatted about a remarkable book just out— *A Man of Honor,* an autobiography by Joseph Bonanno, one of the five original Crime Capital bosses, written long after he had retired and moved to Arizona. Bonanno, whose father was an old-world don in Sicily, said his noble "tradition" had been corrupted by a new-world worship of money; soldiers born in America were reckless and impatient. Bonanno also wrote about the Commission, which was something he, like Angelo, would live to regret.

Castellano regarded the book as "interesting reading" because he knew some of its characters; he said Bonanno had accurately described the landmark conference of Families at upstate Apalachin in 1957 and the no-drug rule adopted there. But he was shocked that Bonanno didn't seem to realize the consequences of writing in such detail about the Commission.

"He don't know what the government is looking for. The government is looking to make us be one tremendous conspiracy. And anybody that they know who [is] a member, they can lock him up on conspiracy ... this guy's explaining [the Commission]!"

Astute prophecy aside, the Pope listened as Gambino, a power in the garment district, explained the Mercury Pattern problem. The owners had borrowed $50,000 from Angelo—"backed by Gotti"—after Marty got out of prison in 1980. Earlier, they had borrowed from a Luchese Family shylock, who "forgave" the loan when "the Jew went to the can." Now, however, the shylock had learned that Marty and Tommy were back in business and paying Angelo; he felt it was only right they start paying him again.

"So, it could get sticky, you know?" Gambino said.

Castellano asked if the Luchese soldier was beginning to really "push" for his money.

Gambino said he was, which meant that the shylock might use his Family's union influence to incite an organizing movement at Mercury Pattern, which was paying the Gambino Family to keep a union out. In the garment trade, as with trucking, sanitation, and construction, the Families always worked it both ways.

"Ya gotta bring it to a head," Gambino added, "because [the Mercury owners are] borrowing from Gotti."

Castellano said the situation would have to be approached delicately because "you know, [we could be] opening up a can of worms and you want to make sure you don't open it too much." He didn't want to stir the union pot, so he decreed that the Mercury Pattern owners take on the first shylock as a "partner" and take less out of the business. However, the Luchese man must understand that Mercury would have to keep paying Angelo and Gotti, too.

The competing loan sharks, Uncle Paul added, should be told: "You get some of yours; they get some of theirs."

Castellano told Gambino to spread the word, and if the terms were not satisfactory, to be sure to tell the participants to "talk to Paul" before taking any action. "Get to Paul some way, anyway you can," he told his nephew to say.

Just then, future underboss and murder victim Thomas Bilotti came into the dining room—just off the kitchen, where the bug was—and helped to demonstrate why Paul, despite his misgivings, went to sleep with the Gotti crew. It was more than its leader's skill in intimidating balky union officials; it was the money the crew seemed to attract.

As the White House bug recorded the sound of rubber bands popping off bundles, Bilotti began counting cash—its history and purpose were not made clear.

"There's only twenty-seven [thousand] there. So I got to pick up three more tomorrow morning. John gave us twelve because he's dealing with it. Genie gave us ten and this is your four thousand.

"I better hold on to it," Castellano said.

"You want me to do it, Paul?" asked Bilotti, a papal favorite, but not in the same way as Gambino, who was blood. "Here, I'll do it."

A different FBI–Strike Force team out of the Eastern District had installed the White House bug as part of a conspiracy case against the entire Gambino hierarchy—bosses and capos. In fact, all over the Crime Capital, similar teams were investigating each Family.

While carrying out his duties for Neil, John Gotti kept looking over his shoulder, expecting an indictment, according to Source Wahoo. His worry was shared by Michael Coiro, who knew the Angelo tapes were dynamite. "Mike is drinking a lot," Wahoo said.

Angelo, however, was spending $40,000 on remodeling his home and saying "the bugs in his house were a bunch of bullshit and nothing is coming." His confidence would later seem ridiculous, even to his confederates. In court one day, John Carneglia would toss off this line: Dial any seven numbers and there's a fifty-fifty chance Angelo will answer the phone.

Early in 1983, Angelo was overheard on another bug, in a Brooklyn restaurant, where he was having lunch and spreading poison, by trashing Castellano and talking about murder.

"To me, he bad-mouths you," Angelo told Gennaro Langella, acting boss of the Colombo Family. "He bad-mouths everybody ... he bad-mouths his own Family."

Langella, who thought Castellano had cheated his Family out of a $50,000 construction-industry payoff, said that he had predicted that "Neil and Johnny will die" in a Gambino war.

This was another opening for the Brutus in Angelo. He said he had spoken to Neil, who had sided with Langella on the payoff dispute and was angry at Castellano. He said Neil regretted ignoring the advice of Langella's boss to kill Castellano back in 1976.

"It's a fucking shame," Angelo said.

"Most of [Castellano's] guys got guns, and you know he ain't going easy." Langella replied.

"No. I know, and Neil knows it and Johnny knows it. If anything happens to Johnny and Neil, I'll come see you. I don't trust nobody else."

"I don't blame you. It's not a nice way to live today."

Langella was currently keeping the chair warm for Carmine Persico, the boss whose advice Neil didn't take. An incident involving Carmine's son soon showed how seriously some took advice on the no-drugs issue.

Alphonse Persico, age 29, was arrested on heroin-conspiracy charges along with Colombo soldier Anthony Augello. The Family felt Persico was dragged into the case by Augello, who was told to do the right thing. Augello, age 59, said good-bye to his family from a pay phone and then fatally shot himself in the head.

In August, the Angelo bugs finally came home to roost. Angelo, Gene Gotti, John Carneglia, and Mike Coiro were arrested pending return of an indictment. Five others—the Gurino brothers of Arc Plumbing, Edward Lino, Anthony Moscatiello, and Mark Reiter—were arrested, too. A day earlier, Reiter, once identified with Carneglia as a member of an auto-theft gang, also had been acquitted of heroin charges in a separate federal case in the Southern District.

Four other defendants could not be found. They included Salvatore Greco and William Cestaro, whose brother Philip would later plead guilty to helping hard-headed Edward Maloney buy drugs. Most of the group had direct links to the Bergin crew, whose boss, despite his worry, was not charged. Nothing on the tapes implicated him; Source BQ's observations were not evidence.

Unknown to most until later, two more Bergin associates, the brothers Michael and Louis Roccoforte, who would plead guilty, were arrested in Manhattan that same day as they tried to sell about two kilos of cocaine to an undercover cop.

"John Gotti is on the carpet with Big Paul Castellano over the drug bust," Agent Abbott wrote after Wahoo reported in, "as Paul feels John was either involved himself and if he was not, then he should have known his crew was involved and therefore he cannot control his crew."

Source Wahoo, on the other hand, said Dellacroce "is backing up Angelo's version of the drug bust as cleaning up his brother's operation." Even retiree Carmine Fatico was letting Angelo know he supported him; but the Pope was so angry that Wahoo said Carmine might be unretired "if Gotti cannot convince Big Paul he was not involved in the drug operation."

Because the men were arrested on a sealed complaint, not many details were immediately available to either side.

A few days later, FBI agents picked up rumors that murder contracts had been let on the lives of Special Agents Edward Woods and Donald W. McCormick of the Gambino squad. The rumor ran contrary to Family practice, but had to be checked.

"We spoke to the appropriate people," an agent recalled, "including Gotti, who apparently did not know about it. He was really annoyed." Gotti, he added, said: "That's just Angelo, shootin' off his mouth, blowin' off steam."

Another appropriate contact, Wahoo, "advised that no personal recriminations will be made on any FBI agent as they would have to be approved by Big Paul and at this time Gotti and Ruggiero are lucky they have not been clipped themselves."

The FBI had acted on the case as cautiously as possible for fear the targets might learn in advance of the impending arrests. A week before, Source BQ had stated "that most of the crew will disappear if they know there are [arrest] warrants [out] for them. Only Mike Coiro will not flee."

Once arrested, defendants who secure bail with a deed to a house or cash are more likely to stay around for their trial. This is what happened with the main players, who were released after posting property. Angelo's bail was the highest—$1 million. After making his $125,000 bail, Coiro told a judge: "You can rest assured, Your Honor, I'm a fighter and will be here."

Soon after this, agents visited Coiro to test his state of mind: Would he want to deal? But Coiro stood on ceremony and did not go bad; he "went straight to John," Source Wahoo said.

Amid all the turmoil, before the indictment, John and Victoria Gotti's eldest daughter, Angela, was married. Among the guests was Wahoo, who told Agent Abbott: "When the indictments come out and Castellano [is] made aware of the particulars, then it is quite possible [those arrested] will be in serious trouble and Ruggiero may yet be killed."

Weeks later, the indictment arrived. Angelo, Gene, and John Carneglia were hit hard: racketeering, conspiracy, obstruction of justice, and harboring a fugitive. As far as Family matters were concerned, Count 2 was the most serious: It stated that the three men were the "organizers, supervisors and managers" of a heroin ring.

Knowing the case was based on tapes, Castellano sent word he wanted copies of the transcripts as soon as prosecutors turned them over, as required, to Angelo's lawyers.

Near the end of 1983, he got a taste of the trouble the tapes might cost his papacy; a grand jury at that time tried to force Little Pete Tambone to talk about Uncle Paul's proposal to the Commission that Tambone be killed. Little Pete would hang tough—he went to court in his pajamas to support a Polisi-type gambit, and when that failed, he kept silent and went to jail for contempt—but, nonetheless, for Castellano the episode was a disturbing harbinger. Just a little while later, when he found out he had been bugged, the Pope knew the swallows had come back to Castellano.

The Pope pressed Angelo again for the transcripts of the tapes, but Angelo kept making up stories and excuses, which was good for Thomas Gambino and Thomas Bilotti, but bad for John Gotti.

That summer, before the Angelo, et al. indictment, a cash-heavy cocaine dealer anchored his yacht in Sheepshead Bay, Brooklyn. Willie Boy Johnson figured the man was a perfect mark for James Cardinali. As with the bodega-owner hammering, John Gotti's pal hid in the background. Since Willie Boy's lecture that Jamesy should not indiscreetly litter streets with bodies, Jamesy had gone to Florida several times to rob drug dealers. He refrained from killing any, he later said.

In the middle of the night, Willie Boy called Jamesy and scripted the score. He told him to meet some accomplices in an after-hours bar. One of these told Jamesy:

"The boat is leaving in a few hours. Go by my house, wake my wife, get the bag with the guns and badges, and come here."

At 4:30 A.M., many fishermen clogged the way to the *Lucky Lady*. The others wanted to call it off, but Jamesy strolled past the unknowing anglers and onto the unguarded yacht, opened an unlocked door and began handcuffing the surprised occupants, except for one.

"The captain of the boat was giving me a hard time. When I woke him and said, 'Police,' he was trying to get up. I kept pistol-whipping him with the gun."

The *Lucky Lady* gang got about $10,000 in jewelry and cash. But Jamesy's luck had just run out. He was arrested for the murder of Michael Castigliola, who was killed for ratting Jamesy out to Gotti.

Jamesy was looking at 25-to-life, and he spent the night in a Brooklyn jail, alone with his thoughts.

Some of these arrived later in a letter to a *Daily News* reporter. "I would be willing to sell a story ... or possibly doing a book. I have a lot of interesting stories about Johnny and our crew. Johnny and I were exceptionally close."

At the jail, for cops the next morning, Cardinali summed up his thoughts this way: "I would be willing to talk."

Late in August, he was taken to the Brooklyn District Attorney's office and began talking about one of his other murders—the one he felt bad about, the collegiate-looking kid at the Riviera Motel at JFK Airport—but he told Mark Feldman, deputy chief of the homicide bureau, that he wasn't the shooter. It wasn't a candid start for someone seeking to deal down a big charge. Feldman, however, told Jamesy to continue talking and so long as he told the truth, nothing he said would be used against him.

Blessed with this absolution, Jamesy admitted he was the Riviera Motel triggerman, but offered nothing about the three victims whom nobody with a badge knew anything about: the two coke dealers in Florida and the Brooklyn dealer anchored in Jamaica Bay. He did offer another body, however, and when he connected the murder of court officer Albert Gelb to John and Charles Carneglia and the Gambino Family, he was on his way to protected status.

Jamesy told Feldman he knew little about Paul Castellano, but he knew a lot about John Gotti.

"Who?"

"He'll be the boss after Paul and Neil are gone."

Feldman worked homicide in Brooklyn, so it isn't surprising he hadn't heard about the capo from Queens. He called then-NYPD Detective Kenneth McCabe, who verified Jamesy's Family observations and called in Detective Billy Burns, who was still working with FBI-less Diane Giacalone.

Giacalone was ready for good news. She had recently lost an extortion case against Castellano's cousin, the case that had caused tension between her and some FBI agents even before the FBI pulled out of her RICO case. Her lost case was based on tapes, but the most memorable line of dialogue came from a witness who quoted an enforcer as saying: "This is *La Cosa Nostra*—what's yours is ours and what's ours is ours."

Now, Diane told Jamesy: "Tell me everything you know."

Though Jamesy kept his three other murders a secret, he talked all day. It was the first of many marathon sessions and the beginning of a tortuous, fateful relationship between him and Diane, kids from Queens born a year apart who grew up as polar opposites. They fought constantly. To him, she was a deceitful bully. To her, he was a remorseless punk. But as much as they hated it, they needed each other.

After that first day, Giacalone felt her investigation was taking off. Jamesy's stories would have to be tested against others before any deals were made, but they sounded true. In the meantime, Jamesy was transferred to federal custody and lodged in a special dormitory, a prized murderer.

Multiple murderers were part of Paul Castellano's camp, too, and now he began to pay the price as the first shot in the federal Family assault was fired. Early in 1984, the Pope was indicted as a beneficiary of a conspiracy to steal luxury cars and sell them overseas.

The announcement was made by the new U.S. Attorney in Manhattan, Rudy Giuliani. Paul and 21 others were indicted, making it one of the largest RICO cases ever. The charges were a bloody lesson on how quickly the Family kills, and not just its own. The defendants were accused of varying roles in 30 murders tied to the ring's car-theft enterprise. Most of the victims were hoodlums, but one was a twenty-year-old man who happened to witness a double homicide; a second was the nineteen-year-old girlfriend of a suspected informer.

Besides Paul, the key figures in the case were Anthony Gaggi, in whose house Paul had been crowned, and a dead man, Roy DeMeo, whose name had popped up in the death of the Howard Beach service manager, John Favara. The indictment stated that Paul ordered Gaggi to kill DeMeo, a maverick Gambino hit man who fell into disfavor when one of his victims was found in a barrel and the Family got some bad publicity. DeMeo then sealed his fate by refusing to show up for a sitdown.

DeMeo's name had also popped up in an FBI affidavit in support of the White House bug. The affidavit said Paul had "put out feelers" to the Gotti crew about killing DeMeo. It paraphrased one of the last conversations secretly recorded at Angelo's house in 1982—a lengthy Angelo-Gene chat in which Gene seemed wary of accepting a contract on DeMeo because DeMeo had a "small army" around him.

Gene said he and his brother John had "done" only seven or eight "guys" while DeMeo had "done" 37.

DeMeo's army apparently deserted him early in 1983, when he was found dead, shot five times, in the trunk of his car. While DeMeo was alive, the indictment in the stolen-car ring case now charged, Paul had ordered him, Gaggi, and a third man to kill a father-and-son Gambino team who helped stage a phony charity event attended in 1979 by First Lady Rosalynn Carter. The scheme was said to have embarrassed Paul, the upright businessman.

Like Carlo Gambino had been, the Pope was only vaguely acquainted with courtrooms. But now, at age 68, he realized his retirement years might be spent behind bars.

John Gotti realized it, too, and was pleased, according to Source BQ, an associate of the crew, but not as active as Wahoo—and also not as big a Gotti fan. Days after the indictment, Gotti and friends were "already contemplating their rise to power." Gotti knew Paul's problems "will only mean better times for himself." Gotti had been at a restaurant in Little Italy and "was quietly gloating in the troubles that have recently befallen" Paul, who was pressing for details on the Angelo heroin-trafficking indictment, but was still being denied "the whole truth."

Wahoo didn't comment on Gotti's state of mind, but he did express surprise that Angelo and the others hadn't met up with no-drugs-enforcer Chin Gigante on some rooftop; he offered this explanation, as rendered by Agent Abbott:

"Angelo, et al. may have drafted a phony indictment to display to Big Paul and Neil to tailor their excuses and get them off the hook."

Wahoo also added a bulletin from another front: "James Cardinali has become a rat because he is jammed up with a murder charge." Jamesy had "given up" Willie Boy and was talking about assaults on a cocaine yacht and a bodega owner.

Another rat was about to crawl into a trap laid by cops in Queens. Crazy Sally Polisi was arrested in Ozone Park as he handed over serious cocaine to an undercover detective. Polisi was dealing again because he was broke. He had moved upstate and sunk all his money, including the $90,000 shopping bag of 20-dollar bills from John Carneglia, into a 50-acre weekend retreat for go-cart fans. The property had two tracks, a house, a restaurant, and few go-cart fans. Polisi lost $600,000.

Like Cardinali, Polisi was facing 25-to-life. Lt. Remo Franceschini, who convinced Wahoo to become a Queens informer, knew Polisi had mob ties. He invited him into his office and pointed to a photo gallery of Family men, Queens branch.

"Would you be interested in helping us?"

"Never, never, never."

Polisi was unable to make bail and was jailed. Over the next two months, "never" became "maybe." But what he was maybe ready to give had too much to do with Queens. He was afraid to trust anyone from Queens and so he called the federal probation officer he met on his bank robbery case in 1975 and asked him to take him to Edward McDonald, boss of the Eastern District Organized Crime Strike Force.

McDonald wanted to use Polisi in the case that he and the FBI had underway against the Gambino hierarchy, but Polisi set another agenda when he said: "I can give you a judge in Queens. I paid Mike Coiro $50,000 to fix a stolen-car case against me, my wife, and brother-in-law, and he did. Mike Coiro is the man who can fix cases in Queens."

When Giacalone's boss, Raymond J. Dearie, the U.S. attorney for the Eastern District, was told about Polisi, he took control of him because his staff was probing corruption in Queens County courts; Polisi went into the witness-protection program, was wired up, and set out to get a judge. He would make a bribery case against one who had fixed Family cases for 15 years. As part of the deal, his case in Queens was dropped in favor of a less-punitive federal charge. Instead of 25-to-life, he faced zero-to-15, closer to zero if he continued to cooperate, which is why dates with Giacalone and the trial of John Gotti were in his future.

Giacalone was busy arranging Cardinali's deal. Jamesy had proven his value in appearances before her grand jury. And now he would plead guilty to the Castigliola murder in state court, for a 5-to-10-year sentence. As to his other crimes, including the "I-felt-bad" college-kid murder, forget about it. He would not face any punishment for any as long as he continued to tell the truth and testified at trial against Dellacroce and Gotti.

Minutes after his deal was signed, Cardinali revealed a truth to Edward Magnuson, the DEA agent assisting Giacalone. He had killed two drug dealers in Florida; when Giacalone was told, she screamed bloody murder.

"Tell me everything now! Don't hold back!"

"Well, there was this other murder in Brooklyn."

Jamesy had sandbagged Giacalone. She could respond in either of two ways: She could revoke the deal and cripple her investigation by depriving it of the main witness, or she could carry on with the unseemly baggage of a five-time killer in her corner. She knew that defense attorneys would capitalize on that, but it was nothing new for the government to use creepy witnesses. Often, it is the only way to make a case. Giacalone carried on. It was a legal calculation with an unspoken moral ingredient: The men she was after were more important than the killer of drug dealers.

Jamesy returned to the witness-protection program. He had dealt away five bodies—including two in Florida, which has the death penalty—for one, for which he would get a short hitch in the more palatable federal prison system.

"I think that I made a fantastic deal," Jamesy said.

22

BETRAYERS BETRAYED

IN THE CRIME CAPITAL, 1984 was the year of mobspeak and, for FBI informers, the beginning of doublespeak.

New-age surveillance—a bug was placed in the Jaguar of the Luchese boss—was producing miles of transcripts detailing all the Family monopolies. In addition to Giacalone's case and the Family hierarchy cases, a Southern District team—just as the Pope predicted—was targeting the Commission, which Rudy Giuliani was defining as one tremendous conspiracy.

Author Joseph Bonanno was made to regret his anecdotage; he was forced to review passages in his book pertaining to the Commission for a grand jury. Later—when prosecutors feared he might die before he could testify at trial—they sought to preserve him on videotape. The ailing Bonanno refused, and, at age 82, he and his oxygen tank were thrown in jail.

In October, the dominoes started falling. Eleven men described as the entire leadership of the Colombo Family were indicted in the Southern District. The announcement was made two weeks before the 1984 national election, and Attorney General William French Smith came up from Washington to hold a press conference with Giuliani and take political credit.

"We're one down and four to go," Smith said.

In the Colombo wake, the first sketchy public report on Giacalone's case appeared in the *New York Daily News*. The newspaper said a grand jury had been working on it for 18 months. No targets were named, but a source was quoted saying that soon "Smith might be in a position to say, 'Two down and three to go.'"

Several insiders snickered when they read this; they were the agents and attorneys on the Gambino hierarchy case, based in part on the White House bug. Castellano, Dellacroce, and several capos—not just John Gotti—were all targets.

Gotti tried out a low profile. Worried about bugs, he opened a satellite office on 101st Avenue. He was concerned about "the possibility of a rat in the Family," Source Wahoo reported; and he also worried about Neil, now stricken with cancer and undergoing chemotherapy.

Angelo called on Neil almost every day and still refused to turn over to Paul any tapes or transcripts—they contained, he said, too many embarrassing remarks; he, Gene, and Carneglia had already spent about $300,000 in legal fees.

Neil won a small legal victory in the fall. The U.S. Tax Court ruled the IRS had incorrectly assessed him taxes on an unreported bribe. He was able to savor it only briefly. In a month he was arrested on another tax case, by some of the same IRS agents who had arrested him 12 years earlier.

The tax men found a shrunken Neil at the Ravenite Social Club, in the company of Gotti, Angelo, and others who spotted them coming. Neil ducked into the men's room, followed by Angelo. Most of the others skipped out a back door, but not Gotti, who hung around as the agents coaxed Neil out of the toilet.

Gotti was about to acquire his second son-in-law. The bridegroom would be Carmine Agnello, 24, proprietor of Jamaica Auto Salvage. Agnello had recently beaten a counterfeiting case and, in 1980, had been the victim of a beating authorized by his future father-in-law; but all was forgiven, if not forgotten, and on December 9, 1984, he married Vicky Gotti, the former beauty pageant contestant his company had sponsored.

The wedding was unlike the bride's parents' wedding in every way but the "I do." More than 1,000 people attended the reception, which was held at Marina Del Ray in the Bronx. FBI agents observed from two vans near the entrance as the guests arrived, and saw most of Gotti's associates, except for Paul Castellano. One guest recalled that at least 30 tables were occupied only by men, who took turns paying their respects to the bride's father.

The men played a find-the-agent game all night long, and thought they had spotted many among the waiters and musicians. Actually, none were inside to review the entertainment, which included singers Connie Francis and Jay Black (of Jay and the Americans), who was related by marriage to a Gambino soldier, and comedians George Kirby, Pat Cooper, and Professor Irwin Corey.

Despite the snoopers outside, it was a happy event, and was followed in a few weeks by another. Self-made and made, John Gotti, age 44, became a grandfather. His daughter Angela gave birth to a baby boy, whom she named Frank—a tribute to her 12-year-old brother, who died on a minibike in 1980 and who was still listed as a member of the family when Angela's mother, in 1983, submitted an item about her family to the local newspaper.

All during the fall of 1984, "the real Italian lady" was lining up her targets. Finally, Diane Giacalone put the names and the evidence into a memo, and was promptly accused of jeopardizing a man's life to get her revenge on the FBI.

One of Giacalone's targets was Source Wahoo. Not only would she ask her grand jury to indict him, but she would reveal that he was an informer. This was, of course, a pressure-coated invitation for him to seek a deal and testify against the Family within a Family.

Wahoo was highly regarded at the FBI. He had provided so much about so many. "Most of this information could not have been obtained by other investigative means," said a memo in his file. "Incalculable hours of investigative time has been saved by this informant's specific information." Several memos ended with cautionary footnotes such as "This informant can in no way testify to the information supplied by him since to do so would … place the lives of his family, as well as himself, in extreme jeopardy."

The FBI had not told Giacalone about Wahoo. Once into her investigation, however, she could have deduced it in a number of ways. For instance, the Queens District Attorney's detective squad was helping her by turning over its Bergin gambling tapes; Wahoo had helped the Queens D.A. squad back in 1981, after he was squeezed on an attempted-bribery rap. It was reasonable to suspect and conclude: once a snitch, twice a snitch.

By including Wahoo in her case, Giacalone was setting up a mechanism for disclosing his informer status. Even though her case was not based on information he had given the FBI, she would argue that defense attorneys would be entitled to information he gave about codefendants.

The FBI felt Giacalone was playing games, and trying to shore up a case at the last moment by pressuring Wahoo into the witness-protection program and onto the witness stand. If she wanted to have him indicted, she should do it separately. Then she would not have to expose Wahoo—and thus ruin forever a "top-echelon" informant, while undermining the confidence of other informers in the ability of the FBI to keep a bargain.

Two top FBI officials in New York, Thomas Sheer and James Kossler, protested to Washington to get Giacalone to back off. But she had the backing of her boss, Eastern District U.S. Attorney Raymond J. Dearie, and of her underboss, Susan Shepard, chief of the major-crimes unit. Dearie and Shepard had recently been married. The Justice Department brass understood the FBI angst, but gave the decision to Dearie, who admired Giacalone's devotion to duty and gave her his approval.

Wahoo, playing ends against the middle since 1966, was cornered. He was warned by Agent Abbott that he might be revealed, and he was horrified.

"I will be killed," he said. "My family will be killed."

Abbott told Wahoo there was a way out, the way Giacalone wanted: He could take a plea, testify for a light sentence, and fade away in the witness-protection program, like Cardinali and Polisi.

"I will never testify," Wahoo said.

———

In February 1985, the federal hammer raised by the Angelo bugs slammed down on the Crime Capital. In Manhattan, Paul, Neil, and bosses, acting bosses, or underbosses of the other four Families were indicted on charges of operating an illegal RICO enterprise—the Commission.

The indictment began with a history of Family crime dating to 1900. It said the Commission was formed in 1931 to "regulate" Family relationships, and that its current members had used murder as a regulatory tool. The contemporary group had also formed a "club" of contractors, and used extortion to gain control of all concrete jobs in New York City over $2 million.

Many top officials joined Rudy Giuliani to toast their work. "The indictment exposes the structure of organized crime on a scale never done before," said FBI director William H. Webster. "The mob is on the run and we ask you to help drive the Mafia out of New York

City and out of the United States," said Steven Trott, chief of the Justice Department's Criminal Division and the official who gave Dearie the decision on Wahoo.

The media turned to its sources and asked who was running the Gambino Family now that Paul and Neil each had two federal cases pending.

This resulted in John Gotti's public debut, a half-page splash in the Sunday, March 3, *Daily News* under this headline:

NEW GODFATHER REPORTED
HEADING GAMBINO GANG

Reporter Paul Meskil said Gotti was being identified as the "new 'acting boss' of the Gambinos, a position that could make him the most powerful leader of the New York underworld."

The speculation was a bit rich. The Pope was still the boss, and though quite sick, Neil was underboss. It was true that Gotti was in a position to move up, but so were others, like the two Thomases, Gambino and Bilotti. Two photos ran with the story. One showed the "home of new reputed godfather John Gotti in Howard Beach." The second was a mug shot from Gotti's hijacking days, in which a young man with black hair stares into the lens, daring it to capture any emotion except defiance.

On March 18, Agent Abbott and his boss, Frank Storey, met Giacalone to turn the Source Wahoo files over to her. She had won the battle to indict him, but they still wondered why she planned to tell defense attorneys about him if her case was not based on his information. She said the defense was entitled to all his prior statements to authorities. Not all lawyers would argue it had to be done voluntarily. Why not at least wait until asked?

Sorry, boys, Giacalone said.

———————

John Gotti knew he was about to become another Family defendant, but on March 20 he was able to joke about it.

The government was about to "knock the fuckin' nuts off of me," he said to Peter Mosca. "They figure instead of givin' ya 10 years, they give ya 30 years."

Mosca visited Gotti in the company of Dominick Lofaro, the wired informer who was working off a heroin charge after telling the state Organized Crime Task Force he was a made man in Ralph

Mosca's crew. Ralph Mosca, Peter's father, had sent the pair to tell Gotti that a card game about to open in Maspeth—near the Gotti-controlled Cozy Corner Bar—was not Mosca-sponsored, despite its operators' claims.

The messengers arrived on 101st Avenue and exchanged greetings with Gotti and Angelo, still hoarding his heroin tapes, which the government had turned over during pretrial discovery in his case. Gotti already knew of the rival operation from his Cozy Corner nominee, Philip Cestaro, and was amazed at the operators' gall.

"I cleaned [out] that neighborhood when there were junkies down there, fifteen years ago when we were on the lam," he said, referring to his McBratney era.

The men nodded respectfully.

"Yeah, we got a game right there and we got a club there ... so now this fucking pimp went around and told all the storeowners, 'We gonna open up a game.' He was making like he's got a license!"

Gotti said he had dispatched Cestaro to tell the two men in Maspeth that they should just sell coffee because "John" had a game at the corner. But the men didn't know a "John."

At this Gotti paused to poke fun at himself. "That's all right ... I don't even know who I am myself sometimes."

The men laughed respectfully.

Gotti completed the story by telling Peter Mosca that the two men told Cestaro they were "with" his father.

Mosca wanted to know, "Which one?"

"I don't know which one of them. I didn't even go see them yet. But if I go see them, maybe I'll ... you know, I'll crack one."

Gotti told Mosca and Lofaro to visit the men and find out who they were really with and report back to him. Later that day, they did. Mosca said the men wouldn't name their sponsor, perhaps not until they could find one important enough to match up against Gotti.

"Well, forget about that," Gotti said. "I got four thousand guys, I'll send 'em from every neighborhood."

"I wanna know who they're gonna come up with," Peter said.

"I don't give a fuck who they come up with."

Gotti said he wouldn't even let the men host a friendly game of poker. "I'll tell you right now, I need the exercise. They're not gonna play nothin' ... let someone come forward ... I want somebody to come forward. I'm dying to see who's gonna come forward."

"Yeah, me too," Lofaro said.

"He better go to Russia and get a guy. He can't get nobody from the five crews we know."

Five days later, on March 25, 1985, Czar Gotti and nine soldiers were indicted.

The indictment was sealed pending the arrest of John and Gene Gotti, Neil and his son Armond, the brothers Carneglia, Willie Boy Johnson, Anthony Rampino, Nicholas Corozzo, and Leonard DiMaria. Corozzo was named as the leader of another crew in the other mob that included DiMaria and Armond.

All were charged with two RICO counts: racketeering and conspiracy. Each faced 40-year sentences and fines of $50,000. Each was accused of varying "predicate acts"—that is, specific crimes committed to benefit the illegal enterprise.

Three of Gotti's seven predicates were crimes he had been convicted of and served time for—two hijackings and attempted manslaughter in the McBratney case, which the RICO indictment elevated to murder. John Carneglia was accused of the murder of court officer Albert Gelb; Willie Boy was accused of conspiracy to murder Anthony Plate, the loan shark whose disappearance led to Neil's beating a case in 1979.

It was Neil's third federal rap in five months—the mortgage on a life in crime was coming due in his final months. He was accused of supervising both the Gotti and Corozzo crews over an 18-year period. Gene and John Carneglia were not in a good spot either; they were already under indictment in the Angelo drug case.

On March 28, NYPD detectives and DEA agents moved out to make the arrests. A little after 4 A.M., they found John, Gene, and Willie Boy playing cards at the Bergin.

"What'd we do?" John asked.

"Don't worry, you already did it," DEA agent Magnuson replied. "Your crimes have caught up with you."

Raymond Dearie issued a press release after the arrests. He said an investigation had reconstructed the organized acts of an illegal enterprise by interweaving almost 20 years of information from state and federal files.

"The investigation revealed that what appeared initially to be unrelated investigations, prosecutions, and convictions of the defendants for the commission of numerous state and federal crimes was, in fact, the organized criminal activity of the two crews under the supervision of underboss Aniello Dellacroce," Dearie's statement said.

Dearie didn't say that most of the interwoven probes had produced no indictments. But he did salute the work of the Manhattan, Brooklyn, Queens, and Suffolk County district attorneys, Billy Burns of the NYPD major-case squad, DEA agent Edward Magnuson, and assistant U.S. attorney Diane Giacalone. A veteran reporter noted the remarkable omission of the FBI and asked for an explanation. Dearie answered that the DEA was the federal agency on the case because, early on, it involved drug-trafficking allegations.

United States of America v. Aniello Dellacroce, et al. was called for arraignment and bail applications later that day in Brooklyn, with Judge Eugene H. Nickerson presiding.

Michael Coiro, then under indictment, too, appeared for John and Gene and pleaded them not guilty. John was released on $1 million bail secured by his brother Richard's home and his own home, which was in Victoria's name and said to be worth $230,000. Gene was released on the same bail he posted in the drug case, $250,000 secured by his home.

Anthony Rampino was released to the facility at which he had been arrested—a heroin detoxification center in the Bronx. Neil was not able to appear; he was hospitalized for a chemotherapy treatment and would have to plead not guilty by telephone.

"Your Honor, unfortunately, I think Mr. Dellacroce's stay with us is somewhat limited," said his lawyer, Barry Slotnick.

After bail for the others was decided upon—two defendants, Buddy Dellacroce and Charles Carneglia, had not been found—Giacalone told Judge Nickerson that Willie Boy Johnson, now the only defendant in the courtroom, should be jailed immediately because "no conditions of bail would secure his appearance."

The judge's eyes requested an explanation.

"The reason is that Mr. Johnson has been an informant for the Federal Bureau of Investigation for a period of over fifteen years, including a period up through the present time."

Willie Boy remained as still as a courthouse statue, although his fists were clenched so tightly the words "True" and "Love" tattooed across his knuckles stood out clearly. His close friend John Gotti was headed home to Howard Beach, but he had been told earlier that day about Willie Boy—by Willie Boy—as they and others were brought to the courthouse in handcuffs.

"They're accusing me of being an informant," Willie Boy told Johnny Boy. "It ain't true."

Gotti was stunned, not by truth but by untruth. Giacalone had to be lying. The idea of Willie Boy as a rat was crazy. Willie Boy had been around too long. He knew *too* much. Calling him an informer was a devious effort to make him go bad.

"I don't believe it," Gotti said.

By denying it, Willie Boy was keeping a vow he had made in 1966 when he said that's what he would do if it surfaced. That was when he was "very bitter with *La Cosa Nostra* members who never helped his family while he was in prison" and was described by the FBI as a "tough, standup guy" and "muscle man for Gambino" who "moves with fluidity through the underworld," but would never be made because he wasn't Italian.

Willie Boy, a rock-solid 51-year-old former boxer, listened as Giacalone urged that he be jailed without bail.

While informing on his codefendants, he had been "simultaneously participating in serious criminal activity," and it would be legally impossible to keep his informer status a secret. She recounted how in December, when first warned by the FBI, he said he would be killed if he was revealed.

"It is an assessment with which I cannot disagree. We have indicated to Mr. Johnson that we are prepared to protect him as a result."

"Not true, Your Honor," Willie Boy protested.

It was true, but Willie Boy was trying desperately to avoid going off to jail as a protected inmate. He feared his codefendants would regard it as proof that he was an informer. He wanted to make bail and take his chances on the streets, but Giacalone held all the cards. Earlier in the day, she and her supervisor, Susan Shepard, had informed him he would be compromised, but they were prepared to offer him protection.

"I will be killed," he had said. "My family will be slaughtered."

Giacalone now told the judge about the earlier meeting. "He also said ... that he would at some point tell them himself in some way, his codefendants, that he had been an informant."

The judge asked Willie Boy to tell his story under oath; Johnson denied being an informer, though he did admit: "I spoke to the FBI many times."

"Did you give information to the FBI about Messrs. Gotti and those?" the judge asked.

"No sir."

You never mentioned Mr. Gotti?"

"No, sir."

Willie Boy, who, in addition to many other crucial tips, had fingered Gotti in the McBratney case and set him up for apprehension, hesitated briefly before continuing.

"I might have mentioned the name. Yeah. Mr. Gotti. They mentioned it to me."

"What did you say about him?"

"They said he's the boss. I said, 'He's always the boss.' Things like that."

After a few minutes more, Nickerson decided Willie Boy was a serious no-show risk for trial. He said the FBI files showed Willie Boy had been an informer about his codefendants and about the specific crimes they had committed.

"It would be irresponsible of me, it seems to me, to release him on bail ... and so I order his detention."

Willie Boy was led away to the Metropolitan Correctional Center. Because of a report filed the next day by Source BQ, he was locked in a special pen—sealed off from the other inmates like a man with a deadly disease.

Source BQ reported that three Bergin men—whom he would not name—had discussed killing Willie Boy without Gotti's permission—to protect him "from embarrassment." As a ruling member of the Gambino Family, "John would immediately fall into disfavor if it became known on the street he was so closely aligned with an FBI informant." BQ said crew members were surprised that Willie Boy's status as an informer had been disclosed in court. "Because this fact is known, Johnson's life will forever be in jeopardy."

Willie Boy was confined in his cell 23½ hours a day. His access to showers and recreation was restricted. A glass door to the pen enabled other inmates to taunt him. In a few days, he complained he had found blood in his urine and needed medication. On Easter Sunday, his wife, who had sent messages from Wahoo to the FBI many times, was denied visitation. When his lawyers visited, he was led to them in leg shackles.

The lawyers demanded a hearing to protest this "cruel and inhumane" treatment, which they said was Giacalone's attempt to force Willie Boy to become a witness, and to reapply for bail because "his life is not in danger."

On April 9, the hearing was held and now Gotti would learn that two more informers were talking to the FBI about the Bergin crew. Without identifying him, Special Agent Storey described BQ's report. He also disclosed the FBI had received a tip from a recently developed source who said the crew wanted Willie Boy freed "so they could talk to him and find out more about" the extent of the damage.

The hearing was adjourned without change in Willie Boy's habitat. He would spend the next 16 months in the special pen while the pretrial moves in the case were played out. His had been a most unusual saga, soon to be reprised by a second mystery man, Source BQ—who, like Wahoo during the past decade, had received about $35,000 in small, periodic payments from the FBI.

Peter Mosca and Dominick Lofaro's visit to Ozone Park to discuss the Maspeth card-game situation was the probable cause that the state Task Force needed to go up on John Gotti, and plant bugs in the Nice N EZ Auto School, next to the Bergin annex. The state bugs went in 13 days after Gotti's indictment, so no conversations taped by them could be used in Diane Giacalone's case.

Gotti was overheard only once—complaining about "severe" gambling losses—before he motored to Florida and rented two rooms on separate floors of the Fort Lauderdale Hilton under the name Dom Pizzonia. His bail required Nickerson's approval for trips outside New York; Gotti thought that Bruce Cutler, who was handling pretrial matters, had arranged this. In fact, Cutler hadn't, and on April 24, Gotti was arrested for violating bail as he and three other men clad in bathing suits sat by the pool. As they took Gotti to his room so he could dress, FBI agents noticed what appeared to be a tattoo of a serpent on his right shoulder.

Working the phone, a frantic Cutler got Gotti out of jail by 9 P.M. The next day, in court, Cutler apologized for a "misunderstanding." He said he thought when he arranged for Gotti to be excused from a routine court appearance he had also "indicated to Miss Giacalone that John Gotti was going with his family down to Florida." In the future, Cutler said he would notify Judge Nickerson when Gotti would be away.

"You are going to notify us?" Nickerson said icily. "You are going to notify us he is going to break the bail limits?"

Cutler said no, he meant to say he would ask the court's permission and, meantime, his client was still in Florida and wouldn't be able to be in court to be admonished until April 30. "He is emotionally ... he doesn't fly, Your Honor."

Early in May, to help identify people overheard on the bugs, the state Task Force put a video camera atop a Long Island Railroad trestle over 101st Avenue a few hundred feet from the Bergin annex. On May 8, the Task Force learned how paranoid—and vigilant— that part of Ozone Park is: The camera was stolen.

"Right this instant we're going on tape," Gotti crowed that night in the annex, "and we know their [listening post] is [at] Ninety-fifth Street and Ninety-ninth Avenue. And I want them to know and that's why I'm talking the way I'm talking right now here."

Within hours, the Task Force moved out of its post, which hindered timely "observations necessary in identifying those ... in intercepted conversations," according to an affidavit.

Though certain he was being overheard, Gotti continued to create a record of his verbal ferocity and gambling. On May 11, he complained about a man who owed him money and hadn't made a payment despite a pocket full of cash. "I'll kick his fucking brains in. Six thousand in his pocket Tuesday and he don't tell me nothing. I ought to whack him." On May 12, he bet 15 dimes on a pro basketball game. "I got on the [Philadelphia] 76ers, taking two [points]. That's a $30,000 decision."

Now and then, officers monitoring the bugs tried to count the profanities in Gotti's tirades, a difficult pastime. On May 19, they heard him describe sitting in a restaurant the night before near

"Val," a jeweler who belonged to another crew and owed him money. "Right behind me is that fuckin' dick sucker Val, that asshole jeweler with the big mouth family, big mouth, fuckin … [I] told him you better come and check in every week. You miss one week and I'll kill you, you cocksucker, fuckin' creep." The next day, Gotti said Val "might be tough in that crew, but that crew ain't got nobody tough anyway."

On the day Gotti derided Val's toughness, Source BQ filed a blockbuster report; it suggested a reason why Gotti, even by his standards, was talking tough in May.

After saying Gotti still didn't believe that Willie Boy was a rat because he had been "involved in too much criminality" to be working for the FBI, BQ said he had been at the Our Friends Social Club in Ozone Park and seen the future. Although he didn't say so, his report indicated Gotti may have had his own Wahoo in Castellano's camp, because he seemed well informed.

BQ said John, Angelo, Gene, and John Carneglia had received "sensitive street information" that the Pope was "contemplating contract murders" on them "because of internal strife within the Gambino Family and, in part, because John is being touted" as his replacement. He said Castellano "wants to make Tommy Bilotti the new head of the Gambino Family and is therefore considering wiping out a strong portion of the Gotti faction. Gotti is contemplating striking first before Castellano can formulate his own plan."

Special Agent Colgan summarized BQ's assessment of the situation this way: "Source believes John Gotti would definitely consider a hit on Castellano and others, including Bilotti, and if he was successful, Gotti would surely be one of the most formidable and youngest heads of an organized crime Family."

BQ's most dramatic report for the FBI was his last. Diane Giacalone had decided to reveal him, too.

BQ, whose trade in later years was bookmaking, was an unindicted co-conspirator in Giacalone's case; he had turned up on gambling tapes that she intended to play at the trial. Once again, the FBI argued it was unnecessary because BQ turned up innocuously on only a few of the hundreds of gambling tapes at her disposal. Once again, the FBI accused her of trying to force an informer to testify and thus jeopardize his life. And once again, the FBI lost, and Agent Colgan warned BQ.

For nine years, BQ had told Colgan he would get in the wind if exposed. And later that summer he did, leaving his wife and child behind. Until January 1986, when Giacalone got a warrant for BQ's arrest, only Colgan and Mrs. BQ knew where BQ was, but then all contact had to end.

Later, Colgan said BQ was not a "top-echelon" informant—"he never made the big-time" of FBI informant ranks, but he was highly valued. Colgan, who had welcomed BQ into his home during their odd-couple relationship, also said he was "personally and profession-ally devastated by the actions of the government in this matter."

William Battista, age 53, the old Brownsville-East New York hijacker-bookmaker who never appreciated Gotti's bully ways, hasn't been seen since.

23

THE LAST STAGE

Tommy and the other guy will get popped.

—*John Gotti, June 13, 1985*

IN JUNE, THE FEDERAL FEVER infected Aniello Dellacroce's home in Staten Island. A bug stayed only for that month, but long enough to capture some remarkable talk by the other mob about a sharp upturn in Family tensions and an insinuation that Neil had lost his marbles.

Neil was furious at the man who suggested he was senile—Buddy LaForte, son of Joseph, the Staten Island capo. Neil also was angry at Michael Caiazzo, another captain and Neil's former driver who had appointed Buddy acting capo of his crew without asking his underboss, a friend for 50 years. Caiazzo, before checking into a hospital for an operation, had gone over Neil's head and told the Pope, which infuriated Neil even more.

On June 8, Castellano and Thomas Bilotti stopped at Neil's house to discuss the Caiazzo-LaForte affair.

"You know what I heard [about LaForte]?" Neil began. "That this fuckin' punk called me senile ... I think I'd kill him ... Paul, if it wasn't for you, I would kill him."

"Watch out for people telling you stories," replied Castellano, who was experienced on the subject. "Sometimes people tell us stories."

Castellano said that Buddy LaForte had denied being disrespectful to Neil, and suggested, gently, that Neil was his own worst evidence. "You know what it is, Neil. You have some good days and you have bad days."

The next day, Gotti and Angelo went to Neil's to review Castellano's newly persistent demands for the heroin tapes; Angelo had been holding on to them since the government, as required, had turned them over to help him prepare for trial. But the Pope was saying he needed them now for his own trials. Both were set to start before Angelo's, which was delayed partly because of a change in prosecution teams; U.S. Attorney Raymond Dearie had taken the case away from the Eastern District Strike Force and turned it over to a special drug unit in his office.

The heroin-tapes talk between Neil and his disciples may be the most evocative Family tape of all. A dying man is heard extolling *La Cosa Nostra* and seeking a way to avoid bloodshed, but acknowledging that—to save Angelo—it may be necessary to go to "the last stage."

It began with Gotti and Angelo learning what Neil had decided to do about Caiazzo and LaForte. Little Pete Tambone had been "chased" for six months for dealing drugs, but now Caiazzo was booted out forever for naming LaForte acting capo without Neil's approval. Buddy's penalty was a demotion to soldier in James Failla's crew; in a bow to Neil's anger, the Pope had blessed both moves.

As he would throughout the heroin-tapes talk, Gotti was quick to agree with Neil. He said that since Caiazzo "was the brains" of the Caiazzo crew, he should be dumped.

"I don't think he was the brains," Neil said, "But he was the boss. He's responsible for all the mistakes."

In this, Gotti saw a corollary: "You don't kill a guy just because the guy's a tough guy. It ain't right. You kill the guy that gives the order."

Now, the monitors of the Neil bug got to overhear Angelo make up a story to explain his refusal to turn over transcripts of tapes made by the bugs in his house in 1982.

"If you two never bother with me again ... I ain't givin' them tapes up. I can't. There's good friends of mine on them fuckin' tapes. If it was some fuckin' asshole like Buddy, or somebody like that, I'd give it to [Paul] in three seconds flat. There's good guys on them fuckin' tapes."

"Don't call them good guys whatever you do," said Gotti. "Don't look for them when you're in trouble, the good guys."

"That's right," said Neil.

Angelo announced he intended to meet Castellano and a papal lawyer because "I want them to tell me how these tapes could help them."

"If he shows you how, he's the boss," Gotti said. "While he's the boss, you have to do what he tells you."

Gotti was expressing loyalty to a boss who, according to William Battista, was "considering wiping out a strong portion" of the Gotti crew. But he also was speaking in the presence of the terminally ill underboss, his mentor.

"You don't understand *La Cosa Nostra*," Neil said.

"Angelo, what does *Cosa Nostra* mean?" Gotti chimed.

Neil answered first. "*Cosa Nostra* means that the boss is your boss."

Angelo said he wasn't going to give up the tapes so that his boss could turn *Cosa Nostra* against him and his friends. "I won't do that," he said.

"Forget about it," Neil said.

"I won't do that."

"Forget about it. *La Cosa Nostra*. Boss is the boss is the boss."

Neil then accused Angelo of "making up stories" so that he wouldn't have to cough up the tapes, but Angelo denied it.

"What I'm trying to say," Neil said again, "is a boss is a boss is a boss. What does a boss mean in this fuckin' thing? You might as well make anybody off the street."

Angelo protested that Neil was singing "a different tune" from the last time they talked about the tapes.

"You don't know what the fuck you're talkin' about," Gotti interposed. "Why don't you keep quiet, and shut the fuck up?"

During the Tambone crisis, Neil had warned Angelo that he would kill even his own son if he dealt drugs, but his frame of mind was different now. He was going to bat for Angelo. He said he had told Paul he would try to talk sense to Angelo because he "didn't want anybody to get hurt"—but Angelo was making it rough on all of them.

"Now, what do you want me to tell him? 'The guy says, "Fuck you," he don't wanna give you these fuckin' tapes.'"

Neil recalled trying to take Angelo's side at the start. "I've been tellin' [Paul], 'The guy can't give you the tapes because his family is on there.' I've been trying to make you get away with these tapes, but Jesus Christ Almighty, I can't stop the guy from always bringin' it up. Unless I tell the guy, 'Why don't you go fuck yourself?' ... Then we know what we gotta do then, we, we go and roll it up and go to war."

In what was a reference to an earlier, untapped comment by Angelo that Paul would order him killed if he knew what was on the tapes, Neil said, "I told you, that's in the last stage. Let's wait. Let's take it easy. That's the last stage. If it has to come to that, it'll come to that."

The boss was a boss was a boss—up to the last stage. Neil was saying, in the end, he would support a strike against Castellano if it meant saving Angelo, who had been very loyal to Neil. "For Christ's sake, I ain't saying you're wrong, [but] don't forget, don't only consider yourself ... a lot of fellows'll get hurt, too. You could get hurt. I could get hurt. [Gotti] could get hurt."

As Neil finished, Gotti gave his own lecture, lambasting Angelo for speaking out of school about the Commission to an unmade man like Edward Lino. "You're not supposed to speak to every fuckin' guy [who is] not a friend. About a Commission meeting! You ain't the only guy that done it, but you ain't supposed to do it. Right is right."

Joseph LaForte, father of the offending soldier, and James Failla, the soldier's new captain, also dropped by Neil's house that same day, June 9. At the time, Gotti was not there, but Angelo was.

Angelo reminded LaForte of "three" killings "we did" for "you, you know, for the thing." He reminded him of the time "Willie Boy and the kid [Cardinali] put the guy [the Staten Island bodega owner] in the hospital." The remembrances were for the purpose of asking LaForte what his son Buddy had done for the thing lately.

"Nothing," the father said before making a comment about the beating Cardinali and others gave Antonio Collado, who was suspected of intruding on a LaForte numbers operation.

"No, forget about that one," Angelo said, "I'm talking about McBratney [the man Gotti and Angelo killed]."

"[Buddy] had nothing to do with it," LaForte said.

"Definitely not, I was there. It was a suicide mission."

"I didn't even know the guy."

"I didn't know the guy either. When I walked in the bar, I met him."

When Failla entered Neil's parlor, he expressed surprise that Caiazzo had been thrown out of the Family completely.

"Jimmy, I've been carrying him for fifty years," said Neil. "Mother-fuckin' lice cocksucker that he is."

"Your mind is good. You seen it straight."

Back by the Nice N EZ Auto School, Gotti was overheard talking about mail he had received from Italy. He paraphrased an apparent fan letter this way: "[It's] good to see a young guy, a young healthy guy there now, instead of those old fucks."

The seventy-year-old Paul Castellano and John Gotti sat down together on June 12—three weeks after William Battista said Gotti and others learned Castellano was contemplating killing them. The fact of this meeting indicated Castellano had assured everyone it wasn't true, or that the "sensitive street information" reported by Battista had originated on 101st Avenue.

Castellano now assumed he was headed to jail, not because of the stolen-car case or even the Commission case. He thought he had a chance to beat both; but he thought he was a loser on a case that hadn't even been filed yet—the Gambino hierarchy case. As required after the fact, the government had recently notified him that his home was bugged in 1983.

"I musta said so many things," he told Gotti. "That's the way it goes."

Certain of going to prison and Neil's death, Castellano met with Gotti to discuss a "peaceful transition." Despite a streak of independence, Neil, as long as the Family within a Family got its share of the bounty, had been a loyal underboss, the kind Thomas Bilotti could be for Thomas Gambino. Castellano was less sure of Gotti, but knew he must be appeased, and so he proposed that Gambino, Bilotti, and Gotti have operating control of the Family while he remained the behind-the-bars boss.

With Paul still the boss, and with two Thomases in the frame, Gotti thought the picture at the top was looking too busy. *Consigliere*

Joe N. Gallo, age 73, another "old fuck" who was, Gotti had said, an "asshole weak cocksucker," would not have any real influence, no matter what happened.

A day after his sitdown with the Pope, Gotti reviewed it for a crony. He suspected Castellano was patronizing him and was angry that Paul had "disregarded Neil" in formulating his plans. Gotti saw the demise of the other mob.

"He told me again last night, he said, 'Well, I'm gonna try to make a peaceful transition [and] switch the Family over to two [or] three guys.' [But] we ain't gonna get nothin'."

According to Gotti, Castellano said, "You come with me, Tommy, and the other guy." Gotti said he replied that Gambino and Bilotti didn't want to share power. And then Gotti told the crony what would happen if Paul was patronizing him and he was cut out of the picture when Paul went to jail:

"You know what we're gonna do then. Tommy and the other guy will get popped."

———————————

The former Rockaway Boy was supremely confident during these pivotal times in Family history. At the Bergin annex, he told a soldier: "I know what's goin' on. See, you don't … you're oblivious … guys like you, your brother, and other soldiers, God bless ya, [but] you're oblivious to what's goin' on, but I ain't … Me, I'll always be all right."

Gotti also was supremely active, as he complained: "I got appointments and favors coming out of the asshole. I can't keep up with them."

One appointment he couldn't keep up with was an unusual pretrial hearing held at Neil's house—because Neil was too ill to travel. Judge Nickerson brought his court to him on June 25, so two legal issues—involving potential conflicts of interest among lawyers in the case—could be resolved by having Neil waive any later objections.

The first issue did not involve Gotti, so it did not matter that he and Bruce Cutler were late. Court was convened—the FBI had silenced the bug in Neil's house for the day—in Neil's bedroom. The underboss, clad in white embroidered pajamas, sat propped up on a king-size bed.

Nickerson explained how the potential conflict might affect Neil, and did he still wish to waive an objection?

"Your Honor, I have been sick and I have had three angina attacks and whatever my lawyer, whatever my lawyer does, is okay with me. I don't understand the law … I don't understand the points of it."

The participants recessed to Neil's living room to await Gotti and Cutler; they chatted while a Viennese waltz played softly in the background, according to the only reporter present, Philip Russo of the *Staten Island Advance*.

"Have you seen *Prizzi's Honor?*" Nickerson asked Diane Giacalone. "… [T]hat had some funny scenes."

Giacalone, surprised by the judge's mention of a sardonic movie about mob assassins, merely nodded.

"Gotti," Russo later wrote, "a big man clad in a dark brown suit with matching brown shirt open down the first three buttons, arrived after a short delay." Then, Gotti, Cutler, and the others all filed back into Neil's bedroom.

Once again, they heard a dying man wish them whatever they wanted.

Twenty years after entering Neil Dellacroce's world, Gotti was in command of it. Neil would survive another five months, time enough for the man acting in his stead to grow accustomed to his place.

One of Gotti's first challenges was solving a problem between a dead loan shark and a blind bookmaker. The family of the loan shark, who died of natural causes, felt it was entitled to a share of the gambling operations he had built up. Gotti called in the blind bookmaker, who worked for the loan shark, and said he should "do the right thing" and pay the man's family $1,000 a week, to be divided equally among his former wives and children.

"[He's] the best [bookie] in the country," Gotti said after the blind man left. "He takes $250,000 [in bets] a night."

As always, Gotti seemed as prone to violence as to diplomacy on some problems. Late in July, the state Task Force bug overheard him urging ill will on a pizza shop operator.

"Why didn't you give him a beatin' then?" Gotti asked a crew member.

"Well, 'cause uh ... "

"I told ya. Forget this other shit. Give him a fuckin' beatin'."

"Well the, uh, I was waiting to hear from you."

"I told you yesterday ... what are you, Chinese? Hit 'im. This guy's nobody, and if he's somebody, I don't give a fuck."

And so it went that summer and early fall. Gotti farmed out a $20,000 shylock collection to a New Jersey soldier who needed a payday; he assured a contractor he would help him collect a job payment; he told a garment-district trucker: "If they're embarrassing you now, I promise you they'll apologize tomorrow and you'll get the matter settled."

Gotti was riding high—at one point, he was even winning at the track. And when he won, he didn't appreciate it when his winnings were miscalculated, as he demonstrated when he called a runner for a Manhattan bookmaker and asked about his "figure" for the week.

"Twenty-five [hundred]," the runner said.

"Your ass, twenty-five."

"Why, why my ass?"

"Because it's thirty-five fifty, tell him."

"All right."

"Six winners and two losers, the asshole, tell him."

"Six winners and two losers."

"Yeah, that fuckin' idiot mother fucker that he is."

When he started losing again, Gotti went into a rage about bookmakers. "I can't wish them cancer 'cause I'm half a bookmaker myself. I got three guys hanging around me. Otherwise, I wish 'em all cancer."

In September, Gotti was notified he had been overheard on the Neil bug. "The FBI is all over the place," he said at the Bergin annex, which was about the only Family place the FBI wasn't all over.

State Task Force cops, however, were watching as a parade of Gambinos and other Family men were calling on Gotti, who was heard to complain that Angelo and others should be helping him out more as he tried to deal with "good fellows from all over the country."

"They all come to me," Gotti said. "I ain't got nobody here. I got to listen to everybody. I forget what things there are. I write notes to myself."

That month, Willie Boy Johnson, still in segregated confinement, forgot two important things: that the authorities at the Metropolitan Correctional Center sometimes tape phone calls; and that the people he was locked up with were professional informers. And so Willie Boy was taped while calling his son and arranging a heroin deal. The DEA set up the son and arrested him as he turned over $25,000 to an undercover agent. Father and son were indicted.

Willie Boy, as Wahoo, always told the FBI that he and John Gotti were not part of any drug deals. Billy Battista, as BQ, always said Willie Boy and Johnny Boy were part of the Angelo crowd.

In October, Barry Slotnick told Judge Nickerson that Neil would most likely be dead by December 2, when the Dellacroce-Gotti trial was scheduled to start.

If Neil died, Gotti would become the lead defendant in the case; his name would be at the top of all court papers. Some assumed that Slotnick, who had defended many RICO cases, would then begin representing Gotti and become the lead attorney while Cutler dropped down to one of the lesser defendants. But they didn't know of the friendship developing between the two dynamos out of Brooklyn, John Gotti and Bruce Cutler; they didn't know Gotti didn't care that Cutler had never defended a RICO case, and had lost his only federal trial.

Around Thanksgiving, in the aftermath of a murder, Cutler dispelled any doubt about who would be lead attorney, and thus get his name in the newspapers hundreds more times.

The year before, in Howard Beach, a young man named John Vulcano Jr. had been shot in front of his girlfriend's house as he changed a slashed tire. En route to the hospital, Vulcano was told he would not live and he told Detective John Daly that the man who shot him was John Gurino Jr., whose uncles ran the Arc Plumbing Company. Vulcano and Gurino had been arrested together in a truck filled with illegal fireworks in 1982, but had since fallen out.

The day of the incident, Detective Daly took Gurino into custody and then to the hospital, where Vulcano identified him as the man who had shot him. Gurino was charged with murder not long after Vulcano died.

Days later, Willie Boy told the FBI that Angelo and Gene "were trying to help [Gurino] out," and soon Slotnick's partner, Cutler, former deputy chief of homicide in the Brooklyn District Attorney's office, was defending Gurino. Slotnick had a big mob practice and had recruited Cutler after beating him in a case in which several Hasidim—member of a Jewish sect—were charged with beating a black man to near death.

Now, in November 1985, as the trial got underway, Vic Juliano, an investigator for Slotnick and Cutler, visited Vulcano's girlfriend to question her about the case. The next morning, she told assistant D.A. James Quinn that her boyfriend, Vulcano, told her before he died that he had lied about Gurino. Until this time, she had refused to discuss Vulcano with the A.D.A., but now she became a witness for Gurino. A group from Bergin attended the trial every day—to see and be seen.

"They had thirty or forty people in court staring at the jury for days," said Quinn. "I never saw a jury that frightened when they came in to give their verdict, and they acquitted."

In one of the many curtain-raising articles preceding the Gotti trial, Cutler would cite his performance in the Gurino trial as the reason why he became Gotti's trial attorney. He said the interested Bergin observers were "amazed at how great the performance was. They joked, 'No wonder you're Barry Slotnick's partner. With you around, who needs Barry Slotnick?'"

On December 2, 1985, the day the Dellacroce-Gotti trial had been scheduled to start, Neil beat the case. The 71-year-old underboss, the Family peacekeeper, passed away at Mary Immaculate Hospital in Jamaica, Queens.

The former Albert Anastasia gunman whose ambition was blocked by the blood bond between Carlo Gambino and Paul Castellano had entered the hospital two weeks earlier using the name Timothy O'Neil; he liked that alias more than the name

E. Grillo, in which his home telephone was listed. Obituary writers noted that his name, Aniello Dellacroce, meant "Little Lamb of the Cross."

Neil's death was the beginning of "the last stage"—his term for the penultimate chapter in the Angelo tapes story.

On December 3, John Gotti was spotted by detectives walking up and down Mulberry Street in Manhattan with Frank DeCicco and other capos, to be sure to avoid bugs. On December 4, at Neil's wake, Neil's protégé was treated like a grieving son, according to the surveillants.

The Pope did not attend the wake. He might have felt he wasn't wanted; he might have felt the certain publicity would hurt him in his stolen-car trial, which had gotten underway; he might have simply wished to defer to Gotti. Whatever he felt, his judgment was not good. The other mob was astounded he did not pay his respects—wakes were a serious ritual. Gotti, who regarded Thomas Bilotti as a "fuckin' lugheaded scumbag," had, even so, recently gone to a wake for Bilotti's mother.

In a few days, Castellano's error was compounded—at least in the view from Queens—by naming Thomas Bilotti as underboss. And in a few more days, of course, Paul Castellano and the other guy, Bilotti, would be popped and their families would be planning wakes.

Thomas Gambino, who had gone to an exclusive prep school with future congressmen and rulers of countries, mourned the loss of his uncle, but he wasn't about to challenge anybody from Queens. He would be happy with all the companies he owned in the Manhattan garment district.

The murders set off a torrent of publicity, but readers never learned that a few days after the executions, Gotti was overheard on the Nice N EZ bug saying that whoever was with the Pope that day was to be killed, too. But Gotti and Angelo also were in the dark; they did not know that—at least for the past year—Castellano had been occasionally sitting up late at night—reading transcripts of Angelo's heroin tapes.

Paul, who had told Neil to watch out for people telling stories, obtained the transcripts legally; they had surfaced in pretrial motions connected to Angelo's case. Under his rules, he had all the evidence he needed, but beset by his own burdens, he did not summon the will to act against the Bergin crew; he had a final test of loyalty, though, and its failing grade figured in Bilotti's promotion.

On December 16, as he and Bilotti got out of the Lincoln at Sparks Steak House—to have dinner with DeCicco, Failla, and two other men, one of whom didn't show—Castellano was well aware of the anxiety in Queens. Still, he wasn't afraid. It was just another business meeting with Family at a crowded restaurant in the middle of Manhattan during the season of goodwill.

At the end of his reign, the Pope had forgotten the nature of his realm.

24

LET THE PLAY BEGIN

BY AUGUST 18, 1986, JOHN GOTTI was the boss behind bars, thanks to a double-parking dispute with a refrigerator mechanic.

He rose early from his bed in the federal prison in Manhattan, the Metropolitan Correctional Center. He had unfinished business in Brooklyn—his RICO trial. It had been adjourned in April after Judge Nickerson, in the wake of the bomb-murder of new underboss Frank DeCicco, had trouble finding jurors willing and able to serve.

As Gotti showered, federal marshals were arriving to take him to court. In an hour, he would get into a van and enter the world outside for the first time since May, when his bail was revoked because Romual Piecyk was intimidated into forgetting who had assaulted him outside the Cozy Corner Bar.

In the meantime, more big headlines had appeared in the papers. At a hearing to decide whether Angelo Ruggiero's bail should be revoked, an FBI agent testified that an informant said that Gotti and Angelo choreographed the Sparks murders. His freedom on the line, Angelo complained, "This is like Russia." Later, when a judge ordered him to jail, Angelo lost his temper and appeared to threaten a prosecutor when he pointed his finger and said, "Go home and celebrate with your family! Go ahead and laugh!"

Other news hadn't been so good either. As the Colombo Family hierarchy case ended in guilty verdicts for all, the Gambino hierarchy case had been indicted. With Paul and Neil dead, and with Gotti eliminated from the Gambino case because of Giacalone, the lead defendants were *consigliere* Joe N. Gallo and DeCicco's replacement, Joseph Armone. Family capos Joseph Corrao and James Failla—as well as Angelo—also were indicted. As "John Doe," Gotti was merely an unindicted co-conspirator.

Gotti had tried to focus on the matter at hand: his date with Diane Giacalone. Over the summer, at the MCC, long strategy sessions with Bruce Cutler and attorneys for the other defendants were held. One burden was the guilty plea by Armond Dellacroce after his father died. He had disappeared a few months later, prior to sentencing, but his plea would be introduced as evidence. He had also admitted that the Gambino Family existed, that it was an illegal RICO enterprise, and that he had conspired with John Gotti and the others to commit enterprise crimes.

"I conspired with others known to me for gambling, loansharking," Armond had told Judge Nickerson.

After Armond failed to appear for sentencing, another defendant came to court to plead guilty, but Leonard DiMaria backed out at the last moment. DiMaria and Nicholas Corozzo were two other guys thrown into the case against the other mob to show a conspiracy of crews—both reporting to Dellacroce.

DiMaria bolted when he realized what his plea meant. His attorney, Frank Lopez, explained to Nickerson: "He is willing to say that he did these acts [but] he doesn't want to be placed in a position that he has admitted to being a member of the Gambino Crime Family."

DiMaria's decision to stay in the fold was part of the strategy—it would be a joint defense—that was emerging at Gotti's behest. A lawyer's instinct is to pursue a client's best interest, but in this case the interests were diverse. Though each defendant was accused of conspiracy and racketeering, individual "predicate acts" were very different. For instance, the other guys, DiMaria and Corrozo, were not accused of any violent crimes, unlike Gotti and the rest, who were named in three murders—McBratney, Gelb, and Plate. Still, Gotti would have his joint defense.

After his shower at the MCC, Gotti donned a blue, tailored, $1,800 double-breasted suit, similar to the gray one he was wearing in a photograph accompanying a recent *New York* magazine cover story on "The New Godfather." In July, Cutler had asked Nickerson to let Gotti come to Cutler's office for two hours every morning so they could prepare for trial, strategically and sartorially.

"My client takes great pride in his appearance," Cutler had said. "Physically coming into court haggard and worn and not impeccably attired does him a disservice when he is fighting for his life."

The judge had said no, but somehow Gotti would manage to come into court every day dressed for success in a series of chief-executive-officer ensembles that turned reporters into fashion writers. In fact, as the trial progressed, Cutler would begin to resemble his client, from his crisp white collars down to his see-through hose, which always matched his shoes.

As Gotti checked himself in the prison mirror on August 18, two codefendants in the MCC also were getting ready. One was DiMaria, already serving time for one of the predicate acts he was accused of in Giacalone's RICO case: smuggling contraband cigarettes. The other was Willie Boy Johnson, serving time for denying he was Wahoo and not becoming a witness.

Around 8:30 A.M., after breakfast, all three men were led to the van for the trip to the United States Court House in Brooklyn. For the next seven months, Wahoo and the man he ratted out rode to court together. Willie Boy acted as if nothing was wrong, and so did Gotti.

In Courtroom No. 11, a modern arena of polished mahogany and marble, the trial was about to begin. The lead defendant, after coming into the courthouse in handcuffs and riding up a back elevator, entered with a smile, and defendants out on bail greeted him with kisses and hugs, the start of a daily ritual.

After some debate, the defense table was realigned into a backward "L"; Willie Boy ended up a seat away from Johnny Boy, along the tall line of the reverse "L," facing the jury box across the room. Willie Boy was not ostracized; in fact, he was welcomed home because, when it counted most, he stood up to the pressure and did not become a witness. He and Gotti ate lunch together each day.

Diane Giacalone and co-prosecutor John Gleeson occupied a table directly in front of the jury box; Cutler objected, to no avail. Once the trial began, defense lawyers would often accuse the prosecutors of playing to the jury, as if they wouldn't think of it.

Playing to the jury was what the trial would be about. It would not be a search for truth, but a search for freedom, and for reputation. The jury would hear a million facts—the trial transcript would run 18,250 pages—and it would be impossible to keep a line on them. The facts would arrive out of sequence because of delays brought on by illness, bad weather, and even a railroad strike. And at the end of many days, after some turns in the defense blender, the facts would make hardly any sense.

Even so, it was a mob case, and the government wasn't losing any lately. Now that the boss of the biggest Family was taking his turn in the dock, the media was playing it big; Gotti had more charisma than the usual "old fucks." The hoopla was on the minds of the defense attorneys, seven wise men and a very wise woman in the service of seven wiseguys, as jury selection began.

"The government and press have made John Gotti the most feared man in America today," one lawyer told the judge during a salvo of last-minute pretrial motions. "This case against Gotti is the biggest media event since World War II," said another.

The press ignored most of the lawyers' agonizing and concentrated on Gotti: Would he say anything?

Around noon, after a squabble over where the defendants could eat lunch, pens scurried across pads when Gotti grumbled sarcastically, "Judge, why don't we just not eat? Why should we eat? We don't deserve to eat."

It was his only public remark of the day, and it was reported like a pronouncement. No matter how innocuous his words were, Gotti's flash and dash, combined with his presumed treachery and violence, was regarded as good for circulation and ratings. In a few weeks, in fact, the "Dapper Don," an unknown Queens capo the year before, would appear on the cover of *Time*, in one of Andy Warhol's last drawings.

The chief correspondent of Soviet television and radio even came by to see the man about whom so many were saying so much.

"If I were the director of a *Godfather* movie, I would be happy to find someone who looks just like him," said Vladimir P. Dounaev, who had interviewed Henry Kissinger the day before. In a sly punch at the American way, Dounaev added: "I am a bit puzzled, however, why men like him in your country always seem to have the best lawyers."

Romual Piecyk, the refrigerator man, was another surprise visitor. He knew that—despite his retractions—he was the reason why Gotti was in jail. He tried to see Nickerson, to urge him to be nice to Mr. Gotti, but Nickerson told him to put whatever he had to say in writing. Piecyk, however, held a press conference outside the courthouse and twisted in the wind.

"I honestly feel Mr. Gotti should be out on bail. I was never threatened or harassed or intimidated by Mr. Gotti."

In such a climate, Nickerson had to pick a jury. He had decided, in the aftermath of DeCicco's death, to seat an anonymous jury, a phenomenon in many Family cases. He began by having potential jurors complete a questionnaire to detect bias and knowledge of the case. Then he called them into the courtroom one by one to introduce the cast and ask more questions. Anyone aware of the case wasn't automatically rejected; the test was having an open mind, a willingness to base a verdict on a million facts.

The routine took a month, mainly because many potential jurors plainly wanted to be elsewhere and gave disingenuous answers. The seven wise men ranted and raved throughout the ordeal, saying, on the one hand, the press made it impossible to find an impartial jury and, on the other, anybody who hadn't heard about the case was too dumb to be on a jury.

"Anyone with half a brain has to have read about my client even if they read the paper only once a month," said Cutler.

Finally, on September 16, a jury of 6 men and 6 women was picked from a pool of 28 approved by Nickerson. The defense had 10 automatic challenges, the government 6. All the defense selections were subject to a veto by Gotti, the team's quarterback. Because the choices were so limited, Cutler complained that a nurse's aide—who made it onto the jury—was so "uninformed" she wasn't "from the planet we're from."

A pretty Italian-American woman, age 24, was one of Gotti's personal choices. She was Brooklyn born and bred, and single. She was "The Girl." The defense gave others nicknames, too, based on who or what they looked like. A black man was "Willie Mays." An ex-marine was "Larry King," after the talk show host. Another Italian-American woman was "The Heavy Lady." A man who the defense thought was against it from the start was "Death."

The jury also included another black, another ex-marine and another Italian-American. By and large, the jurors were middle age, middle class, and middle brow and they were about to embark on a raucous, memorable half-year journey through the world of John Gotti, hardly one of their peers.

Opening statements, the time to color the case, were held on September 25. Giacalone showed up in a power red suit, and thus the "real Italian lady" became "The Lady in Red."

"Good morning," she told the jury. "Jimmy McBratney was a big man." She had chosen to begin her effort to put Gotti away for the rest of his life by recreating a scene in Snoope's Bar on Staten Island 13 years ago:

"This was no simple barroom brawl. It was part of a pattern of criminal activity ... John Gotti killed Jimmy McBratney out of ambition—ambition to have himself in an organization known as the Gambino Crime Family."

Giacalone went to a blackboard to draw a Family tree. She explained the two counts in the indictment: the first charged a conspiracy, an agreement, to commit crimes; the second charged racketeering through commission of specific crimes. She warned that the witnesses she would call as to both counts were "just horrible people."

After 90 minutes of earnest argument, Giacalone sat down and Bruce Cutler got up with a fury. Settling back to watch the performance from the other end of the defense table was Barry Slotnick, who was representing John Carneglia. Cutler—"Who needs Barry Slotnick?"—had recently left the law firm of Slotnick and Cutler.

Cutler, prowling like the champion wrestler he formerly was, said Giacalone's statements were "half-truths and lies." Her case was a "fantasy." He went over to her blackboard and erased the Family tree because "it tells you about a secret underworld that doesn't exist."

Erasing the blackboard was a two-point reversal, and now Cutler came in low for a takedown. His client wasn't hooked up to any enterprise! The government just didn't like him because of his lifestyle! But Gotti grew up poor, was "denied Harvard," and so he ran with old friends, people like—here came a name that didn't mean anything to the jury—Angelo Ruggiero.

"What's wrong about that?"

The Bergin Hunt and Fish Club was not a "nefarious place" but a social club where nuns, women, and children came! The government would use a gang of murderers and drug dealers—perish the thought that John Gotti would even know drug dealers!—to lie about a man whose only family was his wife and kids! The government didn't like Gotti because he cursed and placed bets and took pride in his appearance!

"So when he sits there resplendent in his suit, it's not out of being bold! It is out of pride; that's what made this country great!"

Time for a big finish. The indictment "stinks" and a "fancy wine dressing" called RICO doesn't make it taste better! "It still is rancid! It's still rotten! It still makes you retch and vomit!" Cutler grabbed a copy of the indictment and—shouting "This is where it belongs!"—slam-dunked it into a waste can.

Veins still bulging, Cutler walked back to the defense table and sat down next to his client, who shook his hand.

The stage was set. Let the play begin.

25

BRUCIFICATION

IN ACT I, IT BECAME CLEAR: If John Gotti were a lawyer, he would be a Bruce Cutler.

"Hit 'im ... hit him with a baseball bat. I want that as soon as you find this guy on the floor, you give 'im a beatin'."

That was Gotti, in 1985 on the Nice N EZ bug, telling a minion how to handle a pizza-shop owner, and apart from the bat, it was the way Cutler handled witnesses at Gotti's trial; anyone with anything bad to say, one defendant later said, was "Brucified."

All lawyers in the case were adroit cross-examiners, but none insulted and rattled witnesses, and then pounded them to a pulp, the way Cutler did. Throughout, he had an air, a swagger, a look that said, "I'm great and you're a piece of shit."

Judge Nickerson, reluctant to use his authority, let Cutler get away with courtroom murder. Cutler punched after the bell and below the belt; he called Giacalone a tramp and got a witness to call her "a slut and a blow job." When it seemed the judge might slap him down, Cutler drew back, apologized, and promised to be good, usually after accomplishing what he wanted, an unfair question, an insulting remark, a sly inference, a gambit for the jury—which ultimately elected "Larry King" its foreman.

On the first day of testimony, Cutler let Nickerson know that John Gotti wanted to know and hear everything that was to go on. He didn't want the judge and lawyers to hold many sidebar conferences. "It's our position we'd like to keep sidebars to an absolute minimum," Cutler said, except for "an emergency situation."

The Gotti trial would have many emergencies—every day.

Cutler was only one of the able lawyers on the defense team. Their strategy was simple—show the case is a lie. It was unveiled early in the trial by the brothers Santangelo, Michael and George, and Susan Kellman, who represented the other guys, Leonard DiMaria and Nicholas Corozzo.

As the prosecution set the scene with several police witnesses, the Santangelo brothers chopped away. At the outset of their careers, they were Legal Aid Society lawyers—working for the poor—but now they were well-to-do gunslingers, and every time they stood to cross-examine a witness, they dripped contempt for the case, implying that every cop and agent was lying or merely mouthing facts from the ambitious table of Diane Giacalone, "that lady in red."

Her case did have problems. One was hardheaded Edward Maloney, once part of a kidnapping gang with James McBratney, the man Gotti helped kill. He was the first major witness to be Brucified.

Maloney was an easy target—it was hard to figure out why he was testifying. Having failed to get Willie Boy Johnson or Billy Battista as witnesses, and anticipating the defense would clobber Polisi and Cardinali, Giacalone put witnesses on the stand who didn't have much to offer, except their own terrible résumés.

In his questioning of Maloney, Cutler established with a rapid volley of questions that Maloney had spent half his life in prison for kidnapping, armed robbery, and other violent crimes. Then he raised his eyes from a rap sheet he was reading and, granting Maloney a look for the first time, shouted:

"You'd agree with me, sir, you are a menace and have always been, haven't you?"

"No."

"Were you a menace to society when you went into jewelry stores and held people up with a loaded gun?"

"Yes."

Through more questions—accompanied by smirks, sneers, and mocking chuckles—Cutler set up how "a bum" like Maloney was given immunity, wired up, and sent out to catch a small-timer like Philip Cestaro, the bookmaker at the Cozy Corner Bar.

"Did you ever meet John Gotti in your life, sir?"

Cutler turned toward the jury. A look of disgust. Then of wonder. And now triumph.

"No," Maloney said.

Giacalone had wanted Maloney to testify that he was targeted for murder because he and McBratney had kidnapped mobsters. But before Brucification began, Nickerson accepted a defense motion that the recording in which Maloney said Gotti "got his wings by whacking" out McBratney should not be played, because FBI agent Edward Woods had spoon-fed the idea to Maloney. There was no doubt that Gotti had helped to kill McBratney, but the jury had to wonder: What was the motive? Was it for the enterprise? Or a bar fight?

The jurors got to hear only harmless conversations between Maloney and Cestaro.

"And you know quite honestly," Cutler continued, "that as far as Phil Cestaro was concerned, he was afraid of you, wasn't he, sir?"

"Yes."

"As a matter of fact, Mr. Maloney, isn't that why you maintained a relationship with him? Because monopolizing the weak, and the sick, and the infirm is something that you know about, isn't that true?"

"No."

"Didn't Phil Cestaro tell you throughout these tapes that his friendship or relationship with you was not known to John Gotti?"

"No."

"Didn't he tell you that the reason it was not known to John Gotti was because he wouldn't want Cestaro associated with a menace, a lowlife, and a drug dealer like yourself? Isn't that what he told you, sir?"

"No."

Nickerson would remind jurors many times that questions are not evidence; only answers matter. But when questions are repeated often enough, sometimes they do matter, subliminally if not consciously, especially if a witness repeatedly answers "no."

If Maloney had replied "yes," Cutler would have moved on, but now he paused and found a transcript in which Cestaro told Maloney that they would have to meet a drug dealer in secret.

"Why?" Cutler asked. "Tell the jury the truth."

"Because he [the dealer] was involved in narcotics."

"And Phil Cestaro knew the only way to meet an individual like that would be unbeknownst to John Gotti, isn't that right, sir?"

"That's the way I understood it."

Cutler turned to look into the jurors' eyes again. An I-told-you-so look this time. *Like I said in my opening, John Gotti doesn't have anything to do with drug dealers.*

Later, when Maloney refused to confirm that the government had spent $52,000 taking care of him, Cutler waved a document and said, "Do you see a figure for the fiscal year nineteen eighty-three, eighty-four, eighty-five?"

Nickerson said the question was improperly framed, so Cutler put it another way: "Does it refresh your recollections that you received from the government in toto some fifty-two thousand dollars—well, let's see, put it this way, Mr. Maloney, that it cost the United States of America some fifty-two thousand dollars to give you a new identity, to give you a new home, to give you a new job, to cut your hair, and give you a suit, a menace and a bum like you?"

"Objection!"

"Sustained."

Cutler wasn't through. He demonstrated how the trial would at times sound like a Gotti tape recording when he asked Maloney if he were a "fucking cocksucker." He began by paraphrasing an earlier remark by Maloney that someone "gave him up," and asked, "Is that what you are, a giver upper?"

"I would say that right now."

"You used expletives like fucking cocksucker and bum on the tapes quite often, didn't you?"

"Yes."

"Is that what you are?"

"Objection!"

"Sustained."

Cutler's questioning of Maloney was enhanced by a prosecution decision to play hardball. Though not required to turn over information the government has about its own witnesses until after they testify, prosecutors usually do so beforehand, so that the defense is ready to cross-examine and the trial moves smoothly.

Citing concerns about witness safety, Giacalone and Gleeson withheld material about another member of the witness-protection program, Crazy Sally Polisi, until after his direct testimony. When the defense argued it had no time to prepare its questions, Nickerson delayed the trial and then because of a scheduling problem allowed Maloney to go on the witness stand before Polisi got back on for cross-examination by the defense.

Cutler's cross-examination of Maloney introduced Larry King and his colleagues to the idea that what is heard in direct testimony is not always all there is to know. When Polisi came back for his turn in the defense shredder, the point was made consecutively.

———

In the Polisi material that was turned over to the defense were transcripts of tapes that Polisi—the ex-marine who defrauded the Marine Corps—made with a writer who wanted to feature him in a book. On October 15, Barry Slotnick began exploring the tapes for the benefit of the jurors, especially Larry King, Willie Mays, and the other ex-marine as well as the other black on the jury.

"I think I left off ... asking you about the fight you had in jail with a black man. Is that correct?"

"That is correct."

"I believe I asked you whether you had expressed some opinions about the fact that you believed that black people were the lowest form of humanity?"

"That is correct."

"And later on when you start kidnapping black people you indicate that ... is [a] reason why you kidnap black people."

"Correct."

"You told the author ... that black people could not count, right?"

"Correct."

"When you told her this, you claim to this jury you were normal and sane. Is that correct?"

"Correct."

Polisi had nowhere to hide, and Slotnick kept him in a corner, asking Polisi if it were true that when he faked a judge into giving him probation, all he had on his mind was getting out of jail "to go out and steal."

"That is correct."

Slotnick asked if it were true that Polisi fraudulently took $300,000 from the Veterans Administration over a 20-year period after feigning insanity to get out of the Marine Corps.

"Sounds like a reasonable estimate."

As Slotnick demolished Polisi, the defendants couldn't contain their glee, and cracked jokes and laughed.

"Excuse me, Your Honor," interrupted Giacalone. "May we have an admonition as to the comments coming from behind me?"

"Yes, please don't talk."

Nickerson would use the word "please" a lot in the days ahead.

Slotnick picked up where he had left off. In addition to the VA fraud, he revealed that Polisi got a $400 monthly disability check from the Social Security Administration.

"Isn't it a fact that every day of your life, you woke up and said to yourself, 'Who can I rip off today?'"

"At one point in my life, I would say that's correct."

Cutler also got in his licks at the would-be antihero of a never-published book whose working title was *Kicks.*

"Mr. Polisi, haven't you spent your adult life taking advantage of the weak, the infirm, the diseased, and women?"

"No, sir."

Cutler called Polisi a "yellow dog" for punching a black inmate, running away, and causing a race riot while in prison. He got him to agree that Gotti was "loved and revered" in the Queens neighborhoods that Polisi had polluted with drugs.

Nickerson raised his voice when Cutler inserted the name of federal Judge Mark Constantino into the trial. The judge had been quoted in newspapers as calling Polisi a "lowlife" because Polisi had said a case in Constantino's court was fixed.

Cutler wanted to use Constantino to bash Polisi some more. Nickerson tried to stop him, but Cutler kept punching, after the bell.

"Did you find out yesterday that Judge Constantino called you a lowlife and a liar?"

"Objection!"

"Stop, stop. Don't do that again, Mr. Cutler."

"I wanted to know if he knows it."

"Stop. The objection is sustained."

"I wanted to know if he knows it."

"The objection is sustained."

"I won't ask." Cutler asked again.

Later, at sidebar, Giacalone asked Nickerson to admonish Cutler if he "continues to behave improperly before the jury."

"You shouldn't ask a question like that about Judge Constantino," Nickerson told Cutler. "Don't do that."

"I just asked if he was aware."

"Don't do that. You know it's improper."

"I don't believe it's an accident," Giacalone said. "It's happened over and over again. I don't believe the government will be able to get a fair trial if counsel continues to use these tactics."

"I think you will get a fair trial," Nickerson said.

When Giacalone got her chance to question Polisi again, on redirect, she tried to establish that he was a reformed man.

"Mr. Polisi, are you proud of the way you played your life in the past twenty years?

"No. I think it's completely un-American, and I'm ashamed of the way I lived my life."

Moans from the defense table. Cutler objected to the answer and asked that it be stricken. Giacalone asked that Cutler's "performance" be stricken. Cutler denied performing and the judge overruled another lawyer's request to strike Giacalone's characterization of Cutler's objection.

In a recross of Polisi, Cutler got in a final shot when he asked him when he had acquired "this new religion? Tell us so we can free the jails of lowlifes like you."

When Giacalone, unable to do much with Maloney, put on other witnesses about the McBratney case, Cutler agitated her more. Her contempt for him was now heartfelt and she would soon make her first demand that he be cited for contempt.

A man in Snoope's Bar the night McBratney died was on the witness stand. During his cross, Cutler sought to plant the fact that the first state trial in the McBratney killing—when John Gotti, on the lam, was not a defendant—had ended with a hung jury.

Each time Cutler tried to plant, Giacalone objected and Nickerson sustained and told Cutler to stop, but Cutler ended up just shouting out what he wanted the jury to hear.

As Giacalone rose to object again, Cutler said: "Ms. Giacalone is getting up. I don't know if she is doing it for the exercise of getting up ..."

"Those comments aren't useful," Nickerson said. "Please."

After two more objections were sustained, Cutler yelled: "Will the government stipulate there was a hung jury ...?"

"Just a moment, please, please don't shout like that, Mr. Cutler."

"I'm asking if he knows it."

"Please don't shout like that. Please disregard those comments, members of the jury."

Later on, Cutler sneaked in an appeal to the jurors' sense of fairness by suggesting there is a double-jeopardy issue with the RICO statute—an idea held baseless by appeals courts on the theory that when a punished crime shows up as a predicate act in a RICO case, it's merely evidence of a new crime—the crime of racketeering to benefit an illegal enterprise.

"Did you ever hear of someone going to jail twice for the same crime?" Cutler asked.

"Objection!"

"Sustained."

A turn, a look of woe. "Thank you," said Cutler.

"All right," said Nickerson. "Let's have lunch."

After the jury had filed out, Giacalone asked Nickerson to cite Cutler for contempt. Cutler had made it "very obvious" he intended to introduce improper evidence and questions "that contain facts that are irrelevant." He intended to "shout" and "make comments" and "take this courtroom and turn it into a music hall for Mr. Cutler."

Though he agreed, Nickerson demurred. "I don't think I am going to hold him in contempt now, but the questions were plainly improper and have been with respect to several of the witnesses."

"You know what I think?" asked Cutler. "Ms. Giacalone doesn't like the way I question people because I show the jury the scum that they are." Cutler said witnesses in the case had called him to complain about how "Ms. Giacalone threatens them, how Mr. Gleeson threatens them. And then they get up in a nice little dress and a nice suit and say in front of the press, 'John Gotti is going to influence witnesses.' ... I don't care, Your Honor. I care about my client most of all. The government doesn't like it. Their case is sliding down the tubes."

Richard Rehbock, Willie Boy's attorney, spoke up here. He implied Giacalone was "floating" stories in the press. The "most famous" one—that as a schoolgirl she had walked by the Bergin Hunt and Fish Club in the 1960s—was "absurd."

"You will see, Your Honor, it didn't exist there. It wasn't in Ozone Park [then]," Rehbock said.

The jury didn't hear this factual offer, but near the end of the trial it would hear a completely contrary one—from a defense witness.

Cutler's comment about witnesses contacting him was a tipoff that some big surprises lay ahead in the trial of John Gotti. Some would involve James Cardinali, who had spoken to Cutler months earlier, after a shouting match with Giacalone. Some would arrive with a man from the past: Matthew Traynor, who had known Gotti since their teenage gang days. Giacalone had intended to call Traynor, who was in jail for bank robbery, but dumped him after another squabble. Traynor then called Cutler.

"I went to see Mr. Traynor," Cutler told Nickerson on October 20, "and ... we were together three hours."

Cutler and others executed trial strategies approved, and sometimes conceived, by Gotti. A key strategy: rattle Giacalone, get on her nerves, get her to lose control in front of the jury, put her on trial.

Gotti got into the game on occasion, once while Victor Ruggiero, a former NYPD detective, was on the stand. Michael Santangelo was giving Ruggiero a hard time and Ruggiero was being hard right back, dodging questions in a challenging way—if Ruggiero were still a cop, his bosses would not have been happy. At one point, Nickerson ordered him to be responsive.

Snickers in the court. Giacalone asked for a sidebar: "Something happened on the last question."

Nickerson sent the jury and Ruggiero out of court.

"Your Honor, as you were explaining to the witness, Mr. Gotti said distinctly, 'He is doing it because we threatened him, that is why.' If I can hear him [being sarcastic], there is a chance the first juror could."

"It's not true, Your Honor," Gotti said, arms out, palms up, a look of exasperation. "If anybody is making comments, it's her."

"My client doesn't make comments unless I am there," Cutler added. "Is this really necessary? She cleared out the courtroom and does a little song and dance. We would like to try the case."

As the trial dragged on, Gotti began regularly tossing off lines for reporters. "They got no case," he would say. "If my kids ever lied as much as these guys lied, they'd have no dinner." All the while, Gotti, his codefendants, and their lawyers kept studying the jurors—looking to see if "Death" was showing any sign of becoming "Life."

26

THE ART OF BEING MENDACIOUS

"THIS IS OUT OF GRIMM'S *Fairy Tales*," was a line John Gotti tossed off on December 2, after two days of listening to James Cardinali link him to what certainly sounded like an illegal enterprise.

Gotti was putting on a good face. Cardinali had come across as the "critical witness" he was billed; he had spoken calmly and in great detail and tied Gotti and the others to all three murders cited in the racketeering count. Cardinali had put Giacalone's case back on track, and the defense was alarmed.

Despite his murderous pedigree, whacking out Cardinali on cross-examination wasn't going to be the tea party it was with Maloney and Polisi, even though the defense was holding a few extra cards.

Several months earlier, during the pretrial preparations, Cardinali had become furious at Giacalone and written angry letters to, among others, Senator Alfonse D'Amato of New York, who wrote a "What's-going-on-here?" letter to Giacalone. More importantly, from prison, Cardinali called Cutler and trashed her in tape-recorded comments. As it turned out, some of his anger was based on a misunderstanding, and by the start of the trial, he had made his peace with her and stopped talking to Cutler.

Once, however, would be enough. Knowing he was on tape, Cardinali could hardly run from his earlier comments; moreover, he could hardly deny the blood on his hands and his motivation for cooperating. The way to handle these realities, he decided, was to be agreeable, almost cheerful. During much of his cross, he came across as a happy-go-lucky killer who had snookered the government into an incredibly generous deal. The defense used him to implement part of its strategy: put Giacalone on trial.

The carnage began on December 4 and lasted two weeks. Gene Gotti's attorney, Jeffrey Hoffman, a former assistant district attorney in Manhattan, was first up. His job was to test the witness's candor, and from the start Jamesy was very candid.

"Would it be accurate to say that you have one primary reason for testifying?"

"Correct."

"And have you described that primary reason as to save your own ass?"

"Exactly."

"Did you have meetings where she [Giacalone] or others in her presence threatened you?"

"Yes."

"[Did] Miss Giacalone ever lie to you?"

"In my opinion, yes."

Hoffman got Cardinali to admit he was looking to do well in his testimony to attract book-and-movie deals. He got him to admit he knew when he began to cooperate he wasn't going to get a good deal if he didn't have good evidence.

"They very specifically let you know that you have to produce for them, right? Or, you were valueless?"

"Absolutely."

As Jamesy answered questions, he occasionally looked over to the defendants, as if to say, *I'm sorry, but I couldn't do the time; I'm still one of you, you know that.*

Now, Jamesy was about to put Giacalone on the floor, by doing for Hoffman what he did for her, tell her the truth.

"Did [Giacalone] ever tell you about any things that go on between she and [Nickerson], how he treated her?"

"Objection! Objection!"

"No, I will let him answer that," Nickerson said.

"Not during this trial," Cardinali said, inviting a follow-up.

"Did you ever say that she said that he treats her like a daughter?"

"She told me that."

"And that she gets whatever she wants from him and the defense gets nothing. Did she tell you that?"

"I've heard her say something like that."

Later, in an embarrassing moment at sidebar, Giacalone would not deny that she had spoken so freely in front of Cardinali. It was an admission that she had trusted a criminal with something of value, even if her boasts were merely careless chatter.

After only a few hours of Cardinali's candor, Gotti felt better and felt like swaggering. During a recess, he strolled over to the audience section; smiling confidently, he pointed his finger at three men— John Gilmore Childers, John Savarese, and Michael Chertoff, prosecutors from the Southern District who had just won guilty verdicts against all the bosses and underbosses in the Commission case and who later told friends that the atmosphere in the Nickerson court was much more tense.

"Childers, Savarese, Chertoff," said Gotti. "You know who I am. Now I know who you are. It's better when everybody knows each other."

The job of leading Jamesy through his catalogue of crimes fell to David DePetris, former chief of the narcotics unit in the Eastern District. DePetris's client was Tony Roach Rampino, the Gotti gopher who had become a heroin addict. Because Tony Roach tested positive for drugs early in the trial, DePetris had to assure Nickerson every day that Rampino wasn't stoned and was able to assist in his own defense.

Under DePetris's probing, Cardinali admitted using drugs while in the witness-protection program awaiting his debut as a star witness. He admitted that while at the MCC, he assaulted an inmate who ratted out a guard who was supplying him with heroin. His punishment was a transfer to a prison in California, where he again was caught using drugs.

Most of Cardinali's direct testimony would remain intact despite the whacks of seven lawyers; he would be tripped up on only a few discrepancies. But details about his behavior, atop all the slime about his murders, were having their intended effect on the jurors—during jury selection, Larry King himself had said he would "have a problem" with the testimony of criminals singing for their freedom.

Halfway through DePetris's questioning, Slotnick complained at a sidebar that Giacalone and Gleeson were making "facial expressions" as Cardinali testified. Giacalone denied it, the judge said he hadn't seen it and called a recess. As the jury began to file out, Giacalone heard a murmur from the defense table, and once the jury was gone, spoke up:

"I think it's ironic. On the way back from a sidebar in which counsel made claims about the behavior of the government, which they were unable to articulate, Mr. Gotti said quite loudly and I'm certain loudly enough for the jury to hear ... "

Gotti cut her off, "She's lying to you!"

Giacalone finished her sentence: " ... 'she's trying to protect that murderer, she's the murderer, that mother.'"

"Judge, do I have to go through this all the time?" Cutler inquired.

"Those are lies!" Gotti said.

"Please," Nickerson said.

Giacalone asked the judge to instruct the defendants to keep their comments to themselves when the jury is present.

"I sit here and I have to watch Ms. Giacalone making faces, grimaces, smiles, comments to Mr. Gleeson," Cutler said. "I don't like it ... I don't know why she's brought this out now."

"Because she's a liar!" Gotti said.

Nickerson told the prosecution not to make faces, the defense not to make comments.

Later, Gotti said to a reporter: "Mendacity. The word for today is mendacity. It's the art of being mendacious."

On December 15, the start of Cardinali's third week on the stand, Giacalone sought to rehabilitate him. Jamesy said he had told the truth in court; the only threats Giacalone had ever made were to prosecute him for lying; and he would be killed by the defendants if he ever returned to Ozone Park.

Jamesy said he was "frequently abusive" to Giacalone and "yelled" at her on the phone.

Giacalone used this response to get in a shot worthy of Cutler. "Did you ever speak to John Gotti the way you talked to me on the telephone?"

"Objection, judge!" Cutler cried.

"Sustained."

"Are you kidding me?" Cutler said in disgust.

Several more times during the remainder of Cardinali's testimony, Giacalone and the defense lawyers exchanged barbs. The defense, however, had a numbers advantage; they could rest on the bench while their teammates rushed Giacalone and Gleeson all over the field.

Giacalone ended her redirect by getting Jamesy to say that Cutler was pleasant, a "gentleman, soft-spoken," when he spoke outside of court, unlike the way Cutler "behaves in court."

As Giacalone sat down, a defense lawyer asked for a brief delay, but Cutler, who was to re-Brucify, was already up and storming toward Jamesy and one of the trial's many low points.

"You made up with Ms. Giacalone, did you?"

"Yes."

"So she's no longer the same individual you described in May of 1986, is that correct?"

"That's correct."

"In other words, she's no longer a slut, is that right, in your mind?"

"Correct."

"She's no longer a blow job in your mind?"

"Correct."

"Excuse me a minute," interrupted Nickerson. "Please keep your voice down."

"Yes, sir, sorry, sir ... I apologize to the court."

"Please don't make those comments and please keep your voice down."

A few questions later, Cutler ignored an objection and the judge's ruling—and kept punching.

"Mr. Cutler, please don't do that. The objection is sustained. Please don't do that."

"Yes, Your Honor."

More questions, more objections, more questions.

"Please, Mr. Cutler, please."

A little later, Cutler asked Cardinali about the "free ride" he got for his multiple murders.

"Objection!"

Another put-upon look from Cutler. "It's all right if Ms. Giacalone interrupts me, but it's not okay if I interrupt her, Your Honor?"

"Just a minute," Nickerson said. "She's entitled to make an objection."

"I don't want a speech from her," Cutler snarled.

On many occasions, Cutler and the others tested the limits of Nickerson's patience, and almost always found them expansive. And many times they stated grievances against Giacalone and Gleeson without the slightest compunction about their irony.

The next day, for instance, Slotnick moaned about Cutler-type tactics from Giacalone during his recross of Cardinali. "I would wish that counsel would follow the rules," he said.

At a sidebar, Cutler complained that Giacalone was getting on Gotti's nerves. "Your Honor, Ms. Giacalone is making a lot of comments ... a lot of facial gestures. I spoke with my client. He's very upset about it ... He's going to do the same thing, judge. He's upset about it. I want you to know about it and I would like you to try and put a stop to it, judge."

Giacalone fired back: The defense had decided "it is advantageous to harass me" and "create a record that is absolutely false" in "the face of the most extraordinary harassment" ever seen "in either a federal or state court."

Giacalone said she sometimes could barely hear witnesses because the noise at the defense table was so loud—"I can hear them say, 'The rat is dead.'"

"This thing about harassment is not true," Cutler said.

On December 16, as Act II was winding down, FBI agents and cops handed out leaflets to Christmas shoppers on East Forty-sixth Street in Manhattan. The leaflets asked if anyone had been on the street the year before and heard or seen anything about the murders of Paul Castellano and Thomas Bilotti outside Sparks Steak House.

"If witnesses to the killings would only come forward, these murderers could be brought to justice. We need your help to solve this crime. We need your participation to keep the streets of our city safe for all. It is imperative to the maintenance of a civilized society."

The Sparks investigation had stalled. Informants had stories, not evidence. One story recently out was that John Gotti's driver and also Gene Gotti and seven crew members were at the scene of the crime.

In court a week later, John Gotti stood at the railing of the visitors' section to accept season's greetings from many crew members. After a dozen or so had passed in review, exchanging handshakes and kisses, Gotti jovially turned to reporters: "See all these good people. They come to wish me a merry Christmas."

The New Year began with another "major" witness: Dominick Lofaro, who had worn a body wire for the state Organized Crime Task Force, which had touted him—once he was surfaced for trial—as the first made man to secretly tape-record other soldiers.

On January 6, 1987, the Feast of Epiphany, Lofaro pleaded guilty to racketeering—two of his predicate acts were murder. For his plea, Lofaro got immunity for anything he would say at Gotti's or any other trial. The government requested that Lofaro be held at a "safe house" until sentencing, but Jack Weinstein, chief judge of the Eastern District, sent Lofaro to the MCC.

"After what this man told me, he is clearly a danger to the community," Judge Weinstein said.

However, an interested observer, Bruce Cutler, predicted that at sentencing time, "Lofaro will walk."

In reality, Lofaro didn't have much to offer against Gotti. He had provided the probable cause the state Task Force needed to instill the Nice N EZ bug—his body wire recorded Gotti talking as though he ran a gambling operation—but none of the Nice N EZ tapes were part of Giacalone's case; all of them had been made after Gotti was indicted in March 1985.

All Lofaro could testify about was the two times he taped Gotti, and though these were colorful conversations, they were not terribly incriminating. Giacalone already had plenty of colorful conversations, but state Task Force director Ronald Goldstock, eager to get credit for getting Gotti, had promoted Lofaro in the media and Giacalone was desperate for witnesses.

A day after his guilty plea, Lofaro caused more damage—to Giacalone. He told the Gotti jury that he had suckered the state Task Force and lied about being a made man; he was merely a lowly associate. He also had exaggerated the number of his murders, figuring, as only a denizen of the Crime Capital would, the more murders, the bigger catch he would appear to be.

"I figured I could get a better deal from them," he said.

Lofaro self-destructed without defense help. He described his two murders, an attempted murder, dealing kilos of heroin, and how the Task Force—to set him up as an informer—let him keep $100,000 in drug money that he had when arrested.

A week later, just before her final witness—now-federal investigator Kenneth McCabe—took the stand, Nickerson ordered Giacalone to use the time during a recess to search for documents that the defense lawyers complained had not yet been turned over to them.

As the jury filed out, Giacalone approached George Santangelo and wagged her finger at him: "You're lying!"

"Get your finger out of my face and stick it up your ass," said Santangelo.

During the recess, the newspaper reporters who regularly covered the trial—Pete Bowles of *Newsday*, Leonard Buder of *The New York Times*, Daniel Hays of the *New York Daily News*, and Philip Messing of the *New York Post*—called their offices and picked up bulletins about another big case.

Across the East River in Manhattan, the defendants in the Commission case had just been sentenced. The aging bosses of the Colombo, Genovese, and Luchese Families, none of whom had made the cover of *Time*, got 100 years each.

"A hundred years! A century!" exclaimed Gene Gotti's attorney, Jeffrey Hoffman, as he came into the courtroom to inform the Gambino boss.

Johnny Boy was cool. He moved over to the rail separating the well of the court and spoke to the reporters clamoring for a reaction: "Those cases got nothing to do with us. We're walking out of here."

The next day, January 14, on the forty-sixth day of testimony, after calling 78 witnesses, the government rested. Before it did, Cutler got Kenneth McCabe to say that in all the times he surveilled John Gotti he never saw him commit a crime. Cutler strutted away: Chew on that fact, Larry King and friends.

Very few people know the facts behind some facts that Jeffrey Hoffman had drawn out of Cardinali weeks earlier.

Cardinali testified that he learned in April 1985 that without his testimony, Giacalone had "an extraordinarily weak case." Cardinali's discovery was made when prison officials mistakenly showed him a letter intended for their eyes only. The letter was written by Giaca-lone's supportive boss, Raymond Dearie, who wanted the prison personnel to make Jamesy's life better.

Getting the star witness—who was about to be made into a villain—to say that without him Giacalone had a poor case, was another clever move by the defense. But Cardinali, Hoffman, and the jurors never learned that a top government official—before the indictment was handed down—told his Washington bosses and Giacalone's boss, Raymond Dearie, that the case was a loser, even with Cardinali's testimony.

In an October 23, 1984 memo, Edward McDonald, chief of the federal Organized Crime Strike Force in the Eastern District, said Giacalone's case had "little likelihood of success." He said it would prevent the Strike Force, which had been created to battle organized crime, from including Gotti in the Gambino hierarchy indictment it hoped to obtain the following year.

On March 8, 1985, two weeks before Gotti's indictment, McDonald wrote a much stronger memo. Gotti and Dellacroce should be a part of the hierarchy case because Giacalone's case "was especially weak against Gotti and Dellacroce and with respect to Gotti, could very well result in his acquittal." This, he warned, would "immunize" Gotti from future RICO prosecutions involving gambling or loan-sharking conspiracies through 1984, the endpoint of the conspiracy charged in Giacalone's case.

McDonald obviously was interested in protecting his own turf, but the Strike Force had been given the job of fighting the mob, and Giacalone was getting in the way. He proposed she give up Gotti and Dellacroce for the Strike Force case and proceed against Tony Roach Rampino and John Carneglia on conspiracy charges involving the armored-car heists, which had prompted her to go after Gotti. McDonald also said Willie Boy Johnson should not be in either case.

The memos would make for interesting cross-examinations, if McDonald, Giacalone, or Dearie ever got on the stand. But the star witness of the trial was James Cardinali, who, during his testimony, had this to say about John Gotti:

"He is the finest man I ever met."

27

WAY TO GO, MR. G!

IN ITS FINAL ACT, THE GOTTI play because a farce. Diane Giacalone, for example, was accused of offering her underwear to a witness.

It happened during the defense part of the case, which began with Andrew Curro and Peter Zuccaro, two of the armored-car robbers, who testified they did not give any of the loot—about $1 million, never recovered—to anyone at the Bergin.

"What am I, Santa Claus?" said Zuccaro.

While Giacalone was cross-examining Curro, Judge Nickerson called for a sidebar, but Cutler stayed seated. As the other lawyers passed behind him en route to the bench, Cutler said: "See if the tramp will give us an offer of proof."

The wording of Cutler's request that Giacalone state the relevance of a point she was making was a little too insulting to let go by. "In quite a loud voice," she told Nickerson, "and I believe loud enough for the jurors to hear ... Mr. Cutler said, 'Ask this tramp if she'll give us an offer of proof.'"

"Do you want me to respond?" asked Cutler, buying time while he contemplated an escape move. "Or do you just assume because Ms. Giacalone says it, it's true?"

Nickerson began to speak, but Cutler interrupted, which caused the judge to say:

"You will wait for me to finish, sir."

"You can call me Mr. Cutler or Bruce. You don't have to call me 'sir.'"

Cutler pushed and stalled some more, until he had calculated his escape, which would be an offensive move.

"I'm ashamed that she is part of this government in this courtroom. And what I said ... was to ask her to give us an offer of proof ... this is a dangerous woman. She's trying to inhibit me and intimidate me and she is not going to do it, Your Honor. I beg the court to open your eyes, Your Honor, and I say it most respectfully, to see this woman for what she is. I'm not ashamed to say it."

After more thrashing by both sides, Nickerson told everyone to calm down and forget about it. A former county executive on Long Island and an erstwhile candidate for a seat in the U.S. Senate, the 67-year-old Nickerson now wanted to steer the case toward a conclusion—without a mistrial.

After Curro and Zuccaro went back to prison, the star of the defense case came into the courtroom. The man who came to save the former Rockaway Boy was Matthew Traynor, the former Ridgewood Saint who became a thief, bank robber, and drug dealer— *perish the thought that Gotti would even know a drug dealer!*

Traynor was another Giacalone mistake. Prior to the trial's original start, he was her witness. Desperate for witnesses to complement Cardinali, she had decided to use a man who had once tried to con his way out of prison by lying to the FBI about a nonexistent murder plot against a cop.

Giacalone had spent many hours preparing Traynor for his testimony, but then she caught him in what she felt was a lie. He told her that while he and Cardinali were cellmates in the MCC, he had overheard Cardinali tell Cutler that he had lied to the grand jury. Giacalone didn't believe it and dumped Traynor from her witness list. Once the trial was underway, Traynor, seeking to shave some time off his bank-robbery sentence, volunteered his services again, but Giacalone shunned him.

So Traynor called Cutler and told him some Giacalone stories. Some on the defense team were opposed to putting Traynor on the witness stand. They felt he was an unguided missile who might detonate over them. In addition, his FBI files—which would come into the case as evidence—were heavy with details about murder, drug dealing, and other crimes by the Berginites.

Gotti, however, felt that what Traynor wanted to say about Giacalone was more important and of course, he prevailed.

Traynor, age 40, took the stand on February 2, wearing a smirk and a pullover sweater. He promptly said that the prosecution had plied him with drugs to induce him to invent stories about the defendants. He said he was frequently "zonked out" when he appeared at Giacalone's office for a preparation session.

"I was so stoned I didn't want to go home," he said.

It only got worse, as the defense "sucked the hate"—as the process was known—out of Matthew Traynor, who referred to Giacalone as "the woman with the stringy hair." Finally, he cocked his fingers like a gun and pointed at her; he said when he told her he wanted to "get laid," she "gave me her panties out of her bottom drawer and told me to facilitate myself."

The defense had put Giacalone on trial during the cross of Cardinali. Traynor was used to keep her there.

"She said, 'Make do with these,'" Traynor said.

"She really wanted me to frame Mr. Gotti and the others," he continued. "She didn't like them ... because many years earlier they had ridiculed her for being skinny when she used to walk through the neighborhood where they hung out."

But wait. At sidebar months earlier, a defense lawyer had accused Giacalone of "floating" an "absurd" story about walking past the Bergin as a schoolgirl. The Bergin wasn't even in Ozone Park then!

One fact for the judge, one fact for the jury.

Traynor slugged on. He said that DEA agent Edward Magnuson had given him drugs and when he begged for more, he was sent to a doctor with a fat pad of Rx prescriptions and got Valium and codeine. He said he was so "zonked" that once he vomited all over Giacalone's desk, and she screamed, "Get him out of here!" He said agents drove him around to sober him up.

Over three days, Traynor was crossed, redirected, and recrossed. It added up to a numbing record of confusion and conflict, all for the get-Giacalone defense.

After it was mercifully over, Nickerson, whose patience had ceased being a virtue, made his strongest statement about the defense—on a day when the trial was in recess, to a virtually empty courtroom. Nickerson finally spoke his mind after coprosecutor John Gleeson spoke his; Gleeson came into court to complain that the defense had gotten too personal.

It had served a subpoena on a hospital for job records of Gleeson's wife, a nurse. The doctor who prescribed the drugs for Traynor was on the staff of the same hospital. Gleeson, age 33, who left a big-time Manhattan law firm to become a federal prosecutor, told Nickerson the subpoena was "harassment," pure and simple.

Gleeson was speaking up and asking Nickerson to control the defense because the harassment had "reached outside the courtroom" to "someone very close to me for a reason that I think is patently pre-textural." He said David DePetris had apologized for the defense, which was "appropriate" but not sufficient. He asked Nickerson "to exert some control" over a defense effort "to create issues of impropriety where none exist" in order "to take this jury's eye off the ball."

DePetris showed up to take the heat for the defense, which had wanted to establish a link between the prosecution and Dr. Harold Schwartz, the doctor Traynor was sent to. DePetris told Nickerson he was unaware until late the day before that other defense attorneys had decided to try and make the link by causing a subpoena to be issued.

"How is it conceivably relevant?" said Nickerson.

"How the government got to Dr. Schwartz," said DePetris. "Because the government got to Dr. Schwartz presumably through Mr. Gleeson's wife."

"It is just so off the wall, completely off the wall," Nickerson said about the notion that the United States government had to use Gleeson's wife to get a doctor to write prescriptions for Traynor.

Nickerson quashed the subpoena with words that showed how he felt, but not how he ever acted: "This case is not going to turn into any more of a circus than the defendants' attorneys have already made it."

After calling 11 witnesses, the defense rested on February 11. Giacalone then announced she would call 17 witnesses for a rebuttal case.

"Seventeen?" Nickerson wearily asked.

At the six-month mark, everyone was weary, especially Larry King, Willie Mays, The Girl, and all the rest, who wanted to go back to being people again, not numbers. They had been told it would be a two-month trial.

The defense, however, had succeeded in putting Giacalone on the defensive. She felt Traynor's statements could not go unrebutted. She felt the jury had to see how reputations—hers, Dr. Schwartz's, DEA agent Magnuson's—had been besmirched on behalf of John Gotti.

Over three more weeks, the 17 testified. Agents, prison officials, detectives, and Dr. Harold Schwartz, who did not know what lay ahead when he was asked a year earlier to examine a federal prisoner apparently suffering a loss of nerve.

When he saw him, Schwartz said that Matthew Traynor was "suffering from a massive anxiety reaction" about testifying against Gotti. "He was pacing back and forth. He was sweating profusely. He was flushed. Very, very agitated." The patient, the doctor added, was "very anxious" and "afraid for his life." He feared he would say something that would help the defendants find him, and kill him, even if he were in the witness-protection program.

Schwartz said Traynor was "embarrassed and humiliated" that he didn't have the strength to be a stand-up guy, like Willie Boy Johnson was in the end. "He mentioned the phrase, 'If you can't do the time, don't do the crime.'" Schwartz said he prescribed Valium and Tylenol with codeine for the pain Traynor felt from a separated shoulder. The drugs were given to prison officials, who dispensed them as indicated.

That was direct and now Cutler got up, to indirect.

As Schwartz tried to answer his questions, Cutler kept cutting him off to twist, shape, bend, and contort, which finally caused Gleeson to get personal, too.

"I object to cutting off the witness," Gleeson protested.

"Yes," said Nickerson.

Cutler started Brucifying again.

"Let him finish his answer, Mr. Cutler."

Cutler started up again, the same way.

"I object to Mr. Cutler's manner, which is peculiarly offensive," said Gleeson.

"[It] really isn't helpful," said Nickerson.

"I am doing the best I can, Your Honor, I am not a doctor."

"You are a lawyer," reminded Nickerson.

"He is not a lawyer, either," said Gleeson. His Cravath Swaine & Moore decorum had departed.

Nickerson excused the jury to hear Willie Boy's attorney, Richard Rehbock, sail away on a long discourse that ended this way: "This whole trial is not a search for the truth. It's become a massive cover-up where they can do whatever they want and we are restricted from bringing out the truth for the jury."

It was a little too much, even for Nickerson, who didn't even respond. He turned to Gleeson and Cutler and told them to cut the crap. Please. He wanted to bring the jury back in and get the damn case over with.

"Please don't make comments," he said. "Hopefully, we are coming to the end of this trial—someday."

The jurors filed back. A few lawyers were sure they had recently seen signs of Life in Death. One was sure The Heavy Lady had been saying with her eyes, *I know what you are doing, and it is working.*

Cutler started in on Schwartz again and kept on going even after Nickerson called for a sidebar.

"I am going to ask you not to talk over me," said Nickerson when he finally got Cutler's attention.

"I have not heard you."

"You have talked over my voice throughout the trial. I think it is most discourteous. I will not stand it anymore from you."

"I have not done it on purpose."

"You have done it constantly."

"Judge, I really don't need this in front of the jury. I don't think that's right. If I am talking over you in the heat of battle, so to speak, I apologize. But I didn't hear you ask me to come up until you asked me to come up."

A few more exchanges and Nickerson said, "Let's finish this. Please. Please. Let's finish."

Then to the jury: "If you heard any comments made by anyone at the sidebar, please disregard them."

Later in the day, Cutler asked if Gotti could be excused from court on the same day that Nickerson was to meet the attorneys to decide what to tell the jury about the applicable law before it began deliberations.

"I don't mind," Nickerson said. "All I want to emphasize to you, Mr. Gotti, I think it's important to you ..."

"If I'm here I can say something?" said the boss who always had a lot to say.

"No."

Well, then, forget about it.

At the end of the rebuttal case, Gleeson came close to accusing Cutler of suborning perjury, so close the defense thought he had. Afterward, for the first time in 18,250 pages of trial transcript, Cutler remained quiet and asked another lawyer to respond to Gleeson's comments.

This revealing moment came during a discussion about the Cardinali-Cutler interview that was tape-recorded. The story that Traynor, who was in the MCC at the same time as Cardinali, told about that interview—that Cardinali told Cutler he lied to the grand jury—was why Giacalone dumped Traynor as a witness; she felt he was lying and that Cardinali had said no such thing. A tape would prove it and could be used to prosecute Traynor—and maybe Cutler.

When Cutler spoke to Traynor, Gleeson charged, he "found a person" willing "to tell a lie to hurt the prosecution." At the time, however, "Mr. Cutler had in his possession ... proof that the lie he had at that point, that Traynor was telling at that point, wouldn't work, wouldn't fly."

Gleeson continued: "It turned out later on ... Mr. Traynor came up with some more allegations against the government, some more and different ones, that wouldn't be refuted by the tape that we believe exists."

"All right," said Nickerson. "Who would like to be heard on the other side?"

"Mr. Hoffman," said Cutler.

"Mr. Gleeson," Jeffrey Hoffman began, "has indicated that he believed that Mr. Cutler had a witness who he knew would lie and that he suborned that witness's perjury by calling the witness in that case," said Hoffman.

"That's not what I understood him to say," said Nickerson.

"I didn't say that," said Gleeson.

Gleeson didn't say it, but he had inferred it, and after the trial, a grand jury would begin a perjury investigation.

Nickerson ended the discussion by telling the lawyers not to destroy any tapes or notes.

On March 2, for almost five hours, Diane Giacalone summed up her case. She was tired and even thinner than she was at the start of trial seven months earlier. Her voice was raspy and weak and several times she identified people using the wrong name.

She played portions of tapes made at Neil's house, when Neil booted a capo out of the family. But she was not allowed to play the parts featuring Gotti asking Angelo about *La Cosa Nostra* because the tapes were made after Gotti was indicted. Nonetheless, she said, the evidence showed the Gambino Family was a "frightening reality" whose members "exercised their power without regard to the law or human life."

Over at the defense table, two men dressed almost exactly alike, John Gotti and Bruce Cutler, sat stoically as Giacalone dealt with the million-facts problem. She said the jury's job was "not to look at the pieces of the puzzle one at a time." Rather, "each piece of evidence is to be considered in the context of the other pieces of evidence."

Now, it was Cutler's turn. Like Gotti, he wore a gray double-breasted suit, white shirt, red tie, and matching pocket hanky. Only the shade of the suit was different as he rose to make a last pitch for his client. And now, for the first time in the trial, he turned down his volume and sounded like a discussion leader in a book circle.

He pointed out that no witnesses had testified they saw Gotti commit a crime, or shared the proceeds of a crime with him, or were ordered by him to commit a crime.

"You want to get John Gotti? Get some evidence on him. You want to bring him to trial some other place, go ahead and do so. Find that he did something wrong. Find a witness. Do it the right way. The ends do not justify the means."

The jury couldn't convict John Gotti, Cutler said, merely because the government didn't like his lifestyle.

"The government is people. It's my government, it's John Gotti's government. It's your government. But it's people. People do things wrong. You are the only shield we have against abuse of power, against tyranny."

The jurors deliberated for a week. They asked that parts of Cardinali's testimony be read back, but not Traynor's. That was considered good for the government. The day before they came in with a verdict, they asked for a chart prepared by the defense showing all the crimes committed by the witnesses. That was considered good for the defense. But it was all guesswork, as it always is.

On Friday the 13th of March, juror No. 10, Larry King, the foreperson, sent a note to Judge Nickerson shortly after the lunch recess: "We have reached a unanimous verdict." The agonizing wait for the only judgments that mattered was over.

"We're walking out of here," John Gotti said with the surety of a man betting on a fixed race, as he and the others took their places one final time.

The news that a verdict was in swept the courthouse and now the courtroom filled up as it did on the trial's opening day. After so much farce, the play was ending on a moment of pure drama.

All rise, please. Jury entering.

In walked the keys to freedom, anonymous but so familiar by now. Eyes cast downward, they showed no emotion. They were a solemn file staying their secret to the end.

Suddenly it was overwhelmingly quiet.

"Would you take the verdict from the foreperson?" Nickerson asked his clerk, William Walsh.

Walsh read from a form: "Count one, the conspiracy count, how do you find John Gotti, guilty or not guilty?"

Larry King's voice was diplomatically even: "Not guilty."

A collective gasp seemed to suck all the air out of the room. Gotti clenched his fist and suppressed a smile. What would the jury do with the others?

"Count one, John Carneglia, how do you find?"

"Not guilty."

Another gasp. And now whispers and murmuring. And an electric momentum as the clerk kept calling for the fates of the five others. And five more times, "Not guilty," the words crackling like sparks from a downed power line.

Gotti punched Cutler in the shoulder, but it wasn't over yet. The jurors had said no as to a conspiracy, but what about the racketeering count? Would they even the score?

"Count two. How do you find John Gotti?"

"Not guilty."

Exultation at the defense table. Raised fists and cheers from the Family section. Disbelief on the press row. In front of the jury, sunken prosecutors. On the bench, a crumpled judge.

Once again, around the table, the clerk kept calling, and the foreperson kept answering: "Not guilty."

"Justice!" someone screamed.

Pandemonium now in the well of the court, on one side. Hugs, slaps and, suddenly a standing ovation by the defense for Larry King and the others.

"Please don't do that," Nickerson said.

Nickerson then ordered the release of John Gotti, and the release of the keys to his freedom—the jury—which had heard the facts and found reasonable doubt that Gotti and the others conspired to commit crimes for something called the Gambino Family.

"Does the court exonerate all bail conditions for all defendants?" Jeffrey Hoffman asked.

"Yes, of course."

Those three words brought the curtain down. And as the press rushed Gotti for reaction, Diane Giacalone and John Gleeson slipped away, silently.

"Shame on them!" Gotti said, wagging his finger. "I'd like to see the verdict on them!"

Gotti put off the press by saying he might talk later, but he had no intention of doing so. He might make pithy remarks, but he didn't hold press conferences. Cutler would do that. Gotti was led out of the courtroom by the back way and taken down an elevator to clear up some paperwork at the federal marshal's office, which Philip Messing of the *Post* had staked out.

"I told you so," Gotti told Messing.

Gotti wanted to avoid the melee going on outside the main courthouse exit; surrounded by marshals, he headed toward a basement garage. Messing tagged along.

"They'll be ready to frame us again in two weeks," Gotti said.

Messing tried another question, but Gotti didn't want to say much, so Messing asked the man with a penchant for sports betting which baseball teams would be the best in 1986.

"Come on, you know how I do on those things. You don't really want me to answer that."

For a few minutes, Gotti waited by the garage door for his driver to pull up. He fidgeted and paced; everything had happened so fast. One minute he was facing the rest of his life in prison, the next he was free, and now he was going home. So much had happened in his life, so fuckin' much.

Finally, his car pulled up and Gotti dashed out the door toward it; *Post* photographer Don Halasy captured him hopping over a curb, aided by a bodyguard.

In the lobby of the courthouse, federal Strike Force prosecutor Laura Brevetti called her boss, Edward McDonald.

"I can't believe it," she said. "They beat the whole case."

McDonald looked out onto the street from his office, three floors up. He saw more cars pulling up to pick up the defense lawyers and other defendants who were shouting and punching air. He rummaged through his desk and found a copy of his memo predicting Gotti's acquittal, glanced through it, and flung it across the room.

The reporters went back into the courthouse and up to the United States Attorney's office. "A jury verdict is the end of the case," said Giacalone without any visible emotion. "My personal feelings are mine."

Up and down 101st Avenue in Ozone Park, the word was spreading, "Johnny beat the case! Johnny Boy beat the case!"

A man in a coffee shop across from the Bergin said to another man, "Queens has two world champions—the New York Mets and John Gotti."

About 4:30 P.M., a gray Cadillac with Gotti inside pulled up outside the Bergin. Several club members came out to greet him and he went inside for a few minutes. Then he went down the street to the barbershop. The only boss acquitted in the federal assault on the Families—fueled partly by the loose tongue of Angelo Ruggiero—got himself a trim.

Next, the chief suspect in the murders of Paul Castellano and Thomas Bilotti climbed into another car and was driven home to Howard Beach. He ignored another crowd of reporters and, escorted by his son John, moved grandly up the sidewalk to a side door.

"Way to go, Mr. G!" called out a passing driver, who surely never heard Gotti say, "Tommy and the other guy will get popped."

Gotti's daughter Angela, holding his grandson Frank, opened the door and Gotti went inside his home for the first time in nearly a year. Up and down the street, people had tied yellow ribbons around trees—a welcome home message for their hostage mob star.

28

THE FIX

WHILE JOHN GOTTI AND HIS SUPPORTERS celebrated, his opponents retired to their boss's office and gathered near a case of beer. It was their boss's idea. Andrew Maloney became U.S. Attorney for the Eastern District after the case began, and while he knew the FBI and the Eastern District Strike Force, among others, had opposed putting Gotti into Giacalone's case, he strongly backed her and John Gleeson throughout the trial.

For reasons he could not tell them about earlier, he also harbored suspicions that somehow Gotti—despite the secrecy surrounding the jurors' selection and their deliberations—managed to fix the case.

"Look, you will be replaying the trial for the rest of your lives," Maloney said as the prosecutors and their colleagues began to relax. "It'll never go away, but I'm telling you, Gotti was too cool during the trial, especially for the verdict."

Maloney was standing up for his troops, but also believed what he was saying. A former commander of an elite United States Army Ranger unit, he was good-natured and informal—most people called him "Andy"—but highly combative; while at West Point in the early 1950s, he was a welterweight boxing champion.

"I don't care who they are," he continued, "when the jury's out for a week, defendants start to sweat."

Giacalone and Gleeson thought Maloney was just being gracious until he began describing a memo the FBI's Gambino squad sent weeks earlier. It quoted an informant saying Gotti had reached someone on the jury. Maloney had not shared the memo with his lawyers or Judge Nickerson; that likely would have caused a mistrial, and without anything but the unsubstantiated word of one informant, would have been foolish.

Because one of its agents was a witness in the trial, the Gambino squad asked another FBI squad to investigate. The Eastern District's chief judge gave that squad the identities of the anonymous jurors, and checks led to vague suspicions about two, but without anything more specific from the informant, the agents could go no further.

Giacalone and Gleeson remained dubious as Maloney told the story. They instead wondered whether they had failed. If they had performed better, they reasoned, at least a few jurors would have believed enough in the case to refuse to go along with an acquittal and would have fought for a hung jury—which would have meant a retrial—no matter how much a secretly crooked juror trashed the case in deliberations.

Maloney wasn't dubious at all. "We may never prove it, but the case was fixed," he was soon saying, as the mood in his office lightened. "What happened in Nickerson's courtroom wasn't justice. It was fraud. We may not get Gotti for that, but we will get him."

In a few months, Maloney got the Justice Department to give Giacalone and Gleeson $5,000 bonuses for their work. Giacalone's statement at a post-acquittal conference with the press—"my personal feelings are mine"—were her last public words on the subject. In a few months more, despite her promotion to special prosecutions chief, she resigned for a job with the local transit authority.

Gleeson, who clashed with Bruce Cutler during a fiery moment in the trial—"he is not a lawyer"—would stick around.

Gotti celebrated his first night of freedom in nearly a year with a five-hour dinner at his favorite Queens restaurant, Altadonna's. Over the next couple days, he visited son Frank's grave and attended a wake for Angelo Ruggiero's father. Angelo himself stewed in prison on the heroin charges, much to his chagrin.

In the days after, Gotti vacationed in Florida without his wife. Persuaded now more than ever by Salvatore Ruggiero's death to stay off airplanes, he took the train and stayed in a $730-a-day suite at the Marriott Harbour Beach Resort in Ft. Lauderdale under the name "Russo." This was a gag on the FBI, which had recently arrested a little old lady by that name, a federal courthouse clerk, for passing secrets about gangster cases to a Family capo.

While in Florida, he and his entourage—including son Junior—piled into a sleek cigarette speedboat owned by Carlo Vaccarezza, a New York restaurant owner whom he had befriended a few years earlier. Vaccarezza had named the boat "Not Guilty," and the men reveled in the in-joke left for boaters tossing in their wake.

Gotti also visited Lewis Kasman, a Garment Center businessman whom he also had befriended a few years earlier. Kasman had a winter home at tony Williams Island, where actress Sophia Loren and singer Whitney Houston also had homes. The acquitted don caused a stir at the resort's clubhouse; actor-comedian Eddie Murphy, a guest of Houston, stopped by to say hello and congratulate him, as did Sophia herself.

In addition to Junior, Vaccarezza, and Kasman, the Gotti group also included two other men who had become close friends in recent years—Jack D'Amico, a roguish type who, like Gotti, looked straight out of Central Casting's gangster division, and Joe Watts, who became part of the inner circle by doing some of Gotti's dirty work. The in-group also included Eddie Lino, who again put the lie to Gotti's claim that he avoided drug dealers. Lino was out on bail in the heroin case involving Angelo and Gene.

The Florida contingent did not include a man who also had grown close to Gotti in recent years—a man who would now become increasingly important, Salvatore Gravano. Virtually no one knew him by that name, however; in the Family and in the construction trades that provided him seeming legitimacy and growing wealth, Gravano was known by either of his two nicknames, Sammy Bull or Sammy.

Sammy didn't like to travel, much less hang out in places where he could be seen associating with known gangsters. He thought the gangster life meant being undercover, and that is how he tried to live. He looked like a construction foreman, and usually wore clothes to match. So far, he had managed to avoid much law enforcement scrutiny, even though he had been living the gangster life since 1968, when at age 23 he joined a Mafia farm team in Bensonhurst, Brooklyn, where he grew up. He committed his first murder two years later; the victim was a friend who had broken some gangland rule. It was the beginning of Sammy's reputation for cold-bloodedness.

Unlike Gotti, Sammy grew up middle class. But the Mafia pulse in New York beat loudest on the streets of Bensonhurst, and Sammy embraced it as a teenager when he saw his father—who owned a small dress factory—and other ordinary people give cash and respect to the neighborhood's "connected" men. Their status appealed to him. Growing up, Sammy was badly teased because he was short and people thought he wasn't that bright.

But Sammy was bright; he did poorly in school because his dyslexia was never diagnosed and because he stopped trying. As a criminal, he quickly proved how capable he was. Unlike so many others, he didn't throw his money away gambling. He built up businesses. At 32, Sammy became one of the "connected" men. The business-minded Gambino boss, Paul Castellano, gave Sammy his "button" in 1977, the same year as Gotti but in an earlier ceremony. Over the next eight years, he became one of the Family's most respected "earners" and also one of its most steely killers. By 1985, however, he was among the many who were unhappy with Paul's leadership. They believed Paul was only interested in accumulating personal wealth. With the crisis ignited by the heroin case involving his men, Gotti's reasons for disliking Paul were different, but he and Sammy became secret allies.

When Gotti's bail was revoked in the Giacalone case, he asked Sammy and two others to run the Family. Sammy accepted, but did not attend any of Gotti's trial. A *Daily News* story had recently described him as a little-known gangster on the rise. He didn't want to bring more attention to himself by going to the biggest media event in town.

Behind the scenes, however, Sammy was the trial's most pivotal figure. He was the person who arranged to do exactly what Andy Maloney feared had happened—fix the case.

It was fixed almost from the beginning, when the jurors were chosen. Soon after taking his seat in the jury box, George Pape, a middle-aged suburbanite with a drinking problem, contacted a man he thought might know someone in the Gambino Family and offered to sell himself. That man, Bosko Radonjich, the boss of a gang of mostly Irish-American thugs known as the Westies, took the offer to Sammy, who bought Pape for $60,000. Pape would vote "not guilty" no matter what.

It was the best-kept secret in New York. Only Gotti, brother Gene, Sammy, and Radonjich, who passed the money from Sammy to Pape in installments, knew the story. Someone got wind of it—the informant who tipped the FBI—but did not know enough to give agents anywhere to go. Pape gave Gotti the confidence to predict acquittal. Gotti devised the get-Giacalone strategy to give his ringer on the jury something to work with in deliberations, but he knew almost from the start that he would get at least a hung jury.

Radonjich and Pape had met on a construction job years before. Radonjich moved into the Westies and Pape into odd jobs and periodic unemployment. He was 48 years old and lived on Long Island with his wife, two children, and his drinking problem. After reporting for jury duty and realizing he might get picked for the Gotti trial, he recalled that Radonjich's gang, the Westies, was affiliated with the Gambino Family. Suddenly, jury service became a financial opportunity.

During jury selection, Pape lied several times when asked questions designed to eliminate jurors who might know people connected to Gotti or who had participated in legal cases that might affect their independence—as Pape had when he was a character witness for Radonjich in a deportation proceeding nearly ten years before.

The special steps taken by Judge Nickerson to assure the jury's integrity were no match for one man's greed. His decision to empanel the jury anonymously was meant to prevent defendants from contacting jurors; it did not imagine the opposite problem. But soon after the trial began, Pape contacted Radonjich, who contacted Sammy, who sent word to Gotti through brother Gene, free on bail and able to visit him in prison.

"Unbelievable that this fuckin' drops out of the sky like this," Gene said during a meeting with Sammy in Gene's lawyer's office. "My fuckin' brother has nine lives."

Pape kept his end of the deal. In the jury room, on the first day of deliberations, he said: "This man Gotti is innocent. They are all innocent, and as far as I am concerned, there is nothing left to discuss."

Several jurors thought otherwise and urged Pape to deliberate. He said it was a waste of time; obviously, Giacalone was out to get Gotti, but had not proved her case. For three days, the others deliberated almost as if Pape was not there. Most leaned toward conviction.

At night, at the hotel where they were sequestered, Pape refused to mingle. Some jurors began to suspect that somehow the defendants had threatened Pape. This suspicion heightened the danger some felt in the courtroom stares of Gotti and his men, and made them dwell on unpleasant thoughts. Over the last two days of deliberation, an unspoken group paranoia took hold and the tide turned, creating a beach of reasonable doubt upon which early beliefs in the government case were gradually discarded. Not guilty.

Naturally, the verdict—the only not-guilty one in all the recent Mafia cases—fed the wildest blizzard yet of myth-making publicity. Gotti did seem a genuine phenomenon, a modern-day Al Capone, an underworld "untouchable," and a headline writer gave the Dapper Don a new tabloid handle that captured that idea perfectly: "Teflon Don."

All the stories soon to be written about the Teflon Don—that he was a modern-day Robin Hood, that his acquittal symbolized the nameless little guy's contempt for the faceless government bureaucrats who run his life—were built on the lie that he had won fair and square. The coverage awed and intimidated even the cynical men in his Family. Like the rest of New York, they didn't know the fix was in. Even to them, Gotti was a phenomenon.

———————

In the previous five years, in cities across the U.S., the government had critically wounded or decimated all 23 *Cosa Nostra* families. In New York, it had won a virtual life sentence against Philip Rastelli, boss of the Bonanno Family, and actual life sentences against three other bosses who pillaged the city for decades with nearly the same impunity as Carlo Gambino—Carmine Persico of the Colombo Family, Antonio Corallo of the Luchese Family, and Anthony Salerno—a Chin Gigante stand-in—of the Genovese Family.

If the gangster from Central Casting had not come along, any of those bosses would have been an apt choice to illustrate, as Gotti was when his trial began, a *Time* magazine cover story on the *Cosa Nostra* crackdown. But now that he was the boss who got away, the *Time* cover became a dartboard for agents and prosecutors; by wagging a finger at Giacalone and Gleeson, and taunting them while celebrating, Gotti also made sure that agents and prosecutors would come at him with the kind of gusto reserved for those who have been personally wronged.

Just as there was the get-Giacalone defense, there would be a get-Gotti offense, and it would begin that very day, a Friday the 13th in March of 1987.

Bruce Mouw, boss of the FBI's Gambino squad, was driving across the Brooklyn Bridge with his car radio tuned to an all-news station when an announcer broke in with a bulletin about the Gotti acquittal. Mouw cursed the announcer's voice. He had just left a meeting at FBI headquarters in Manhattan and was bound for the courthouse in Brooklyn to meet the Eastern District Strike Force lawyers on the so-called "Gambino heirarchy" case against Armone, Gallo, Angelo, and others—a case Gotti would have been in, had the Strike Force won its turf war with Giacalone years before.

The courthouse was just a couple minutes over the bridge. Mouw calculated that by the time he arrived, Gotti, his men, and their lawyers and supporters would be spilling into the streets and dancing to their cars—sights he did not care to see. He instead drove to the FBI's office in Queens, and began reviewing his squad's latest intelligence reports on Gotti.

Mouw had been investigating the Gambino Family since 1979, when the bureau's New York bosses reorganized their organized crime section into distinct squads—one for each of the city's five families—and Mouw was plucked out of a desk job in Washington to lead one. Organizationally, the squads were like crews and Mouw was like a capo.

It was a long way from his first job—sports reporter for his high school paper in Des Moines, Iowa. He did so well in school, he won an appointment to the United States Naval Academy, then his commission. In the Navy, he was involved in the highest-stakes game the world has ever known—the underwater hide-and-seek game pitting the navies of the U.S. and the former Soviet Union. He was a navigator on a submarine capable of killing millions; tracking Soviet subs, but never provoking a response the world would regret, was a game requiring skill and patience.

He joined the FBI in 1972. After a year in St. Louis, he went to New York, where he spent two years investigating Genovese Family loansharking. The FBI was just then beginning to learn how the families were organized, thanks to illegal eavesdropping it conducted in the 1960s and to a hood named Joseph Valachi—the first to reveal the existence of *La Cosa Nostra*.

In 1979, Mouw took over the Gambino squad just as the FBI
decided on a major *Cosa Nostra* offensive. In 1981, after Ronald
Reagan's election and after Congress gave the FBI more money and
eased restrictions on electronic surveillance, the campaign was
launched. With his background, Mouw was inclined to surveillance,
and his squad's first major target was Angelo Ruggiero, who had
bragged that his home telephone was "safe."

The Angelo Ruggiero tapes led to many unforeseen consequences—
bad ones for Paul Castellano and Thomas Bilotti. But they also shot
Gotti to power, and Gotti's victory now made the squad's triumph
against Angelo, who hadn't even been brought to trial yet, look small.
It really was time to start a new case.

Three months after his crooked victory, Gotti annoyed authorities
even more. His muscle-bound son Junior, who had been accused of
slugging an off-duty cop in a bar brawl a few months after his father
slugged refrigerator mechanic Romual Piecyk, was found not guilty.

In a virtual replay of the Piecyk case, a waitress forgot what she had
seen, and a man hurt during the brawl—the man whom the cop was
trying to help—testified for the defense. Gotti went to the courthouse
to escort Junior through the media pack.

"They gotta try to rig a case to get us," he crowed.

29

TEFLON DON

"TEFLON" WAS A MORE APT METAPHOR for John Gotti than headline writers knew. Because of the law's double jeopardy provisions, his pre-paid acquittal on racketeering charges also immunized him for crimes committed prior to indictment in March 1985. He had been in prison nearly half the time since. Maloney, Mouw, and several others in law enforcement would have to build cases from scratch. They needed time and mistakes by the target, who would get what he was overheard asking for on the Bergin bug, shortly after Sparks: "If I can get a year run without being interrupted, get a year, I'm gonna put this thing together where they could never break it, never destroy it, even if we die."

Potential interruptions abounded. Many gangsters in and out of his Family—notably, Chin Gigante of the Genovese Family—were angry that Gotti was now boss of the Gambinos. They did not like him, or how he grabbed power. Traditionalists like Chin believed in the Commission rule that a boss cannot be removed from office by murder unless the other Family bosses agree.

Gotti believed he could get away with this infraction by simply denying he had anything to do with Paul's murder. Still, in the weeks following the verdict, many reprisal rumors reached him. Several involved avenging relatives of Paul and Bilotti, and so Gotti always had several bodyguards around. In the post-Sparks atmosphere, trigger-happiness was never far away, and six weeks after the verdict, it led to the murder of a man in the wrong place at the wrong time.

The man was walking past a florist's shop opposite the Bergin when a truck backfired. Gotti had just walked out the door, and, fearing gunfire, he ducked back in as a bodyguard pulled a gun and pointed it across the street at Jeffrey Ciccone, a mildly mentally disabled distant relative of a Gambino soldier. He saw the gun and ran. Several Gotti men gave chase; chief bodyguard Bobby Borriello fired a single shot that hit Ciccone in the buttocks.

In view of bystanders who later claimed to have seen nothing, the men tossed Ciccone into the trunk of a car that glided up from the Bergin. It was driven by another bodyguard, Dominick Borghese. He and Joe Watts, one of the men who helped Gotti celebrate in Florida a few weeks earlier, drove to a store owned by a Gambino capo on Staten Island, so that there, in the basement, Gotti's men could interrogate the wounded and presumed would-be assassin before killing him.

But the more Ciccone was beaten and questioned, the more he wailed that he didn't know what his tormentors were talking about. He denied firing a shot and frantically quoted Bible passages. In time, Gotti's men began to suspect he was not an assassin, but a disturbed man who decided on his own to try and kill Gotti.

Meanwhile, of course, back at the Bergin, Gotti played dumb.

"Nothin' happened here," he told George Gabriel of the FBI, after Gabriel heard of a "shots-fired" report from the NYPD and went to the Bergin to inquire in his newly acquired role as Gotti "case agent" for the Gambino squad.

"We're nice guys," Gotti continued. "We don't have to duck nobody. You're the ones who should be duckin', the way you treat people."

"You're right, John. But just make sure you stay indoors. We don't have the manpower to protect you from your enemies."

While Gotti and Gabriel bantered, Gotti's men continued to believe Ciccone had fired a shot. They also concluded he was a crackpot acting on his own. Joe Watts, the main inquisitor, grew tired of pummeling Ciccone and sent Gotti a message asking what they should do with Ciccone.

"Kill 'im," the Teflon Don said.

Watts, a Paul loyalist before switching to Gotti, and Dominick Borghese, a 400-pounder, bound Ciccone's feet and hands; someone produced an orange body bag, into which Ciccone, bawling and pleading, was stuffed. Watts zippered it shut; aiming to please, he fired six shots into Ciccone's head.

Intending to return and remove the body once they arranged a disposal site, Watts and Borghese left the store for a few hours. Amazingly, while they were away, burglars hit the store. They did not enter the basement, but left the store's metal gates open. A passerby called police, who searched the basement and found the body.

Back at the florist's shop, lips were sealed when the cops came by. "It looks like what we have here is a John Lennon-type situation," a top police official soon announced, as the case went into the unsolved murder files. "It looks like some individual had a thing about John Gotti."

Ciccone's only thing was bad luck. He was an occasional carpenter, 38 years old, who lived with two aging aunts in Queens, one of whom later said he had "mental problems." His distant relative, Sonny Ciccone—a Gambino capo who ran what rackets were left at the city's aging, Mafia-ransacked shipping piers—rushed to the Bergin to emphasize how distant.

"Forget about it," Gotti said boisterously. "But good thing he was a lousy shot!"

———————

A gambler on a hot streak, Gotti set about cementing his control of the Family. He promoted Sammy Gravano to *consigliere* after seventy-seven-year-old Joe N. Gallo, tired and on trial in one of the Strike Force cases, asked if he could retire. He agreed to allow sixty-seven-year-old Joseph Armone, on trial in the same case, to remain underboss if Armone were found guilty, but this was only symbolic thanks for Armone's treachery toward Paul. He made Frank LoCascio, a bookmaker and loan shark who had moved into the inner circle, acting underboss with non-acting authority. He also made brother Gene boss of the Bergin crew after Angelo from his prison cell—without Gotti's okay and for some personal slight—tried and failed to orchestrate the murder of an important gangster in another Family.

Beyond his Family, Gotti shored up relations with other bosses, including the sly stickler for Commission rules, Chin Gigante of the Genovese Family. They even met after Mouw and Gabriel visited Gotti and warned that FBI agents had overheard two Genovese men discussing a plot to kill Gotti and Gene to revenge Paul and Bilotti.

The men were overheard in a bathroom where agents had installed a listening device; in such cases, FBI policy requires agents to warn the targets.

"We have solid information about a threat against you and Genie, a legitimate threat," said Gabriel on the doorstep of Gotti's home in Howard Beach in the fall of 1987.

"There's a million plots, so what?" Gotti said.

"All we can say is that this one is for real." Gabriel rubbed his chin mischievously. "By the way, John, it's coming from the Genovese Family."

Gotti frowned. "There're my friends. Chin is my friend. Everybody's my friend."

The warning may well have saved Gotti's life because he decided to let Chin know he knew. Sammy set up the summit, and also invited Luchese Family leaders; the man Angelo had conspired to kill from prison had become Luchese underboss, and Gotti thought it best to at least try to repair the damage. With three of the five New York bosses in the same room, it was the first Commission meeting in years—and probably the most preposterous ever. Everyone in the room was lying and everyone knew it.

"Whatever was said, if it was said, was not authorized by me," Gigante told Gotti, referring to the plot captured by the FBI's bathroom wiretap. "We got enough problems with the FBI all over the place, to bring more problems on ourselves. Our Families have always had a good relationship."

"I agree with you, hundred percent," Gotti said. "We can't fight amongst ourselves. We fight the government!"

"Paul was fightin' the government when he was killed. He was standing up to two RICOs, like a man."

"I swear to you," Gotti said. "I'm as angry about that as you. We don't know who killed Paul. I've been tellin' Sammy and everyone else, the fuckin' cops might've killed Paul."

Feeling ever more flush, Gotti revealed he was making the Ravenite Social Club in Little Italy—the clubhouse of his mentor, Aniello Dellacroce—his headquarters. He also announced he would hold weekly meetings there of top associates, attendance required. The news shocked his men. The Ravenite was within a few blocks of the headquarters of almost every important law enforcement agency in New York, including the FBI and the NYPD.

As *consigliere*, Sammy Gravano was obliged to speak up about these decisions, albeit politely. He did so at a meeting with Gotti and acting underboss Frank LoCascio at a Little Italy restaurant owned by Joseph Corrao, a Manhattan crew leader, a few blocks down Mulberry Street from the Ravenite. Corrao, or "Joe Butch," fell quickly in step with Gotti after Sparks. Some had even urged Gotti to make Joe Butch, not LoCascio, acting underboss.

"I know the idea of being in [Dellacroce's] club feels good, John, but we maybe oughta be more undercover," Sammy said.

"I've been comin' down here fifteen fuckin' years! What's the big deal?"

"You're the boss now. You gotta be more careful."

"I could stay in bed like the Chin, and they'll still come after me!"

"Maybe, but what I was thinking, you could put Frankie in charge of The Bronx, let everybody up there answer to him. You and Genie stay out in Queens. Joe Butch will stay in Manhattan. I'll stay in Brooklyn. We'll get together when we gotta, in the middle of the night when the fuckin' agents are sleeping, in a graveyard or some place."

"We don't have to run and hide! What're we afraid of? It ain't a crime to meet and get together. We're Italians. That's the way the Italian people are."

"The old-timers used to hide and sneak and stay in the neighbor-hoods," Sammy said.

"But look at Neil, he was here on this street all his life. I'm not gonna be a back-door boss. It's better this way. Everybody sees the boss and the boss sees them. Keeps everybody happy."

"Times are different."

"Times are the same. Except this here is a Cosa Nostra now. I ain't Chin, and I ain't Paul, hidin' out in my house."

Sammy let it go. Gotti's mind was made up. Soon after the Ravenite "shape-ups" began early in 1988, Gotti also showed he would not indulge non-compliance with the mandatory-attendance requirement.

The men who squawked about the recklessness and inconvenience of weekly trips to the Ravenite included Thomas DeBrizzi, a 64-year-old soldier. He ran a loan-sharking and gambling operation in Connecticut for Carlo Gambino's son Tommy; per his to-the-manor-born image, Tommy had authority over operations in the nutmeg state.

Unlike Tommy, DeBrizzi lived in Connecticut, two hours by car
from Mulberry Street. He barely knew Gotti, and was in prison during Sparks. But then he made the mistake of complaining too much,
in the presence of his crew leader, about the Ravenite meetings.

Falling into line, too, Tommy told Gotti, and it was all Gotti
needed to hear. DeBrizzi was found dead in his car's trunk on
February 5, 1988, killed by men in his own crew eager to show they
were not complainers.

"A guy don't want to come in, he's gone, that's all," Gotti told
Sammy.

Gene Gotti also considered the Ravenite meetings a reckless
idea—and not just because his bail terms in the heroin case required
him to avoid such places. "Why don't we just draw the fuckin' feds a
picture?" he complained to Sammy.

"I know, Genie, but he don't think it matters."

Gene believed the Ravenite meetings symbolized narcissism more
than homage to the past and Dellacroce. But Gene believed it pointless for him to be the one to tell his brother that.

"That's your job, Sammy, you're the *consigliere*. He'd never listen
to me. He'd think I was jealous, but John, he just wants to be the
center of attention all the time."

"He loves bein' boss, that's for sure. You know how Paul made
people come to him in small groups. John seems to like it when an
audience comes."

"This guy, you oughta seen him when his name started gettin' in
the papers. Fuckin' loved it. And when his face was on the tube?
Forget about it. It was like he was gettin' off for free."

To Sammy, Gene wasn't exaggerating. Once, he and Gotti were
dining in a restaurant when they noticed a young couple staring at
them.

"Look at the guy and the girl over there, lookin' at us," Gotti said
solemnly. "They love me."

Sammy cringed inside. He accepted someone who had been called
Robin Hood and a folk-hero of "the little people" might believe
strangers found him fascinating, but to hear Gotti say "love" was so
startling Sammy didn't know what to say.

"They do. They love me. They can't stop lookin' over here."

"You're fuckin' nuts," Sammy smiled before trying to steer the
subject elsewhere.

"I'm tellin' ya, they love me," Gotti insisted again, lifting a second martini, Boodles very dry.

Gotti also remained highly visible in Ozone Park. He usually stopped at the Bergin Hunt & Fish Club to hang out for a couple hours each afternoon, before heading into Manhattan. The club and neighborhood were part of his identity. He still sponsored the community's annual Fourth of July celebration. Thanks to his larger-than-ever profile, the 1988 version drew many reporters and led to another round of big headlines that made official New York appear powerless next to Gotti.

"This is just something we do for the neighborhood," Gotti said early in the day, during a brief bow in front of the Bergin coinciding with the arrival of television cameras.

In past years, the celebration always ended with an unauthorized fireworks display, but this year the NYPD had warned it would enforce a law requiring sponsors to get a permit by which the sponsor agreed to safety rules. Gotti ignored the warning, and that afternoon, NYPD trucks took away two dumpsters where his men planned to launch the 'works.

As day became evening, the crowd grew restless. "We want the 'works!" about two thousand people outside the Bergin began chanting. "We want the 'works!"

They grew more excited when Gotti, wearing an all-white ensemble, appeared in the Bergin doorway again, smiling and waving like a political nominee addressing a convention. He had given away a grocery store of food and soda; his men had erected carnival rides and strung patriotic bunting along 101st Avenue. He would have been elected mayor by that crowd.

Although the dumpsters were gone, the fireworks remained inside the Bergin, and now the crowd began chanting again. Several dozen cops stood by on sidewalks south of the club; a block north, more sat in squad cars. But they had underestimated the crowd that now swelled and screamed between the cops on foot and cops in cars.

"We want the 'works! We want the 'works!"

Gotti stepped back into the Bergin and a bonfire suddenly arose in the street. Gotti's son Junior then exited the Bergin, lugging a crate of fireworks. He was followed by several muscular young men. As the crowd roared, each began throwing Roman candles, cherry bombs, and other small-size devices into the fire. Some others stood metal canisters by the fire and were soon launching larger-sized rockets and starbursts.

The crowd grew more rowdy. They were mainly teenagers, but to the police captain in charge, they had been drinking something besides soda all day and seemed drunk enough to be both stupid and dangerous. He told his men to do nothing as the fireworks burst over Ozone Park. Two firetrucks also arrived, but firefighters wanted no part of a possible riot either and soon left.

Gotti again appeared in the Bergin doorway to gaze upon the frenzy. The cops made no arrests and issued no tickets, prompting the eldest Gotti brother, Peter, a newly made man, to a gleeful and widely reported taunt:

"All the police did was make themselves look foolish."

It was hard to argue. The next day, officials in New York punted. The fire commissioner, responsible for licensing, quickly passed the buck to the police commissioner, responsible for enforcement; he would not even answer questions.

Editorial-page writers flogged away. One opined that while it was regrettable that so many citizens in Ozone Park admired that "All-American Yankee Doodle Dandy Don, John Gotti," cops standing around like helpless children was even more so: "That's a pretty dangerous image to risk adopting. Even worse is the image it promotes: That the masters of organized crime are above the law, sneering as they put the city's law-enforcement establishment where they believe it belongs—in paralysis and humiliation."

A month later, Gotti decided to end the game he was playing on one of his oldest and most reliable men, Willie Boy Johnson, and make him pay for betraying him to the FBI all those years. The game began three years earlier, when Diane Giacalone exposed Willie Boy as an informer and Gotti promised to forgive him so long as he didn't take the stand in her case.

Willie Boy stayed at the defense table. Then, after the fix came in, Gotti banned him from the Bergin, but told him to go on with his life without fear: "I'm gonna give you a pass and I give you my word no one will bother you." Willie Boy did not believe it, but could never stop wanting to. He wanted it so much he deceived

himself and his wife that somehow his refusal to testify was atone-
ment for his betrayal. The only place he ever lived was New York.
He didn't want to ask his wife to give up the nice home they had in
a choice neighborhood and join him in a life on the run.

In almost everyone else's mind, payback was only a matter of
time. FBI records turned over to Gotti's lawyers in the Giacalone
case showed that Willie Boy was the one who led police to Gotti
when Gotti was on the lam in the early 1970s. They showed that it
was Willie Boy's information that helped the Gambino squad build a
heroin case against Angelo, Gene, and the rest.

It was what Willie Boy had not told the FBI that gave him a period of grace. "The rat will pay," Gotti told Sammy after the Giacalone case. "But we'll let 'im get comfortable first. We can't make any
mistakes. There's a lot he didn't talk about. He didn't talk about
killin's he knows about."

Grace ended August 29, 1988, after Gotti heard from the Colombo Family. Willie Boy had given information about some Colombo men as well, and Alphonse Persico, son of the imprisoned
Colombo boss, urged Gotti to lower the boom. Gotti handed the hit
to Sammy, who enlisted Gotti stalwart Eddie Lino.

As a defendant in the heroin case, Eddie also had a personal
motive. He knew able killers in the Bonanno Family, which also had
suffered Willie Boy's sting, whom Willie Boy did not know. He con-
tracted them, and they surprised their target at just past dawn, outside his home, as he left for the legitimate construction job he had
taken.

The first shot brought Willie Boy to his knees; six more tore
open the back of his head. The killers were gone before his wife ran
out and cradled his body in her arms.

Later in the day, Richard Rehbock, the lawyer who represented
Willie Boy in the Giacalone case, spoke about the murder with
reporters. In their stories, none noted that Rehbock had gone on to
win an assault case for Junior Gotti and that he was in the Gotti
camp more than the Willie Boy camp.

"He never expressed any fear [of Gotti]," Rehbock said of Willie
Boy. "The only enemy that this man had in the world was the government."

30

HEROIN REDUX

AFTER FOUR YEARS OF PRE-TRIAL MATTERS, the case that led to Sparks—the heroin-dealing charges against Angelo, Gene, and others—finally began after Gotti's pretend peace pact with Chin Gigante in the fall of 1987. Several more crooked turns in what was already a twisted journey lay ahead.

In addition to Gene, Angelo, and Lino, the defendants included John Carneglia, a Bergin crew soldier and salvage operator who had been close to the Gotti brothers most of his life, and Mark Reiter, the heroin dealer whose arrival at the Bergin started *babania* madness.

The prospect of conviction weighed heavily on Gene Gotti. He faced a 50-year sentence if found guilty at trial. For months, his lawyers had been discussing a guilty plea in return for prosecutors recommending a 14-year sentence. Lawyers for Angelo and Carneglia were involved in similar talks for recommended pleas of a couple years more. Lino and Reiter, who faced lesser charges, intended to go to trial.

Gene was 42. Under sentencing policies at the time he was indicted, he would qualify for parole after serving two-thirds of the 14 years. That meant something of a life after he got out. Angelo and Carneglia, a few years older, felt the same.

As the trial neared, however, all were reminded of John Gotti's earlier edict—prompted by Neil Dellacroce's son Armond's plea in the Giacalone case—that no one in the Family could agree to a plea in which they were required to acknowledge the Gambino Family existed and they belonged to it.

U.S. Attorney Andy Maloney and Robert LaRusso, the heroin-trial prosecutor, wanted plea deals, but would not budge on the Gambino issues, and so Gotti ordered his men to trial. Suspicious about the verdict in the Giacalone case, Maloney told LaRusso to be wary of jury tampering. "These people will try anything!" he said. "They don't believe we have the right to put them on trial!"

Attempts to tamper began soon after the jury was seated. An informant told agents that two private detectives working for the defense were trying to acquire the identities of jurors. As in the Giacalone case, the jurors served anonymously. Next, agents learned that a Brooklyn stockbroker offered to give a new car to a man who had been chosen and then excused from the jury for personal reasons. The stockbroker wanted to ask the man about the remaining jurors.

Maloney ordered John Gleeson, the assistant prosecutor in the Giacalone case, to start a jury-tampering investigation with the FBI. As before, because the Gambino squad was part of the prosecution, non-Gambino agents began conducting checks of the jurors.

In the absence of proof, Gleeson still did not fully share Maloney's suspicion that his case was fixed. And he continued to feel that way—even after he and agents found evidence suggesting the heroin defendants might have already bribed one juror and had learned the identities of five more.

"They did it again!" Maloney exploded.

"Maybe; it looks like it, but it'd be tough to prove," Gleeson said. "This time, we're taking it to the judge."

Late in 1987, after he and other judges reviewed the evidence, the trial judge, Mark Costantino, found a high probability of jury tampering, and declared a mistrial.

For Gene and the rest, a mistrial was not as rewarding as what brother John got—an outright acquittal—and it meant they would have to go to trial a second time.

Publicly, Maloney said his office would mount a new trial and pursue the case to verdict or plea. Privately, he fumed. For a second time, the Gotti wing of the Gambinos had embarrassed his office. It was hard for him to feel much better when, a few weeks later, the Eastern District Strike Force, the special squad of prosecutors attached uneasily to his office, won the Gambino Family hierarchy case. Jurors returned guilty verdicts against Joe N. Gallo and Joseph

Armone, the old-guard Gambino leaders who had warily given their support to Gotti.

Gallo was released on bail, pending sentencing two months later. He was 77 and an informant correctly told agents he was no longer the *consigliere*. Bail meant the old man could spend a last holiday season with relatives. The judge proposed another plan for Armone, 70: He, too, could get bail and the holidays with his wife and daughter— but only if he made a statement publicly renouncing a life in crime.

The certainty of a sentence condemning him to death behind bars broke Armone's normally iron will. In court, he indicated he would agree. The judge told lawyers to draft a statement and return to court the next day, Christmas Eve. Before Armone was returned to the Manhattan jail where federal detainees are kept, the judge told him the statement should show that Armone was renouncing any connection he might have ever had to organized crime and was resigning any position he might currently have.

That night, "Joe Piney," as Armone was known, asked a nephew to send the new Gambino boss a message asking permission to make the statement. "Piney doesn't think he's ever gonna get out when he goes away, so he just wants this time with his Family," the nephew told Gotti. "He doesn't think it matters what he says, it's just legal bullshit."

Having told Gene and the other heroin defendants that they could not make such agreements, Gotti could not let Armone off the hook. Frank LoCascio might now have the position, but Armone, at least officially, was still underboss.

"I'm surprised by Piney!" Gotti shouted. "This is a Cosa Nostra! We don't make no official statements! He can't do it! You tell him that's an order! He's my underboss, even if he's in fuckin' jail, until I say different!"

Armone got the message Christmas Eve morning. In court that day, he dutifully announced he had changed his mind about making a statement. He was promptly jailed to await sentencing. In two more months, he got 15 years in prison; the judge gave Gallo 10. Gallo became the oldest inmate in federal custody anywhere, but he served his time and got out. On the other hand, in 1992, Armone died of natural causes at a federal prison hospital.

The second trial of Gene, Angelo, and the rest began in the spring of 1988. The details differed, but the result was the same—mistrial. The case actually got to the jury, but after a couple days, jurors told the judge they were hopelessly deadlocked—the word "hopelessly" immediately raised suspicions in the minds of Andy Maloney and prosecutor Robert LaRusso.

It takes someone like George Pape, refusing to talk or negotiate, to make a jury hopelessly deadlocked, Maloney believed. After hearing from the jurors, the judge told them to keep deliberating. Unlike in the first trial, it was too late for agents to start an investigation into whether the case was being fixed again.

As deliberations continued, federal marshals found cocaine hidden in a jogging outfit that a woman brought to a friend on the jury. If a juror's girlfriend felt free to bring cocaine into the case, what else was going on? Maloney and LaRusso became convinced something else was going on when two jurors next told the judge in the case that they suspected FBI agents had tampered with the tape-recorded evidence.

"Too incredible to believe," Maloney said to LaRusso. "Somehow, they got to these people too."

When deliberations failed to break the deadlock, the judge declared the mistrial. There would have to be a third trial. Meanwhile, the judge decided it was no longer fair to keep Angelo Ruggiero in jail without bail. Angelo had been boiling and plotting in a federal lockup in Manhattan for 25 months while his main codefendants, Gene, Carneglia, and Lino, remained free.

At a hearing on Angelo's request for bail, his lawyer told the judge his client was a good candidate for bail because he was a good father who cared for his six children and was providing for two others left fatherless by the death of his brother, Salvatore Ruggiero, in a plane crash. To no avail, LaRusso argued the opposite: "He's got the greatest motive to flee with the evidence we have on him. If this defendant is released, he probably will not return—he will not return."

The statement was prophetic, but not in the way LaRusso intended. Free at last, Angelo fell ill before he could devise a plan for either getting "in the wind" or working his way back into the graces of the friend whose coattails he grabbed on to long ago and once telephoned each morning to go over the day's dirty agenda.

Ruggiero was diagnosed with diabetes and emphysema. Depressed by these illnesses and his legal predicaments—in addition to the heroin case, he faced a separate trial on the same charges that brought Gallo and Armone down—Angelo actually obeyed the terms of his bail. He hung out in his house on Long Island, the one in middle-class Cedarhurst that he had remodeled with heroin cash even as Gambino squad bugs documented the progress.

The bail conditions forbade him from contacting anyone in the Gambino Family, but it depressed him that his old Fulton-Rockaway pal, Johnny Boy, never attempted a clandestine visit or even sent a secret message of goodwill.

Instead, several times over the next several months, Gotti told Sammy that rather than forgive Angelo, he should kill him. "He's caused us so much fuckin' trouble, and not just us," Gotti said. "He don't deserve any passes."

The change of heart was breathtaking. The trouble Angelo caused was a big part of why Gotti was now boss. Then there were the personal ties; Angelo was Gotti's oldest friend, and his eldest son's godfather. Each time Gotti talked of killing Angelo, Sammy and Frank LoCascio pointed out that Angelo's declining health made it pointless.

Late in 1988, Angelo's doctors delivered a last bit of bad news: lung cancer, and they said he probably did not have long to live. Still Gotti did not visit or send a message, and Gene—now facing a third trial because his brother would not let him plead guilty—was particularly perturbed.

"I told him the other day," Gene told Sammy. "I said, 'The guy Angelo is broken-hearted. He don't understand why you're so hot still. This guy would've jumped in front of a car for you. Ain't it time to let your beef go?'"

Gene said his brother shrugged and turned to other subjects. The indifference surprised even stone-cold Sammy. It would cost John Gotti nothing to bestow a little absolution—insincere as it would be—upon a dying old friend.

Illness would take Angelo to bed and out of the picture, but the heroin trial would have a third and final act. It would be a year more in coming because of a legal fight over whether it was fair to put the defendants on trial again. After they won that issue at the Supreme Court, trial prosecutor LaRusso and his aides chose to narrow the case by cutting loose some defendants, such as Eddie Lino, for separate trials.

It proved to be a good strategy. With fewer defendants, they were able to build a strong, simple case. Gene and Carneglia were convicted—but, incredibly, not before yet one more attempt to buy a juror. Without a break as lucky as the one John Gotti got in the Giacalone case, when a man already on the jury announced he was for sale, Gene was left to devise something on his own, and he did, quite ably, without telling his brother.

The plan relied on one of John's sons-in-law, Carmine Agnello, and Gene feared John would object; it also involved Lino, who agreed to secretly help and risk the boss's wrath, because of his special bond with his former codefendants. The plan was to force the disqualification of a seated juror and thus cause the selection of an alternate juror assessed by Gene during jury screening as sympathetic and bribable.

After employing private detectives to learn the names and addresses of the jurors, Gene found that one lived on the same leafy street as Billy Noon, an FBI agent who sat at the prosecution table with LaRusso. He sent Lino to the juror's home with orders to leave an unsigned note questioning the juror's fairness when everyone knew he was friendly with his FBI neighbor.

Gene assumed the note would provoke a hearing and the juror's disqualification, and it did. In the meantime, Gene sent Carmine Agnello to the home of the first alternate juror, the one judged sympathetic and bribable. It turned out he was both. And after the other juror was excused on grounds that the note might have rendered him incapable of objectivity, the alternate took his place.

It was an artfully crafted scheme, but doomed. Rather than stay strong during deliberations and refuse to discuss anything but an outright acquittal, the alternate's feet turned to clay. He sent a note to the judge saying that he was concerned about his and his family's safety and must get off the jury because the wrong people knew where he lived. He didn't mention the $25,000 he'd been promised.

Still, the judge smelled something rotten. He granted the alternate his wish, then ruled the case would be decided by the eleven remaining jurors, who took only three hours to lower the boom on Gene and Carneglia and bring down the curtain on the longest federal prosecution in history.

The judge allowed both to remain free on bail, pending sentencing. But both had already decided they were not going to flee. Because the case began in 1983, it fell under federal sentencing rules that were not as punitive as rules that came into effect in 1985 and that John Gotti had confronted in the Giacalone case.

A few weeks later, however, Gene and Carneglia got much stiffer sentences than they expected—thanks to the scrapyard czar, Carneglia. He had reverted to his Fulton-Rockaway days and promised a reporter that some day he would "piss on the grave" of the trial judge, John R. Bartels, an 89-old jurist who had dozed off a few times during the more boring parts of testimony.

Bartels, a Harry Truman appointee, remembered the slight at sentencing, and gave Carneglia and Gene sentences requiring them to serve more than 20 years before they had a chance to qualify for parole—and, in Carneglia's case, carry out an ill-advised vow.

The end of the case continued the devastation of the original core of the Bergin Hunt & Fish Club. Peter Gotti, John's older brother, was still around—and John made him acting captain of the Bergin—but Gene, Angelo, Willie Boy, John Carneglia, and Anthony Rampino were now in jail, dead, or dying.

Their boss had no time for regret or remembrance. The night before Gene was to surrender and begin serving his sentence, brother John told Sammy he had bawled Gene out after Gene finally spilled the details of his artful but failed fix.

"I told him, 'You used Eddie and you used my son-in-law and you don't think you have to tell me.' He says, 'I didn't want to involve you.' Involve me. I'm the fucking boss and he don't want to involve me! He says, 'Well, maybe you wouldn't have let me do it, 'cause Carmine's your son-in-law.' Well, yeah, maybe, but I am the fuckin' boss!"

Sammy, though growing weary of Gotti's rants, listened as Gotti ranted on.

"I don't mind them trying to fix a case. That's what we do, but I'm the boss. I'm gonna wring the neck of that no-good son-in-law of mine. Can't believe he didn't tell me!"

31

MULBERRY STREET

SOON AFTER HE REVEALED IT, informants told the FBI that Gotti was making the Ravenite his headquarters and requiring men to report weekly. The news astonished Gambino squad boss Bruce Mouw and his case agent, George Gabriel. The club opened onto the sidewalk of a narrow street in one of the city's busiest areas. Until late at night, because Little Italy and the adjacent Soho and Chinatown neighborhoods were all tourist centers, the area was jammed with people and cars. It seemed the worst place for regular meetings between the boss and his men.

Surveillance showed that the informants were right. In January of 1988, Gotti began going to the Ravenite almost every weekday, arriving between five and six in the evening. A special FBI surveillance squad also saw dozens of other men—including many they recognized, but many they did not—entering and leaving the club over several days. The Ravenite meetings promised to open rich veins of information about the breadth and depth of the Gambino Family.

"Some secret society," Mouw gleefully said, when he informed Andy Maloney.

To both men, the biggest implication of Gotti's moves was immediately clear. Mouw, the former nuclear submariner who believed mightily in the value of electronic surveillance, had been mulling where to launch an eavesdropping attack on Gotti. The target had just provided the answer.

Mouw now decided to complement eavesdropping with video surveillance of the sidewalk in front of the club. Visitors frequently loitered there. The video surveillance would help identify them and, if a case could be brought against Gotti, help establish the "enterprise" requirements of the RICO law. Defense lawyers would find it difficult to argue their clients did not belong to the Gambino enterprise if jurors could see them on videotape meeting regularly, hugging, cajoling, and taking furtive walks around the block that the FBI dubbed "walk-talks."

The key question with the video was where to install the camera. The buildings directly across the Ravenite on Mulberry Street were not options; many residents were as fond of Gotti as they had been of Neil. Gotti was a familiar figure on the street for nearly 15 years. Now that he was such a celebrity, many loved having him in their midst even more, and would quickly let him know if they noticed something odd in the windows of the buildings across from the Ravenite.

Telephoto lenses made it possible for Mouw to consider locations farther away, as long as they afforded a view of the Ravenite entrance. After scouting locations, he settled on a high-rise apartment tower two and one half blocks north of the Ravenite—far enough out of the Little Italy milieu, but near enough for a long lens. The building was at the northeast corner of Mulberry and Houston Street. One of its apartments, which was for rent, offered a view directly down Mulberry.

In February of 1988, a federal judge secretly authorized the squad to begin audio and video surveillance of Gotti and several others at the Ravenite after Gabriel submitted an affidavit saying rather unsurprisingly that the FBI had cause to believe crimes were being committed there.

The "video plant" was quickly set up. The next trick was getting a listening device or "bug" inside the Ravenite, a ground-floor storefront in a plain four-story, brown-brick building. The club, just two large rooms filled with cheap chairs and tables, had its own street-level entrance, but it also could be entered through a door in the hallway of the building's main entrance, which was used by tenants of the apartments on the upper floor.

It would take time to discover the significance of this, but the tenants included someone important to Gotti, an elderly woman named Nettie Cerelli. Her late husband, a Neil soldier, had been the club's longtime caretaker.

While at the Ravenite, Gotti normally sat at a table in the rear room, beneath two framed photographs—one of Neil and one of Gotti. The latter was a copy of a photo on the cover of a newly published book chronicling Gotti's rise to power. It was a tight head shot, taken when a scowling Gotti was outside the Brooklyn federal courthouse and stared directly into a photographer's lens, and thus now into the eyes of anyone who looked at it.

Mouw wanted the bug as close to Gotti's table as possible. With informants' help, Gabriel diagrammed the Ravenite interior for the bureau's Special Operations squad. In February of 1988, S.O. agents—maybe the best locksmiths in the world—descended on the club long after Norman Dupont, its caretaker and Nettie Cerelli's nephew, closed for the night.

While others waited in the shadows, ready to distract passersby, two S.O. agents walked into the tenants' hallway, picked the lock of the side door and entered the Ravenite. Dressed all in black, they ran wires, tapped into power sources, and installed a tiny transmitter that was never found—even though Gotti and his men were always looking for one. After the S.O. agents left, agents at an "audio plant" a few blocks away at the main New York FBI office could operate it from their desks.

Maloney beamed when Mouw reported the FBI now had an electronic ear in the Ravenite. "Fantastic!" he said, "the big mouth's going to talk himself right into jail!"

Not so fast. Optimism spawned by the installation of the video camera and the bug soon faded. The camera worked fine, but agents in the audio plant could overhear only fragments of conversations and sometimes only the unintelligible noise of several men talking at once, coughing, laughing, and dragging chairs across floors.

Gotti's arrival also always raised the decibel level. It was just too many people talking too excitedly in too confined an area for the bug to capture coherent talk. It also became apparent that Gotti—having been burned by the Bergin bug—was being cautious. The few times it sounded as if he might be talking about something incriminating, his voice dropped to a barely audible whisper. Frequently, he left the club and—joined by Sammy, LoCascio, or others—went for a "walk-talk."

Though frustrated by the problems with the bug, Mouw was delighted with the video. Every morning, he reviewed the tape from the day before, and began compiling physical descriptions and other data on all the men making their required appearances.

"This is great," he told Gabriel. "John is introducing us to everyone in his Family. We got guys coming in cars from New Jersey and Connecticut. We're gonna get to meet everybody."

Men they didn't recognize were listed as "unsubs," for unsubstantiated. But depending on with whom the unsub arrived, agents would know which of their files to pull, which informant to contact, or which law-enforcement agency might be able to help. Steadily, they began identifying many previously unknown soldiers and associates in the Family's 21 crews—as well as men from other Families who dropped by.

"The secret society meeting in broad daylight!" Mouw exclaimed on another day. "The administration of the Gambino Family strolling down Mulberry like tourists!"

The audio tapes were not as pleasing to review. But while they did not add up to anything incriminating, they did offer enough snippets to satisfy the legal requirements for keeping the bug in place—and to open the window on Gotti's world a little farther. They showed, for instance, he was still worried about the Sparks stories heroin junkie Anthony Rampino might have told after his arrest several months before. And although Roach had decided to stay loyal and was sitting in a state jail awaiting trial, Gotti still wanted to kill him.

"Go ahead, I want him dead," he said, after another man wondered if it was possible to kill Roach in jail.

"You want him dead?" the man asked again.

"Yeah, I feel sad. But that's what he gets for being dumb. He can carry away everybody."

After overhearing this conversation—and others in which a contract on Roach also was discussed by Gene Gotti—Gambino agents alerted jail officials, who enhanced their security around Rampino.

On another day, Gotti was overheard using the words "ice" and "hit" and "whack" while apparently discussing a series of homicides. "You get that sort of respect with murder," was the only intact sentence to emerge from the jumble of whispers.

At other times, the bug overheard fractured comments about construction jobs, waterfront shakedowns, union extortions and ghost payrolls, loan-sharking schemes, and gambling percentages. Taken

together, however, they only proved that the Ravenite was not a
Boys Club.

"We've got to get a microphone on the street," Mouw told
Gabriel, "or find out where they talk when they really want to talk."

———————

The fruits and frustrations of the FBI operation were not shared
with other law enforcement agencies, some of which had their own
get-Gotti ambitions. In the fall of 1988, a gangster trying to save
himself offered information that fortified these ambitions and gave
the media a story to rival Johnny Boy's still seemingly legitimate
acquittal in the Giacalone case.

The gangster was James McElroy. Along with members of the
Gambino farm team known as the Westies, he was convicted in a
case that led to Bosko Radonjich—broker of the juror, George Pape,
arrangement—becoming Westies boss.

Like Rampino, McElroy was a violent, drug-addicted gopher;
unlike Rampino, he felt no loyalty for Gotti. "I have done some
things with Johnny Gotti," he told the state's Organized Crime Task
Force, which earlier had failed to persuade Andy Maloney to mount
a Gotti prosecution based on tapes made when it bugged the Bergin
in 1985 and 1986.

McElroy was puffing his connection to Gotti. But one thing he
said resonated: He was at a wake in 1986 when a former Westies
leader departed a meeting with Gotti and said Gotti had just
enlisted the Westies to deliver a stern warning to some union leader.

The story seemed to fit with other facts the state agents and
others—including NYPD cops on the Manhattan District Attorney's
detective squad—had collected since the May 1986 shooting, in
Manhattan, of John F. O'Connor, the corrupt boss of Local 608 of
the United Brotherhood of Carpenters and Joiners, the largest local
in the United States. One of the main facts was an excerpt from the
Bergin tapes in which Gotti seemed to be promising some malice:
"We're gonna, gonna bust 'im up," he said in his often repetitive
way, or so it sounded.

O'Connor survived the shooting, but would not even answer
questions about motive. However, the state agents thought they'd
overheard Gotti providing the motive two months before, in
February of 1986, when underlings told the new boss that

O'Connor ordered a squad of carpenters to ransack a Gambino-backed restaurant newly built by non-union carpenters.

Another Westie who cooperated in an earlier FBI investigation had also secretly taped one of the four O'Connor shooters saying the "greaseballs" had given them the assignment:

"Oh yeah, [it was] for the greaseballs, something they needed quick. You know what happened? This guy O'Connor got a bunch of construction guys from his union. They went on the job and wrecked it. He was supposed to get kneecapped, but the bullets ended up high and one went in his asshole. He's got an extra asshole."

Alone, each of these facts hardly made for a case against Gotti. In court, even his "bust-'im-up" remark could be turned him into harmless chatter by a man famous for exaggerated speech. But the state agents believed McElroy's claim that the Westies leader told him the shooting was for Gotti, and McElroy's willingness to testify about it tipped the case into prosecutable range.

Maloney, among many on the federal side of law enforcement, did not agree. But the state Task Force did not need Maloney. The O'Connor shooting was a state crime in Manhattan, which gave jurisdiction to the elected Manhattan District Attorney, Robert Morgenthau. The 68-year-old Morgenthau was a powerful local prosecutor who had once been the federal prosecutor in Manhattan. He also had a history with the Mafia, having in 1963 talked a run-of-the-mill hoodlum, Joseph Valachi, into becoming the first Mafioso to break the vow of *omerta* or silence.

With the usual concerns about imperfect evidence and reliance on a lowlife witness such as McElroy, who once slit a man's throat for 100 dollars in drug money, Morgenthau and his rackets chief, Michael Cherkasky, came to agree with Ronald Goldstock, the state Task Force boss, that the case was winnable.

Neither would say their decision was affected by the accolades a Gotti victory would bring, but his notoriety guaranteed it. Still, a prosecutor's code requires only belief in the defendant's guilt and the possibility of conviction, not the beauty of the case. In addition, a provision in New York law dramatically raised the reward of convicting Gotti of ordering the assault of John O'Connor.

In the 1970s, Gotti was convicted of three felonies—attempted manslaughter and two hijackings. In New York (and many states), three-time losers can be deemed "predicate" felons—incorrigible career criminals who ought to be treated as such at their fourth felony conviction and locked up a long time. So rather than the five-to-fifteen-year sentence a judge would give for an ordinary conviction for assault, Gotti faced a twenty-five-years-to-life sentence.

It took a couple months to seal a deal with McElroy. A murder charged was dropped, his girlfriend got a pass on drug charges, and Morgenthau and Cherkasky agreed to write a letter on his behalf to the federal judge who sentenced him to 60 years in the Westies case. Worse criminals have gotten more, but not in such a theoretically simple assault case.

In January of 1989, for the third time in four years, Gotti was indicted. His arrest came on January 23, when 23 NYPD detectives and Task Force agents took up positions near the Ravenite and waited for him. Escorted by three bodyguards, Gotti left the Ravenite about 7 P.M. and walked north on Mulberry. The cops and agents stopped him just as he reached the adjacent neighborhood of Soho and the street of his Machiavellian dreams, Prince Street.

The suspect quickly fell into character. "I'll lay you three to one, I beat it," he said to Joseph Coffey, the Westies expert who had left the NYPD and joined the state Task Force, as Coffey told him the charges and slapped on handcuffs.

"I ain't goin' nowhere. Why're you doin' this shit?"

"Forget it, jerkoff, get in the fucking car," Coffey said.

Booking at nearby Manhattan Criminal Court took some time. Gotti fumed in a crowded holding pen behind the bail judge's court. Many two-bit drug dealers, thieves, and muggers—the detritus of the NYPD's other efforts that night—were startled to see him led into their midst and responded with a standing ovation.

Gotti was held overnight for a bail hearing the next morning. Prosecutor Cherkasky did not expect the judge to refuse Gotti bail—as a defendant, Gotti had always shown for court, the main basis, in state law, for determining bail—but he argued for it anyway. He said Gotti led a major criminal organization and had "enormous financial resources" enabling him to flee.

"He has never missed a court date," Bruce Cutler replied. "He gets to court before the building opens. He's always on time. He has never run away from a problem."

The lawyers argued several more minutes, long enough for Cutler to rhapsodize about Gotti the loyal husband, devoted father, and doting granddad unmercifully hounded around the clock by agents and cops who never saw him commit a crime. The judge pretended to pay attention, then set a bail that set the suspect back for about a week's worth of gambling: $100,000—or half of what Gotti spent the month before on a Christmas party for 1,000 gangsters and their wives, children, girlfriends, and lawyers.

Exiting the courthouse, Gotti broke into a familiarly sly smile when asked whether the new case caused him any concern.

"Did I ever worry yet?"

The reporters clamored for more and he indulged. "I have nothing to be worried about. They have nothing."

The questions kept coming in a hail, striking all around, accumulating in nothing, until Gotti heard one he felt it was productive to answer. It involved James McElroy, and his words tipped the tried-and-true strategy sure to be employed at trial: "This case is from the word of lowlifes."

The performance charmed the media beast and, for the most part, produced the desired result. The lead paragraph of one newspaper story actually began with Gotti's statement, in 1987 after the Giacalone case, that in no time at all, law enforcement would try to frame him again.

32

NETTIE'S PLACE

MORE THAN HE KNEW, Gotti was right that the law was coming after him. Besides the O'Connor case, the FBI was cutting a video-and-audio record that might play well before a jury some day. In Brooklyn, meanwhile, Andy Maloney and the Eastern District Strike Force were about to use their generous grand jury powers to apply more pressure. The idea was to start giving people near Gotti a choice: go before a grand jury and talk truthfully, or go to jail.

In Manhattan, rival federal prosecutors got the same idea after they rekindled an investigation of the Sparks murders. This was the piece of Gotti turf Rudolph Giuliani reserved when he and Maloney discussed Gotti after the Giacalone case. In 1989, with always annoying and sometimes dire effect, Manhattan federal grand jury subpoenas began landing on the doorsteps of Gambino Family soldiers.

Through Sammy and the crew chiefs, Gotti repeated standing instructions on how he expected soldiers to handle grand jury testimony: Tell the truth about things that don't matter; fail to remember when questions get pointed; lie when there is no choice.

Several men would be squeezed, including Thomas Spinelli, a Brooklyn soldier whose only link to Sparks was that his captain, Jimmy Brown Failla, was one of the men inside Sparks waiting to see Paul and Bilotti that night. Still, this made all in Failla's crew potential grand jury witnesses. Spinelli had already testified once when prosecutors sent another subpoena. He then made the mistake of saying out loud that he was not going to expose himself to perjury by telling lies his grand jury inquisitors would know are lies.

While uninformed about Sparks, Spinelli knew about Failla's role in the Gambino Family's private-sanitation rackets—the subject of many prior investigations by different agencies. The grand jury subpoena handcuffed him into trying to guess what the grand jury knew as prosecutors fired questions.

Spinelli's fellow soldiers immediately informed their capo of his decision to tell the truth and hope for the best. It would have pleased Failla if Chin Gigante made a move against Gotti, but until then, he had to be loyal to Gotti, so he told him about Spinelli.

"Then he has to go," Gotti responded. "If he don't wanna play ball our way, he don't play."

Gotti gave the job to Sammy, who now believed it was unseemly for a man of his position to be out in the street killing people. But he and a Failla soldier lured Spinneli to a Brooklyn factory owned by some gangster's son. As Sammy waited outside, the soldier shot Spinelli dead.

"It's over," he told Gotti the next day, in a walk-talk at the Ravenite.

"Good, can't have no rats, or would-be rats. People gotta know that by now."

Federal prosecutors use the grand jury cudgel in multiple ways. For instance, they can force people to testify under immunity grants that enable people to talk all they want about their crimes and avoid prosecution—unless they lie. Because this is a powerful tool that could be used to lead suspects into a perjury case, the law prohibits prosecutors from seeking immunity for an investigation's primary targets. It reserves immunity for people on the edges of a case, people less important than their information.

In Brooklyn, Maloney and Strike Force Chief Edward McDonald decided that getting Tommy Gambino was not as important as learning what he knew. It was a dicey call—Tommy was not only a capo but, as Carlo's son, a symbol of Mafia power in New York. Maloney and McDonald had to ask Washington superiors for approval, but the bosses agreed that sacrificing a potential racketeering case against Tommy was worth building one against Gotti.

For Tommy, the pressure of having to testify or go to jail was a new experience. During his father's and Uncle Paul's reigns, he lived a practically anonymous life, so far as the law was concerned, even though until Sparks, soft-spoken Tommy, who was married to the daughter of the Luchese Family patriarch, was set to replace Paul.

In truth, he had little lust for the job. He saw the meaning of the federal onslaught better than most. He was content with the millions he accumulated through his powerful connections. And after Sparks, he had demonstrated his practicality by quickly assuring Gotti that he savored neither revenge nor ambition.

Some of Gotti's reaction to these assurances was voiced within range of the state Task Force's Bergin bug and now provided part of the legal basis for subpoenaing Tommy before the grand jury, not that prosecutors ever have much trouble finding enough basis for a grand jury subpoena.

In the same conversation in which he grandly talked about building a legacy that could never be broken, Gotti told George Remini, one of Tommy's men, that he would appoint only quality men to Tommy's crew—not "hotheads" or "scumbags." He also ordered Remini to act as the crew's capo in sitdowns requiring a menacing nature.

"Tommy don't know how to handle that. He's a sweetheart for everything else, but you would know how to handle it, Georgie."

Putting Tommy into a deeper hole, Gotti also said that since Tommy had been so supportive after Sparks, he would treat him as an insider. "I told Tommy, 'Whatever we do, I want you to know, even if it's bad, off-color. I want you to know it from us. This way here, you're part of it.'"

In the end, Tommy was called before the grand jury four times, the last just before Gotti was indicted in the O'Connor case. He seemed relaxed when prosecutor Leonard Michaels asked about his boyhood, his education, and his business empire in Manhattan's Garment Center. Tommy and his even more low-key brothers Joseph and Carlo Jr. controlled several trucking, leasing, and manufacturing firms that employed 700 people and grossed more than $30 million annually.

Tommy began to prevaricate when he said he had no idea why his companies—which were almost all non-union—were never victimized by union or Mafia shakedown artists, when such was part of the history of the Garment Center. He began stirring in his seat and blinking rapidly when prosecutor Michaels turned to the taped conversation between Gotti and Remini.

"I don't know what is in Mr. Gotti's head," Tommy said.

When Michaels asked about the Sparks shootings, Tommy even refused to refer to them as murders. "I know my uncle was found dead on the street. As far as I am concerned, it was an uncomfortable time in my life. I lost my uncle and that's it."

Michaels pressed on; Tommy's answers began sounding even more evasive and nonsensical. He recalled events from more than four decades before, but not a meeting with Gotti the night before his first grand jury appearance. He admitted he visited Gotti regularly at some social club, but couldn't recall its name, what it looked like, where it was, or the names of many men he saw there.

Tommy's bobbing and weaving and outright lies provided plenty for a perjury charge, or so Maloney and McDonald decided. Tommy was indicted—and, after his arrest by Gambino agents, handcuffed for the first time in his life.

Tommy's lawyers crafted a trial defense relying on an appeal to jurors that the polite gentleman before them was singled out only because of his infamous father and that he happened to know John Gotti, the real target of the case. They thought the case a sure winner, with only slight damage to Gotti, but Gotti was worried; the Teflon Don was starting to feel besieged. The O'Connor case, with its virtual life penalty, was before him; and now he knew that two federal grand juries were behind him, no doubt in league with the FBI, coming at him with who-knew-what kind of cases.

"They're gonna keep comin' until they get something, get a motherfuckin' scumbag rat to say what they want," he ranted to Sammy one day. "It's gonna cost me a fuckin' fortune to fight these motherfuckers off."

The mounting pressure made Gotti more wary than ever about surveillance. But it was impossible for him to be like Chin Gigante, hiding out and faking craziness in public. Gotti enjoyed meeting his men and holding forth in public. It was how he showed power, and reveled in it. As law-enforcement recordings already showed, it also was difficult for him to control his speech. He spoke in big waves, leaping from one subject to the next, quoting himself and others, imagining conversations he intended to have or would have had. This made it sometimes hard to understand him, but also hard for him to edit remarks that might cause trouble if cops and agents were listening.

His verbal exuberance and his constant worry about surveillance led to walk-talks. But Gotti feared that technology rendered walk-talks less than foolproof. The weather also made them impractical at times. More than almost anyone, Gotti needed a place where he felt safe to talk. Starting earlier, but more frequently beginning in 1989, he began feeling safe in two.

The first was a hallway leading to private apartments above the Ravenite. A door in the club opened onto a rear landing of the hall-way, and Gotti could loiter there without anyone outside the club seeing him. He still spoke in low whispers, but about things he never would have spoken about in the club itself.

The second, and more important, place was a small apartment two floors above the club. It was the home of 74-year-old Nettie Cirelli, widow of a Gambino soldier who was Neil's driver and the Ravenite's caretaker. Whenever Gotti wanted to use her home for some secret talk, he would give Nettie's nephew and the club's new caretaker a few dollars and he would tell Nettie to go shopping.

This occurred first in 1986. Gotti had used it sparingly since, and only for meetings with men such as Sammy, Tommy Gambino, and Frank LoCascio. Sammy told Gotti the apartment violated conventional wisdom against speaking in confined places, but Gotti said if Nettie's was bugged, he would already be in jail. Even so, Gotti and his guests usually turned on her stereo to try and muffle their voices.

Gotti's secret places were why Gambino squad agents housed in separate video and audio "plants" frequently argued with each other. The audio plant agents would tell their video counterparts that Gotti could not be in the club during some of the times the video team reported him to be there. Even amid the jumble of voices, they would have overheard some sound from his, so the video agents must have been dozing on the job and failed to notice Gotti had left the club.

Sometimes, the video agents would see with their own eyes the proof that Gotti was inside, which was him walking out the door of the Ravenite. Then it would be their turn to question the alertness of audio plant colleagues.

The video agents were certain they were capturing and helping to identify all the important people in Gotti's life. On occasion, they also were treated to the sight of many older men falling over themselves to greet a much younger man who frequently came to the Ravenite wearing a Walkman.

The younger man was the boss's son, John A. Gotti, and now maybe the youngest "made man" in New York. His father, as a Christmas present in 1988, inducted "Junior" into the Family amid the cronyism whispers one might expect. Junior now had his own crew active in car theft, construction, and extortion. He co-owned or owned expensive properties in two states, including a prosperous trucking company.

At the time, Sammy was among those who whispered. But after the O'Connor case was indicted, and federal grand jury pressure began to mount, he began to believe that by inducting his son, Gotti was being shrewd—cementing his control through his son, in case he had to go to prison.

Junior was still prone to juvenile behavior, however. In June of 1989, he and some body-building pals attacked three men in a disco after one objected to one of the pals ogling his wife. It was Junior's third barroom arrest in six years. The media yukked the story up for a few days; but the wife was actually hurt when someone slugged her, too. Richard Rehbock—the lawyer who moved so quickly from the Willie Boy corner to the Gotti—was called in to try and make the case go away.

Rehbock did not have to do much. In an echo of cases involving Junior and his dad, the victims forgot who attacked them. Though they had identified the assailants for police that night, they were unable to identify them in later meetings with prosecutors.

The outcome was about the only good news for Gotti that summer. He was named lead defendant in a federal civil racketeering lawsuit aimed at breaking the Mafia's hold on the private-sanitation industry. The Manhattan District Attorney's office began an investigation preparatory to a similar suit against Gotti and Mafia control in the Garment Center. Even his Fourth of July party was a bust: So many cops were sent to Ozone Park that Gotti's men managed to fire off only a few rockets from a nearby railroad trestle.

The worst news, by far, came late in June. Gotti learned that the underboss of the Philadelphia Family, Philip Leonetti, had "rolled over" and started talking to the FBI. It was shocking on many levels—Leonetti was the first underboss of a major Family to turn informer—but the level that mattered most was that in 1986, shortly after Sparks, Gotti had met with Leonetti and in vague terms acknowledged he was involved.

He could not recall his exact words, but remembered leaving a strong impression that it was a shoot-or-be-shot situation. But who knew what words Leonetti would recall?

"Can you believe this?" Gotti railed at Sammy. "A fuckin' underboss goes and rats."

"Whatever he says, he'll be wingin' it."

"Mother-fucking rats. We're surrounded by mother-fucking rats."

Gotti was overstating the matter—but not by much. In addition to its video and audio plants, the Gambino squad had launched another operation against him—and that was to increase its stable of informants. By 1989, at least nine men were meeting secretly with agents about Gotti. It was an unusually large informant pool that showed Gotti was resented and disliked more than he could conceive.

The information Bruce Mouw and George Gabriel wanted most was where Gotti felt safe to talk. At first, they suspected a Tommy Gambino-owned office in the Garment Center, then one in Gotti friend Lewis Kasman's building in the same area, but he never used either enough to indicate either was the place. Inevitably, all suspicions led back to the Ravenite, but where and how? In 1986, an early informant had insisted Gotti used an apartment above the Ravenite for an important meeting.

But only a little old lady, the widow Nettie Cirelli, lived there. The federal rules governing surveillance applications are expansive, but a judge needed more than this to allow the FBI to send a black-bag squad sneaking into the home of a 74-year-old widow not suspected of any crime.

The information gathered dust in FBI files. The informants did not mention the apartment again—not until three years later, after Tommy Gambino was arrested and accused of lying to a grand jury, and an informant simply code-named "Source C" told his control agent that Tommy, after making bail, had run right to the Ravenite to meet with Gotti in Nettie's place.

Suddenly, the decision to pressure Gotti by pressuring Tommy seemed a better ploy than anyone had imagined. Agents quickly checked the informant's claim against video-plant logs on the day in question, and there it was: a notation for the time Gotti and

Tommy were spotted entering the club, but nothing for when they left, meaning they must have used an exit not covered by the video camera.

Only two possibilities existed—a rear fire escape for tenants of apartments above the first floor, which was highly unlikely, and the Mulberry Street doorway that tenants used, which strongly suggested that Gotti and Tommy had indeed used Nettie's place.

The FBI pressed "Source C" and the others for details just when Gotti was feeling more in need of secret places to talk. The need for secrecy was already the one unbroken thread of his life—from the time he turned to a life of crime and had to keep secrets from the police, from agents, from his crew, from lawyers and jurors, from Paul, from Neil, and, not least, from wife Vicky, about a longtime affair he had with Neil's out-of-wedlock daughter Shannon.

The need for secrecy was a yoke, and it was tiring carrying it around, especially when some matters, such as Tommy's arrest, demanded urgent focus. He knew the case against Tommy, coming in the wake of the O'Connor case and the reborn investigation of Sparks, was aimed at him. Events were piling up; the need for secrecy was great, but so was the need to talk.

As he told Sammy, Gotti had used the apartment before, with no ill result; so he started using it again. Soon, its existence and use became an open secret among the 50 or so men who shaped up at the club three and sometimes four nights a week, and soon more informants were corroborating Source C. They also reported that Gotti sometimes stepped into the Ravenite hallway when he wanted to talk privately. The informants said they had seen it before, but more often now.

"Now we know why the audio-plant guys couldn't pick 'im up sometimes," Mouw told Maloney, as they decided it was time to ask a federal judge to let the black-bag squad loose. The informants, backed up by evidence from the video logs, pushed gossipy information into solid probable cause justifying more electronic surveillance.

The pessimism brought on by the unproductive bug inside the club now turned to optimism. "Sooner or later, you just know the big mouth's gonna talk himself into a hole," Maloney jubilantly predicted.

By October of 1989, as the Gambino squad won approval to bug the hallway and the apartment, Gotti was using both regularly. The same "Special Operations" team that infiltrated the Ravenite itself almost two years before had no problem with the hallway; the bug was functional on October 15. For many reasons, Nettie's place was not going to be so easy.

"It's obvious we can't go in there at night, even if she's a sound sleeper," Mouw said as he, Gabriel, and team members mulled sneaky scenarios. "She might have a heart attack."

They agreed to wait and hope Nettie took a trip. They knew little about her, except that she was a widow who seemed to stay close to home, so they feared a long wait. Still, her home was such a potential asset it was best to be patient and devise a careful plan. If someone saw them going in, the target would be alerted and stop using the apartment.

Agents began periodic surveillance—to learn where Nettie went on errands, and for how long. She never went far, nor for long. They monitored a pen register—a device that can be placed on a telephone without a court order because it merely lists incoming and outgoing calls—on her telephone, to find out when she stopped making and receiving calls at night and presumably fell asleep.

Usually, she was on the phone every night, but usually no later than ten. Testing this, Gabriel once dialed her number at midnight, and quickly hung up when she wearily answered. Still, a post-midnight break-in was deemed too dangerous, for the effect the sudden sight of figures clad in black would have on her if she woke up.

On November 19, the pen register showed that Nettie didn't use the telephone all day. Knowing nothing, but feeling a hunch, Gabriel grew convinced she had taken a trip, perhaps to visit relatives for the upcoming Thanksgiving holiday. He waited one more day, and again the phone was silent. It was time to go.

That night, after entering Nettie's home and making sure she wasn't there, the FBI's break-in squad scouted it for where they thought visitors would sit and talk. They decided on the living room, which contained a couch and two chairs around a coffee table. The bug went into the ceiling, directly above the table. It was the right location.

33

TICKLING THE WIRE

WITH HIS SECRET PLACES secretly bugged, it didn't take Gotti long to begin talking himself into more trouble. Even before Nettie's apartment was bugged, he was overheard on the Ravenite hallway bug in what amounted to obstruction of justice, a "predicate act" that could be used in a racketeering case. But over the next few months, in the hallway and then in Nettie's, he opened a much more damning window on his world.

He had help. Hoping to make him feel a need to talk, the Maloney-Mouw team contrived a legal squeeze play. The perjury case they had filed against Tommy Gambino after his grand jury lies gave them a perfect setup. The trial on those charges was set to start soon, and so George Gabriel served Gotti a subpoena requiring him to testify.

The subpoena was part of a ploy known as "tickling the wire." Its purpose was to make Gotti believe the Eastern District intended to ask Tommy's trial judge to give Gotti immunity, forcing Gotti to either testify or go to jail—and to talk about this dilemma on tape. In any event, the subpoena would be withdrawn shortly before trial. For legal and strategic reasons, no one wanted to muddy the waters of a future case against Gotti by immunizing him in a comparatively minor perjury case.

The subpoena had its desired effect. A few days later, an agitated Gotti huddled with acting underboss Frank LoCascio and key aides Jackie D'Amico and Joe Watts in the hallway. He said he had just learned that his lawyers Bruce Cutler and Jerry Shargel had met with Tommy's lawyers and devised a plan calling on Tommy to plead guilty in the perjury case. This would moot the Gotti subpoena.

Many clients might appreciate the sacrifice and ingenuity, but Gotti said the plan showed the lawyers did not understand for whom they toiled. He never permitted his men to plead guilty in an important case, even if it meant less worry for him and probably only six months behind bars for Tommy. "Now you tell Tommy to fight it," Gotti said, quoting himself talking to Shargel. "Break their fuckin' holes! And don't worry about us going to jail. Me number one! I like jail better than I like the streets. And do what I'm tellin' ya. And don't ever have these kind of meetings again."

As agents monitoring the bug happily listened in, Gotti added more obstruction. Two other men who also had received "tickle-the-wire" subpoenas would not be allowed to testify either: "Nobody is taking the stand! Tell them to go fight! You go in there and break their fuckin' heads. Don't worry about us. Go in there and fight. Get my cell ready. ... Nobody is taking the stand!" In a few weeks more, per the script, the subpoena against Gotti was withdrawn. On the other hand, Tommy Gambino went to trial—and won. His jurors agreed with his lawyer's argument that Tommy was improperly targeted by a grand jury that really had John Gotti in mind. No one in the Eastern District was too upset. They had a bigger fish on the line. And on November 30, 1989, he hooked himself deeper when—for the first time since the men in black visited nine days before—he visited Nettie's.

He went there just after learning more bad news. In Brooklyn federal court earlier that day, Michael Coiro, the lawyer who defended him during his hijacking days, was found guilty of helping two other clients, Angelo and Gene, hide their heroin money.

Coiro had been arrested in the case with Angelo, Gene, and the rest in 1983, but his trial proceeded separately, and the Angelo tapes hurt him as much as everyone else.

"You're not our lawyer, you're one of us as far as we're concerned," Gene had said to Coiro.

"I know it, Gene, and I feel that way."

Over the long pretrial, Coiro was defended gratis by Shargel. When it was time for trial, Shargel was busy elsewhere, and Cutler took over, setting up a duel with echoes of the Giacalone case. Cutler's opponent was John Gleeson, her former assistant; much ill will remained between them, ever since Cutler called Giacalone a "slut" and Gleeson, in court, ridiculed Cutler—"he's not a lawyer."

Gleeson was starting to share Maloney's belief—based on what they now knew about the attempted fixes in the heroin trials—that the case that shot Cutler to almost as much fame as Gotti was fixed. He thought Cutler should be in prison, not in magazine spreads. He believed Cutler suborned perjury in the Giacalone case by urging a defense witness to invent stories about Giacalone offering him drugs and her panties.

Gleeson now headed Maloney's special-prosecutions unit. He was legally acute and relentless, and in the rematch with Cutler, substance overwhelmed style. Coiro was convicted.

Right after the verdict, Gleeson asked the judge to jail Coiro pending sentencing. The judge refused, ruling Coiro was unlikely to flee. Gleeson then said that Coiro should be barred from visiting places like the Ravenite, but the judge asked for a written motion the next day. After everyone left, Cutler visited the judge's chambers to make a special, fateful request: Could he escort his beaten client to the Ravenite to seek solace from a man who meant the world to him, John Gotti?

The judge, as much in the dark about the Ravenite bugs as Cutler, said yes—and Cutler took Coiro straight to the Ravenite and more trouble.

While Cutler stayed downstairs, Coiro entered Nettie's with Gotti, Sammy, and LoCascio. Audio-plant agents were on high alert because the video agents had reported the arrival of the Gambino troika, and now Cutler and Coiro, suggesting this might be one of those times Gotti felt a need for secrecy.

The audio agents fought their excitement when the voices of Gotti and Sammy gossiping about nonsense arrived clearly into their headsets. One of the agents, Mark Roberts, whispered to another: "This is incredible, they're up there, completely relaxed, talking freely! Tremendous!"

Over the years, Coiro's value to Gotti was based partly on his ability to learn law enforcement secrets from a source he never revealed. Now, as the agents listened in and after a few words of sympathy mixed with a wondrous display of Gotti's endless need to affirm his wisdom, Gotti asked Coiro to tap his source again. This was more obstruction of justice.

"First, you know, we're sorry," he said to Coiro.

"Thank you."

"I don't have to tell you how sorry we are."

"Oh, John."

"I knew you was guilty there. I didn't guess it. I knew it. And I don't think you're gonna go away [to prison] before the [obligatory legal] appeal. So, you got a fuckin' another year on the street, maybe. I think [the judge is] gonna give you ten years. Maybe look for you to do about three or four."

"I'll do it, John."

"Didn't I tell ya? I called the whole shot right down the line."

Gotti then turned to his own problems. Recently, these had flowed from so many directions he believed that both the state and federal governments were preparing cases against him—with both involving Sparks.

"Feds, they got a new statute. Enhancing your position, to commit murder to enhance your position. They're going at it tooth and nail, [to see] who's gonna try me first. I think it's easier to beat a murder 'beef' by the state."

"No doubt about it," Coiro replied. "Federal court, you get the kitchen sink."

While sure his information was accurate, Gotti asked Coiro to corroborate it with his source and learn exactly when the cases would be filed.

"But what you gotta do is you gotta grab this guy. Mike, we've been good to him in the past, we'll be good to him in the future. I never once asked you who he is. Did I ever ask you?"

"Never!"

"You know, Mike, again I'm, I feel lousy for pushing your sins aside, your heartaches aside."

"Forget about it. It's over."

"Now let me ask ya a question, Mike. Can you see this guy pronto?"

"Tomorrow."

"Believe me, it's done tomorrow."

Gotti and Coiro then discussed Coiro's conviction—and how the case was a loser from the start because of Angelo Ruggiero, now dying in a hospital a couple miles away. Angelo jeopardized so many by being so indiscreet in his home, Coiro said.

"You never heard me fuckin' jeopardize," Gotti said.

"You never did!"

"As close as Angelo was, he was never in my fuckin' house talking. Nothin' to put us in fuckin' jail."

"That's the right way," interjected Sammy.

"Because you know why, Sammy?" asked Gotti, about to provide audio agents a particularly sweet moment of irony: "You gotta relax in your fuckin' house. The way we're relaxing right here."

Relaxed, Gotti fixated on Angelo. "That cocksucker, and I hate to talk about people that are dying. He ain't a rat. He ain't a mutt. But I gotta call him a cocksucker. A guy was telling me this morning, 'All your troubles came from two places, 'Willie Boy Johnson and Angelo's house.' Willie Boy Johnson and Angelo Ruggiero decided they wanted to be a big-shot operation. That's all our troubles."

The visit concluded with Coiro repeating his promise to contact his source and report to Gotti the next day; he said he would ask his neighbor and their mutual friend, Lewis Kasman, to telephone Gotti and schedule a meeting somewhere.

With no time to place additional bugs and wiretaps in homes and offices, Coiro's source stayed secret. In any case, Coiro and Gotti got a chance to talk privately only six days later, when Angelo died and they attended the wake.

Angelo had left the hospital to die at home. Gotti still refused to visit, or send a message, and considered boycotting the wake.

"He had to go and be a big shot and get us all in trouble," he complained to Sammy. "Oughta had his tongue cut out."

"Look, everybody knows how you feel," Sammy said, "but it's not gonna look right if you don't go to the wake."

So, Gotti went to the wake, having turned over the first few shovels of dirt from his own legal grave—by being as indiscreet as his old and dead Fulton-Rockaway pal.

Maloney and Mouw were under no obligation to inform other law-enforcement agencies about the breakthrough conversations or the existence of bugs at the Ravenite, and they did not, especially now that it seemed—based on Gotti's exchange with Coiro and another one in the hallway with an underling—that Gotti had access to two corrupt sources in law enforcement.

While elated with the new tapes, the pursuers wanted more than an obstruction of justice case. Gotti's carelessness in the hallway—and his remark about feeling "relaxed" in Nettie's—portended greater things.

For nearly two anxious weeks, however, the bugs picked up little more than Gotti commenting in the hallway that a man who does not gamble "has no compassion." Then, at half past seven in the evening of December 12, 1990, a week after Angelo's death, Gotti made a second visit to Nettie's and turned over darker, deeper dirt.

This time, it was just him and Frank LoCascio—or, as Gotti said as tape rolled, "my acting underboss Frankie." By itself, the remark was a problem, because it tended to establish LoCascio's role in an illegal "criminal enterprise." Similarly, Gotti did himself no favors by calling himself "the boss"—nor Sammy, by calling him "my *consigliere.*"

Gotti, alternately somber and angry, gave his eavesdroppers many more reasons for joy. In an angry moment, talking about a boss's duty to make the tough decisions, he came close to admitting that he killed Paul.

"Who's gonna challenge me? Who's gonna defy me? What are they gonna do? Take a shot? Like I did to the other guy? I'd welcome that. I'll kill their fuckin' mothers, their fathers."

Recalling how Paul's business deals with the Genovese Family hurt Gambino men, Gotti even supplied a partial motive: "That's what made me hate, really, fuckin' Paul. He sold the borgata out for a construction company."

Deeper into his monologue, Gotti became, for him, unusually introspective and self-deprecating. At times, he seemed genuinely melancholy. He had genuinely serious problems, but also sounded like a man gradually coming under the liberating influence of a cocktail—in the background, agents did hear the sound of ice falling into a glass.

For instance, one reason Sammy now had such an active role in the Family, Gotti said, was that he filled a vacuum created by the boss's lesser experience in certain areas.

"I don't know nothin' about building. I don't know anything ... best I ever did was go on a few hijackings."

Gotti also said he found his newfound wealth remarkable, given that he started with nothing. "A fuckin' jerk like me. Never had nothing in my life."

Still, wealth had not made him greedy: "That's not John Gotti. At least I hope that's not me. Maybe I see myself in a light that I'm not in, I don't know. But that's what I feel I am."

At the end of a passage in which he referred to many capos and various grubby issues in the crews, he said about his problems: "[They] break my fuckin' heart. Who the fuck wants to be here? We got nothin' but troubles. I got cases coming up. I got nothing but fuckin' trouble. I don't feel good."

Someone turned on Nettie's radio when they entered, but not so loudly that words spoken directly beneath the bug in the ceiling were lost. But the music coming from it, mainly Italian love songs, contributed to the melancholy aura.

"I'm sick, Frankie, and I ain't got no right to be sick. I'm not goin' partying. I'm not going to race[tracks], [or] popping girls. I'm not doing nothin' fuckin' selfish here."

No, of course not, LoCascio would interject, when it seemed appropriate and when Gotti's mood resulted in paranoid thoughts about the capos' loyalty.

"What the fuck, am I nuts here? If I go to jail, they'd be happy. '... We finally got rid of 'im.' Hah! I'm getting myself sick, Frank, sick."

"You gotta get it out," LoCascio soothed.

"I don't wanna get myself sick."

"You can't hold it in."

"But one thing I ain't gonna be is two-faced. I'm gonna call 'em like I see 'em. That I gotta do 'til the day I die."

LoCascio's support frequently moved Gotti out of self-deprecation and into more familiar self-justifying terrain, and so Gotti again reminded LoCascio of how wealthy he could be, if only he wanted, and what a trusting boss he was because he did not make his men prove with "paper" what they made and, therefore, reveal the level of their tributes. Its legal peril was the reason for Gotti's hatred of paper, a reason a careful old loan shark like LoCascio plainly knew, even as he indulged it.

"I would be a billionaire if I was looking to be a selfish boss," Gotti said. "That's not me. You know I'm taking care of the people. We don't need none of these papers. We're too close for that shit. Ya see, I got that kind of fuckin' trust in *Cosa Nostra*. We're where we belong. We're in the positions we belong in, Frankie, and nobody could change that."

From a law-enforcement view, Gotti's mention, in a single taped statement, of "boss" and "*Cosa Nostra*," was a prosecutorial home run. Still, it got better. Winding down, he gave his opponents a few comparatively easy grounders. The man reporters loved to call the biggest gangster since Al Capone—who went to jail, and died there, only because of tax charges—began talking about what he did to keep the IRS at bay, which included recently taking a fake vice president's job in the Garment Center.

"I just got on the fuckin' payroll. I'm trying to keep my ass out of fuckin' jail, no other fuckin' reason," he said.

Between the Garment Center fakery and his long-time ghost job with a childhood friend's plumbing company, Gotti said he was "showing" for "tax purposes" about $85,000 in annual income.

"Eighty-five thousand, it's good for me, Frank."

"You don't want to spend more than that."

"My wife gets like $33,000. So, now it reads another 33 on top of it."

The December 12 tape contained ample evidence to arrest Gotti. But his pursuers bided time. Gotti was relaxed in Nettie's. He might go again and say more.

Besides, the tape needed analyzing; obscure remarks needed deconstructing; the problems Gotti cited with capos and crews needed checking with informants; the tax trail needed following; much work was ahead, and Gotti wasn't going anywhere. For him, the immediate threat was the O'Connor case, due to go to trial January 8, 1990.

Still, he had other business to attend to, and four days before the trial, he made another visit to Nettie's and gave the world, for the first time ever, an eavesdropper's perch as a *Cosa Nostra* Family discussed one of its sustaining rituals—the making of new members.

Gotti began by announcing he wanted to circulate the names of potential new soldiers to the other Families—and, observing tradition, allow them to raise objections.

"I wanna throw a few names out, five or six," he said to Sammy and LoCascio, adding this qualifying condition: "I want guys that done more than killing."

It became clear the trio had discussed the topic recently, and seriously, because Sammy produced a list of names and began calling out the nominee's first name and sometimes which capo they were "with."

"The kid Richie."

"Right," Gotti replied.

"Tommy. With Frankie."

"Right."

"Tony from New Jersey."

"Right. Fat Tony."

"Johnny Rizzo. With Good-looking Jack."

"Yeah."

"Fat Dom. With Jackie Nose."

"Yeah."

"And Mario, with, ah, Louie Ricco."

Because the video plant had been operating more than two years now, and agents had identified almost every habitue of the Ravenite, the first names of these men about to join the so-called secret society were enough to identify them, especially so when Sammy added their affiliation.

For another half-hour, the Gambino hierarchy discussed the nominees' merits, and the handicaps preventing others from making the list—which, in the case of a "Poncho," was age.

"I like the Richies, the Tommies," Gotti said, "they're young, 20-30 something, [but] these guys like Poncho. [He's] 61, 62! Where the fuck are we going?"

The list contained more men than Gotti wanted to make—some he did not know well, and thus did not trust—and so the "fuckin' hearts" of some "good guys" would be broken.

"This is not the time to make 20 guys," he said, adding that so far as he knew some nominees had never even been "used" in a murder, and capos ought never nominate a man who had not, as the expression went, "made his bones."

Near the discussion's end, Gotti told Sammy to show the list to bosses in the other Families and to explain it was "something that's been on the shelf" in the Gambino Family lately "only because we're caught up pretty good" with other problems.

"Tell them they can go to the bank on these people," he added.

Aside from their evidence value, Gotti's words showed that, for all his faults and defiance of supposed *Cosa Nostra* rules, he adhered to tradition frequently enough that, in his mind, he could present himself as an old-guard, Neil-variety *Cosa Nostra* boss.

His pursuers were almost as happy about the January 4 tape as the December 12. No *Cosa Nostra* boss had ever been captured talking so openly. But there was Gotti, his unmistakable voice unmistakably on tape, talking himself into a grave.

The tape contained one more highlight. After LoCascio left, Gotti told Sammy he planned to announce how the Family would be run if he lost the O'Connor case and was jailed again without bail pending sentencing.

"I'm gonna tell them, 'I'm the [boss] 'til I say different,'" Gotti said, "[but], soon as anything happens to me, I'm off the streets, Sammy is the acting boss.'"

Gotti said he would give Sammy any title he wanted, but whatever, it would mean "acting boss."

"So, I'm asking you, how do you feel? You wanna stay as *consigliere?* Or you want me to make you official underboss? Or acting boss? How do you feel? What makes you feel better? Think about it."

Sammy said he would, but did not think a title "made any difference."

Gotti said it did, because if Sammy remained *consigliere*, LoCascio, as acting underboss, would technically outrank him. "I love Frankie, but I don't wanna [leave him in charge]," Gotti added. "There's nothing I wouldn't do for the guy. But I don't want [that]."

In the face of Sammy's seeming indifference about a title, Gotti decided to pick one for him that would require some maneuvering. He said he would send a message to the imprisoned Joseph Armone and tell him that, nothing personal, but because he was never going to leave prison, he would have to resign as underboss.

Gotti would then make Armone *consigliere* and LoCascio acting *consigliere*. These moves cleared the way for Sammy becoming underboss, he explained.

Finally, Sammy spoke. "It would be my pleasure," he said.

34

INVINCIBILITY LEGEND

THE O'CONNOR CASE JUDGE told a big fib on the trial's first day. He told prospective jurors that because he feared media hounding, they would have to stay in a hotel if they were selected. In truth, he was sequestering them for the trial's duration because prosecutor Michael Cherkasky, fearing Gotti would hound jurors, had filed motions citing the Gambino Family's "notorious record" in that regard.

The judge had no choice. He could not give the real reason without poisoning jurors against Gotti and risking reversal by an appeals court in the event of conviction. It was the first time in history that a state court jury in Manhattan would be sequestered, and to protect jurors further, the judge would give the defense only their last names—making it hard, but hardly impossible, for someone to learn where they and their loved ones lived.

It took several days to pick a jury, and during that time Gotti made another visit to Nettie's that proved the wisdom of trying to safeguard a Gotti jury. On January 17, after receiving updates on the legal troubles of others that appeared to come from a crooked cop, Gotti turned to his own in a meeting with Sammy.

He told Sammy that jury selection in the O'Connor trial was almost complete, and that the last name of one chosen juror was "Hoyle" or "Boyle" and "Irish, I guess." His next remark seemed to imply that because "Hoyle" or "Boyle" was a utility-company lineman, someone in the Irish-dominated Westies gang, which had good contacts in the utility unions, might know him.

"Maybe we can't reach him," Gotti said, "[but] we'll send word out to anybody who knows him."

Gotti's remarks gave the Maloney-Mouw team a dilemma: Was a plot to tamper with the jury afoot, or was it wishful thinking? If a plot, should they tell Manhattan District Attorney Robert Morgenthau and prosecutor Cherkasky? If they did, and Cherkasky asked the trial judge to question the Irish juror, would Gotti get suspicious and stop using the apartment, hurting the increasingly promising case?

Maloney met with John Gleeson, who had learned about the Ravenite bugs a month earlier. Gleeson had suspected something big was up. A day after his win over Cutler in the Coiro trial, Gleeson received an unusual request from the FBI: Would he forget about filing a motion asking the judge in Coiro's case to bar Coiro from the Ravenite?

Now Gleeson argued that even if Gotti's words in Nettie's suggested a plot, they were vague and half-hearted—not serious enough to warrant the potential harm to the Eastern District of disclosing them to the Manhattan District Attorney.

He noted that elsewhere on the same tape, a Gambino soldier gave Gotti secrets apparently provided by a crooked cop—and many cops work for the Manhattan D.A. "Maybe [Gotti's source] is in the Manhattan D.A.'s office, who knows?" Gleeson said. "Unless more turns up, I wouldn't tell anybody. Why, for this, risk our bugs?"

Maloney accepted Gleeson's advice, setting the table for very sour grapes some day. The District Attorney's office stayed in the dark about Gotti's whispers—as much as the Eastern District stayed in the dark about the crooked cop's identity. Only later was Detective William Peist flushed out. He believed the NYPD cheated him out of a full disability pension, and so while in the intelligence division, he took to giving secrets away. In January of 1990, he got a new, temporary, and completely coincidental job: guarding sequestered jurors in the O'Connor case. There's no evidence he tried to influence the third group of New Yorkers who began sitting in judgment of Gotti on January 20.

En route from Queens that morning, Gotti had driven past a large banner that Lewis Kasman had hung from a highway overpass: "Good Luck, John; Love, People of Ozone Park."

In his opening statement, Cherkasky laid out the simple case facts: O'Connor ordered the trashing of a Gambino-backed restaurant built with non-union labor. Gotti ordered the trashing of

O'Connor. Cherkasky ended by pointing a finger toward Gotti: "Like all bullies, he could not allow a challenge to go unpunished."

When it came his turn, Cutler did not disappoint those who recalled how he once slam-dunked Giacalone's indictment into a waste can. Ridiculing Cherkasky's remark that the case was brought in the name of the "people" of New York, Cutler stooped beside the prosecution table like he was peeking up a skirt and screamed: "Where are the 'people?' I don't see any 'people.'"

The trial lasted only three weeks. At the defense table, Gotti exuded his usual public calm in the face of trouble. But then, on January 24, Cherkasky began unreeling the Bergin tapes. Gotti had read transcripts, but this was the first he'd heard them in a court-room. The experience was upsetting.

After the trial that day, he went to Nettie's and unburdened himself to Sammy and LoCascio. He said the only thing that made him feel better was knowing that most of the Bergin tapes were recorded before he succeeded Paul. The crudity on one particular tape—in which he threatened to shove someone's head "up his mother's cunt"—seemed beneath a boss: "Only thing I can comfort myself with [is] ... thank God, this was 1985. If this tape [was] 1988, '89, I would've thrown myself off a fuckin' bridge for embarrassment."

Departing from his usual stroking, LoCascio said he could see why Gotti was upset because he was the one always lecturing about talking in enclosed places: "You've been preaching, preaching, and you're doing the same thing that you're preaching."

Sammy remained silent, but Gotti—to the incredulous delight of audio agents—began sermonizing about the need to watch what is said, and where, in "*La Cosa Nostra.*"

"From now on, I'm telling you that if a guy just so mentions 'La,' I'm gonna strangle the cocksucker. You know what I mean? He don't have to say 'Cosa Nostra,' just 'La,' and he goes. I heard nine months of tapes of my life. I was actually sick, and I don't wanna get sick. Not sick for me, sick for 'this thing of ours,' sick for how naive we were five years ago. I'm sick that we were so fucking naive. Me, number one!"

He recalled the special irony of one tape, in which he was over-heard admonishing Angelo Ruggiero for indiscreet talking in en-closed settings. "'Hey, you gotta do me a favor,' I tell him. 'Don't make nobody talk. This is how we get in trouble, we talk.'"

On this doubly ironic note, Gotti's visits to Nettie's ended. He never returned after January 24. The reason emerged later, and it demonstrated how law enforcement agencies conducting separate investigations of the same man at the same time are bound to stumble into each other's path.

One week before, during a Manhattan federal grand jury session probing Sparks, a prosecutor asked a Gambino capo if he ever met Gotti in "an apartment somewhere." The question showed that the Manhattan team had informers, too—and it strongly suggested to Gotti, when the capo belatedly told him about it, that he ought to avoid Nettie's.

His manner at the defense table in the O'Connor trial did not betray the alarm he must have felt. He exuded confidence until the end, when his lawyers called John O'Connor, a Jerry Vale lookalike, to the stand. O'Connor said he had no idea who shot him, or who ordered it. He wasn't much of a victim—he was facing criminal charges of his own—and he pleaded the Fifth Amendment several times.

In his final argument, Cutler hollered about what a "snake," "rat," "psychopathic killer," "lying bum," and general all-around "swill" James McElroy, the government's key witness, was—and then, on February 5, 1990, jurors got the case.

"The people like me," Gotti replied, when a reporter asked how he assessed his chances.

On their first vote, six jurors liked Gotti, one did not and five were unsure. On the second day, the five unsures made up their minds and voted to convict, deadlocking the jury at six-six. On the next day, the same five changed their minds again and voted to acquit, after listening to a key tape again.

That made it eleven-one for acquittal; the holdout caved a day later, February 9, 1990. Hundreds of people, drawn by radio bulletins that a verdict was in, waited outside the courthouse for Gotti to emerge, then formed a cheering gauntlet as Gotti, escorted by Jack D'Amico, sauntered into a waiting Cadillac.

As after the Giacalone case, yellow ribbons appeared on 101st Avenue in Ozone Park, outside the Bergin, and in Howard Beach, in the yards of the Gotti home and others.

But Gotti did not go home first. He went to the Ravenite, and after a few minutes, fireworks exploded along Mulberry Street. Gotti stepped out for a bow, then invited a few reporters inside.

That day and the next, in the media, the Gotti legend reached its highest elevation; the thin air caused much woozy analysis. One writer said Gotti should be superintendent of schools because he'd "crack a few heads" and drugs would be gone from playgrounds. Another writer loftily described Gotti as the "typical American frontier risk-taker."

The media's problem was that so much had already been written about Gotti, fresh angles were elusive. The legend had already been explained: Gotti had tapped a civic vein of animosity for authority; he dwelled outside the law with style and bravado. But in the excitement of the moment, the media ignored an inevitable truth about the public attention span: As long as Gotti got away with dwelling outside the law, fine; as soon as he tripped up, forget about it. Next legend, please.

Few noticed the most meaningful quote in the coverage. It was spoken by Mouw's boss, Jules Bonavolonta, head of the FBI's organized-crime section in New York. Asked his reaction, Bonavolonta ignored the question and seemed to speak directly to Gotti: "He knows we haven't brought a case against him. And he also knows that when we do, he's finished. He can take all the bets he wants, but he's going to prison."

For an FBI official, it was a rare public display of verbal style and bravado—and there was an exceptionally strong reason for it. Back on December 12, in Gotti's second visit to Nettie's, the one in which he droned on about his troubles, Gotti also admitted he was a murderer. Not once, but twice—according to many reviews of the tape by agents who specialized in decoding Gotti's words, Michael Balen and Carmine Russo.

The first victim he mentioned was Robert "Deebee" DiBernardo, a union fixer and one of those who plotted with Gotti to kill Paul. DiBernardo was murdered in 1986, while Gotti was at the MCC awaiting trial in the Giacalone case. Angelo Ruggiero—lusting to be underboss and considering Deebee a rival—told Gotti that Deebee talked "subversive" behind his back.

Four years later, Gotti said to LoCascio: "When Deebee got 'whacked,' they told me a story. I was in jail when I 'whacked' him. I knew why it was being done. I done it anyway. I allowed it to be done, anyway."

On the same tape, Gotti admitted approving the murder of Louis Milito, a soldier, after Sammy said Milito was complaining about Gotti's leadership.

Gotti could have recalled many murders for LoCascio. That he chose these two did not matter to Bonavolonta or Mouw or Maloney. On top of his other indiscretions at the Ravenite—all his chatter about La Cosa Nostra, obstruction of justice, tax-evasion, bribery, and so on—the murder admissions cooked Gotti's goose. He had talked his way into a clean, easy case.

In fact, the case was even better than the FBI knew. On the same December 12 tape, in a passage yet to be understood, Gotti left evidence of one more murder. At the height of his invincibility legend, Gotti already was—legally speaking—a dead man.

It would take a while for Gotti to find out how clean the case was. It would take that long for the Maloney-Mouw team to analyze the tapes, decide what charges to bring, and fight a turf battle with state and federal counterparts in Manhattan that for anxious months appeared certain to deny Maloney the chance to see Gotti on trial again in the courthouse where the legend-making began in 1985.

Stung by his office's defeat in the O'Connor case, Manhattan District Attorney Robert Morgenthau, the most influential D.A. in the country, also wanted another shot at Gotti. He lobbied hard for a joint state-federal prosecution based mainly on Sparks and featuring his office and the U.S. Attorney in Manhattan. The case should be tried in Manhattan, where the murders occurred, he argued.

In one of many meetings on the dispute, Morgenthau also argued that the jury pool in Manhattan was "better"—a dig at all the jury-tampering that had gone on in Brooklyn during the heroin trials and others involving the Gambino Family.

"The Manhattan courthouse is one subway stop from the one in Brooklyn!" Maloney barked. "Do you think the Gambino Family could find its way there too!"

"All I'm saying is, look at the record."

The rivals exchanged reviews of each other's evidence. The Brooklyn case was based on tapes, Gotti's own words. The Manhattan case was based on turncoat informers, including the former Philadelphia underboss, set to testify that Gotti told him he killed Paul. But defense lawyers fear tapes a lot more than turncoats. In an ideal world, the ideal case would join the proof of both federal offices. And because Brooklyn would bring more to the table than Manhattan, the latter should have conceded the lead role and the District Attorney should have had nothing to say about it.

But Morgenthau did have much to say, and until a final meeting in Washington, where top Justice Department officials controlled the decision, it appeared Gotti would stand trial in Manhattan, in a courthouse just south of the Ravenite. In that meeting, however, momentum shifted back to Brooklyn, mainly because—in one more irony—Brooklyn presented a better plan for guarding against jury tampering.

The plan was devised by John Gleeson. Maloney had put him in charge of the grand jury working with the FBI to prepare the case for indictment. Having led the investigations into jury tampering in the heroin trials, Gleeson was an expert. He told his superiors the problem wasn't the jury pool in Brooklyn, but the defendants. "It doesn't matter where they are on trial," he said, "so how do you attack that problem?"

Gleeson's plan was to ask the judge who got the case to not only impanel jurors anonymously, but to sequester them as well—a highly unusual request. But Gleeson said that with the informants the FBI now had, plus the known Gambino Family track record, a strong legal argument for it could be made. "I think our district's judges, because of recent history, are likely to agree with us," Gleeson said.

Gleeson offered other ideas as well, for screening out pre-disposed sympathizers, and in the end they saved the day for Brooklyn. A key Justice Department official later said that, in contrast to Brooklyn, Manhattan had not given enough thought to how it would guard against tampering.

At the time, however, no reason was given. Instead, a few days later, the official telephoned Andy Maloney. "It's yours, Andy," he said.

Though unaware of the damage he had caused himself, Gotti assumed a federal case was coming because of all the subpoenas floating around Brooklyn and Manhattan. As the jurisdiction issue played out, he tried to learn when he would be arrested—when, as he put it, "the big pinch" would come. But his sources, including Detective William Peist, did not have the federal hooks they needed.

Still, Gotti continued to relish the benefits of office and mold the Family in his image. One benefit was having people shower him with money, directly or indirectly. In the spring of 1990, each Family capo gave at least $5,000 as a wedding gift to Gotti's son Junior; super-loyal capo Jack D'Amico gave $10,000 and Sammy chipped in $7,500. All the bosses of the other families gave nearly the same amounts as D'Amico and Sammy—even Chin Gigante. Some 150 other connected guests gave mostly "nickels and dimes"— meaning, $500 or $1,000. At the end of a day of gift-giving and apple-polishing at a banquet for Junior and his bride at an elegant Manhattan hotel, Junior had $348,700.

A couple months later, Gotti promoted the newly wealthy, 26-year-old Junior to capo. Once again, Sammy among many believed Junior was too young for the job and that Gotti was looking out for his interests as much as Junior's by solidifying his control in advance of his arrest.

Once more, the situation induced speech paralysis. Sammy was now underboss and designated "street boss" if Gotti went to jail. If Sammy objected, how would it look? What was Sammy afraid of? Or planning? Silence was further assured by the manner in which Gotti implemented Junior's promotion to *caporegime*, meaning crew leader.

"I've been thinkin' somethin'," he told Sammy and LoCascio at the Ravenite, "and I want you to tell me if you'd recommend we put Junior up to *caporegime*, and give 'im a crew."

"Yeah, he's ready, be a good thing," Sammy said.

The Gambino squad learned about Junior later, from informers, because all the Ravenite bugs were silent. Because Gotti had stopped using the apartment, and because enough evidence already existed, the FBI had shut down even the hallway bug and was concentrating on marshaling indictment details for Gleeson.

Crucially for one man, the significance of one of the last conversations on the hallway bug was overlooked. Agents failed to link the name of a man mentioned in the conversation to threats Gotti made earlier on the apartment tapes. Consequently, the FBI did not give the man a warning that his life was in danger, and he would be murdered.

In Nettie's on the watershed day of December 12, 1989, the day Gotti talked about killing Robert DiBernardo and Louis Milito, he also referred to another man whose first name was Louis—but agents thought he was still speaking about Louis Milito.

In later reviews of the tape, it became clear he was not—but not in time for Louis DiBono, a soldier in the construction business. By 1989, after he began using cocaine and his business fell apart, DiBono was on shaky ground—particularly after he ducked Gotti's demands for meetings to discuss his delinquent business-tax payments. These threatened Gotti because Gotti, as a secret partner in the firm, was vulnerable too.

"Louie DiBono," Gotti said to LoCascio on December 12, "you know why he's dying? He's gonna die because he refused to come in when I called."

It was easier to see how the agents missed a second threat against DiBono on the apartment tapes. That time, on January 24, speaking to Sammy about someone suspected of bringing an informer around, Gotti referred to the overweight DiBono by a nickname.

"He's gotta get whacked … for the same reason that Jelly Belly's getting it. You wanna challenge [us], we'll meet the challenge! And you're going, motherfucker!"

At the time, agents knew little of DiBono. By the time he got around to meeting Gotti in the Ravenite hallway, they had not yet completely deciphered the two apartment tapes. As DiBono spoke, they didn't realize they were eavesdropping on a doomed man trying to appease his boss.

"I'm in really good shape," DiBono told Gotti, referring to his cocaine problem and a new willingness to fix his tax problems. "I'm paying all the bills!"

"I don't want another thing like this," Gotti said.

"No!"

"We don't need this fuckin' shit. I don't need it!"

"John, I'm working very hard. I'm in the office every day. I'm on the ball."

In time, DiBono paid his taxes, but the penalty for his more serious crime—blowing off Gotti meetings—was not lifted. He must have sensed his apology was no guarantee, because he never returned to the Ravenite and avoided all his usual places.

Louis DiBono lasted until October of 1990, which was when Sammy learned he was on a drywall job at the World Trade Center in Manhattan. DiBono was promptly shot dead by a hit team led by Gotti bodyguard Bobby Borriello. Gambino agents soon learned about the murder and simply regarded it as an unsolved homicide.

It would take a couple more months for them to realize they could have possibly prevented it.

"The system failed," Mouw would later recall, grimly.

35

PROVEN

WITH GOTTI ON THE TAPES, John Gleeson had enough to ask his grand jury to indict not just the leaders of the Gambino Family—Gotti, Sammy, and LoCascio—but virtually every capo, but he and Maloney decided to include only one capo, Tommy Gambino. They liked the case short and simple; the others could be attacked later.

Once that decision was made, in November of 1990, it was time to make the "big pinch." Sammy's brief absence from the scene—he sneaked away to Florida and briefly contemplated fugitive life—delayed matters a little more. On the afternoon of December 11, 1990, the arrest team moved into place. Ten agents and three police detectives would wait near the Ravenite until all the suspects arrived, then move in. One agent would wait for Tommy Gambino outside his office.

LoCascio showed at the Ravenite about five o'clock. An hour later, Sammy arrived. By past practice, Gotti should have arrived 15 minutes later, but did not. After a half-hour more, the arrest team suffered adrenaline letdown. In the video plant, Mouw told his men: "If we take these guys without John, you know what Cutler will do. He'll call a press conference and make a big show of surrendering his oppressed client."

Fifteen more minutes passed. Finally, Gotti's Mercedes inched up Mulberry with Jack D'Amico at the wheel. In a few minutes, after Gotti—wearing a camel-haired coat and jaunty yellow scarf—walked inside the club, Gabriel led his team to the door. Some soldiers recognized him, but did not interfere as he walked in, pistol in one hand, badge in the other.

"FBI! You know why we're here! We're here for John, Sammy, and Frankie, and I want everyone to do us a favor and cooperate."

Smiling, Gotti ambled up, his arms extended in a handcuff-me gesture. A grim Sammy in construction-foreman garb was a few steps behind, trailed by a suited and snarling LoCascio.

"I knew you were coming tonight," Gotti said. "I knew."

This was another example of Gotti's ceaseless need to stroke himself. He did not know. He believed the hammer was going to fall after the Christmas holidays, and so he had continued to book engagements—including one for the next night, when he was to escort a dazzling young woman, Lisa Gastineau, to a Sinatra concert in New Jersey. She was the recently divorced wife of a former All Pro football player whom Gotti had previously squired to the Rainbow Room atop Rockefeller Center.

"I knew," Gotti repeated, trying to bait Gabriel, who thanked him and LoCascio for dressing up so nicely for the arrest, but noting: "You forgot to tell Sammy."

Mouw arrived from the video plant and telephoned Gleeson. "John, I'm in the Ravenite, sitting right across from John Gotti and listening to George Gabriel read him his rights. It's a beautiful sight."

The suspects were denied bail pending a hearing and put in solitary confinement. The first of many hearings on bail and other matters was held in secret a few days later, on December 21, 1990. It would be a very pivotal day for all parties.

A couple hours before the hearing, Gabriel, agent Carmine Russo, and Gleeson assistants Laura Ward and Patrick Cotter went to the courtroom to assure the equipment for playing tape excerpts was working. These would be used to show the suspects were dangerous criminals undeserving of bail.

Gabriel inserted an excerpt from the December 12, 1989 tape and everyone donned headsets. The excerpt was the one that they knew featured Gotti's references to "Louie," meaning Louis Milito, and "Deebee," meaning Robert DiBernardo.

Maybe it was multiple ears hearing the words for the first time, maybe it was that ears were more in tune because everyone now knew about the murder of Louis DiBono, but the words coming out of the machine, into wires and then to speakers mounted around the courtroom provoked a double-edged epiphany.

"Louie DiBono," Gotti said to LoCascio, "you know why he's dying? He's gonna die because he refused to come in when I called."

Until that moment, "Louie" and "DiBono" had been heard—by both prosecutors and agents, during many reviews—as "Louie" and "Deebee," as one confusing reference to two murders mentioned earlier in the tape, not as a new reference to a third murder.

Now everyone heard "DiBono," not "Deebee."

"Holy fuckin' shit," Gabriel said. "Another murder, it sounds like to me." He played the tape two more times, with the same results.

Carmine Russo sank into his chair. "I haven't been back to this tape in a while, but it's there, I missed it, I fucked up."

The agents informed Gleeson, who said, "I listened to that tape myself, maybe a dozen times. I didn't hear 'DiBono' before."

DiBono chose the life he lived. Still, everyone felt an odd mixture of guilt and embarrassment. But it soon gave away to another emotion—excitement. With another murder for the indictment, the nice and clean case had just gotten stronger.

Once the hearing began, it was time for Gotti to realize mistakes. As prosecutors began playing excerpts, the cost of once relaxing in Nettie's place became devastatingly clear. Each excerpt supported a charge in the case; for the suspects, it was like seeing bullets aimed at their heads leave the gun.

Words from the December 12, 1989 tape—the most damning one—resonated with particular impact on Sammy Gravano. He was not in the apartment that day, and so he was hearing the words for the first time—and hearing Gotti lie about the murders of Robert "Deebee" DiBernardo, Louis Milito, and Louis DiBono.

The truth was that Deebee was murdered, over Sammy's objections, after Angelo told Gotti, in jail awaiting trial in the Giacalone case, that Deebee had made "subversive" comments behind his back. At the time, Angelo owed Deebee money and considered him a rival for underboss.

"Deebee," Gotti said on tape to LoCascio. "Did he ever talk subversive to you?"

"Never."

"Never talked it to Angelo, and he never talked it to [Joseph Armone] either. I took Sammy's word that he talked about me behind my back ... I was in jail when I whacked him. I knew why it was being done. I done it anyway. I allowed it to be done anyway."

On the same excerpt, Gotti next turned to Milito and DiBono. Milito had been killed because he noisily questioned the judgment of the new boss. DiBono was killed because he failed to answer a Gotti summons. But now Gotti said the only reason they were killed was that Sammy asked permission to get rid of business partners.

"Every time we got a partner that don't agree with us, we kill him. ... [the] boss kills him. He kills him. He okays it. Says it's all right, good."

In one brief diatribe, Gotti made three murders seem solely Sammy's doing. There would be a price for rewriting history this way, and soon the bill would come due.

Back in solitary confinement, Sammy began spending time with transcripts of the tapes turned over to the defense. The December 12 transcript contained much more Gotti monomania than was excerpted in the bail hearing, and Sammy studied it intently. Time and again, Gotti accused Sammy of having "green eyes"—hoarding money and opportunity for himself.

"That's Sammy ... every fucking time I turn around there's a new company poppin' up. Building. Consulting. Concrete ... where the hell did all these new companies come from? Where did five new companies come from?"

Sammy read on, until on page 30 of the transcript, history seemed to be repeating itself: Gotti compared Sammy to Paul.

"[Paul] sold the [Family] out for a fuckin' construction company. And that's what [Sammy's] doing. I don't know if you could see it, but that's what [Sammy's] doing now. Three, four guys will wind up with every fuckin' thing. And the rest of the [Family] looks like waste."

Unless Sammy was brought into line, Gotti added, the Family was headed down the same path as under Paul—a Family of factions, "a fuckin' army inside an army:"

"You know what I'm saying, Frankie? I saw that shit and I don't need that shit!"

Gotti's words sat in Sammy's craw for months. At one point, when he and Gotti were briefly housed in the same cell, he made his feelings known. Gotti said he was just ranting and that if he believed what he said, he would not have made Sammy underboss.

He also told Sammy that he never believed it when someone came to him and said Sammy was an informer. This enraged Sammy more because, as he told Gotti, he should have been given the right to challenge his accuser, prove him wrong and then kill him.

"As underboss, you owed me. That's *Cosa Nostra*, the life. We do a sitdown. Put me in the basement with pistols. If they prove it, kill me. If they don't, I kill them. It's my right. You took that away. Not telling me, you give credence to a fuckin' lie."

"Sammy, I am your friend, you're my friend. I never doubted ya. I can't remember every little thing I don't think counts."

"I was your underboss!"

"Sammy, this here happened, but it don't mean nothing. Now, we gotta fight hard to get outta here."

As the pretrial stage in Judge Leo Glasser's courtroom moved into 1991, the fight got harder. At the end of a bitter battle fought in legal papers, the judge—at Gleeson's urging—disqualified Cutler and Shargel from representing Gotti and Sammy at the trial because they were too involved in the taped evidence to properly defend their clients.

The legal basis for disqualification was overwhelming. Still, it was controversial. Denying Gotti and Sammy a basic liberty, the right to counsel of their choice, might look unfair. Kicking Bruce Cutler out might look like revenge for the Giacalone case.

Gleeson and his assistants mulled it over a long time. The more time they spent with the transcripts, however, the more they felt the evidence justified it. "The lawyers made themselves part of the evidence, part of what happened," Gleeson argued. "If you don't want to be a fact witness, stay the hell out of the Ravenite."

At the first hearing held after the disqualification, a large media contingent showed up. Gotti noticed and took advantage.

"Why can't I have my counsel, Bruce Cutler?" he demanded of Judge Glasser.

"I made that clear in a decision, Mr. Gotti. I'm sure Mr. Cutler has explained it to you."

Gotti turned toward the prosecution table and shouted: "I think they should be disqualified! I'm not worried about their phony tapes or their phony transcripts!"

He raised his right arm and cocked his thumb and forefinger like a pistol, then aimed at Gleeson—that "Little Lord Fauntleroy," he said, adding: "He says he welcomes a good fight! He says he wants a fair trial! But he can't handle a good fight, and he can't win a fair trial!"

The judge said he would give the defendants two weeks to hire new lawyers, and if they didn't, they would get court-appointed lawyers.

"You can do whatever you want to do," Gotti barked. "It's your courtroom."

Gotti sat down, satisfied with his message of defiance in the face of persecution.

The performance did not impress an increasingly self-interested Sammy Gravano. In the next hearing two weeks later, he startled people at the prosecution table when he smiled and said, "Good morning, Mr. Maloney."

In a few days more, he sent a secret message to the FBI. The message was that he was not going to remain loyal to a man who pinned murders on him and talked behind his back. He was willing to talk about a deal. He had calculated his options carefully. He was facing life in prison if convicted. If he pleaded guilty and helped the government by testifying against Gotti, he might get ten or even five years in prison.

Negotiations took weeks. At the end, Sammy agreed to become the first Mafia underboss to testify against his boss. He also agreed to confess to all his crimes, and in so doing, filled in all the missing details of the Sparks murders.

He identified the 10-member hit team, and where each was placed. It included John Gotti, sitting in a parked car with Sammy, ready to jump out and open fire if the four main shooters had trouble with their targets, which they did not

"Wasn't that kind of reckless?" Gleeson asked Sammy during one of dozens of debriefings. "What if somebody saw you?"

"Nobody knew John then. Nobody knew me, not until John made me and everybody known to you. I always thought Cosa Nostra meant being undercover."

Some wondered about the wisdom of dealing with Sammy. But after debriefing Sammy, Gleeson argued for it. "There's no way we can't use Sammy," he told Maloney. "He gives the case depth. He makes Sparks. At the end of this case, all we will have to do is tell the jury: 'You can convict on the tapes, you can convict on Gravano's testimony—but together, the conclusion to this case is inescapable.'"

In another debriefing with Mouw, Sammy filled in one more puzzle—the 1987 Giacalone case. Mouw asked: "After John's trial in

'87, we got some surveillance that seemed to show people congratulating you for something. Did you have anything to do with that jury?"

"Sure I did!" Sammy replied. "I fixed it! I was in charge of a guy on the jury. Did a good job, didn't I?"

To increase his worth to the prosecution, Sammy agreed to testify against anyone else the government wanted. He would help it dismantle the mob. In return, he would be sentenced to five years in prison. It was the best deal a gangster ever made, and it sealed John Gotti's fate.

Gotti's fourth trial in six years began January 21, 1992. The prosecution severed Tommy Gambino from the case for a separate trial—no use letting any juror sympathy for the gentlemanly Gambino rub off on Gotti.

At the trial's outset, Glasser ruled the jury would be sequestered. This was a first in Brooklyn federal court history, as sequestration in the O'Connor case was a first in Manhattan state court history. Gotti's main hope now was that when deliberations began, jurors would either be too afraid to convict, or too affected by some combination of old and new favorable publicity.

Outside the courtroom, during breaks, Gotti stalwarts lobbied the press. They got reporters to run stories about Gotti buying puppies for sick children and urging thieves to return a religious urn stolen from a church. Jack D'Amico and Carlo Vaccarezza, owner of a favored Gotti restaurant, were the most effective lobbyists. They were charming and always quote-ready—as long as the instigating question was not overtly invasive.

"John's a man's man," Vaccarezza said in his languid maitre d' style. "Loyal, true. He's only on trial because the government hates it that people love him."

"A John only comes along once in a life," added D'Amico. "They broke the mold with John; he's original."

A writer interrupted to ask D'Amico what made Gotti such an original.

"John had two things going for him. He was loved and feared. He's the only person I've seen with both. You call it charisma. He has that, but love and fear was what counted. People don't cross a man they love and fear."

"Sammy apparently has," the writer pointed out.

"Well, because of the situation that happened. But Sammy only ever had one thing going for him. Fear. People were afraid to warn John about Sammy."

At the defense table, Gotti seemed sanguine. But this faded midway through jury-screening, after the *Daily News* broke two big stories. The first disclosed the Giacalone-case fix. The second previewed highlights from Sammy's expected Sparks testimony.

The jury story laid the Teflon Don myth bare just when Gotti needed myth most; the Sparks story showed how much damage Sammy was going to cause. Both stories, widely reported by other media, negated the publicity operation.

As jury screening continued, many obviously frightened people made it plain they did not want to serve on a Gotti jury. One day, Glasser summoned the lead lawyers into chambers to discuss the potential jurors' fears, and Gotti wound up alone with a pool reporter, Gabriel, and some federal guards. The reporter asked Gotti what he thought about Cutler's disqualification on conflict-of-interest grounds.

"Conflict?" Gotti began, pointing to Gleeson's empty chair. "He's the one with a conflict! He's had one for eight years! You know how they say I'm Bruce's only client the last eight years? Well, I'm Gleeson's only case. This guy, you know what he says when he wakes up in the morning, rolls over and looks at his wife? He says, 'Hiya, John.' This guy learned to talk listening to my voice! I'd like to have a bug on him for three hours!"

After an anonymous jury was finally chosen, and Gleeson began introducing the government's evidence, Gotti's behavior grew worse. At the defense table, he smirked, snarled, and swore. He gestured profanely at witnesses and government lawyers.

When FBI agent Lewis Schilero took the stand to interpret Cosa Nostra-speak on the tapes, Gotti muttered that Schilero was a "fuckin' scumbag;" and when Gleeson put relatives of Robert DiBernardo, Louis Milito, and Louis DiBono on the stand to humanize the dead, Gotti blew sarcastic kisses at the prosecution table.

On many days, an aura of danger and imminent violence hung in the air. The menace in the words and gestures of the lead defendant was a major reason why, but so were the abundant federal marshals positioned around the courtroom. Three times, bomb threats forced evacuation of the courthouse. In a sidebar, Judge Glasser revealed that he had received several death threats, and that he was under heavy guard.

Still, on other days, the trial had a light, day-at-the-circus kind of mood, thanks to an odd combination of minor and major celebrities who dropped by to sit with the Gotti lobbyists and sing Gotti songs to the media. The celebrity cheerleaders were procured by Carlo Vaccarezza and included heavyweight boxer Renaldo Snipes, civil rights leader Roy Innis, singer Jay Black, and actors John Amos, Al Lewis, Mickey Rourke, and Anthony Quinn. The testimonials did not always go as Vaccarezza hoped.

For instance, while speaking with print reporters, Mickey Rourke—who met with Gotti while researching a film role—said what Vaccarezza wanted him to say about what a gentleman Gotti was and how he worried about whether Gotti was getting a fair trial.

However, outside the courthouse with television reporters, Rourke grew taciturn. Walking to a car that sped quickly away, he ducked most questions about why he was there and what he felt about Gotti.

Rourke's sudden shyness irked Vaccarezza, who told hallway lobbyists what happened: "What a jerk. He didn't say anything nice. He froze. Despite all the time John spent with him. He's not a man."

Anthony Quinn caused the biggest stir, inside and outside court. At the lunch break, he walked toward the well of the courtroom to shake Gotti's hand, but federal marshals stopped him. Gotti was in custody; even a handshake was against rules.

"Hello, John," Quinn said, with a what-else-can-I-do? expression. "Sorry, John."

"See," Gotti replied, holding his right thumb and forefinger close together, "we're this close to Russia here. But thanks for comin'."

Outside court, Quinn said the trial was "the best drama going on in America right now. This is the greatest theater you can possibly see." The heart of the drama was "the friend who betrays a friend. I'm not here to sit in judgment of Mr. Gotti but in judgment of a friend who betrays a friend. Friendship is a sacred thing. When I was growing up in East Los Angeles, the worst thing was to be a snitch."

Quinn mentioned that he had appeared in 30 "gangster pictures" and that "the boys" liked him because he knew how to portray them. He neglected to say that he was then up for another film project, a starring role in which he would portray a real-life gangster, Gotti's mentor Aniello Dellacroce.

Back in court, Maloney joshed Gotti's new lawyer, Albert Krieger: "Albert, tomorrow the good guys are going to bring in Clint Eastwood."

On the afternoon of March 2, 1992, six weeks into the trial, the high point of the drama, the moment everyone anticipated most, finally came.

"The government calls Salvatore Gravano," Gleeson said.

In short, blunt answers, Sammy described his life's journey—and how, along the way, he was part of 19 murders, because murder was a way of life in *La Cosa Nostra*.

On the third day of his testimony, he finally engaged Gotti in a long staredown.

Sammy's face showed more indifference than anger. Gotti's had a thin, smirking smile. Neither blinked, and Sammy did not turn away until Gleeson began asking questions.

He grew increasingly confident on the stand. "Sometimes I was a shooter," he summarized at one point. "Sometimes I was a backup shooter; sometimes I set the guy up; sometimes I just talked about it. When you go on a piece of work it doesn't matter what position you're in. You're all out there. You're all liable to get charged the same. It doesn't make any difference."

At the end of his ninth and final day on the stand, Sammy drove a last dagger into his former boss that memorably described their relationship: "I was a good, loyal soldier. John barked and I bit."

The case was nearly over, and Gotti didn't put up much of a defense. A day after the prosecution rested its case, the defense rested, after calling one witness—a tax lawyer who testified some-what confusingly that it was he who advised Gotti that he did not have to file income tax returns.

Except in cross-examination, the defense did not address all the other mayhem in the indictment. Coming on top of the tapes, Sammy had made the case indefensible. The only defense, as Gleeson predicted, was the "I'm-guilty-so-what?" defense.

In his final argument, Gleeson stayed between quiet outrage and gentle sarcasm. He called the evidence "suffocating." He noted that the government did not make a sick, serial killer an underboss; John Gotti did. "We'd love to bring you witnesses with absolutely impeccable credentials, of unquestionable honesty and integrity," he added, pointing at the defense table. "The problem is, they don't know any such people."

He reminded jurors that the tapes featured only six hours of conversation. "It probably seems like more because the conversations are so dense with criminal activity. We caught six hours and it's absolute mayhem. Who they've murdered, who they're going to murder, why they have to murder."

For a big federal case, the jury did not deliberate long—only fourteen hours over one and a half days. At one o'clock in the afternoon of April 2, 1992, the forewoman sent a note that a verdict was in, and only 19 minutes later, the judge's clerk stood and asked the forewoman the first of several questions: On the first charge in the indictment, the murder of Paul Castellano, had the jury found whether the government had "proven" or "not proven" the charge?

"Proven," the forewoman replied.

Gotti winced, then smiled and winked at his retinue in the spectator section, as the forewoman kept answering "proven" to every count.

At the prosecution table, Maloney leaned into Gleeson's ear, "Magnificent, John, magnificent."

Moving right along, Glasser thanked the jurors, dismissed them and said he would sentence Gotti in two months. Guards then took Gotti away. Downstairs in the lobby, the lobbyists were still glumly working. Jack D'Amico said Gotti was a "class act" to the end. "When you're born round, you don't come out square."

Meanwhile, 20 feet away, New York FBI boss Jim Fox was in a media scrum. "The Teflon is gone," he said, tossing a line his spokesman Joseph Valiquette had suggested during their hurried ride to the courthouse. "The Don is covered with Velcro."

On June 23, except for Sammy, the trial's main participants returned to court for sentencing. Federal guidelines required the judge to give Gotti and LoCascio multiple life terms in prison without chance of parole. The hearing's only potential drama was what Gotti would say when Glasser gave him an obligatory chance to speak.

But Gotti said nothing. LoCascio spoke for him: "I am guilty of being a good friend of John Gotti. If there were more men like John Gotti on this earth, we would have a better country."

Outside the courthouse, about one thousand people, mainly from Ozone Park and Howard Beach, arrived in chartered buses just as the brief hearing ended and Gotti left the courtroom without even a nod to anyone in the fully assembled press corps. In the end, the media had done him no good.

Chanting "Free John Gotti!" the crowd marched toward the courthouse entrance. Several hotheads, egged on by members of Junior Gotti's crew shouting into bullhorns, began rocking a police car and, before long, three cars lay on their roofs and a riot was on. Just outside the entrance, out-manned cops and Gotti sympathizers slugged it out.

Just inside the entrance, guards barred the doors and stood back from a floor-to-ceiling wall of glass. Standing back, watching the riot unfold with Mouw, Gabriel said, sarcastically, "John always told me he would go quietly if we ever got him. That John, he's a man, a man's man."

By this time, Gotti was back at the federal holding pen in Manhattan. Officials begin implementing his sentence immediately. In a few hours, they shackled him and drove him to an airport. He was put on a plane bound for Marion, Illinois—home of the most punitive prison in the federal system; Amnesty International calls it inhumane. Before the sun rose again, he was in solitary confinement. He would be held that way 23 hours a day, every day—until at some future point in time, prison officials decided that he was a beaten man and could live by prison rules.

A day later, back in Howard Beach, his father, John Joseph Gotti Sr., died of old age—but four months later, Junior Gotti's wife gave birth to a boy, who was named John.

"What's my reaction to the birth?" Bruce Cutler said when a reporter called. "My reaction is that the world is a better place with another John Gotti."

EPILOGUE

SIX YEARS AFTER HE went to prison in chains, John Gotti told daughter Victoria he became a gangster because his early life on the rougher streets of 1950s Brooklyn "dictated" it. Many people, including all those New Yorkers who overcame similar streets to achieve great things, sneer at such rationalization. But Gotti was a great rationalizer; ordering murders requires a gift for it. "My time, all the doors were closed," he said.

In her life, Victoria is achieving the legitimacy her father says fate denied him. She's doing it by becoming part of the same unruly force that made him a household name for gangster—the media. First as an author and now as a columnist for the *New York Post* and correspondent for a syndicated television show, she's become part of the whirl of New York. You have to give her credit; you also have to take some away. She succeeded despite her father's notoriety, but also because of it.

She began creating a public identity in 1995, at age 32, when she wrote a book about a heart ailment she suffers (it would lead to open-heart surgery in April of 2002). A year after that book, she wrote a novel—"It was so bad," she wrote in one of her columns, "that I considered pulling back the book." The novel required her to submit to the publicity rituals publishers employ to sell their products. These "scared her to death," because "the press had their own agenda. This was the chance to finally catch a glimpse of the myth, the man, the enigma. My father."

Fat chance. She was smart enough never to say anything stupid. She danced sweetly around the questions. "The man I knew was a great, loving father," she told *New York Newsday* in 1997, in an interview about her first novel, a legal thriller. Other media jumped on her story—it was and is irresistible. *New York* magazine described her as a "nice person, not a bad novelist, a good mother, and a dedicated volunteer for charity." *Esquire* magazine put her on its "Women We Love" list, along with actress Sharon Stone.

By July of 1998, when Victoria published her second novel, a story about a stalker, media interviews were old hat. She told a writer for her future employer, *The Post*, that her father was the inspiration for one of the book's characters, Dimitri Constantinos. "What I see is that physically, my father had this overwhelming presence. And I just found that when I created Dimitri, it was a great attribute to infuse into that character—that he could have this presence when he walked into a room."

With press clippings like that, Victoria discovered how fawning the popular press can be, how it covets notable names, famous or infamous. She began speaking to gossip columnists and getting her little dramas written up—including one about her three sons announcing that they do not believe in Santa Claus anymore as she ran off to FAO Schwarz to meet her personal shopper. The items were usually decorated with her photograph. Nice face, big hair, long nails, expensive jewelry. Fancy and flamboyant; like father, like daughter.

By August of 2000, when she published her third novel, her name was almost as well known as her father's. The book party celebrating the event was covered by the *New York Times*, whose reporter informed readers that Victoria's husband Carmine was not there because he had just been arrested and jailed on arson and racketeering charges. This fulfilled a prediction made by her father some 20 months earlier. In his absence, Carmine sent five dozen roses and a card declaring how proud he was. After someone read the note aloud to partygoers, Victoria excused herself to a bathroom, reportedly to cry. "I'm very emotional, and they always say a lady never cries in public," Victoria told a scribe for *The Times*' Public Lives column. Now at ease with most reporters, she said she was working on yet another book about someone dealing with terminal illness and, yes, it was prompted by her father's cancer, which had become well known.

"Even though I create fiction, you want a sense of realness," she explained.

The next day, a story in *The Daily News* quoted the congratulatory note from Carmine. He said he was proud of her "as a mother, a wife and a friend. I love you and miss you and the kids."

One thing Victoria seemed to learn on her way to a public life is that it helps to be shameless. One month after bathing in these items, Victoria filed for divorce. Her marriage had been heading south for some time, and Carmine had been overheard on government recordings talking about other women. He would eventually get out on bail, only to be charged and jailed again. The following year, he would plead guilty and take a nine-year prison sentence.

What was now spectacle continued. On December 22, 2000, George Rush and Joanna Molloy of *The News* devoted 23 paragraphs to Victoria's preparations for Christmas ("I have four little trees in the house and one gigantic one") and her recent visit to her now bed-ridden father ("he's doing well, he sounds strong"). Two days later, *The Post* went one better. It crafted a page one screamer out of an emotional letter she wrote her father. It was headlined, "Daddy's Little Girl ... Bares Her Soul," and in it, Victoria expressed her abid-ing love. No surprise there—he had just finished a third round of chemotherapy. What was more remarkable were her assertions, in a *Post* column by new friend Linda Stasi on the same Christmas Eve day, that she was really upset about the story and that officials at a Missouri prison hospital must have leaked the letter.

Ho, ho, ho. Prison mailroom clerks don't commit federal crimes to cloak mob bosses in sympathy. Victoria, or someone close, leaked it.

A half-year later, Victoria went to work for the newspaper she was so mad at. She said yes when *The Post* asked her to become a gossip columnist. Now, she was not just a media object like her father, but a media player. At the *The Post* office, she has the telephone number the well-known writer Jack Newfield once had, before he was canned by the new regime that hired her.

Being a media player had immediate benefits: one week after she took the job, one of her new colleagues at *The Post* shamelessly wrote—in the middle of June, 2001—yet another Gotti Christmas story. The dying don, the article said, had promised to play Santa Claus after he died by donating toys to a children's hospital. Mean-while, he had "secretly sent" Thanksgiving turkeys and toys to other distressed children. The article then paused for some background: Two years before, chip-off-the-block Junior had spent $8,000 at Toys Я Us, buying all the Tickle Me Elmo dolls he could for his father's favorite charity.

As a columnist, Victoria can write virtually what she wants, and one of the first items on her agenda was another salute to her ailing father. It came as she recalled a chat with a public relations woman named Lizzie Grubman: "We kicked around the pros of having tradi-tional patriarchs. Of how our fathers laid the foundation for us early on—rules and regulations and never forget about building character."

The item makes it clear how she intends to have both a public life and deal with her father's criminal life. It is the same way he would have—make no admissions, no concessions, no nothing. The Marion prison tapes, however, show she knows a lot about his Mafia career—at one point, they discuss a list of "made" men—but that column you will never read.

In the Grubman column, Victoria displayed defense-lawyer instincts her father would have cheered, if he had been still well enough to read it. Readers were never told why she and Grubman were chatting or what had happened two weeks before—when Grubman was behind the wheel of a car that veered wildly out of control outside a nightclub and injured 16 people. Without any context, Victoria rose to defend Grubman against the media whipping that ensued: "... [her] dedication is still there ... Amid all the tasteless jokes and unwelcome whispers, she enters her office each morning."

It's easy to understand why the playful *Post* hired Victoria—the name, the glam look, the growing affinity for Manhattan life (she keeps an apartment there now, although she still has her Long Island mansion). It's harder to say if her novels would have been published but for her last name. Her father had his doubts.

This began coming out on the videotapes made in prison in January of 1998, when Gotti recalled for his daughter a talk show he had recently watched on his little prison black-and-white. On the show, a woman said her child was mercilessly teased about a skin condition by classmates, until a cousin came along and straightened the matter out. "He dusted a few of them up and now when they see the kid they treat the kid special," Gotti summarized. "They don't want an ass-kicking. You read Machiavelli, fear is a stronger emotion over love."

Victoria protested that this is what her soon-to-be ex-husband would have done, and had done, after a similar incident years before. "[He] showed them to be the animal they think he is. Proved to them that he was the animal that people said he was ... we're not like that, we're not animals."

"Yeah, but, either you gotta be proud of who you are, and fight for it, or you gotta be ashamed of it and do like some other lowlifes do, and change their names." Gotti then said Victoria's son would not have been teased if Victoria had used her married name, Agnello, instead of Gotti. "I mean, if you ask a guy next door, 'Hey, what do you think about the Agnellos?' He'd say, 'Who are the Agnellos?' … You should stay off television. You should stay off the book covers. You should use Victoria Agnello, and they won't know who the kids are, and they won't be faced with this problem. Am I correct or incorrect?"

"How does me staying off book covers—is that something bad to do?"

"They won't know your name."

"Oh, come on, dad. They won't know who we are?"

"Look, if you think that my name has nothing to do with you, take your mother's [maiden] name."

Victoria didn't reply, but she could easily have argued that the name is at least as much a curse as a blessing. She could have pointed no farther than the case of her brother Junior, who was indicted a week before that conversation. But for his father's name, Junior would not have been acting boss of the Gambino crime Family. But for his father's name, the media would not have cared much about his legal troubles. And but for his father's name, Junior would not have amassed a fortune so impressive he could afford to leave $350,000 in cash wedding gifts hidden in a basement for eight years.

Most likely, Junior also would not have been hit with new charges five months later that alleged he robbed a drug dealer. That one prompted a protest call to *The News* from his mother Vicky, who hadn't been heard from for a while. "He doesn't have enough money, so he gets involved in drugs? Please," she told reporter Greg B. Smith. "Can't they come up with something better than that? "You've investigated what he owns," she said, referring to a story in which Smith described Junior as a millionaire. "He's going to steal $4,000? Please. It's absolutely ridiculous. It's beyond ridiculous. I shouldn't even respond to it. I just want you to know what I feel."

In April of 1999, as sister Victoria was working on her third novel, Junior wrote the end to his mob story—at least for several years. On the day jury selection was about to begin in his case, he broke sharply with his father's tradition and pleaded guilty. He forfeited nearly one million dollars, his wedding money, and multiple vacation homes before going off to prison for six or so years.

His uncle Peter Gotti might be headed there, too. And so might another uncle, Richard Gotti, a low-key member of the clan who had remained in the shadows until early June 2002, when he and

Peter were indicted on labor racketeering charges in the Eastern District. They and others were accused of extorting dockworkers and companies that do business On The Waterfront in Brooklyn. A couple of the others also were accused of extorting Hollywood action star Steven Seagal.

The indictment alleged that Peter, 62, a former sanitation worker who retired on a disability pension in 1979, had become the official boss of the Gambino Family, and that Richard, 59, had become a captain. Bruce Cutler showed up at an early court appearance, representing "Uncle Pete," as he always called him, and naturally he dismissed talk of Peter becoming boss. "There are so many versions of who's in charge," he sneered. "Now it's Uncle Pete's turn."

It almost certainly is Uncle Pete's turn, and not much more need be said about the state of the Gambino crime Family 10 years after John Gotti went away.

In brief, here are accountings of some of the other characters in this book:

Like John Gotti, two important capos in the Gambino Family fought off the government for a while. James Failla, one of those men waiting inside Sparks to meet Castellano for dinner on the night Gotti made his move, also beat a RICO case. So did co-defendant and fellow capo Joseph Corrao.

"Go talk to the prosecutors," Corrao said, sounding much like Gotti after his 1987 victory. "They're the ones who frame people, not us."

The prosecutors, however, would get the last laugh on both Failla and Corrao, thanks to the testimony of a major new cooperating witness, turncoat underboss Sammy Gravano. Together with yet more FBI tapes, Gravano sank dozens of Gambino mobsters following the deal he struck with John Gleeson.

Meanwhile, George Pape, the corrupt juror whose 1987 dive enabled Gotti's reign, was convicted of bribery and sentenced to three years in prison. He served two and was released.

On the first day of 2000, Pape's fugitive bagman, former Westies boss Bosko Radonjich, was arrested at Miami International Airport, aborting a planned vacation in the Bahamas.

Former U.S. Attorney Andrew Maloney, back in private practice with a top Manhattan law firm, was elated. He was confident that with the testimony of one-time underboss Sammy Gravano, who nurtured the Pape-Radonjich deal, Radonjich would be made to pay.

"As imperfect as it is, we consider the jury system sacred and when someone tampers with it, he deserves the maximum possible penalty under the law," said Maloney.

Less than two months later, however, Gravano became a less than ideal witness when he was caught returning to a life of crime and arrested for drug trafficking. Radonjich was cut loose and returned to his Serbian homeland.

Breaking Gotti's rule about making admissions. Failla pleaded guilty to conspiring to kill Thomas Spinelli, the Failla soldier who broke a Gotti rule about grand jury testimony. He got seven years, and died on August 4, 1999, at age 80, at a federal prison hospital in Forth Worth, Texas, about six months before he would have been released.

Corrao also departed from Gotti rules, pleading guilty to bribing NYPD detective William Peist for inside information. He got 70 months. In November 2001, after serving his sentence, Corrao succumbed to kidney failure at age 64.

Peist went to the can too, and was released just before Christmas, 1999.

Dominick Borghese, who helped dispatch William Ciccone, the poor soul whom the paranoid Gotti crew mistook for an assassin, also pleaded guilty to conspiring to kill Spinelli, a murder that resulted in his promotion to "made man." He got seven years.

More than a year after Failla and Borghese pleaded guilty to the Spinelli murder conspiracy, Joe Watts, the unmade man who was Paul's pal, Sammy's pal, and then Gotti's pal, admitted taking part, too. He got six years, one less than the others because he did a little bit of secret spying for the FBI against Gotti and the others during a 13-month period in 1994–95.

In time, Watts also would be called to account for the torture murder of Ciccone. He would beat that charge, but go down for tax fraud and, in June 2002, money-laundering charges. He took a six-year plea deal as Borghese, who helped him kill Ciccone, was waiting in the wings to testify against him, after emulating Gravano and making a deal for himself.

Tommy Gambino, severed from the 1992 trial that ended with Gotti's conviction, was found guilty when he finally went to trial, but of lesser racketeering charges. He served five years and returned to his Family and his Garment Center businesses in May of 2000.

Gotti's 1992 codefendant, Frank LoCascio, went to prison for life, a lot of it in a prison hospital and some in solitary after authorities learned that Gotti supposedly had enlisted jailed members of a white-supremacy group to kill him. Gotti turned on LoCascio after learning that Gravano and LoCascio talked about turning on him had they won the 1992 case.

Retired *consigliere* Joe N. Gallo showed great staying power, until shortly after he got out of prison in June 1995. He died three months later at his home in Queens, at age 83.

Would-be adopted son and assistant press secretary Lewis Kasman served six months for lying to the Eastern District grand jury and resumed his role as Gotti's unofficial spin doctor, especially after Gotti was diagnosed with head and neck cancer a second time.

Gotti pal Carlo Vaccarezza saw his upscale restaurant, Da Noi's, go south very fast. With more FBI agents than customers in the place on some days, Vaccarezza went south, too, to Miami. He helped his old camera-shy acquaintance, actor Mickey Rourke, open a joint on South Beach. Before long, however, he packed that in, and was last heard scouting Chicago.

Another Gotti pal, Lisa Gastineau, became a boutique manager and did some modeling on the side. "I have great affection for him," was all she wanted to say when contacted. "I was really disappointed to learn he was never coming home."

On the other hand, John Gleeson—the young prosecutor when the Gotti saga began, the sage one when it ended—became a federal judge on October 24, 1994, third anniversary of his dramatic face-to-face with Gravano, the first underboss to testify against his boss in court.

The former midshipman, Bruce Mouw—for getting Gotti and a decade's worth of other accomplishments as boss of the Gambino squad—was given the Justice Department's highest award for employee achievement. He helped case-agent George Gabriel and assistant U.S. attorney Laura Ward to build cases against the Gotti remnants, then retired.

Gabriel became head of a squad of Long Island-based FBI agents. Ward became a Criminal Court judge in Manhattan. Robert

Morgenthau remained District Attorney of Manhattan, and the nation's most influential local prosecutor.

The first important lawyer in John Gotti's life, Michael Coiro, was convicted again, this time for lying to the Eastern District grand jury about his one visit to Nettie Cirelli's place. He was released in February 1998, then moved back to Florida to resume retirement.

The most prominent lawyer in Gotti's life, Bruce Cutler, was convicted of criminal contempt for violating an order by the 1992 Gotti trial judge against out-of-court prejudicial statements. He got three months' home detention. A state court panel then suspended him from practicing law for three more months.

He returned with a flourish to represent "young John" Gotti in 1998. Cutler's bald pate was glistening as he rushed into court just as a pretrial conference for Junior was about to begin. He beamed and shook hands all around, then kissed his handcuffed client on the cheek.

Another key lawyer in Gotti's life, Gerald Shargel, was already on the case, handling the pre-trial legal arguments as well as the negotiations that led to Junior pleading guilty in 1999.

Inside the court, Cutler let Shargel handle the legal arguments. But outside, he expounded, "I came today to announce to the court and the world that Jerry and I will be representing John Gotti's son at trial. We helped his father together, and we have a wonderful relationship. It's great to be back in the arena."

Cutler expounded when a reputed Gotti sketch of a lion fetched $2,500 in a Miami charity auction—a Leroy Nieman self-portrait got $700; a Muhammad Ali drawing got $600. "People love John," Cutler said. "He did it (drew the sketch) to help needy, hungry children. And the lion. It's one of his credos: It's better to live one day as a lion than a hundred years as a lamb."

Fifteen years after he was the star defense witness at Gotti's 1987 trial, Matthew Traynor, who admitted lying from the witness stand, is still in prison. After five years in federal prison, he's doing 7 to 14 years for bank robbery and 14 more for parole violation.

By contrast, two more characters from the 1987 trial, Crazy Sally Polisi and Dominick Lofaro, got probation and were released from prison that same year.

Nicholas Corozzo and Lenny DiMaria, the "other guys" in the 1987 Gotti case, fashioned plea deals to satisfy various indictments against them and are due out of prison in 2004 and 2005.

Heroin dealers Gene Gotti, John Carneglia, and Anthony Rampino fared worse. Gene and Carneglia are in federal prison until 2018. Rampino is in state prison until 2012.

After getting away with feigning insanity for three decades, Gotti nemesis Vincent "Chin" Gigante, long-time boss of the Genovese Family, was convicted of labor racketeering and put away for 12 years, thanks again in part to testimony by Gravano.

The Gigante trial was Gravano's last trip to the witness stand for the government. It helped promote sales of his life story, which had come out a few months before. Later in 1999, however, the *Arizona Republic* disclosed that he was living in the Grand Canyon state, and Gravano gave its reporter some quotable words.

"I'm not running from the fucking Mafia," he said. "I was a boxer. I know what it's like to get hit. I know what it is to fight. You lose your fear. I could go to Montana and live 20 years in a cabin and be scared to death. Or I can live here … I choose to live here."

At the time, Gravano ran a Phoenix construction company. He and his supposedly estranged-wife Debra also operated a Scottsdale restaurant. But these were not their most lucrative operations. On the side, they and their two adult children were also running an illegal party-drug business.

State authorities caught up with them first and later the federal government weighed in. For his part, Gravano pleaded guilty and is headed off to prison for a good long time.

Jack D'Amico, who served on a three-capo committee that helped Junior carry out his father's wishes from prison during the mid-1990s, was indicted in the same case that led to Junior going away for six or so years. D'Amico pleaded guilty too, but only to bookmaking, and he served 17 months before getting out in September 2001.

The summer Junior and D'Amico went away, a woman who mounted an impressive Gotti fan club on the Internet and ran it for four years, called it quits and closed the site. She took down hundreds of upbeat items and photos of Gotti, Junior, Victoria, and Cutler.

In a last message to Gotti fans, Melissa (Ravenna) Angelini wrote, "Unfortunately, all good things must come to an end."

The end for John Gotti went on a long time. The first stories hinting that the end was near appeared in the fall of 2000. In the meantime, various treatment crises prompted more stories and transfers between a prison hospital and a hospital in Springfield, Missouri. Each time, his lawyers and spokesmen kept saying what a fighter he was and how, even as they complained about this or that condition of confinement, he never complained about anything. Even if he were no longer in charge of orchestrating public opinion, how the public perceived him remained a large part of the John Gotti story.

If his Family has its way, he will be buried next to his son Frank and father John Sr., in a famous old cemetery in Queens where several infamous gangsters, including Carlo Gambino and Aniello Dellacroce, are buried.

These gangsters from Gotti's life, and most others there, lie in crypts marked only by their names and dates of birth and death. No slogans, no last words. No use giving writers anything to work with. But Gotti leaves his warehouse of tape-recorded words, including those he employed to describe the way he believed things went in his crime Family after he went away for good.

"If I had to give a mark, a grade on how every situation was handled—the lawyers and everything else, jobs and getting jobs and working and all that—I can't put a passing mark on one incident," he told brother Peter in 1998, in prison, before the cancer came.

Naturally, he had his reasons why, and no one who ever knew John Gotti or came to know him would be surprised. "Why do you think this group of people fell apart without me?" he asked, before providing, as he often did, his own answer:

"Everyone became their own boss, set their own moral codes, set their own reasons, their own rhymes, and that's the end of it … that's the end of the ballgame."

POSTSCRIPT

ON JUNE 10, 2002, three days after we finished this book, John Gotti died, giving us this last-second opportunity against a tight publishing deadline to make a few last comments.

We had every reason to suspect it, because we have been on the story 17 years and seen what happens in the media when a big Gotti headline comes along, but we were still amazed at the amount of coverage his death generated. Front-page stories and full-page photographs. Lengthy obituaries. Lots of essays by columnists. Much man-on-the-street. Many sidebars on this or that aspect of the man and his legacy. It went on several days, with follow-ups about disputes that erupted over shipping his body home to New York from the prison hospital where he died in Springfield, Missouri.

We didn't measure the inches, but from the memory of our participation in that story, too, the death of Frank Sinatra—a big hero in New York who had a much longer time at the top—didn't get near the attention Gotti's did.

Naturally, we contributed. The *New York Daily News* published our obituary on Gotti and excerpts from one of our other books. The *New York Post* excerpted this book. *The New York Times* invited us onto its op-ed page. Reporters and broadcasters from Los Angeles to Auckland and New York to London called to ask for our comments.

All of it was evidence that for all the bad he did, Gotti was good on one level—as we said earlier, he lived up to our expectations of what a gangster is. The Gambino crime family is in ruins, because of him, but he looked, sounded, and acted like a gangster, and with such enthusiasm that we all became at least interested in his story, if not captivated. Our expectations come from our gangster movies, and Gotti was right off the big screen.

Ordinary people picked up on that, and used movie terms to talk about him. "He played that tough-guy role to his dying breath," the former warden of the prison hospital where he died told the *Daily News*.

Meeting expectations, Gotti became part of our popular culture—he often was a case of life imitating art imitating life, but people were interested enough to pay attention. This is why the media gave us terrible new details about the suffering and indignity of his last few months of surgically imposed silence. It is why we learned he was to be buried in a crypt alongside son Frank, the boy on the minibike, in that Queens cemetery where so many gangsters lay. It is why we were told that while Roman Catholic officials would not grant his relatives' wish for a Mass of Christian Burial, they would permit a church memorial service, but with no coffin present.

Nobody asked us, but we think his Family should have been able to say good-bye the way they wished. Death is always a sad ending, even for the villain's family.

So long, John Gotti. You were a great story.

Gene Mustain
Jerry Capeci
June 14, 2002

INDEX